BOXED

A VISUAL HISTORY AND THE ART OF BOXING

DAMIANI

PAUL KASMIN GALLERY

TRIUMPH, FAILURE, BEAUTY, EGO, ENDURANCE, COMBAT AND LOVE

Sports have always played an important role in the principle and foundation of Latino Culture, specifically in the Puerto Rican and Cuban culture and its Diaspora. Specifically, boxing and music was a significant presence within my family household. Watching a young Howard Cosell on ABC's Wide World of Sports is still very much a vivid memory. Initially, it really wasn't so much about the sport, but rather a way to connect with my father and spend time with him. It was about being inspired by the energy and cultural identity he brought to the table. Even more so when my father's friends would visit for a cold Schlitz over well-placed vulgarities, quips, and personal barbs that took place in either the garage, the kitchen (my fathers office) or the faux wood paneled basement trophy den that hosted many gatherings throughout my youthful 1970's upbringing. The louder the conversations, the better, since they had to talk over Héctor Lavoe, Willie Colón and El Gran Combo playing at nearly max volume on the tiny boombox while boxing matches with fighters like Ray "Boom Boom" Mancini, Wilfredo Gomez, Wilfred Benítez, Hector "Macho Camacho" Julio César Chávez , Marvin Hagler, Thomas Hearns and "Smokin' Joe Frazier served as a technicolor backdrop on our Zenith TV. My favorite being "No Mas" with Roberto Duran and Sugar Ray Leonard, now considered one of the most famous fights in boxing history.

Obviously, from this I've gained serious interest in the sport and have come to consider the sweet science and history of pugilism as an art form in itself. As an adult and artist seeing classical works by George Bellows, Thomas Eakins and the bronze 'Boxer of Quirinal' along with work by some of my contemporaries who have used boxing as a metaphor has reaffirmed this feeling. Personally, I have come to appreciate the custom made outfits (boxing robes and trunks) as wonderfully handcrafted works of folk art proudly displaying symbols of pageantry and identity. I also cannot help but feel the random yet carefully orchestrated and spontaneous movements young golden glove boxers use to outwit their opponents has a direct relationship to performance-based art. So too the aggressive nature of two boxers at a prized fight in Las Vegas bears a parallel to bloody cockfights between two roosters. My attempt is to create a visual dialogue that convey these stories and memory. The hope is that this publication and body of work will evoke interest and discussion beyond the confines of a squared room into a squared circle.   CARLOS ROLON/DZINE

It surprises me that Carlos (DZINE) Rolon and I have never worked together. It is not only because we share good mutual friends but, because we share certain passions. We are continually amazed by vernacular culture and its infiltration into wider intellectual conversations, especially as visualized in contemporary art. Rolon has spoken in the past of growing up within the setting of his mom's bootleg hair salon, which was also the family living room. An important earlier installation by the artist is called 'Imperial Nail Salon' and was accompanied by the publication 'Nailed'. For me it was, perhaps likewise, the barber shop where I first saw the art of everyday people around me. Those places or sites of community, the barber shop and the hair salon, filled with both intimate and unfamiliar companions in the confines of a space that is at once public but also intensely private are incubators of collective thought and usually adorned accordingly. Aside from my own father, the first images of masculinity that I must have seen would have been the pictures, posters and occasional paintings that decorated the barber shop. This was Harlem, U.S.A. where Earl "the Pearl" Monroe, Walt "Clyde" Frazier and Lew Alcindor, aka Kareem Abdul Jabaar—the local boy who made it big—became my first heroes, next to the portraits of Dr. Martin Luther King Jr., Malcolm X and George Clinton. Music was heard here and fashion was worn and it was all discussed, usually at a feverish pitch. From the most intimate details of people's lives to the fodder of the daily news, life was lived and of course talked about. So private so public, it was Facebook on an infinitesimally small scale. That experience has inspired several exhibitions on sport and society. The music continues to play a role for bridging space, between an active lived place and a space most often defined by its lack of life, the proverbial white cube. Religion and spirituality from the point of view of vernacular culture followed suit.

For Rolon, the exploration of Kustom Kulture has been the direct result of days spent listening to the women who gathered in his mom's salon. Taking that sort of decoration and shine to tricked out bicycles set upon shiny mirrors for pedestals, for instance, was only the next logical step. Resin and crystal covered paintings, with an equally vibrant palette seem to be informed as much by 1970s LSD aesthetics as by contemporary decorative paintings conjured by like minded artists such as Beatriz Milhazes and Mickalene Thomas, among others.

'Dzine: Born, Carlos Rolon, 1970' opens in New York in January 2014 and 'Boxed', this publication, takes Rolon's father as inspiration. Rolon's newest project is one that brings him even closer to seminal past experiences. 'Boxed', continues to demonstrate the power of vernacular art made, presented or discussed in common social spaces. Here he recreates his family's wood-paneled basement where his father, a devoted boxing fan, watched the fights on television. Rolon remembers the scene decorated with gold garlands and vintage beer placards, which become the backdrop for his new paintings and sculptures.

As is demonstrated in this publication, people have been inspired to create art that touches upon the subject of boxing for thousands of years. As far as sport goes, boxing has the distinction of being in the realm of humanity's basic urges: to fight. That we have elevated fighting each other (recreation, sport, gladiatorial entertainment) to a technological discipline—where we kill at the press of a button—belies the sport's claim to fame and fighting as The Sweet Science. Yet, the event and spectacle of regulated boxing continues and as is demonstrated here the images that artists have created inspired by boxing and of pugilists and the apparatus of the sport continue to astonish.

Enlisting the imagery of an incredibly diverse range of artists Rolon's homage to his father and celebration of the sport and its attendant signs and symbols makes for a rich look at a swath of contemporary works of art over the last thirty years. From Ed Ruscha's seminal 'Boxer' from 1979—a text over a burnt orange sunset vertically dominates the canvas—to one-off works like Christopher Wool's 1988 homage to Muhammad Ali (also in text), painters have found a subject in the sport beyond the representational image. Others like Ed Paschke, Andy Warhol and Jean-Michel Basquiat created extended bodies of work around the theme. Warhol and Basquiat used the adversarial pose of boxers to celebrate the presentation of their collaborative paintings at the Tony Shafrazi Gallery in 1985. The two artists donned boxing gloves and posed as if for a boxing poster.

In addition to using the boxing theme as a foil for the jousting that happened in the collaborative process of two big painters facing off in the studio, the duo created 'Ten Punching Bags: (Last Supper)', its title making explicit their content of punching bags adorned with paint and hanging from the ceiling at punching bag height. Warhol had submitted the most famous boxer of all, Muhammad Ali, to the silkscreen treatment for his Athletes Series in 1978. And, Basquiat had already made several paintings on the subject featuring riffs on the images of Ali, in addition to Sugar Ray Robinson and Jack Johnson.

Artists like Paul Pfeiffer and Gary Simmons have explored the theme deeply in video by the former and sculpture, painting and installation by the latter. Both are interested not only in the fight or the history of boxing as subject matter and potentially rich metaphor but in the essence and facts of the sport's history as a reflection of society. Both artists have also looked closely at other forms of sport in this vein, including soccer (or, futbol) and basketball. Pfeiffer examined Ali in three of his most pivotal bouts: the first fight against Sonny Liston in 1964, the "rumble in the jungle," and the "thrilla in Manila." Pfeiffer's 'Long Count' pieces trace the three fights. "These are very important fights at the beginning, middle and toward the end of Ali's career—Clay versus Liston, in Miami in 1964; Ali versus Foreman, in Kinshasa in 1974; and Ali versus Frazier, in Manila in 1975. What drew me to the images of those fights was really that history. These were some of the first sporting events formatted for television. The Rumble in the Jungle, Ali versus Foreman, was one of the very first attempts at a live, global broadcast, and it happens to have originated in Africa. Those three fights are sold today as a boxed set by HBO, so they exist in the archive already as a prepackaged statement."

While Simmons' work has long been inflected by the history of the sport and American cultural politics—as in early works like Step in the Arena (The Essentialist Trap), 1994—recently he has focused in on the sport's tragic heroes. Vintage posters serve as the background imagery for recent paintings and drawings that reference less heralded fighters like Benny Paret, Emile Griffith and Ruben "Hurricane" Carter.

As much as Rolon is also interest- ed in the stories of the pugilists of the past and the present, he is squarely focused on the essence of what the sport has meant to him in his life and art. "The sport was a way to connect with my father. As with my previous project 'Nailed', an homage to my mother, it has brought personal insight of my studio practice. It fleshes out my practice. People now realize where the concept and incorporation of Kustom Kulture, faux luxury and excessiveness come from. I was raised with it, it surrounded me daily." While the contemporary picture of the sport finds visualization in flash, pomp and circumstance—something the artist has clearly tapped into—Rolon, like Pfeiffer, Simmons and the other artists he has selected, has found the essence of substance and style in the history of the sport. "I've come to consider the sweet science and history of pugilism as an art form itself," Rolon says. "Seeing the bronze 'Boxer of Quirinal'—the Hellenistic sculpture of a boxer found in Rome from 330 BC—reaffirms all these feelings."

Franklin Sirmans has organized exhibitions including 'The Beautiful Game: Contemporary Art and Football, For the Love of the Game', and is currently working on 'Futbol: The Beautiful Game'.

FRANKLIN SIRMANS
[Terri and Michael Smooke Curator of Contemporary
Art at the Los Angeles County Museum of Art]

FROM A DISTANCE

Unlike literature and film, both of which have long histories of unguarded devotion to pugilism and pugilists, visual art since 1980, give or take, has assumed a generally arch, harshly critical relationship to the sport and its place in culture. While films ranging in seriousness and scope from 'Raging Bull' to the 'Rocky' franchise have found macho heroes and romance (homosocial and otherwise) in and around the ring, and literary titans including Norman Mailer, Joyce Carol Oates, and George Plimpton have produced reams of hyperbolic fight ekphrasis, visual art has abided by an altogether different orthodoxy when it comes to boxing. Race, class, corruption, commerce and exploitation in various guises (and often in combination), are the prevalent critical themes. One is not supposed to enjoy boxing as it is depicted in art, to behold the spectacle of the good fight in bloodthirsty reverie, or gaze in the grip of admiration at a boxer's intellect and prowess. Rather, one is supposed to frown, to look askance at the brutality of the spectacle, the exploitation of fighters at the hands of their promoters and managers, and to take careful note of the relationship between the boxing game and racial minorities, class inequity, lack of education, and absence of privilege.

A few accomplished examples from the present publication will suffice to demonstrate this point. Gary Simmons' 'Step into the Arena (The Essentialist Trap)', 1994, is a glistening white boxing ring, smaller than regulation, with black dress shoes hung haphazardly by their laces from the ropes. Though the black body is missing from the scene, the shoes mourn that presence though absence, and the title warns the aspirant young man to resist the tug of the ring and the "essentialist" lie that suggests young black men should fight and prosper there. In 'Work Out', 2007, Libby Black has fashioned boxing gloves from paper and acrylic paint, these delicate and improbable tools of the pugilist crudely emblazoned with the word "Gucci", the temptation of quick riches associated with boxing thrown into relief here as a frail falsehood. And then there are Tanner Ceylan's brutal, photorealistic oil on canvas paintings of bare knuckle boxing, the verisimilitude of the image pushed to the point of abjection, the battered flesh, dead eyes, and oozing blood a wordless indictment of the sport. Unabashedly critical yet visually magnetic in spite of that agenda, these are just three examples, many others in 'Boxed' hit a similar note, undoing the possibility of a straightforward critical address, and producing instead an effect that exists on the knife edge of pleasure and aversion, much like the experience of the sport itself. Should we be looking or should we turn away? And if we choose to look, what is the 'correct' response?

Another category of image in the book is made purposefully easier to consume. The romantic toil of training, the warmth of male camaraderie, the ragged glory of the aging, overused gym, the bright lights of the ring, and the sublimity of violence are among the preponderant strains in documentary photography focused on boxing, and it is to the credit of 'Boxed' that images in this vein exist alongside those more orthodox critical accounts of boxing that prevail in the art world. Chris Mosier's photographic account of Gleason's Gym in Brooklyn is an apposite example. Mosier's high capture images, replete with incredible color saturation, describe an interior space defined by attrition on one hand — the material wear and tear of decades of hard use — and on the other, the accretion of equipment, posters, and photographs which, over time, have transformed the gym's interior into an informal archive. Fighters training, posing, or recovering ground this attrition/accretion aesthetic in the serious business of boxing, bringing the viewer close to the action, not with the implied or explicit critical agenda found in a work by Simmons or David Hammons, but with something like an anthropologist's eye, tinged with fandom.

'Boxed' brokers this opposition between the critical and devotional through a parade of images that taken together span both world-views; in its willingness to be bifocal in this sense, the publication may be unique. But whether the person responsible for the image or object has fallen victim to the allure that drove Mailer and Plimpton, or whether they find fault like Black and Simmons, both positions have one thing in common: their subjects remain emphatically 'other', the circumscribed image rendered, symptomatic of the intractable divide that exists between boxers and boxing as a culture, and the sport's intellectual partisans, artist-critics, and popular fan-base. Just as the ring separates the audience from the action - a strikingly thin line between two wildly different worlds - so follows the non-participant's relationship to boxing as an image or idea. Access comes only from a distance, through an image made or an image consumed, the abiding fascination for devotees and dissenters alike being that line, and all it signifies, which cannot and will not be crossed. There are few spectacles in culture as literally circumscribed as boxers in a ring, and few if any literally circumscribed spectacles that enfold a cultural lacuna so vast and complex: how to measure, for instance, the distance between Joyce Carol Oates, the author, and Mike Tyson, her subject? For the vast majority, the act of stepping into the ring is utterly (and justifiably) unimaginable. It is, therefore, very likely the impossibility of identification in life that makes the manufacture of images, critical or otherwise, so irresistible. To gaze in on another may be an inadequate path to understanding, but in the case of boxing, it may also be the only one.

CHRISTOPHER BEDFORD
[Henry and Lois Foster Director of the
Rose Art Museum at Brandeis University]

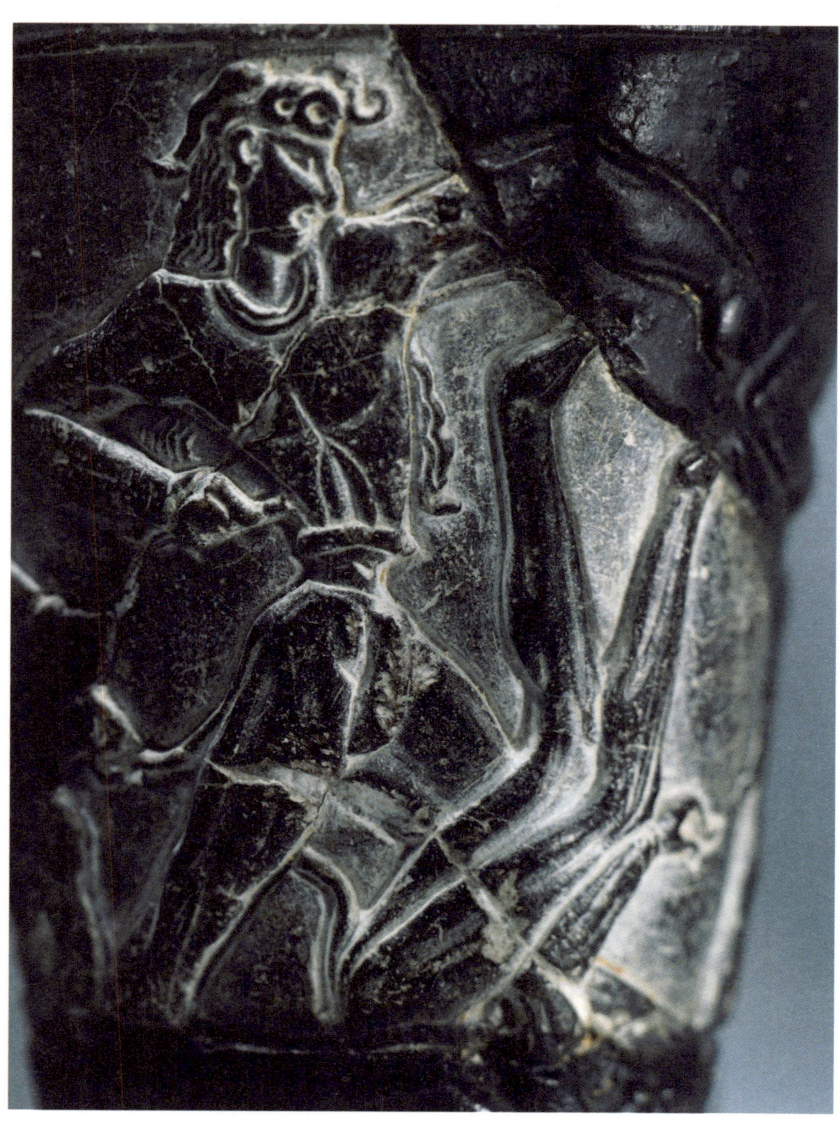

The earliest documentation of boxing comes not from Ancient Greece or Rome, where most accounts place the sport's origins, but from the Fertile Crescent and Minoan Crete. Carved into terracotta plaques or painted onto walls between 3000 and 1000 BCE, these images show human figures engaged in what we recognize as boxing: two bare-chested male figures stand upright facing each other with arms extended and fists balled, apparently prepared to fight each other. Scholars know relatively little about the sport in the ancient kingdoms of present-day Crete, Iraq, Iran, Syria, and Egypt, but images confirm that boxing is one of the world's first known athletic games.

In the majority of these early depictions two fighters appear facing each other, both in composite profile—part of their bodies in profile, part frontal—an illustrative convention employed by scribes and artisans as a means to convey as much visual information as possible. The boxers' legs, in profile, appear to be spread; their torsos are fully frontal; their heads, like their legs, are in profile, so the two figures appear to be looking directly at each other. Their arms are raised, and each fighter's arm that is farthest from the front of the picture plain extends outward, nearly touching or actually overlapping that of his opponent. Each figure holds his front arm bent and pulled close to his torso. Depicted in this manner, the figures appear twisted, and only somewhat engaged in their fight. Indeed, in these fight scenes, the boxers stand slightly separated (their bodies are not entangled as twenty-first-century viewers are used to seeing boxers), so that both figures are fully legible. Though their bodies seem static and slightly contorted, it is apparent from their mutual upright stance and cocked arms that they are prepared to box.

The Boxer rhyton (1600 - 1450 BCE), from Hagia Triada, Crete, exemplifies how boxing was often portrayed as part of a longer narrative sequence. A conical vessel open on both ends, the rhyton is thought to have been used for ceremonial purposes, likely to carry wine (if the smaller, bottom hole was plugged). Four sculpted registers wrap around it. The top register and two bottom registers depict boxers and wrestlers fighting. The stylized curves and exaggerated features of the fighters' bodies emphasize their athleticism and their actions. Their muscles bulge and tendons stretch. Perhaps most interestingly, the figures recur throughout the registers, indicating the progression of their fight and the passage of time. The rhyton is an early stop-motion play-by-play, something that later artists would attempt in different media.

Also from Crete is a fresco, dated to 1550 BCE, that depicts two boys boxing. The two figures stand in the conventional semi-profile stance, but their bodies appear different from the angular Mesopotamian bodies and lack the muscles that mark the figures on the Boxer rhyton. Their long hair, swayed backs and slightly curved stomachs, and generally slender forms signify their young age. The mannerist style in which the boys were painted is the trademark of the frescos at the Minoan Palace of Knossos, where this image was also discovered.

Scholars have speculated about the design and intended meaning of these carvings and paintings. The scenes could document actual fights, or they might represent celebrations of or sacrifices made to leaders or deities. Despite this ambiguity, these various early images suggest that boxing had a prominent place in these ancient cultures.

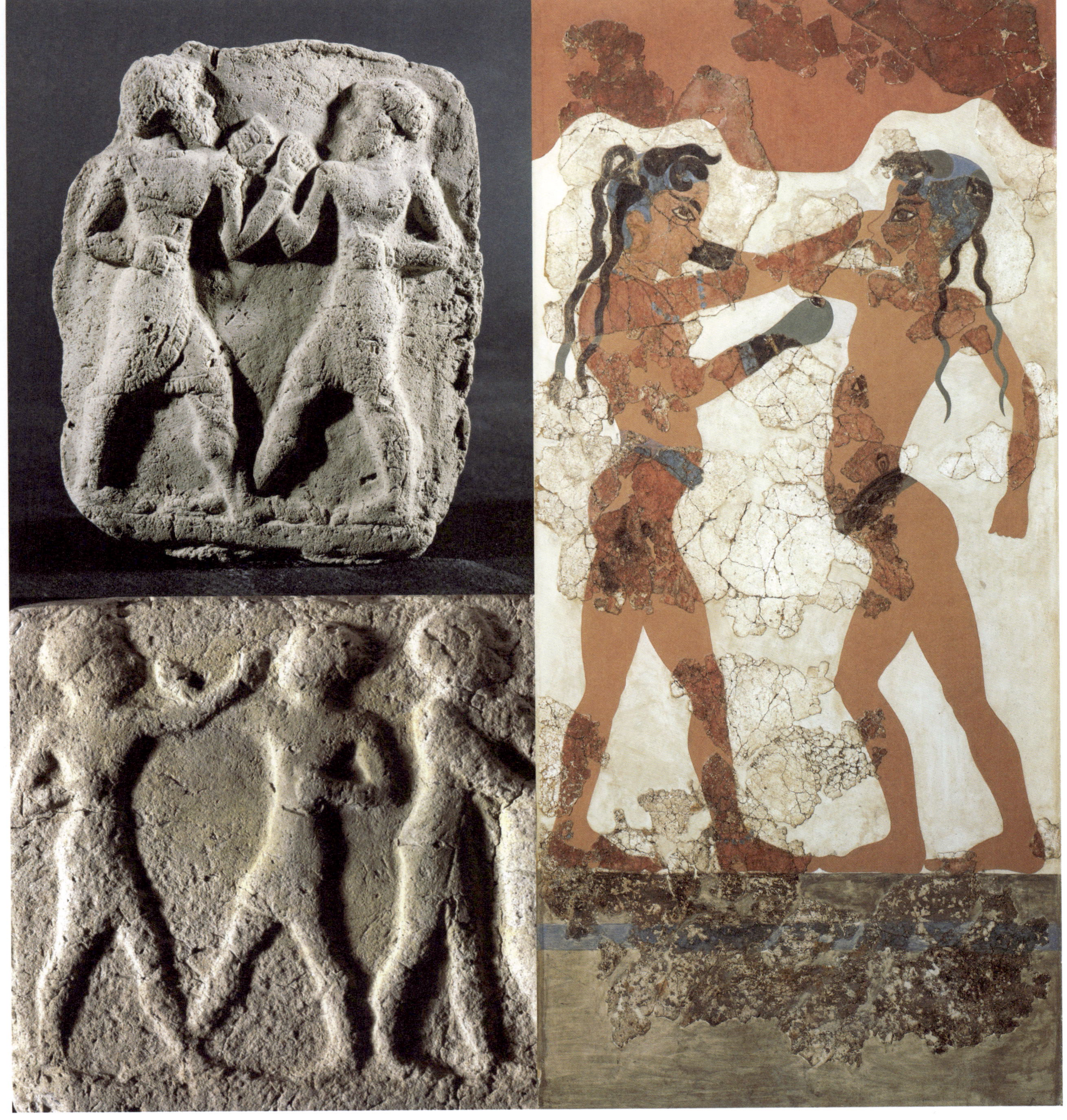

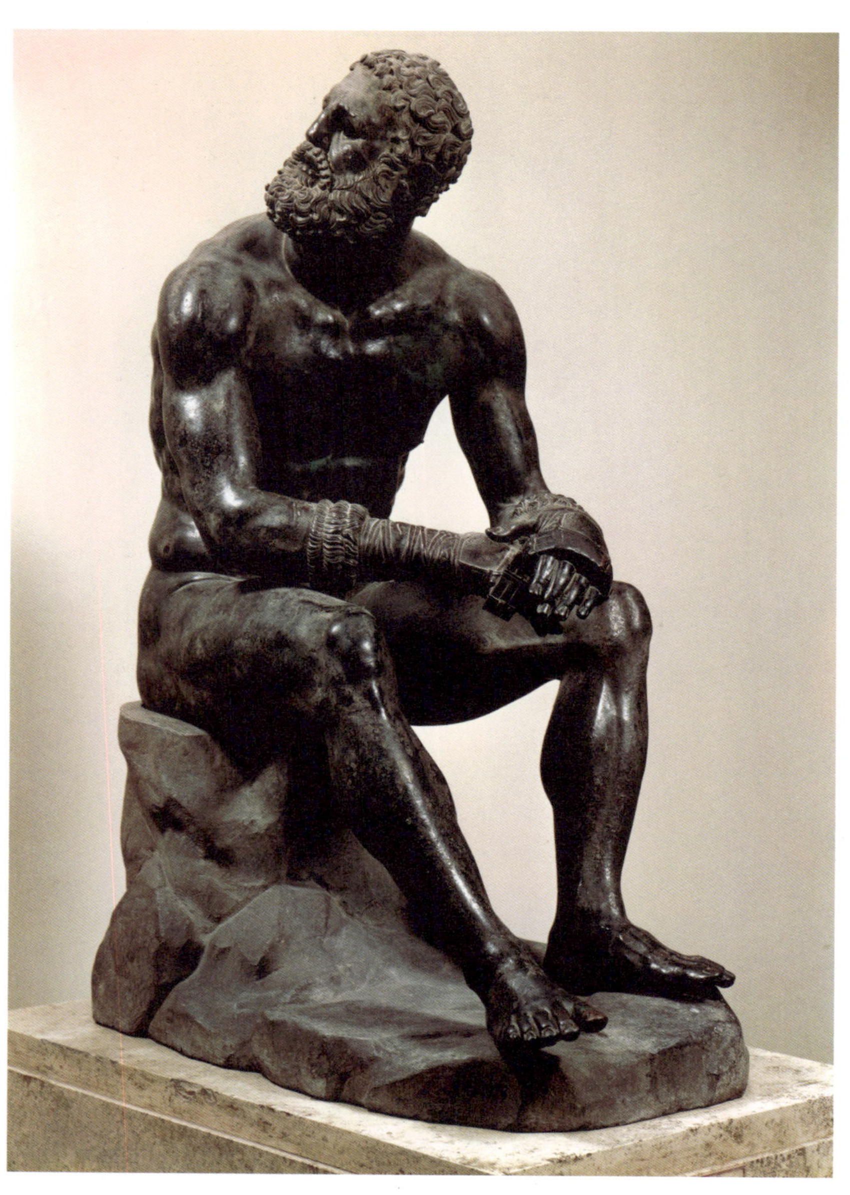

While early artworks prove that boxing's beginnings lay in the Fertile Crescent, common knowledge, based on abundant historical evidence, says that the Greeks originated the sport. Regardless of earlier manifestations of the sport, literary and visual information leaves no doubt that the Ancient Greeks engaged in formalized one-on-one fist fights in which participants wore protective hand gear. Homer refers to something akin to boxing in the 'Iliad' and the 'Odyssey', and ancient records indicate that the sport became an official Olympic event in 688 BCE and was also included in other regular athletic festivals. Visual representations of fighters provide clues about its ancient form, as well as the significance of athletics in Greek culture.

Many such images appear on painted kraters, large vases used to mix wine, made between the 6th and 4th centuries BCE. Vessels used for formal occasions were decorated with detailed scenes—illustrations of myths, battles and other historical events, and real athletic feats. Firing and painting techniques evolved, but athletics, including boxing fights, were consistently portrayed on these vessels. Early vessels painted in the black-figure style show contorted, relatively simple forms in profile that clearly engage but overlap little, similar to Mesopotamian, Egyptian, and earlier Greek depictions. On later, red-figure vessels, athletes' muscles and movements appear more clearly defined and more naturalistic; details, such as wounds, enhance the drama of the scenes depicted.

Athletes were celebrated ambassadors of their respective city-states, on behalf of which they competed, and it is thought that statues were dedicated to victors. Greek statuary form conveys little about how the sport was played, but demonstrates the importance of athletics in ancient Greek society and manifests philosophical theories about the human form. The sculptor Polykleitos extrapolated the mathematician Pythagoras' ideas about symmetry and proportion to create ideal human forms. Athletes' and soldiers' physiques exemplified in real life the balance of form that Polykleitos copied, and perfected, in bronze. Other sculptors after him, namely Lysippos and Praxiteles, similarly attempted to manifest the significance philosophers placed on proportional, beautiful human forms in their work.

'The Boxer of Quirinal' (4th century BCE), contrasts these earlier, pristine bodies and exemplifies Hellenistic sculpture. As is characteristic of sculpture made between the 4th and 2nd centuries BCE, the boxer's form is truly lifelike. He sits in a natural, relaxed position. His slouched shoulders, swollen cauliflower ears, and open wounds suggest the brutality of the fight he has just completed. One of the most well-known depictions of a boxer ever made, 'The Boxer' manifests all that artists have continued to try to convey—the physicality, psychology, emotion, and drama of a fight—in various media and styles.

'The Boxer' was found in Italy, from which a great deal of our knowledge of Greek statuary comes in the form of Roman copies of originals made by Greek sculptors. These copies decorated public spaces and private gardens and villas throughout the Roman Empire, along with new statues made according to Greek stylistic conventions. Another of the many things the Romans adopted from the Greeks was boxing. The sport became part of the gladiatorial 'munera', albeit in a more violent form than that practiced by the Greeks; the Romans added metal pieces to their leather strip "gloves," called caestus, making fighters' hands into horribly lethal weapons.

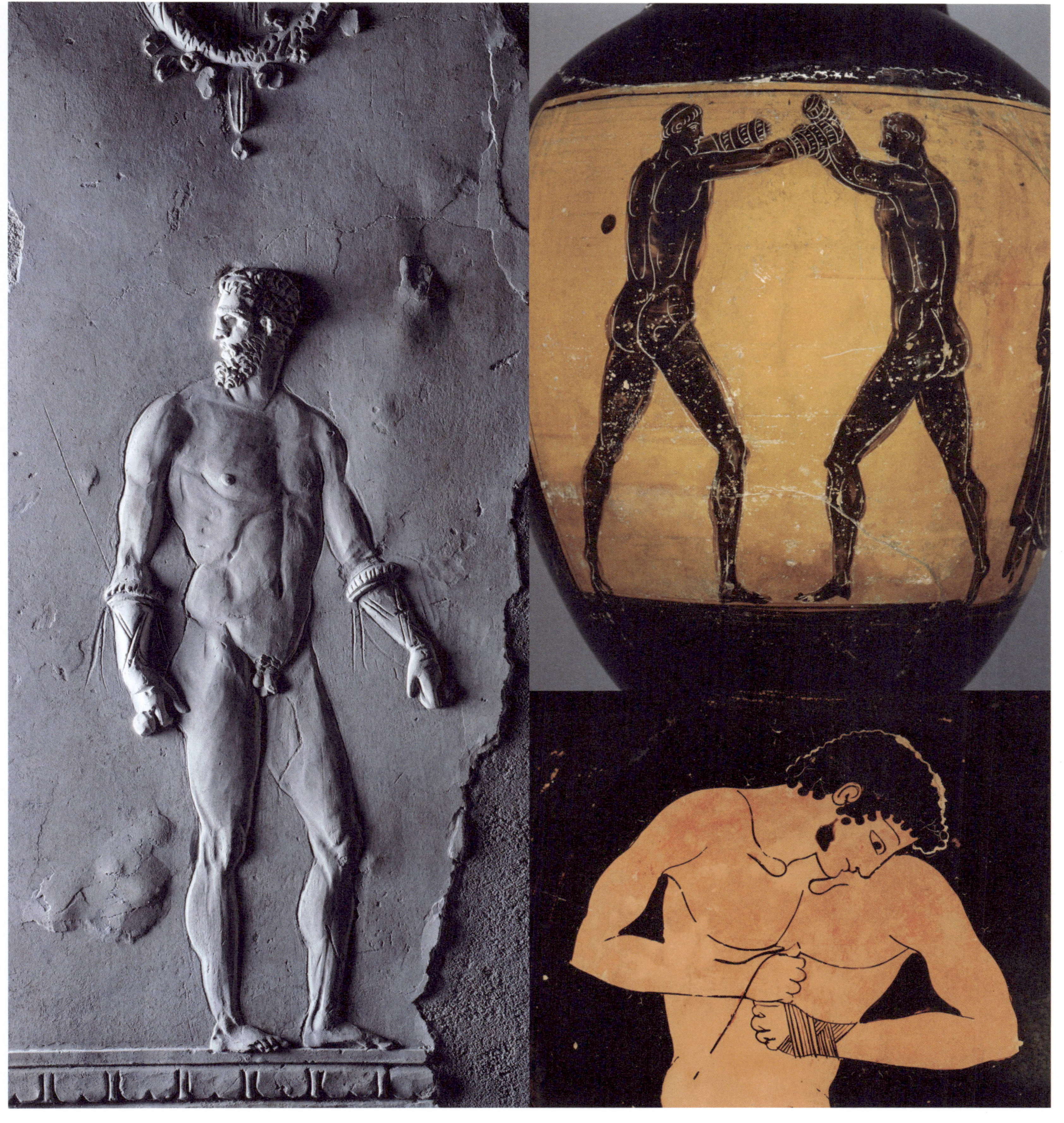

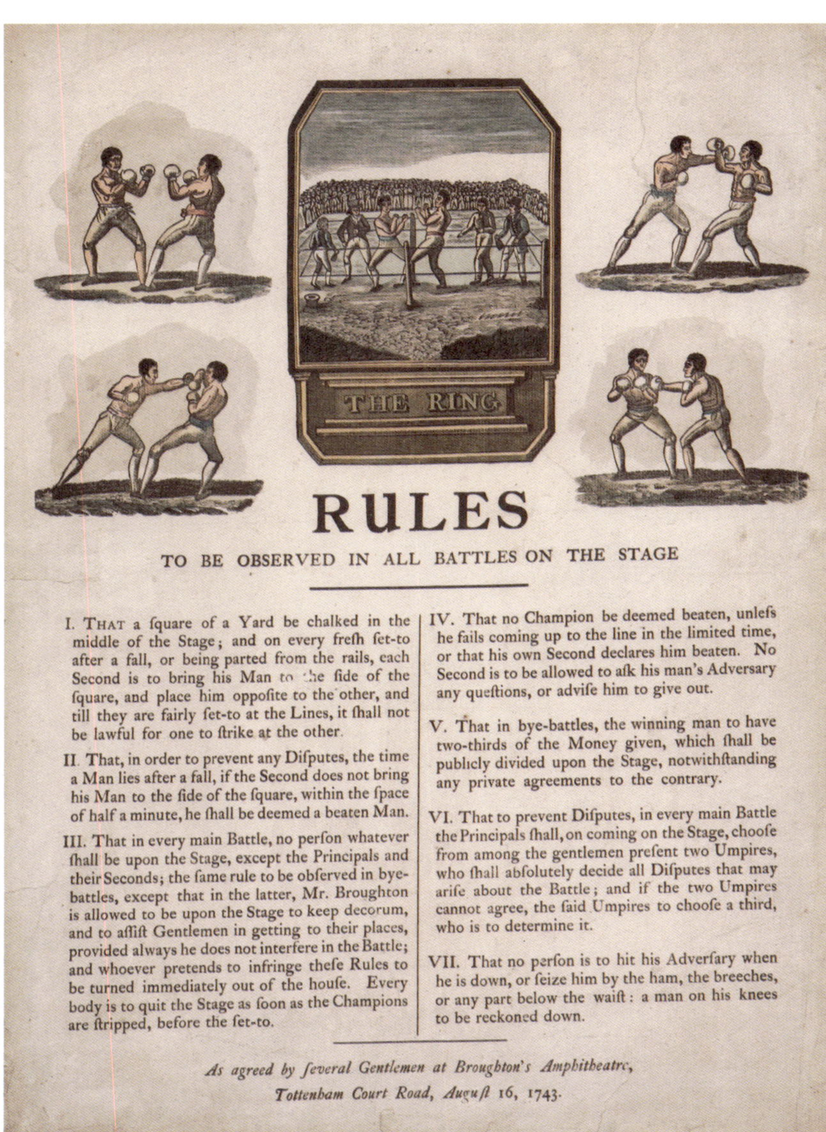

The rise of Christianity in the Roman Empire saw the end of gladiatorial contests, including boxing. During the Middle Ages, the use of weapons was preferred to hand-to-hand combat on the battlefield and in recreational fights, thus it was not until the 17th century, during the Enlightenment, that interest in boxing revived. The Neoclassical celebration of Greco-Roman culture and philosophy that grew out of the Age of Reason extended to athletics, renewing a belief in the value of physical conditioning and competition, at the same time that men began to enjoy more leisure time with the development of industrial technologies. Practiced by laborers for sport and money and by gentlemen for exercise, boxing became a favorite pastime in England.

In his early-19th-century treatise on the sport, 'Boxiana', Pierce Egan describes pugilism as "truly NATIONAL", as it cultivates in men the traits—courage, humanity, good disposition—that he believed at the core of England. He recounts the sport's ancient beginnings in asserting its significance in England, a growing empire.

Like Egan, artists emphasized the classical origins of boxing. Sketches of fighter Tom Tring depict him as a statuesque Olympian standing in quintessential contrapposto. In a portrait by John Hamilton Mortimer, champion Jack Broughton's idealized figure is backed by a pastoral setting; behind him sits the massive base of a Doric column on which is carved a relief resembling 'The Wrestlers', a Roman sculpture modeled on a Greek one of the third century BC, that was copied on canvas and in stone by many artists in the 18th and 19th centuries.

For these portraits and more generic images, artists employed athletes as models. An interest in anatomy developed during this period, as a new emphasis was placed on science and empirical observation. As in ancient Greece, athletes' toned bodies served as excellent samples of the human form.

Other artists were not as reverent in their depictions of boxing. Printmakers employed the sport as a satirical conceit. Cartoons illustrating political issues show members of Parliament and other leaders bare-chested with fists cocked, surrounded by attendants. In representing political tensions or exaggerating national differences between the English and French, artists depicted robust English boxers opposing foppish French opponents. In turn, the French portrayed the English as brutish fighters.

In these caricatures and portraits, and in illustrative prints made for reproduction in periodicals, boxers stand in what was at the time the standard fighting posture: legs wide, feet flat, knees bent, arms extended far in front of the body, fists bare, and torso leaned back. Without gloves, which had not yet been adopted as common gear, boxers used their arms for defense and attempted to keep their heads out of reach of their opponent's fists.

This stance would change, however, when Jack Broughton introduced the use of gloves at the same time that he published a set of rules to regulate boxing matches—the first in the sport's modern history. Though the use of the puffy "mufflers" was not enforced until the late 19th century, they appear in some illustrations from the time and also on metal tokens that were presumably given as medals to victors.

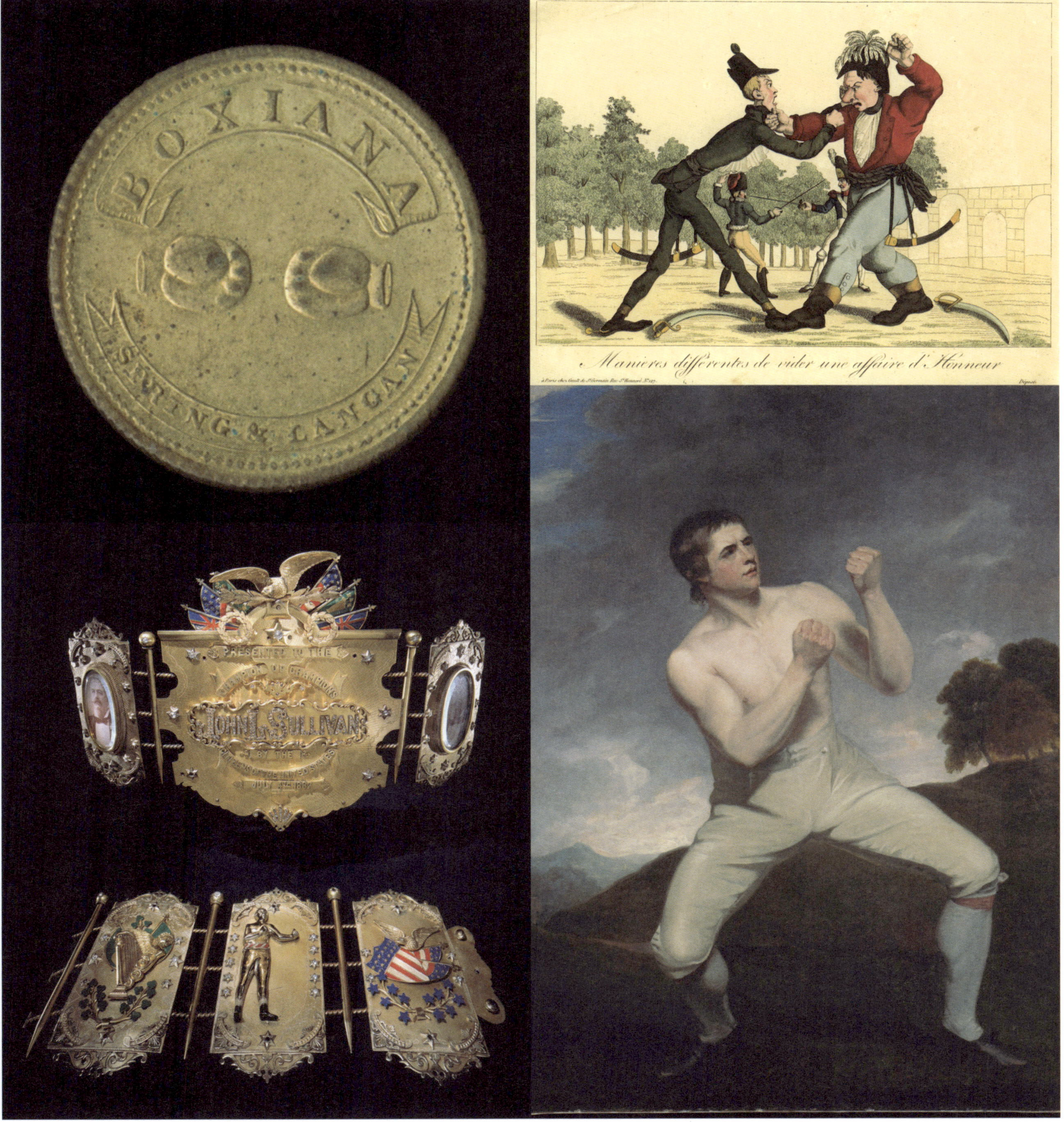
BOXIANA
SPRING & LANGAN
PRESENTED TO THE
JOHN L. SULLIVAN
Manières différentes de vider une affaire d'Honneur

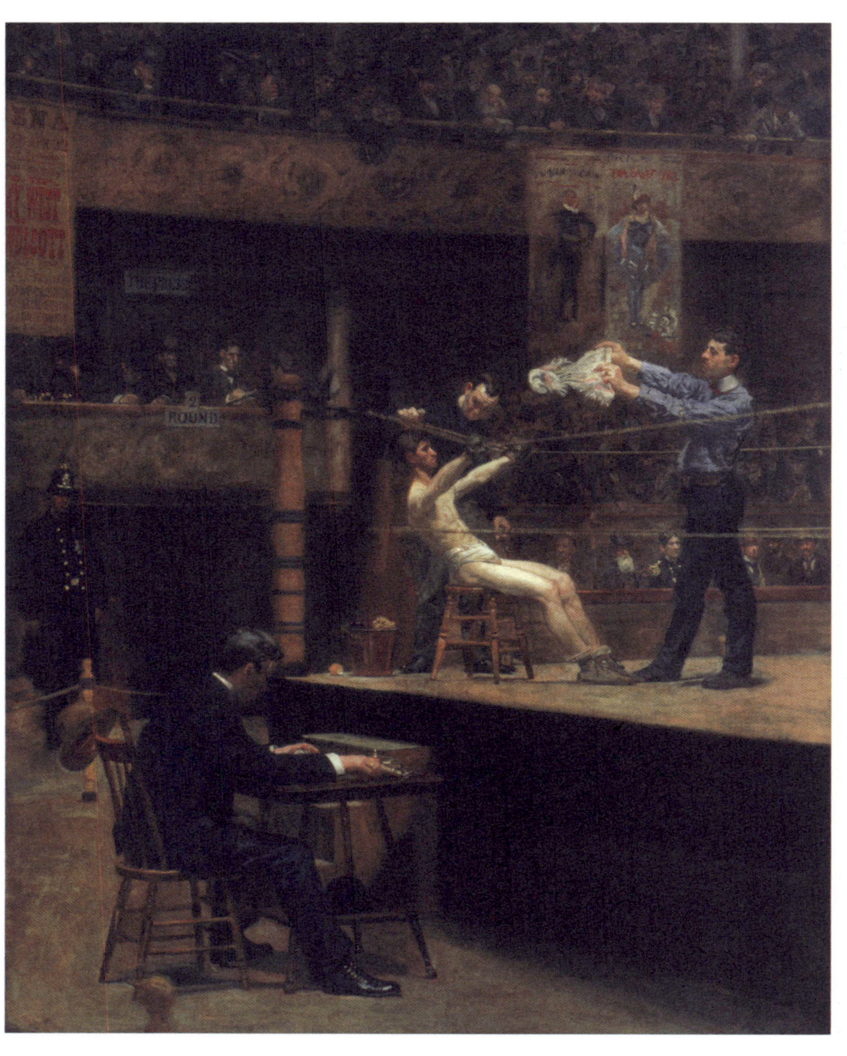

As prize fighting's "golden age" in England began to wane, boxing became increasingly popular in the newly independent United States. Despite the sport's fluctuating legality in America, men around the country engaged in fights. Slaves fought other slaves in brutal contests arranged by their owners, Civil War soldiers boxed in camp for recreation, and immigrants buoyed by national pride fought other newcomers to the country.

In England a new set of rules, published under the name of the Marquess of Queensbury, innovated several regulations that would eventually be adopted in the US and shaped the sport into its modern form. One rule established the length of each round at three minutes, and a mandatory break between rounds at one, a structure that remains the standard for amateur and professional matches. Another required the use of gloves and specified their size. Boxers adjusted their fighting posture to adapt to the gloves, which enabled each fighter to better protect his face. The tucked arms and inclined torso that define the fighter's stance today are a consequence of the standardization of the use of gloves in the 19th century.

Other developments outside the ring had a less direct, but no less significant, impact on the sport. The advent of photography allowed the immediate documentation of fights, which made it simpler for journalists and fans to follow them. Fight stills and portrait photographs of champions alike contributed to fighters' increasing celebrity.

The English photographer Eadweard Muybridge employed photography not as a means to create a single still, representative image of a fight or other extended motion, but as an apparatus for capturing an entire sequence of movement. With Thomas Eakins, Muybridge made series of photographs of animals and people in motion, among them boxers, which when printed in order illustrate the subjects' sequential actions.

Shortly after Muybridge completed his Animal Locomotion project, as the photographs are known, he invented the zoopraxiscope. The new device was a small disc, printed with a sequence of images of a figure in motion, that could be spun quickly to affect the illusion of the figure's fluid action, like a flip book or film reel.

Muybridge was not the only artist to employ boxers as subject for experiments with moving-image technology. Many artists continued to favor athletes' toned bodies as models, as they had in the 18th century. And, because early filmic apparatuses were large and cumbersome, and images could not be created instantaneously, as they are today, boxers confined to a 24-foot square ring were easier to capture on film than, say, sprinters. Some of the earliest films depicted fights, such as the Leonard-Cushing bout, filmed in 1894. Before projection technology was introduced, these could be watched, one round at a time, on a kinetoscope, an individual viewing machine that Thomas Edison created. Anyone could pay to watch a fight or just the final round. The increasing visibility of the sport only augmented its mass appeal.

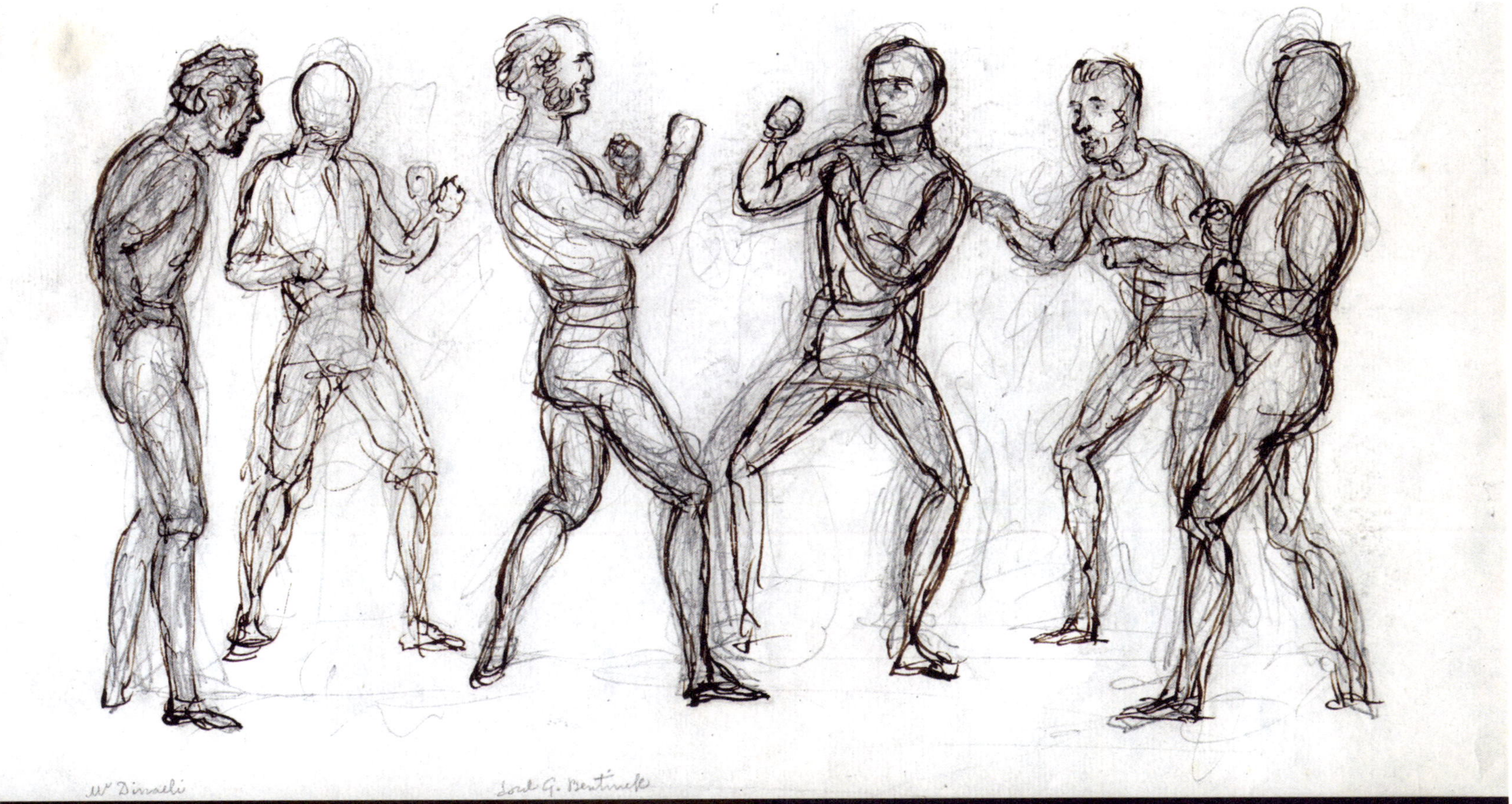

Mr Disraeli
Lord G. Bentinck

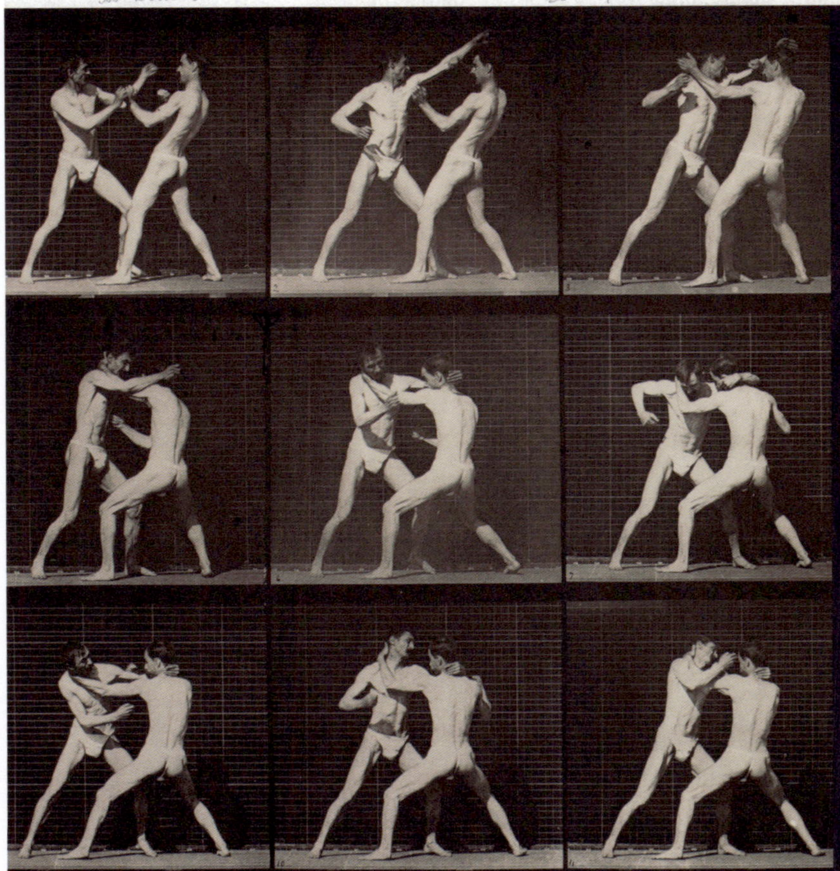

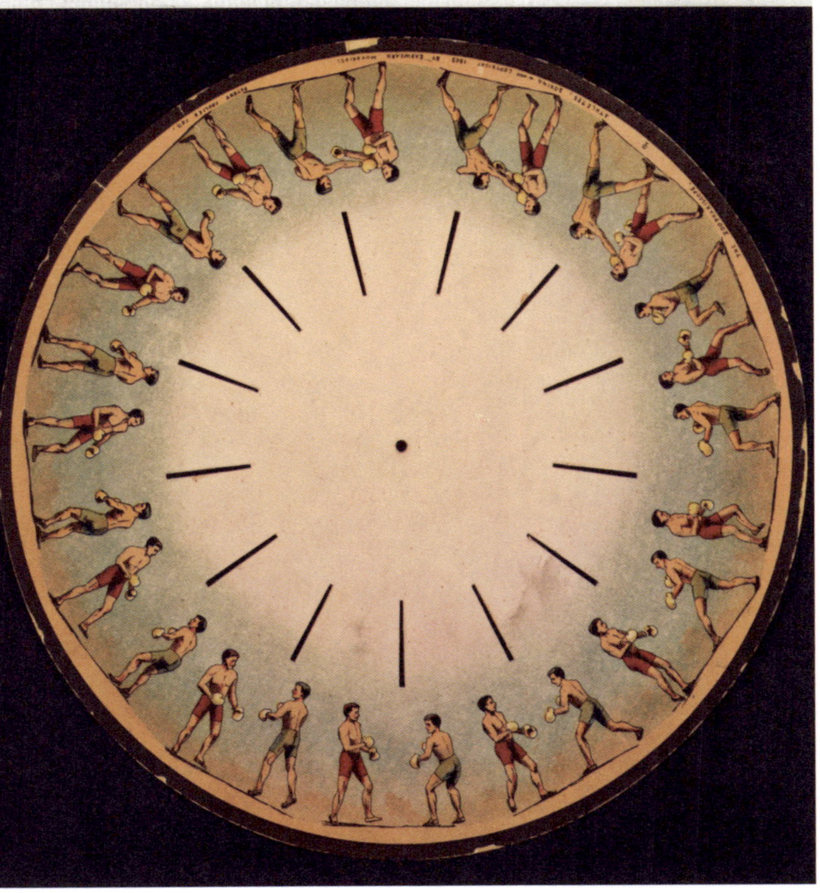

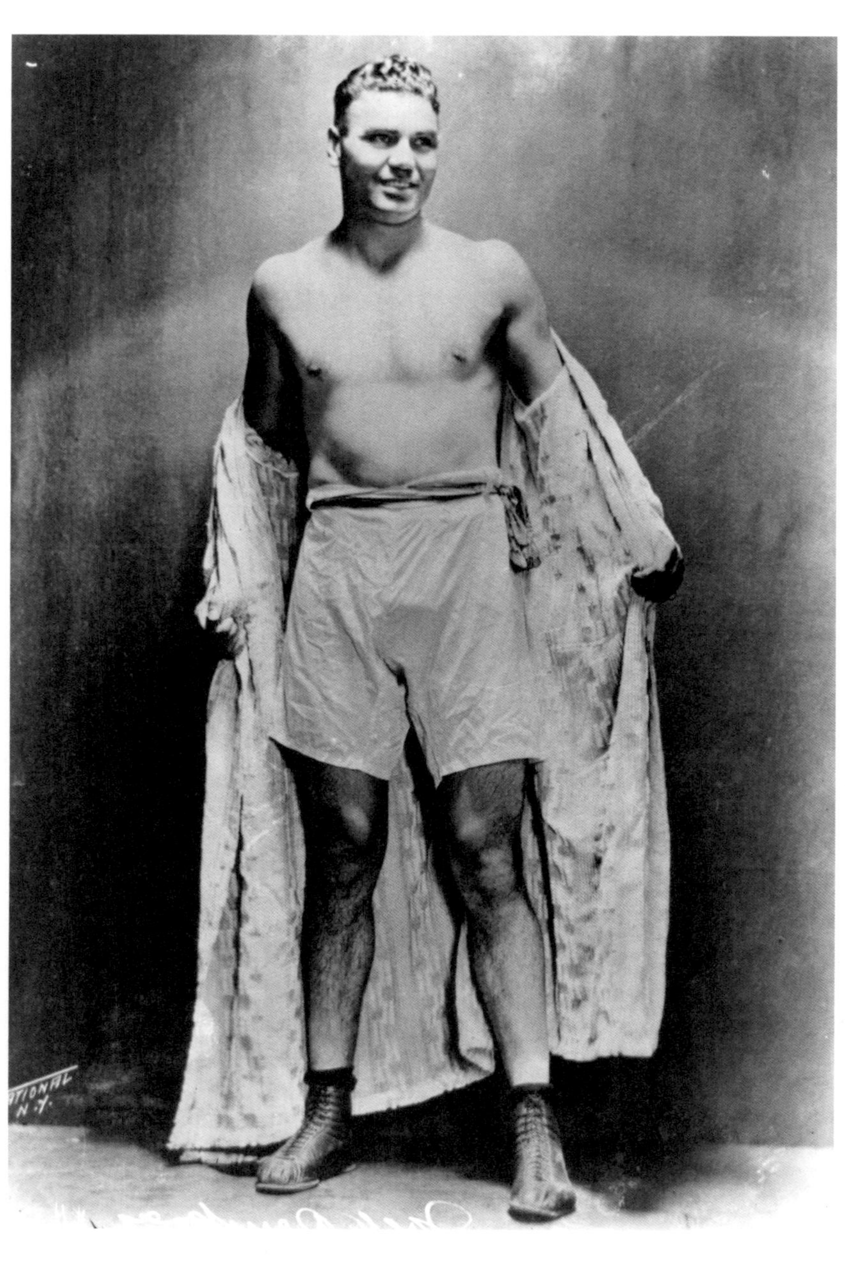

George Bellows (1882-1925), American realist painter who captured the societal exchanges, nuances, and explicit realities
of his urban surroundings, often used the sport of boxing
as subject matter, for here he could combine the expres-
sive quality of his medium with the charged passion of in-
tense body contact and the interim moments of rest. The sport
was inextricable from its reflection of society's desire for
spectatorship and entertainment and its inadvertent tendency
to highlight the athlete's psyche. An integral artist to the
Ashcan school, advocating for the depiction of contemporary
American society, the always socially conscious Bellows focused on individual rights throughout his work and lifetime.
Bellows lived on Broadway opposite the Sharkey Athletic Club,
a prizefighting venue that circumvented the law by charging
a club membership fee to view the fights. One of Bellows's
most famous paintings, 'Stag at Sharkey's' (1909) captures
two fighters in a dark, crowded space of the ring – the essence associated with these prizefighting clubs at the turn of
the century. The promoter's way around the illicit nature of
prizefighting is explored in the title of another of Bellows's
early paintings of the same year, 'Both Members of this Club',
in which two boxers, one black and one white, are "entwined in
a violent dance of naked aggression in the ring, while lurid
spectators cheer."

Meanwhile on July 4, 1910, a crowd of over twelve thousand
people, comprised mostly white men, gathered in a makeshift
stadium in Reno, Nevada anticipating to witness Jim Jeffries,
the retired white Heavyweight Champion of the World, take back
the title from the African-American current champion, Jack
Johnson. Coined 'the fight of the century,' and a significant
moment indeed, for black boxers (with the exception of Johnson) had been barred from fighting for the heavyweight championship title as a result of the inherently racist devices of
the sport. The following morning, Johnson landed front-page
headlines for his unquestioned but shocking and controversial
victory. Mainly portrayed in a negative light in an era when
African-Americans were rarely mentioned in white press (un-
less for a crime), the coverage of Johnson was supplemented
with racist editorial cartoons. As a direct result of the
Jeffries-Johnsons fight, race riots ensued the evening of the
4th of July and in the days following. While blacks across
the nation celebrated Johnson's victory as a racial advance-
ment, whites responded with violence, and in the conflicts up
to 26 were killed and hundreds injured. Johnson would become
an early example of the celebrity athlete in the modern era,
appearing regularly in the press and later on radio and in motion pictures. Actively challenging conventions of the social and eco-
nomic position of blacks in American society, Johnson was involved in three separate turbulent marriages with white women, ridden
with reports of domestic violence, suicide, infidelity, prison sentences, and exiles to Europe. Nonetheless, he remained a major
influence on the history of the sport through his perseverance and presence.

Prizefighting was eventually legalized and the New York Boxing Commission was established as a regulatory agency. By 1923 it was
considered fashionable to attend the more civilized sport of boxing (as opposed to prizefighting). Relics such as Gene Tunney's
boxing gloves preserved from his 1927 'long count' fight with Jack Dempsey, cultural icon of the 1920's who held the World Heavyweight Championship from 1919 to 1926, evidence the increased appreciation and importance placed on the sport.

When men's boxing was introduced at the modern Olympic Games in St. Louis in 1904 as a display demonstration bout, it followed
that men's boxing was then accepted into the Olympics, while women's was not. While the sport was increasingly enjoyed by men as a
'sport like any other,' women during the late 1800s to early 1900s, did not have the chance to fight professionally so they took
to the variety theater stage instead. One of the better known instances, and considered the first female boxing match in the United
States, was the 1876 staged match between Nell Saunders and Rose Harland at the New York Hills Theater. Similar characters, Hattie
Stewart and another fighter named Hattie Leslie were both known as the 'Female John L. Sullivan,' and often they called each other
out in the boxing press, using the media as an extension of the theatrical platform. Throughout the 1920s boxing was part of the
physical training of young women across the United States, and would eventually lead to development in professional women's leagues
at the end of the 1990s before finally being recognized an Olympic sport at the 2012 Games in London.

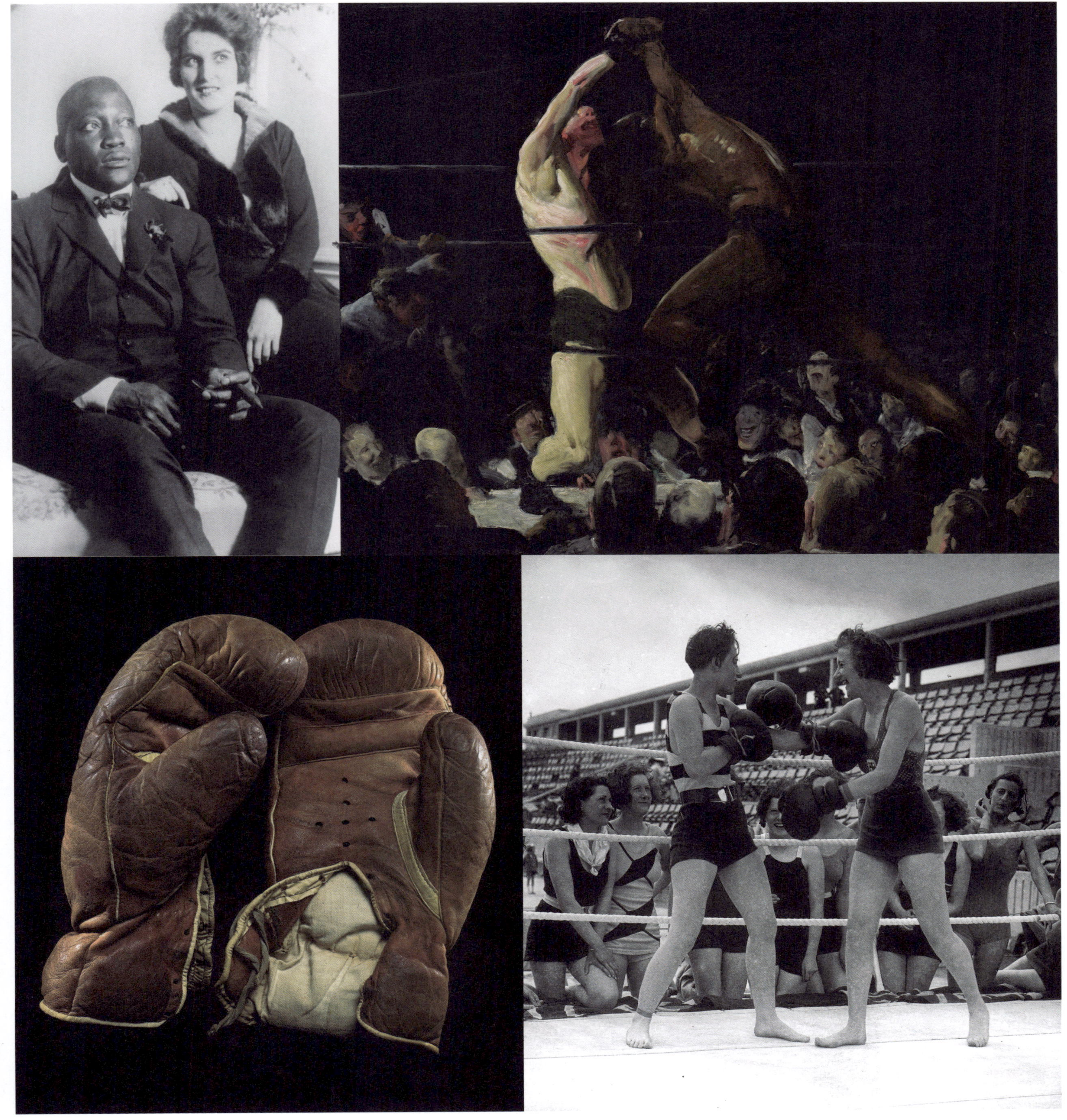

20

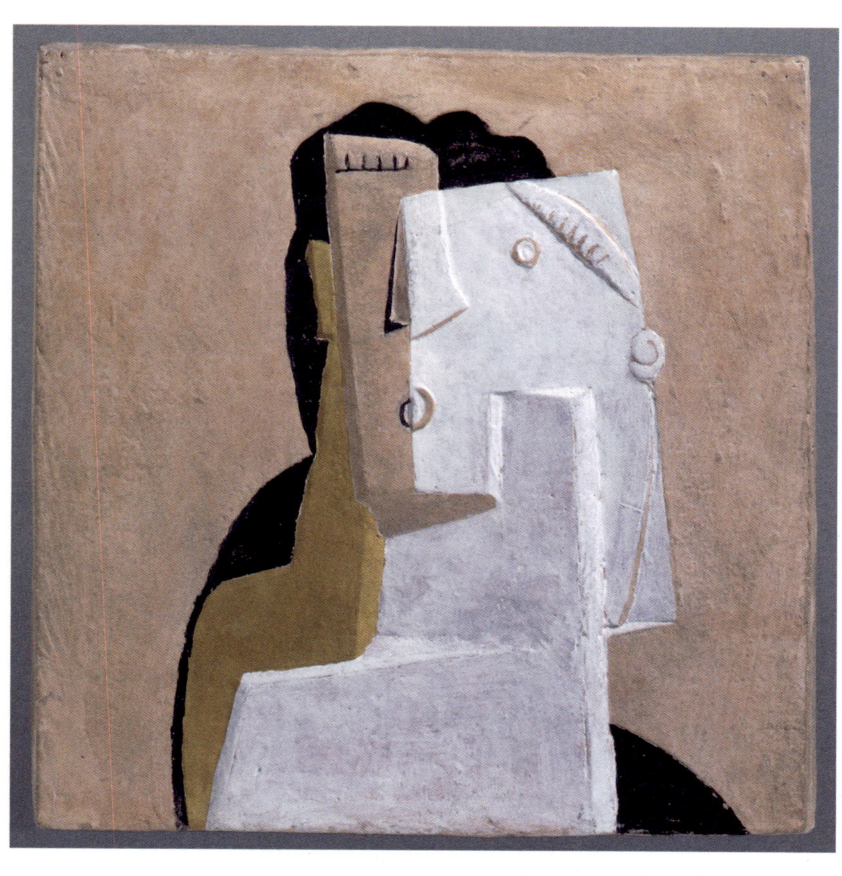

Boxing remained a popular subject among filmmakers and audiences in the first decades of the twentieth century as film technology improved. Audiences continued to pay to watch films of staged and competitive professional fights, and, in an effort to appeal to them, narrative film directors wrote screenplays featuring boxing. The 1927 short experimental film 'Combat de Boxe', made by Belgian director Charles Dekeukelaire, stands out among these films as a stylized, avant-garde portrayal of the sport. In a dynamic montage of footage of a fight that he staged, Dekeukelaire alludes to social politics, capitalism, and human psychology and demonstrates advanced editing techniques and a modernist aesthetic. The film exemplifies a new way of seeing a modernizing world and portrays boxing—and its celebrity champions, international rivals, spectacular fights, and speculating fans—according to that new perspective.

Still photographs from the time similarly evince boxing's popularity in the early twentieth century and manifest a developing snapshot aesthetic (the result of the increasingly common use of photography). Amateur and professional photographs from the period depict fights in outdoor and indoor rings, both typically surrounded by a large crowd consisting almost entirely of white men. It was through the circulation of photographs and films, as well as the inclusion of boxing in the modern Olympic Games for the first time, in 1904, that boxing finally found an audience in continental Europe. Boxing became especially popular in Germany, which gave the world a new champion in Max Schmeling in 1930. (Schmeling is thought to have started training as a boxer after watching a film of Jack Dempsey defeating Georges Carpentier.)

The sport took hold in Germany as the country reeled from the devastation of the first world war. Many artists, some of whom fought in the war and others who witnessed its tragedy as civilians, grappled with the horror of trench warfare and its physiological and psychological effects in their work. In doing so, many reexamined the male body, which signified something markedly different—weakness, pain, immortality—than it had before the war began. Man's powerlessness versus mechanical weapons demonstrated his tragic vulnerability, as did his capability, in operating such machines, to destroy other men.

Considering the impact of war at the time, it is little wonder that boxers, as practitioners of hand-to-hand combat, were among the male figures that artists took as their subjects. Henri Laurens's Cubist 'Head of a Boxer' from the 1920 and ee cummings's drawing, 'Boxer (Puglist)', from 1922, each depict a fighter—in the form of an abstracted, broken face, devoid of any identifying signifier of the sport other than a large, damaged nose. Both images suggest the ruin boxing can wreak on its contestants, and man's fragility more generally.

A number of Dadaist collages, such as Erwen Blumenfeld's 'Marquis de Sade' (1921), make caricatures of the cutout photographs of boxers they include. Boxing was among the sports that became popular in Weimar after World War I, and Max Schmeling a favorite patriot whom Hitler touted as a national hero. In contrast to portrayals of Schmeling as a stoic champion, such as the one, in profile, that George Grosz painted in 1925, these whimsically satirical collages do not glorify the sport or individual fighters but mock them, likely as signifiers of war and Hitler's Nationalist Socialist agenda. The juxtaposition of boxing images with others clipped from newspapers, magazines, and photographs prefigures the advertisements and promotional images featuring fighters that the media would generate during World War II and especially after its resolution.

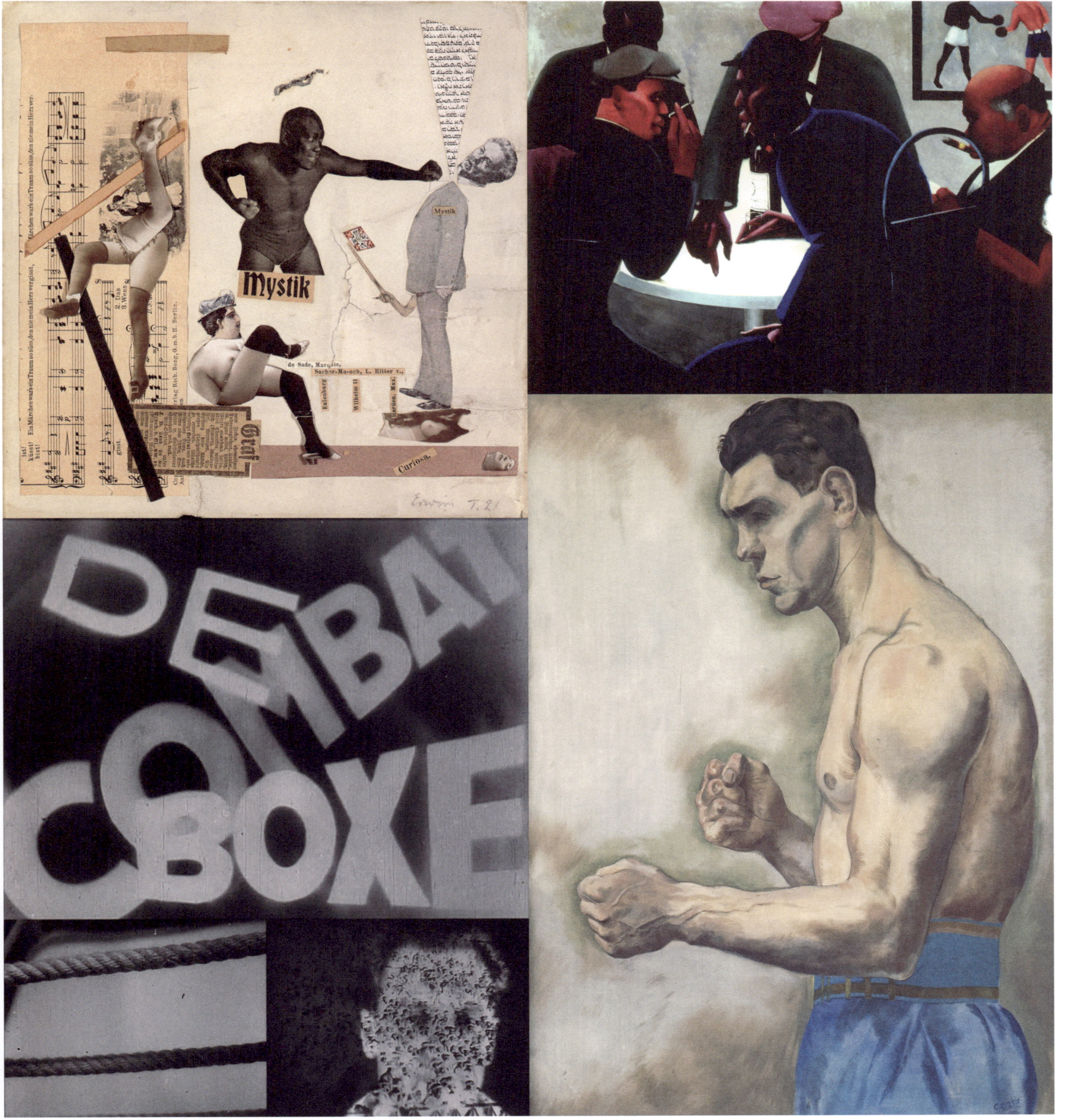

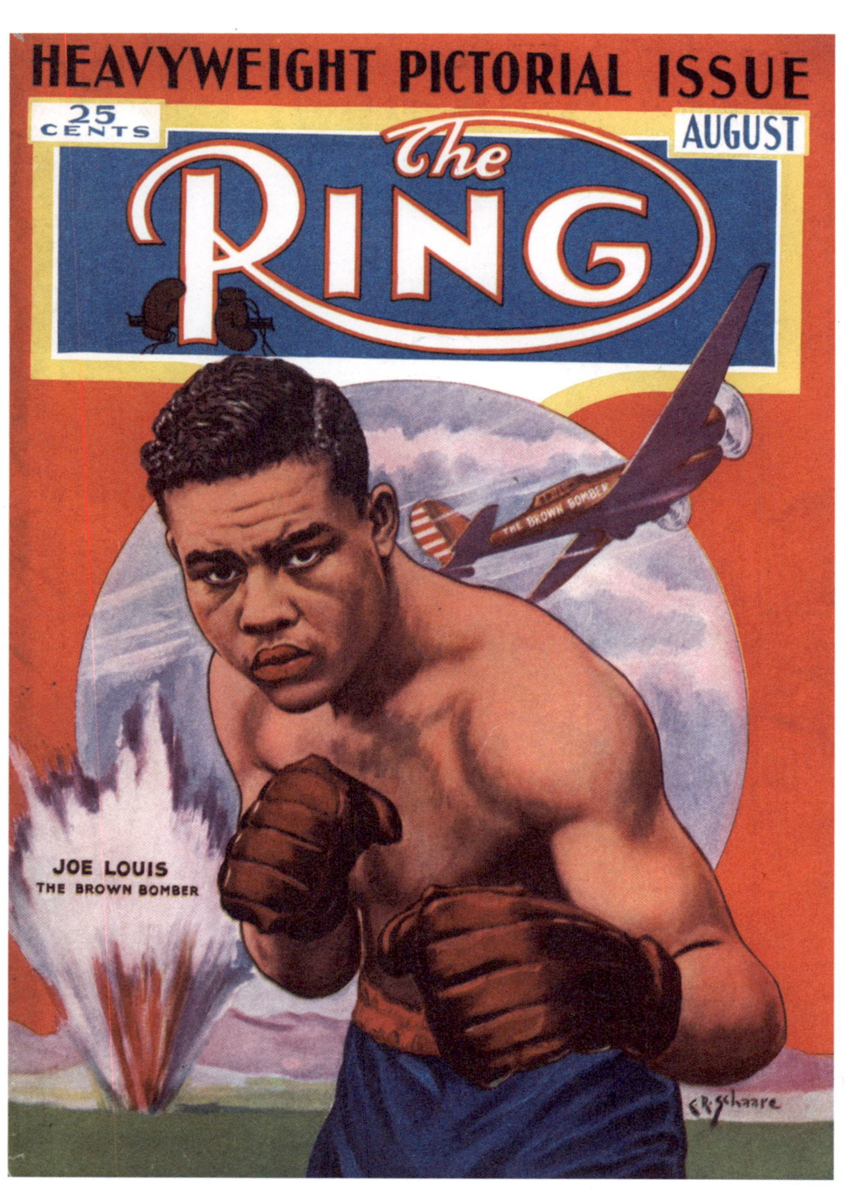

Many great athletes of the 1950s became powerful legends at the mercy of popular culture, and in an earlier era this was foreshadowed by a talented boxer whose passion was true but whose shaping by the collective hand of the American public was a precise reflection of the times. Joseph Louis Barrow, born in rural Alabama to parents who themselves were the children of former slaves, relocated his own family (following an episode of Klan racism) to Detroit in 1926, the city that would later erect a statue and stadium in his honor. When he was 17, the young athlete experienced his first amateur fight, and continued to hide his ambitions from his mother who had hopes that he would play the violin. After a series of wins in the Golden Gloves division, he was on his way to becoming the 'Joe Louis, Brown Bomber' who would go down in the memory of the American public, his nickname an indication of the era's racism. During World War II Louis fought charity bouts, spoke at Relief Fund dinners, and enlisted as a private, his induction and activity captured and reported by the media and complicated in the context of the racially segregated U.S. Army. Louis never saw combat, as he was placed into the Special Services Division and would go on to participate in a celebrity tour with other notables including fellow boxer Sugar Ray Robinson, during which time he staged numerous boxing exhibitions for millions of soldiers. Muhammad Ali would later credit Louis and Robinson as his biggest influences, but also hold criticism toward the amount of malleability on these men from their Caucasian counterparts. Heavyweight champion between 1937-49, Louis' career ended in 1951 with a post-retirement blow delivered by Rocky Marciano. This Rocky (born Rocco Francis Marchegiano) who sent Louis to his grave - career-wise - would go on to retire holding a perfect record title as a world heavy weight champion between 1952-57, his face (unapologetically pronouncing his Italian heritage) donning the cover of countless magazine covers. Sugar Ray Robinson was similarly coveted in the public eye, idolized by the masses and youth culture while accumulating skepticism around his extravagant lifestyle as well as a reputation for traveling with what became called - in perhaps the first usage in sports-history - his "entourage." A new breed of celebrity was born.

The jet-airplane era of the late 1950s allowed for more ease to travel and resulted in more fights occurring outside of the United States, leading to the global growth of the sport. Television became commonplace in the American home in the post-war era and most families looked forward to 'Gillette Friday Night Fights' to watch contestants such Sugar Ray Robinson, Carmen Basilio, Chuck Davey, Chico Vejar, Kid Gavilan, Gene Fullmer, Johnny Saxton, Tony DeMarco, and Charlie Powell — all to the opening jingle of 1954 Boston Pops tune 'Look Sharp Be Sharp.' Rocky Marciano for Hamm's Beer commercial aired on television, showing the great athlete (in post-retirement) comically and effortlessly knocking out the brand's cartoon-bear mascot. 1954, Barbara Buttrick 98-pound flyweight at four feet and eleven inches tall would be the first female fight broadcast on national television.

On September 5, 1960, Muhammad Ali (then still known as Cassius Clay and 18 years old) fought in the Olympic Games in Rome against Pietrzyskowski from Poland in the light-heavyweight championship bout. The judges declared Ali the winner, and awarded him the Olympic gold medal. In 1964, the emerging fighter made a splash from Miami Beach, when he defeated Sonny Liston to gain the title of heavyweight champion. He boasted during his weigh-in that he predicted someone would "die at ring-side from shock," and he wasn't far from the truth. After winning the championship from Liston in 1964, Clay made public that he was a member of the Nation of Islam and took the name Cassius X in order to discard his surname as a symbol of his ancestors' enslavement. Clay would be then be renamed Muhammad (meaning praiseworthy) Ali. A few years later, in 1967, upon his refusal of induction into the U.S. Armed forces for the Vietnam War, the World Boxing Association striped him of his title — anticipating the growing antiwar movement of the 1960's. He would continue as a master of his form who would float and sting his way to victory, through not only boxing but towards battling civil rights and ushering in a new era.

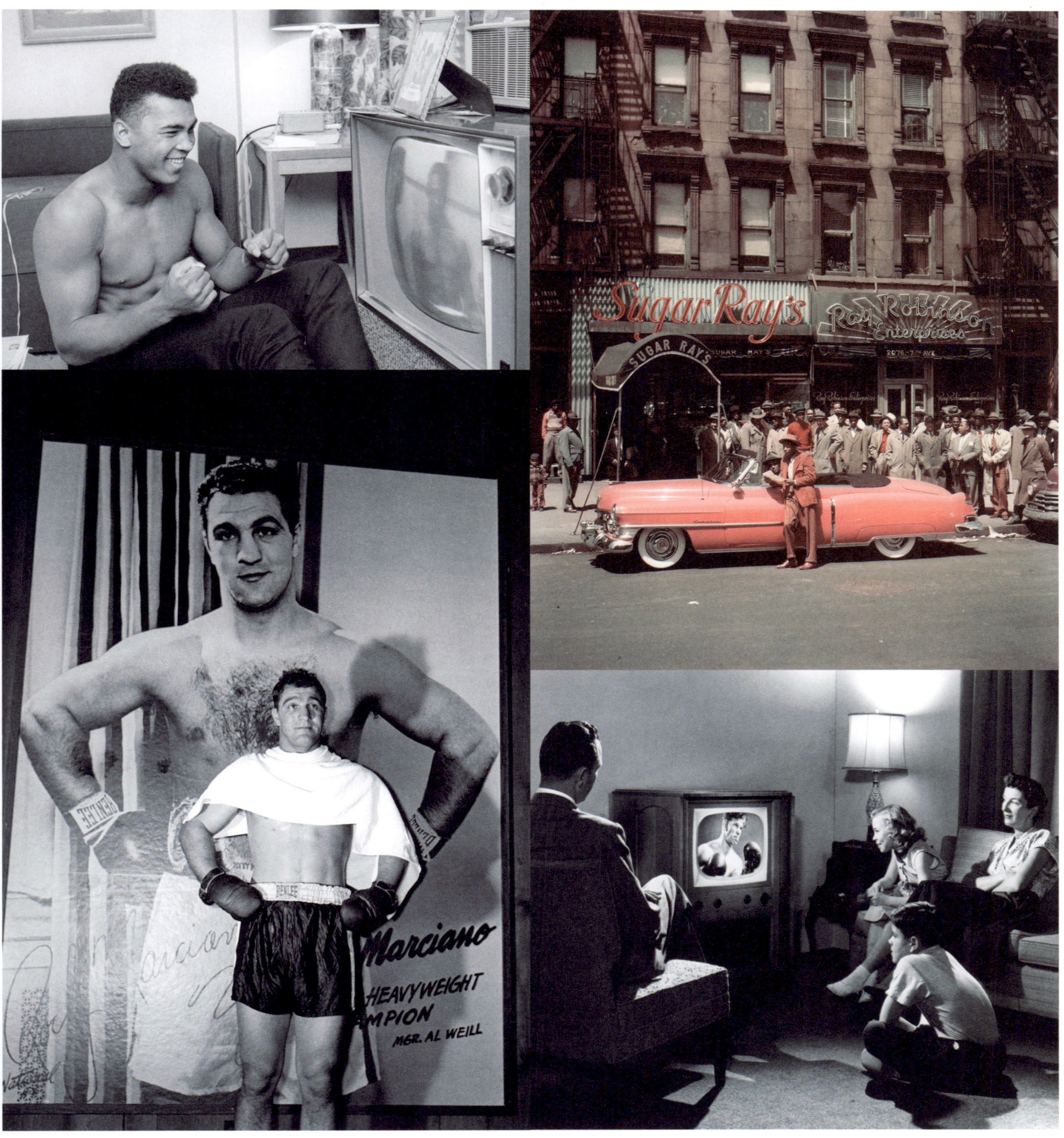

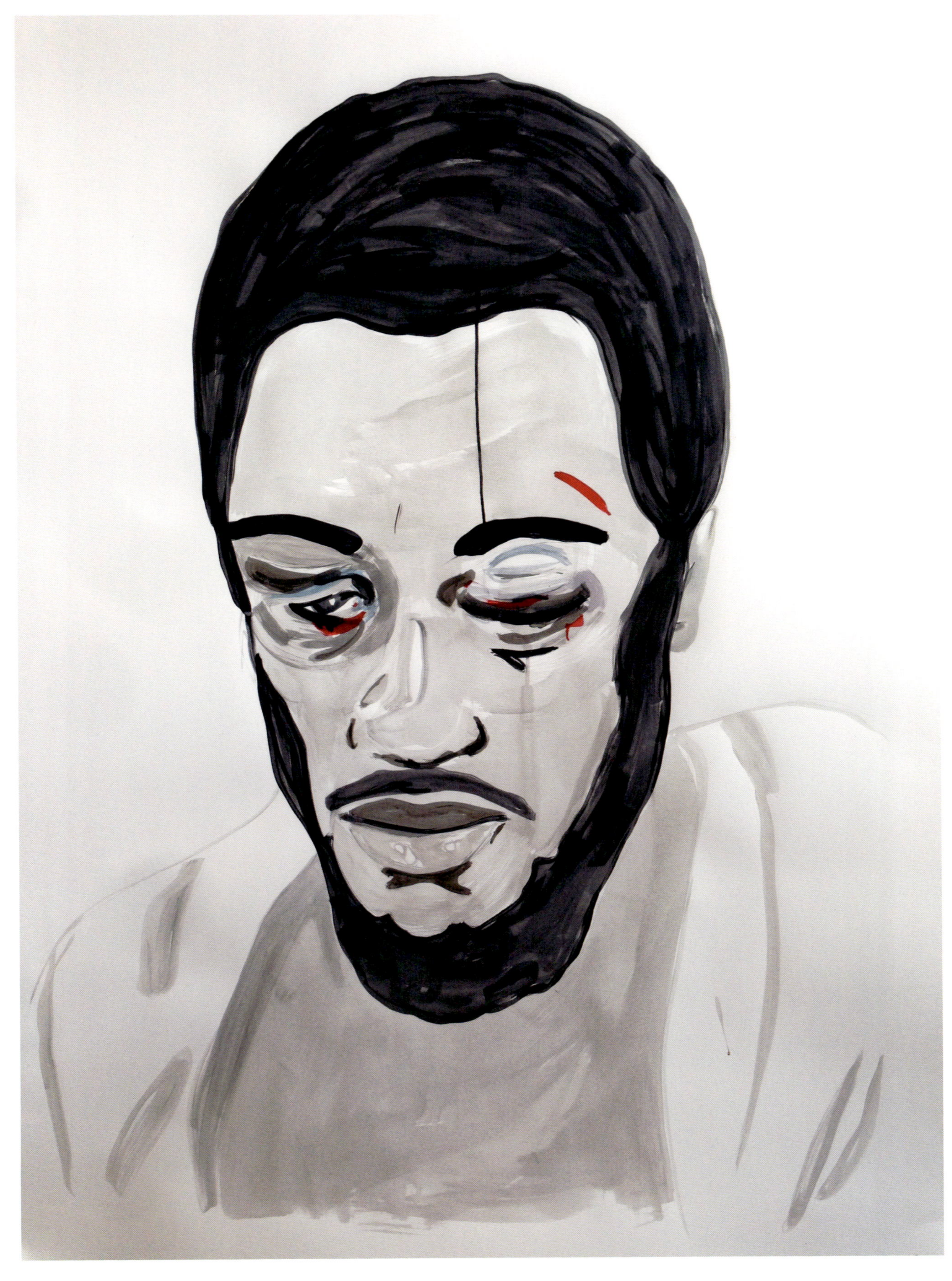

SMOKE, 1983 - AFTER THE FALL / 79 X 34 INCHES
COLLECTION OF SUZANNE JAMES

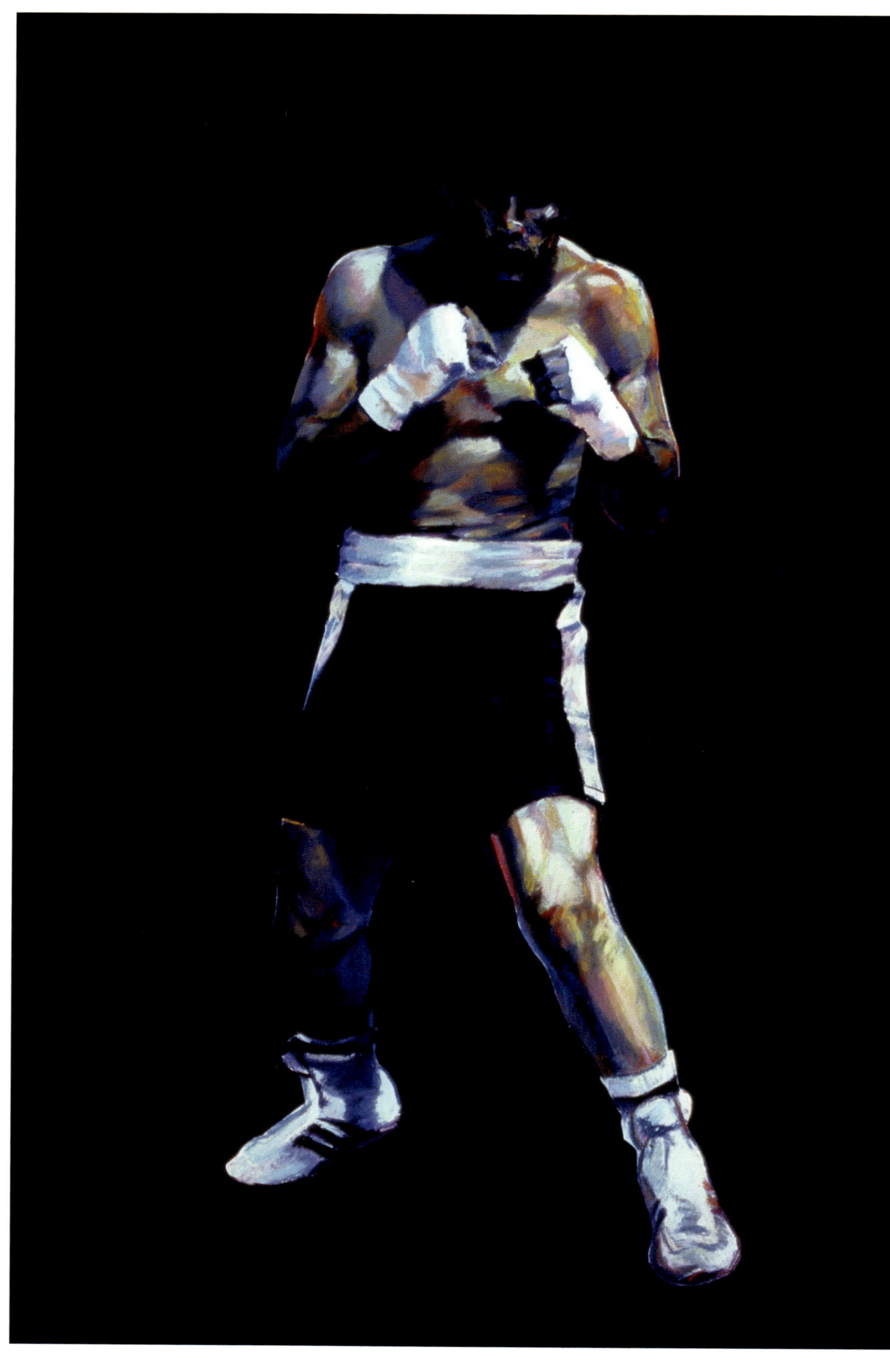

RANDY HAYES

DIDN'T HAVE A PRAYER, 1984 - AFTER THE FALL / 83.5 X 32 INCHES
COLLECTION OF BOB AND MARILYN JOYCE

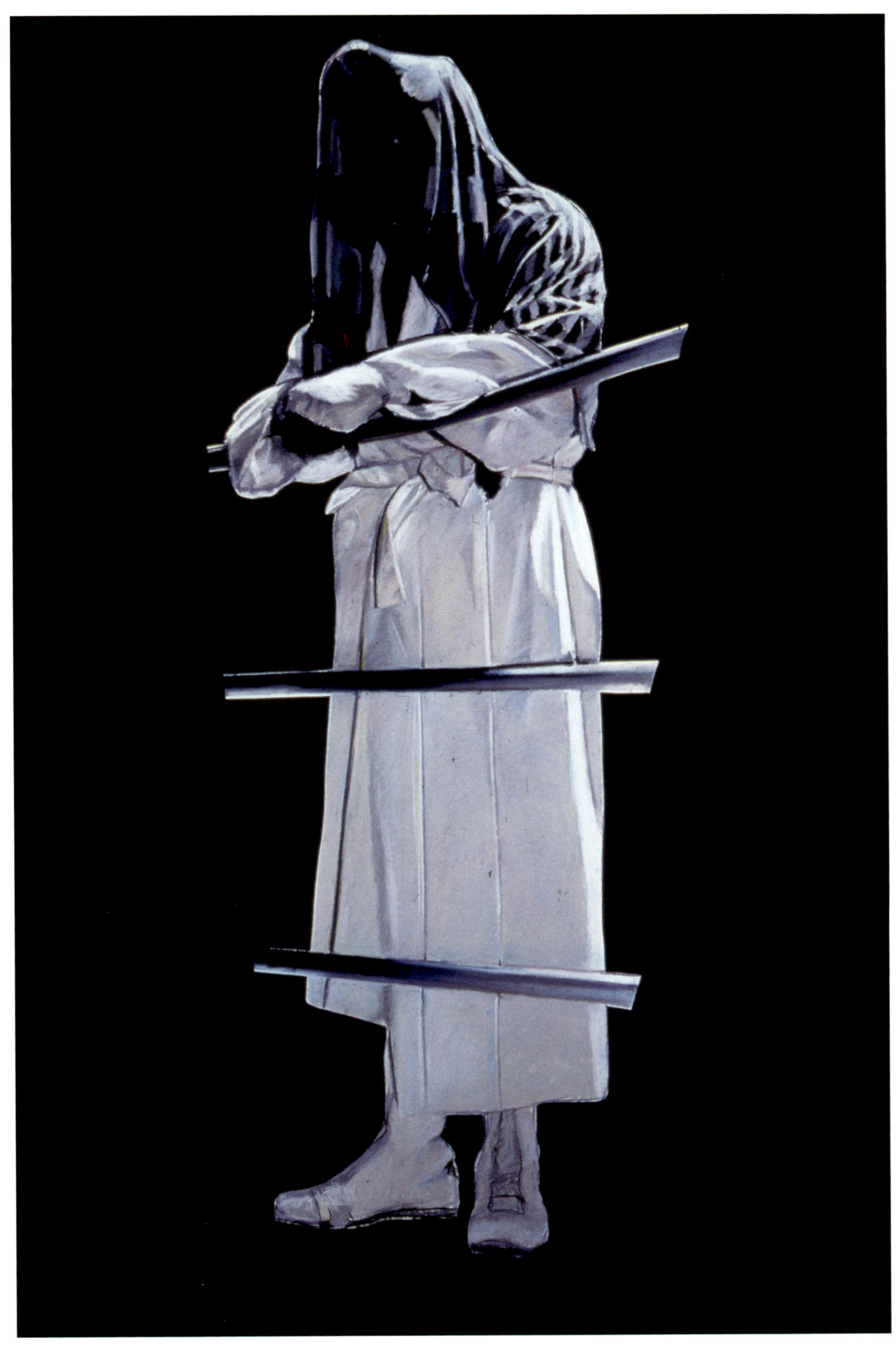

TANER CEYLAN

NIRVANA, 2009 - OIL ON CANVAS / 140 X 200 CM

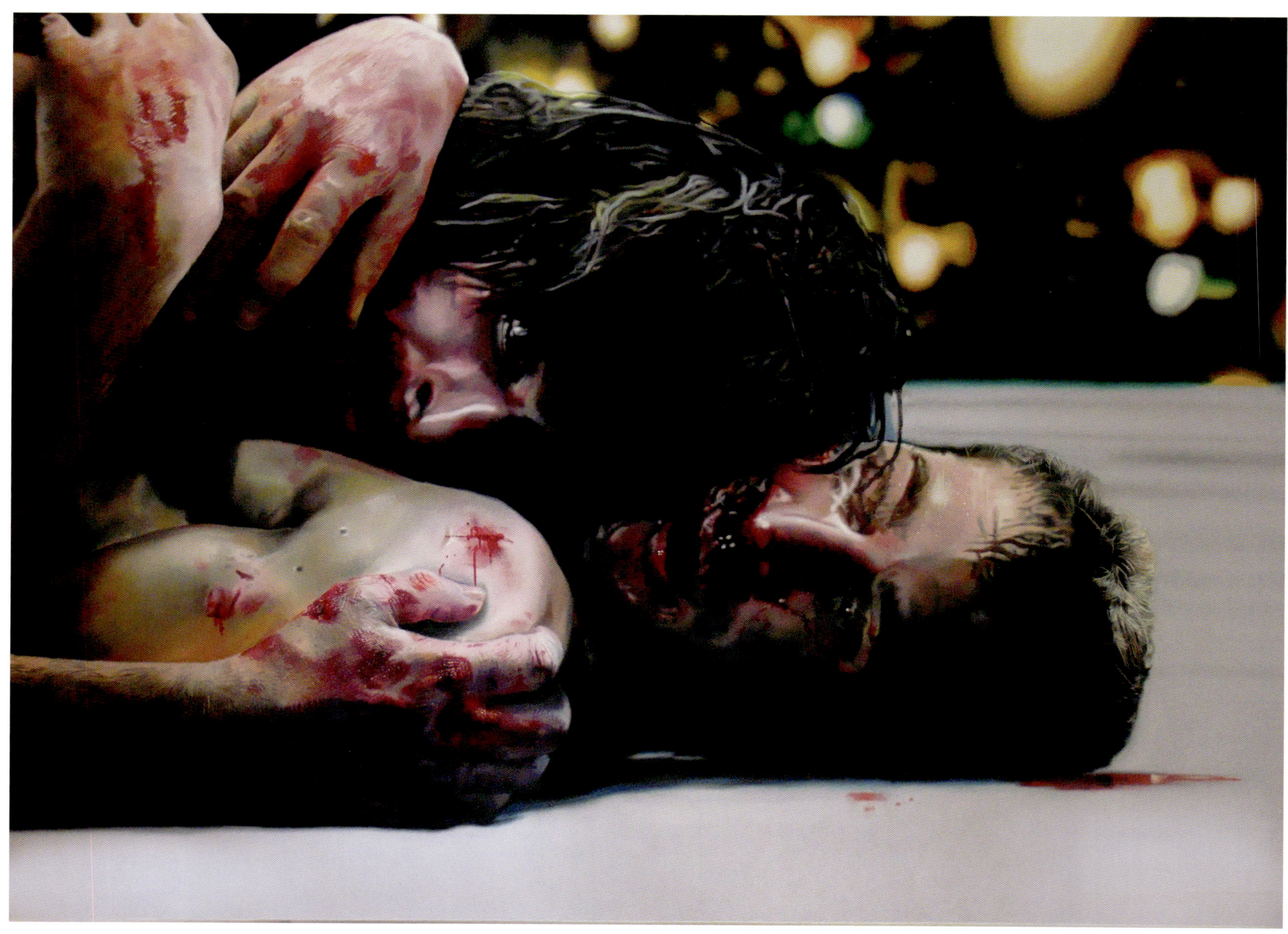

TANER CEYLAN

SPIRITUAL, 2008 - OIL ON CANVAS / 140 X 200 CM

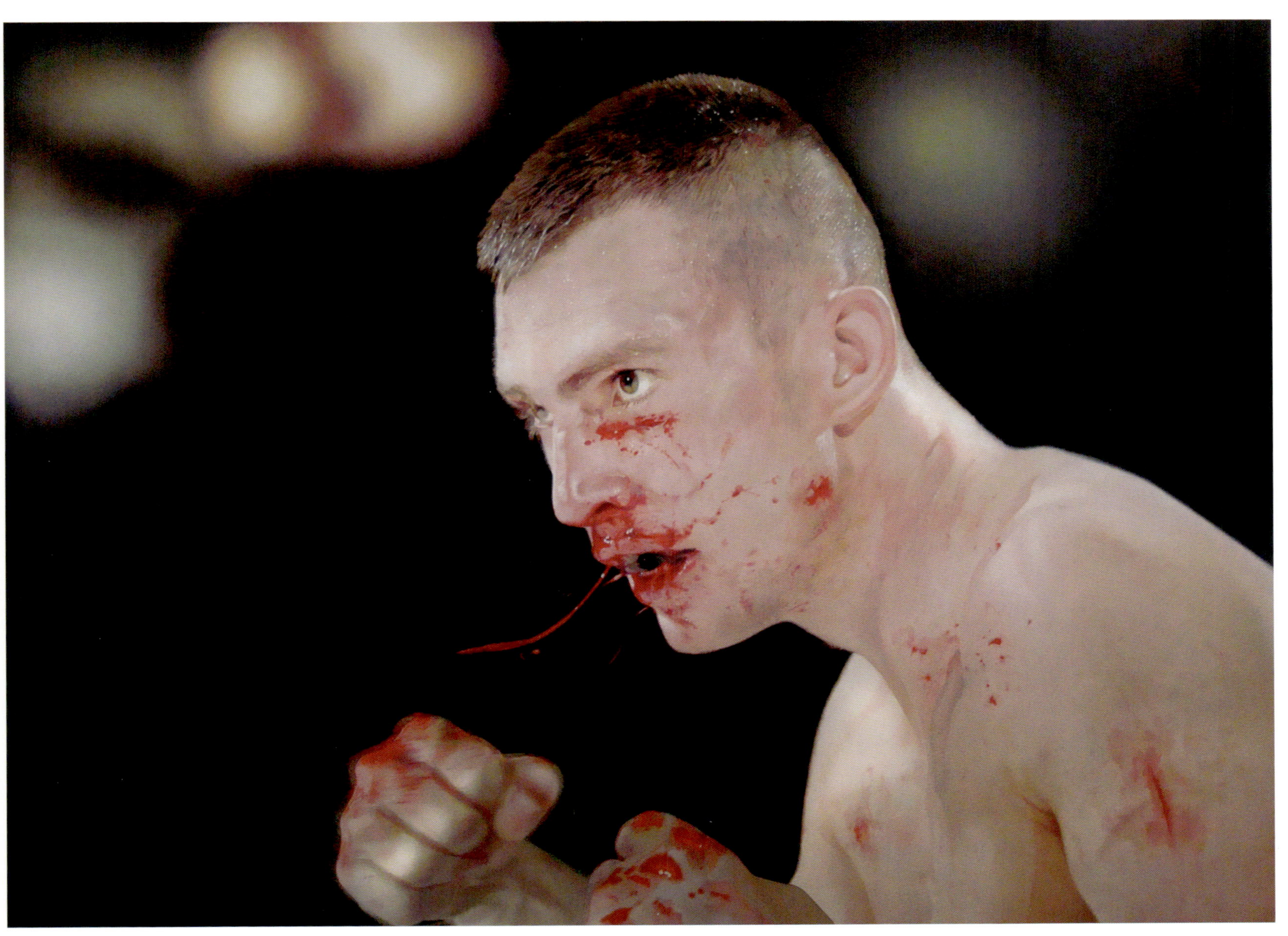

ELLINGTON ROBINSON

WE'RE IN THIS FIGHT TOGETHER, 88, 2008 - ACRYLIC, FOUND OBJECTS, AND LATEX / 96 X 96 X 108 INCHES

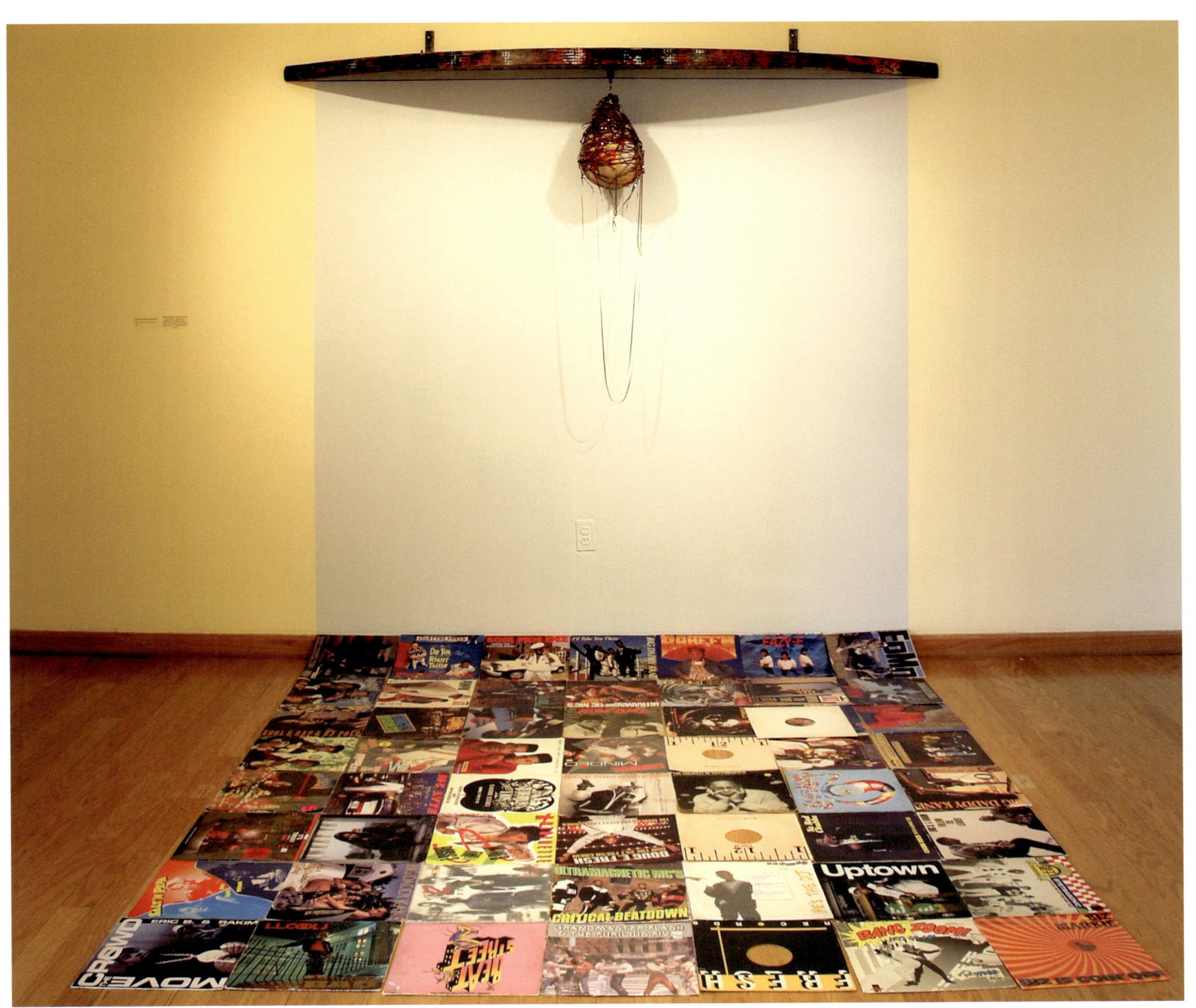

ED PASCHKE

BOXER NARANJA, 2004 - OIL ON LINEN / 50 X 60 INCHES
© ED PASCHKE

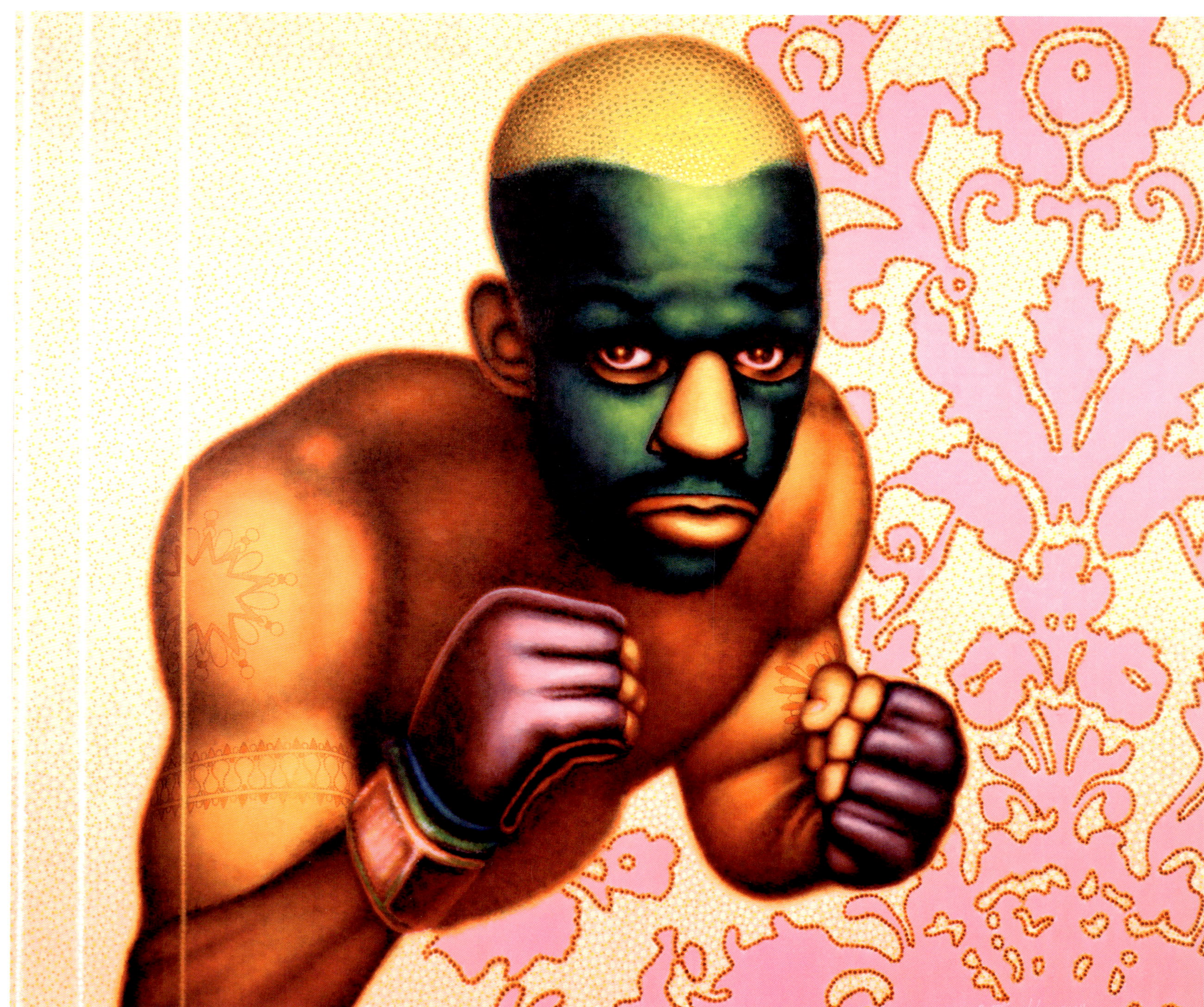

ED PASCHKE

RED BOXER, 2004 - OIL ON LINEN / 50 X 60 INCHES
© ED PASCHKE

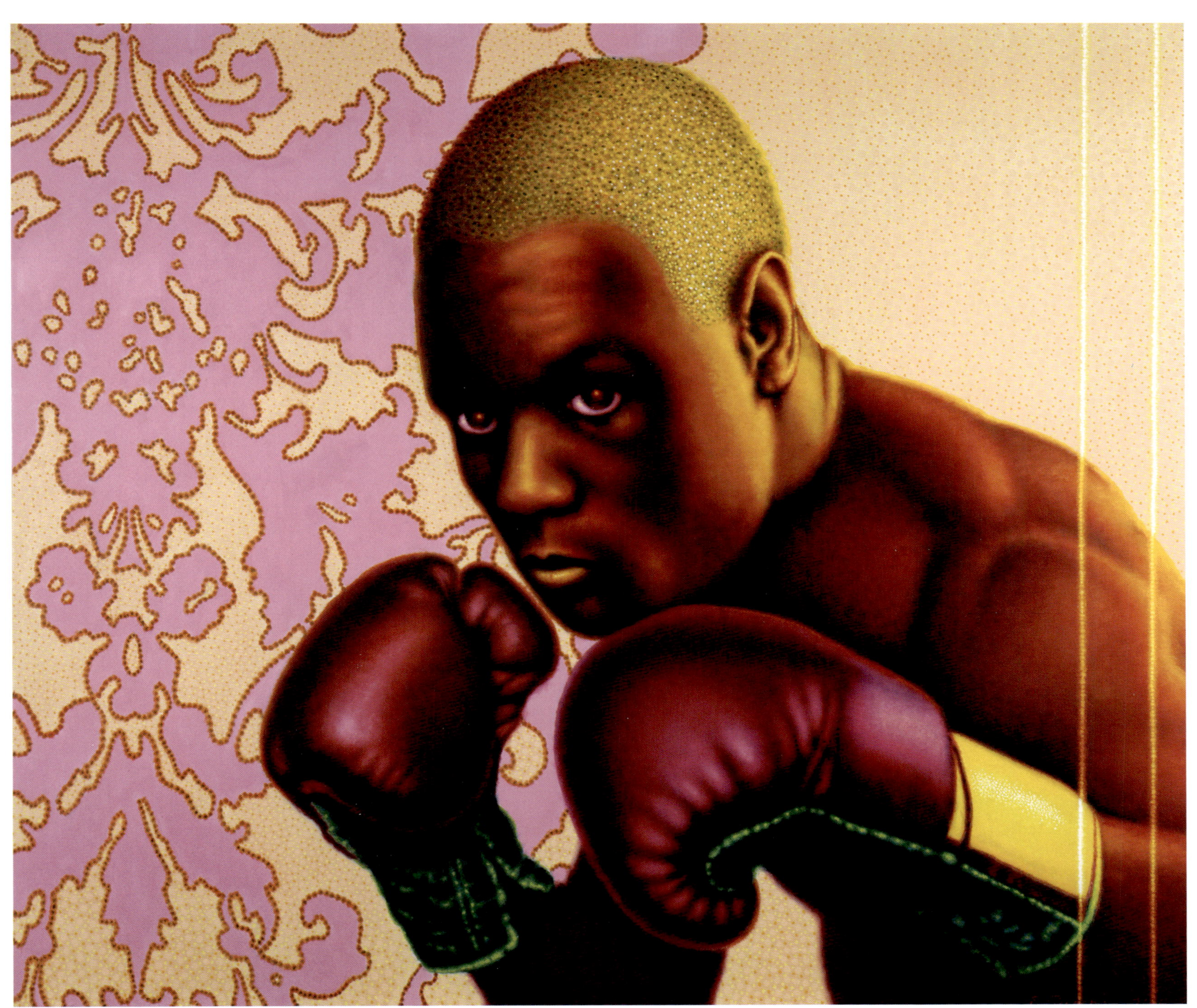

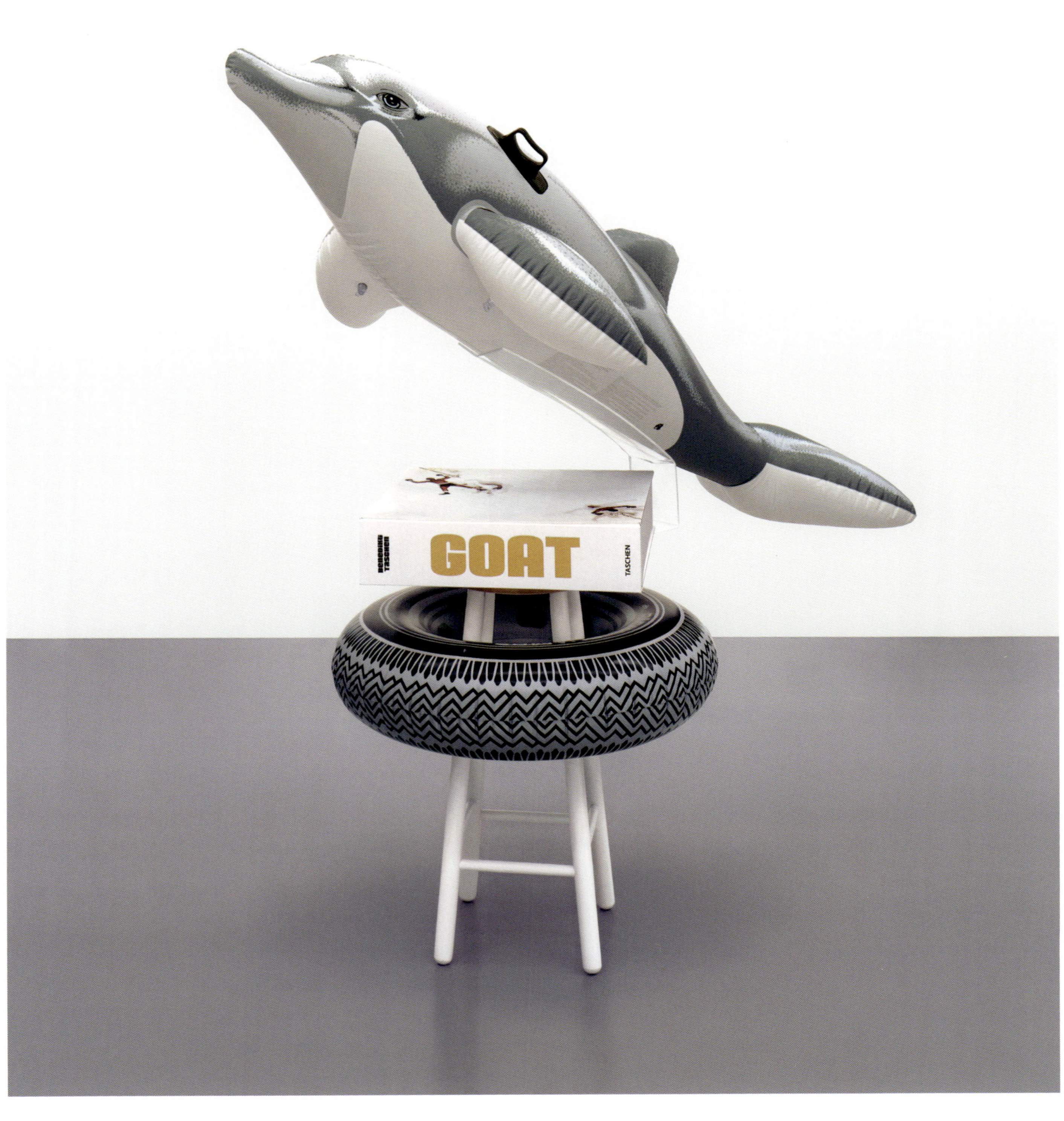

JEFF KOONS
RADIAL CHAMPS (CHAMP'S EDITION FOR GOAT – A TRIBUTE TO MUHAMMAD ALI), 2004 - WOOD, VINYL, CHAMP'S EDITION OF GOAT / 69 X 67 INCHES
© JEFF KOONS

STEP INTO THE ARENA (THE ESSENTIALIST TRAP), 1994 - MIXED MEDIA / 91.2 X 120 X 120 INCHES [900 LBS]
COURTESY OF THE ARTIST AND METRO PICTURES, NEW YORK

36

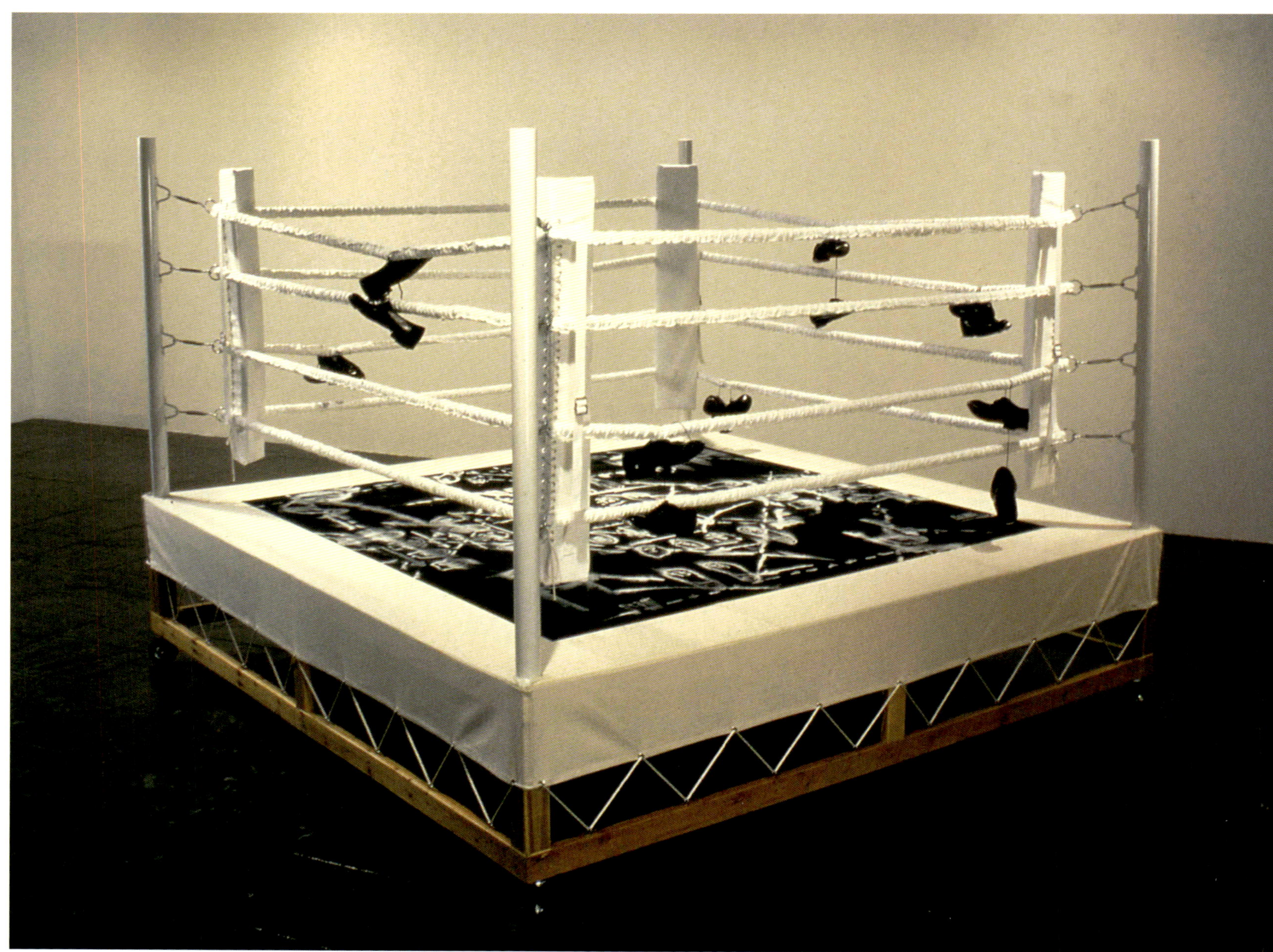

GARY SIMMONS

EVERFORWARD..., 1993 - LEATHER, METALLIC GOLD THREAD, SATIN, LACES, NAIL / 35 X 15 X 6 INCHES [HANGING] / EDITION OF 20
COURTESY OF THE ARTIST AND METRO PICTURES, NEW YORK

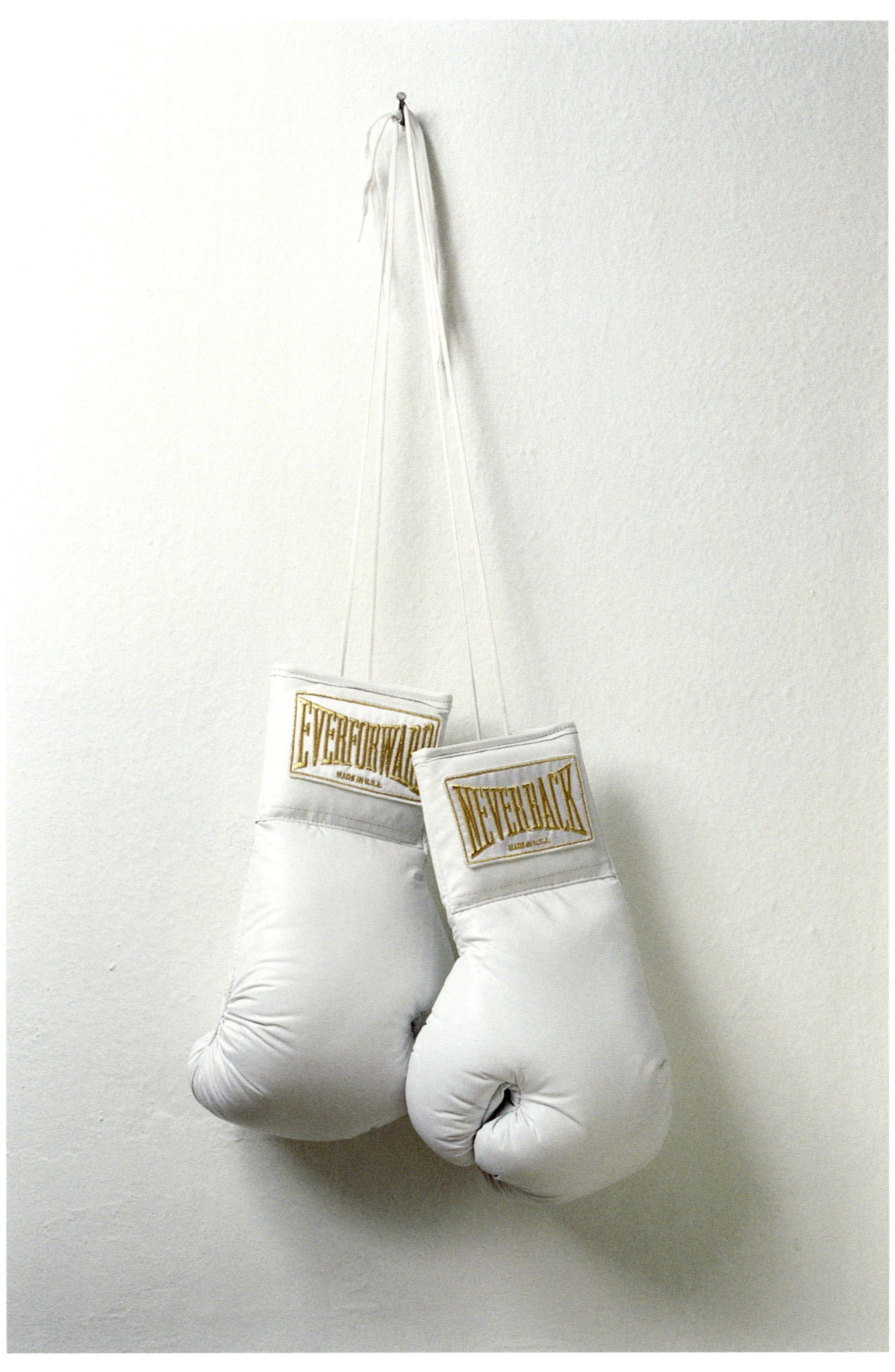

ANDY WARHOL

MUHAMMAD ALI, 1978 - SCREEN PRINT ON STRATHMORE BRISTOL PAPER / 40 X 30 INCHES
COLLECTION OF THE ANDY WARHOL MUSEUM, PITTSBURGH, © 2013 THE ANDY WARHOL FOUNDATION FOR THE VISUAL ARTS, INC. / ARTISTS RIGHTS SOCIETY (ARS), NEW YORK

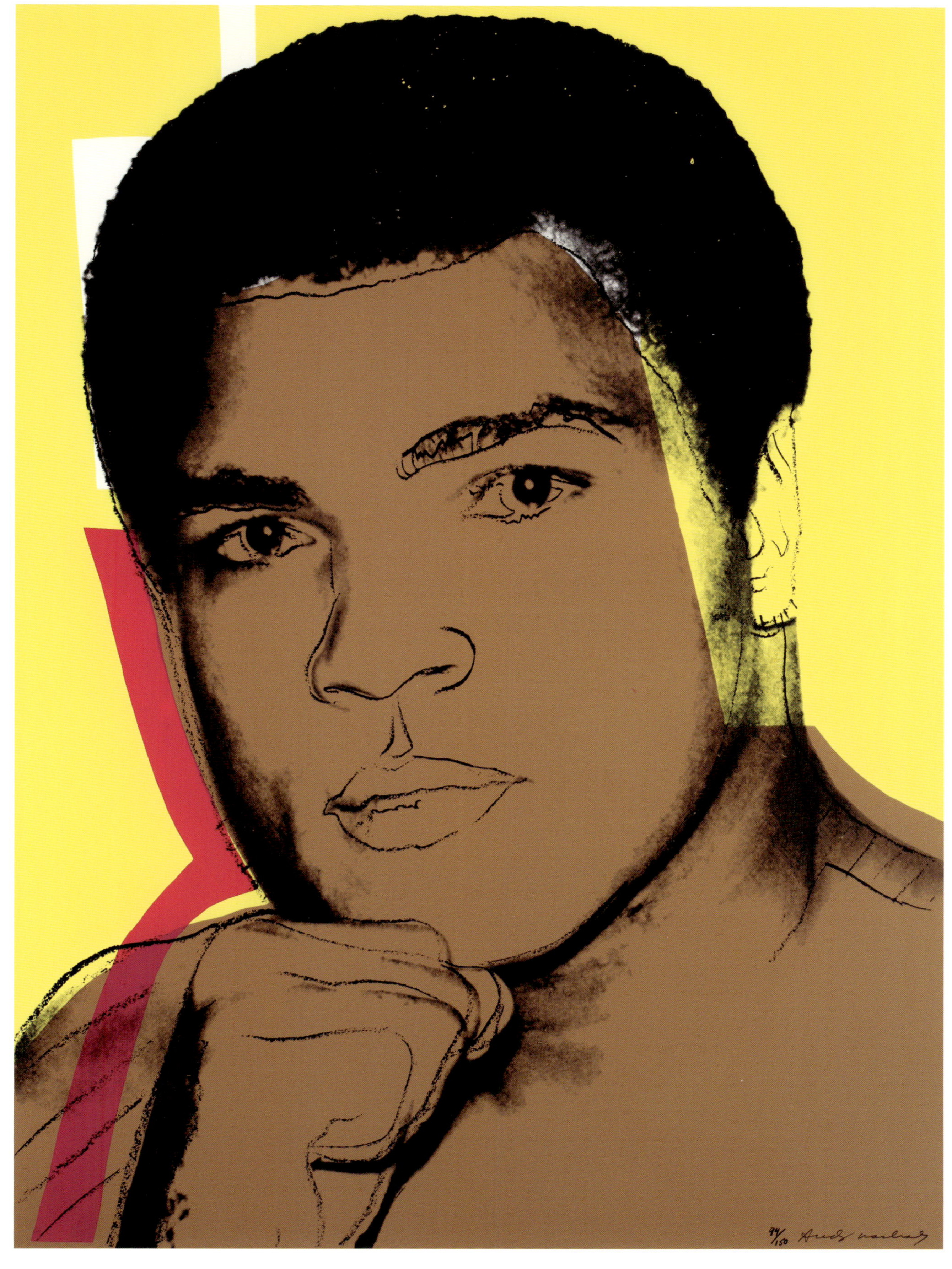

ANDY WARHOL & JEAN-MICHEL BASQUIAT

TEN PUNCHING BAGS (LAST SUPPER), 1985-86 - ACRYLIC AND OIL STICK ON PUNCHING BAGS / 42 X 14 X 14 INCHES
COLLECTION OF THE ANDY WARHOL MUSEUM, PITTSBURGH. © 2013 THE ANDY WARHOL FOUNDATION FOR THE VISUAL ARTS, INC. / ARTISTS RIGHTS

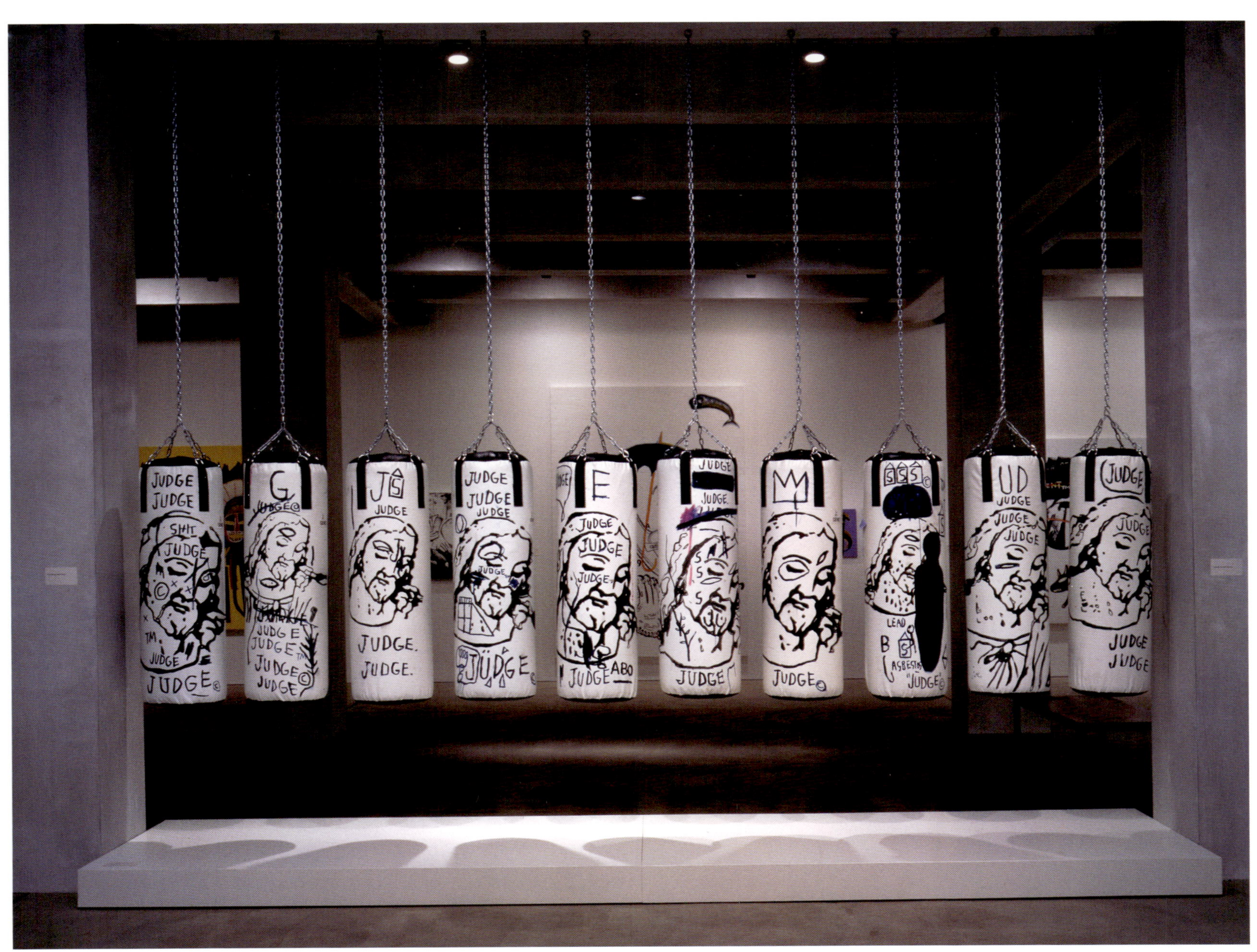

JEAN-MICHEL BASQUIAT

UNTITLED (BOXER), 2005 - ACRYLIC & OIL PAINTSTICK ON LINEN / 76 X 94 INCHES
PHOTO © CHRISTIE'S IMAGES / THE BRIDGEMAN ART LIBRARY, ARTISTS RIGHTS SOCIETY (ARS), NEW YORK

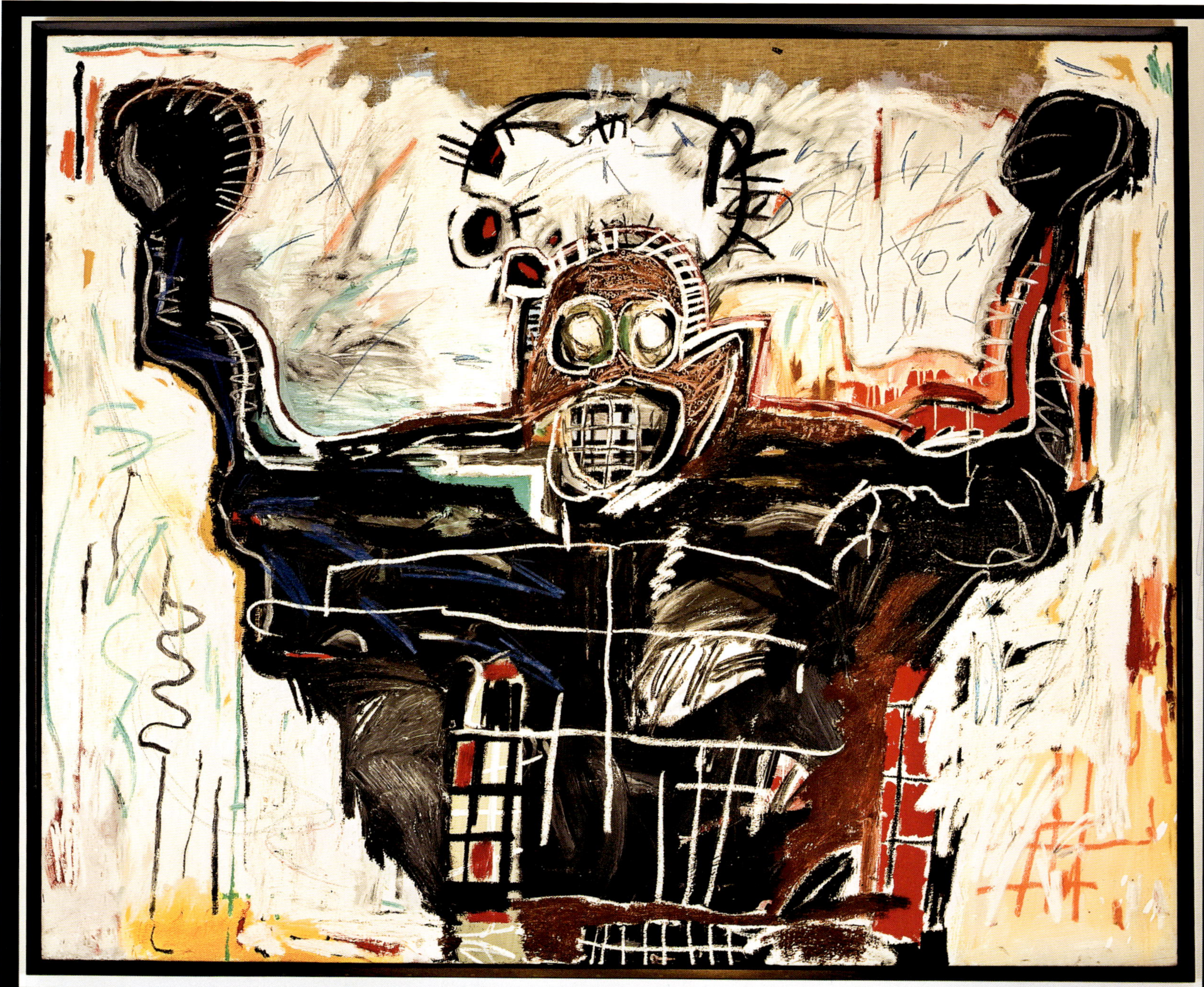

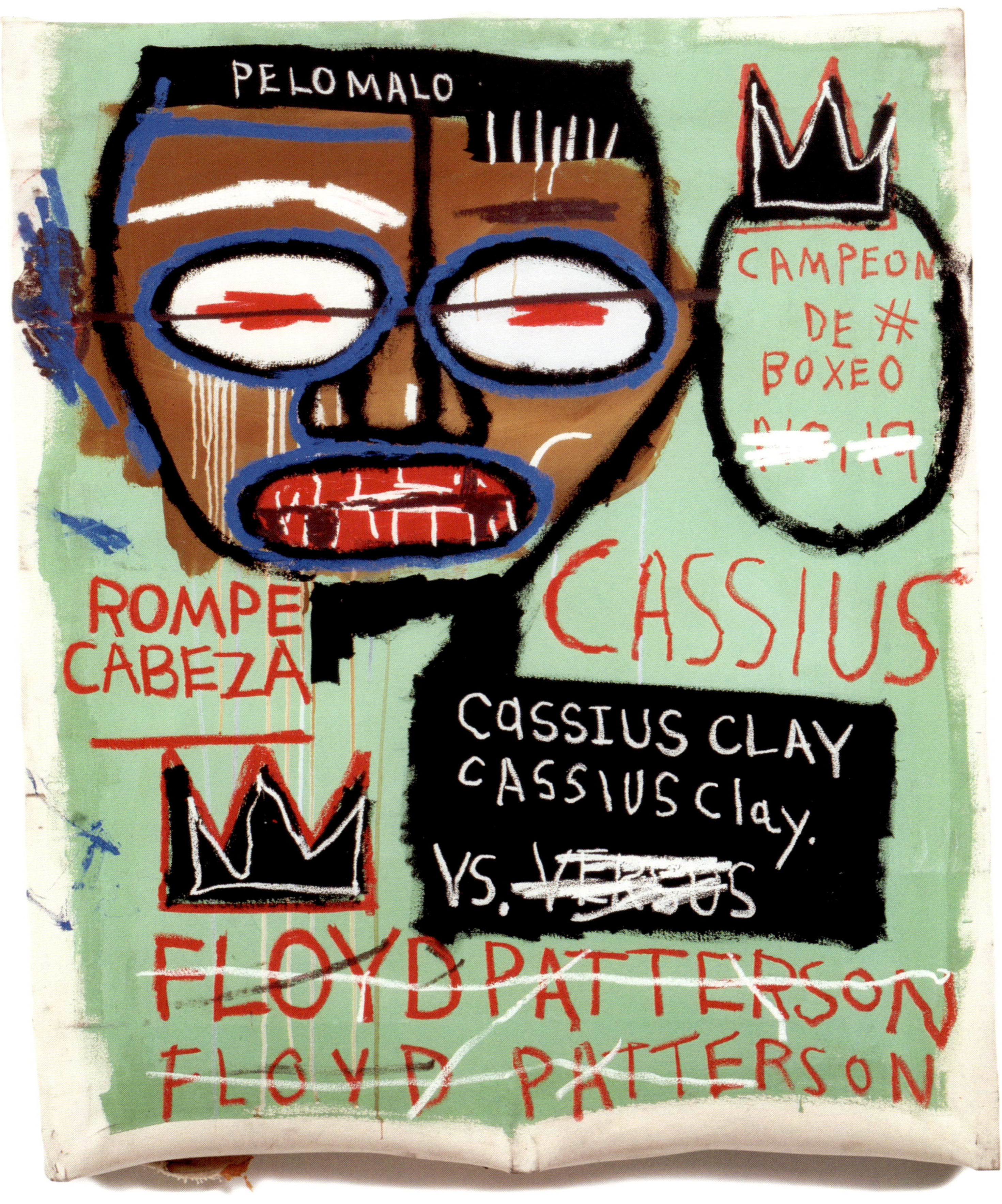
PELO MALO
CAMPEON
DE #
BOXEO
ROMPE
CABEZA
CASSIUS
CASSIUS CLAY
CASSIUS clay.
VS.
FLOYD PATTERSON
FLOYD PATTERSON

BOXERS, 1988 - POLYURETHANE PAINT ON ALUMINUM / 46.5 X 33 X 22 INCHES
© 2013 ARTISTS RIGHTS SOCIETY (ARS), NEW YORK / THE KEITH HARING FOUNDATION

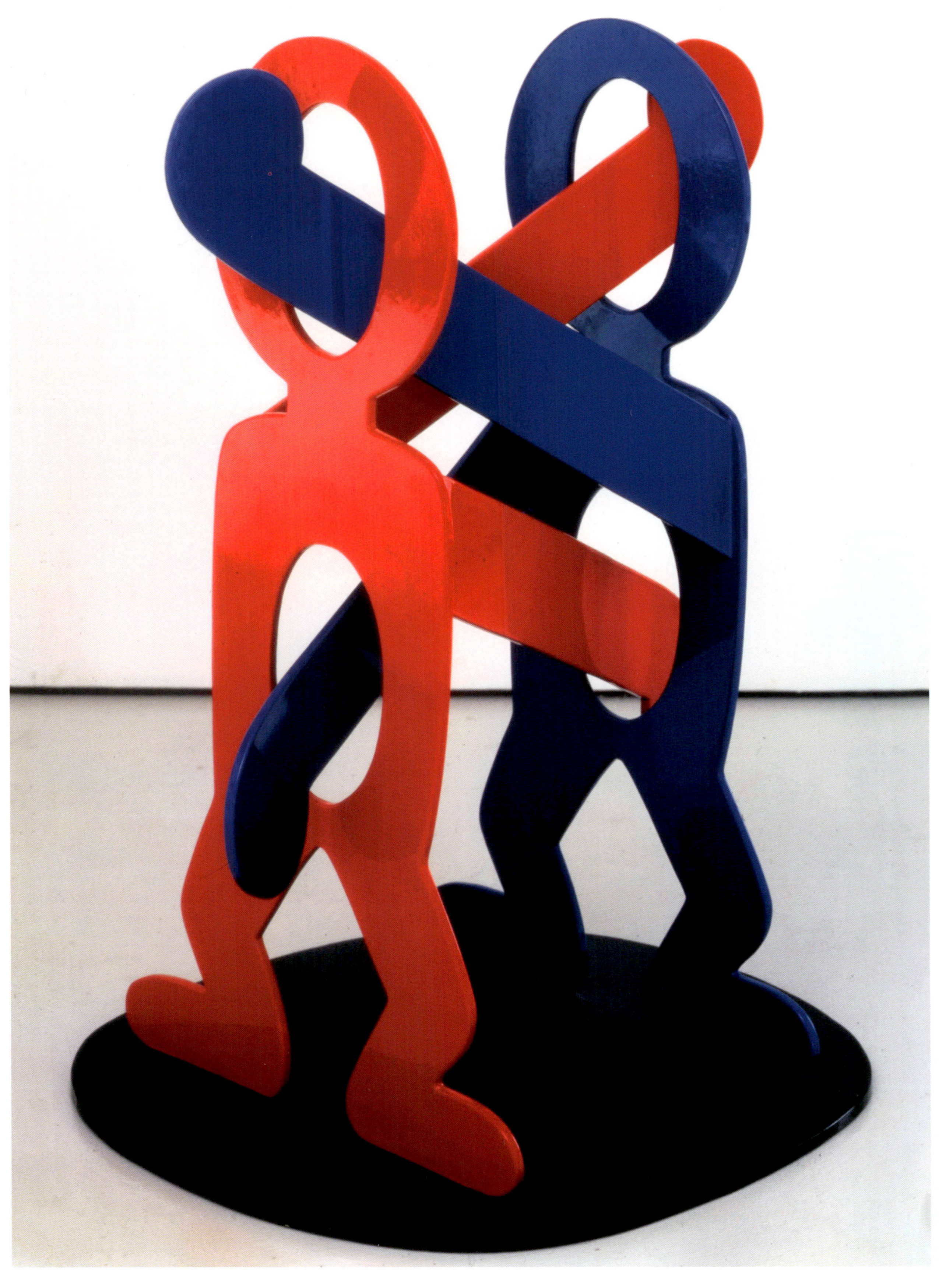

UNTITLED, 1988 - ALKYD & FLASHE ON ALUMINUM / 84 X 60 INCHES
COURTESY OF THE ARTIST AND LUHRING AUGUSTINE, NEW YORK

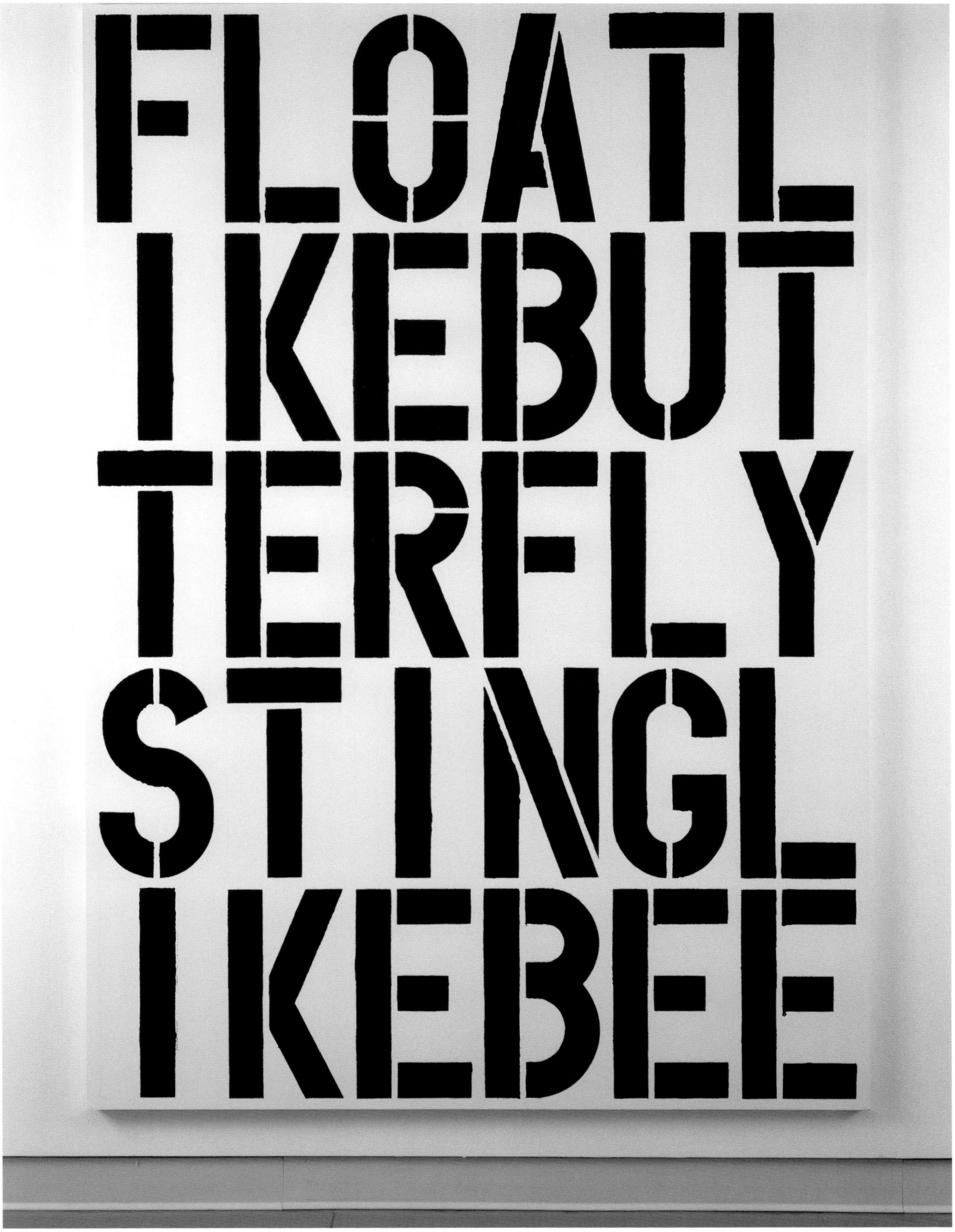

ROBERT LAZZARINI

EVERLAST, 2013 - INK ON PAPER / 3.3 X 5 INCHES
COURTESY OF THE ARTIST AND MARLBOROUGH CHELSEA, NY

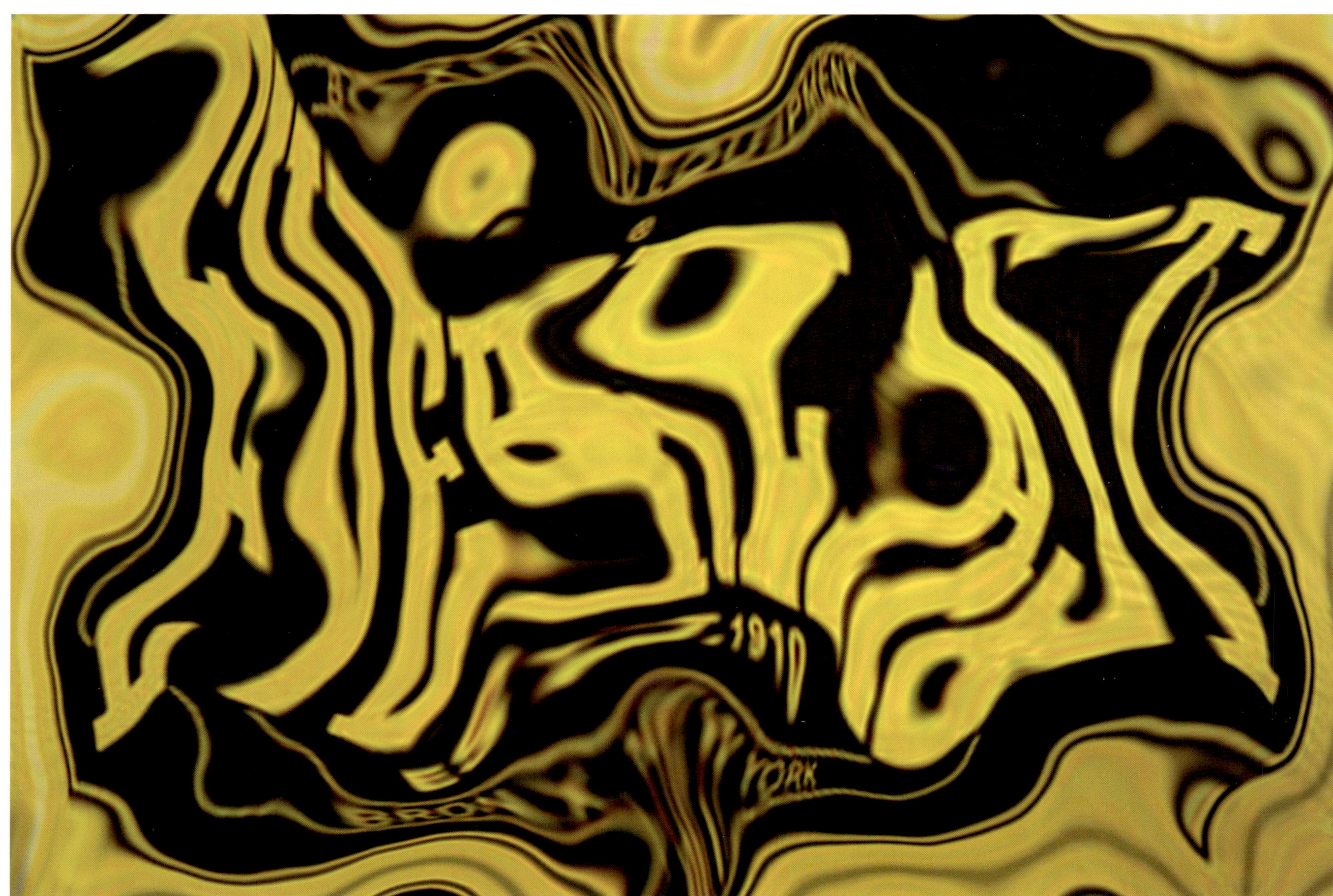

ROBERT LAZZARINI

ARTURO GATTI OBITUARY, 2013 - INK ON PAPER / 12 X 9.6 INCHES
COURTESY OF THE ARTIST AND MARLBOROUGH CHELSEA, NY

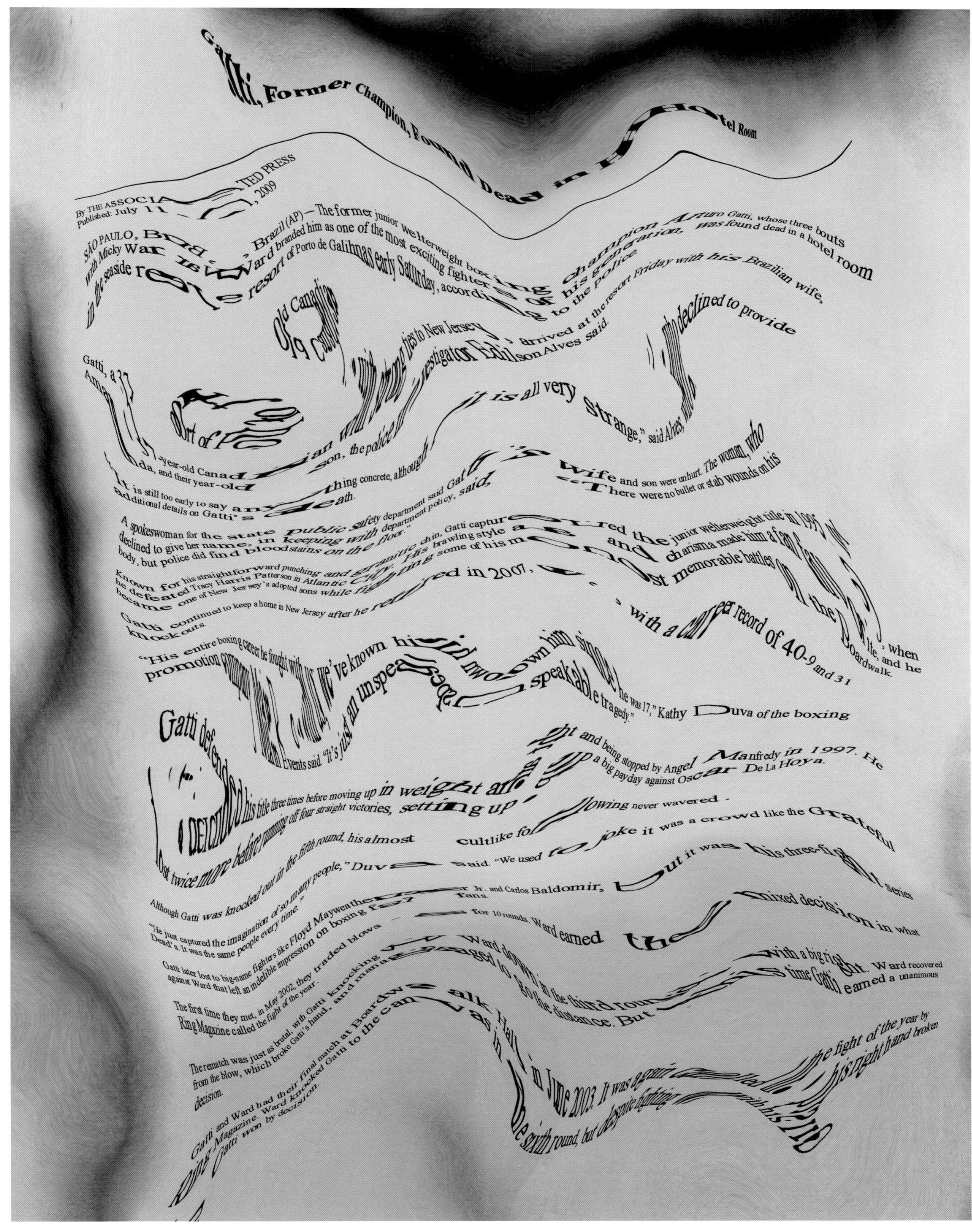

CHERYL DUNN

ROY JONES JR. WITH FIGHTING COCK / PENSICOLA FLORIDA, 2000 - CHROMOGENIC PRINT / 30 X 40 INCHES

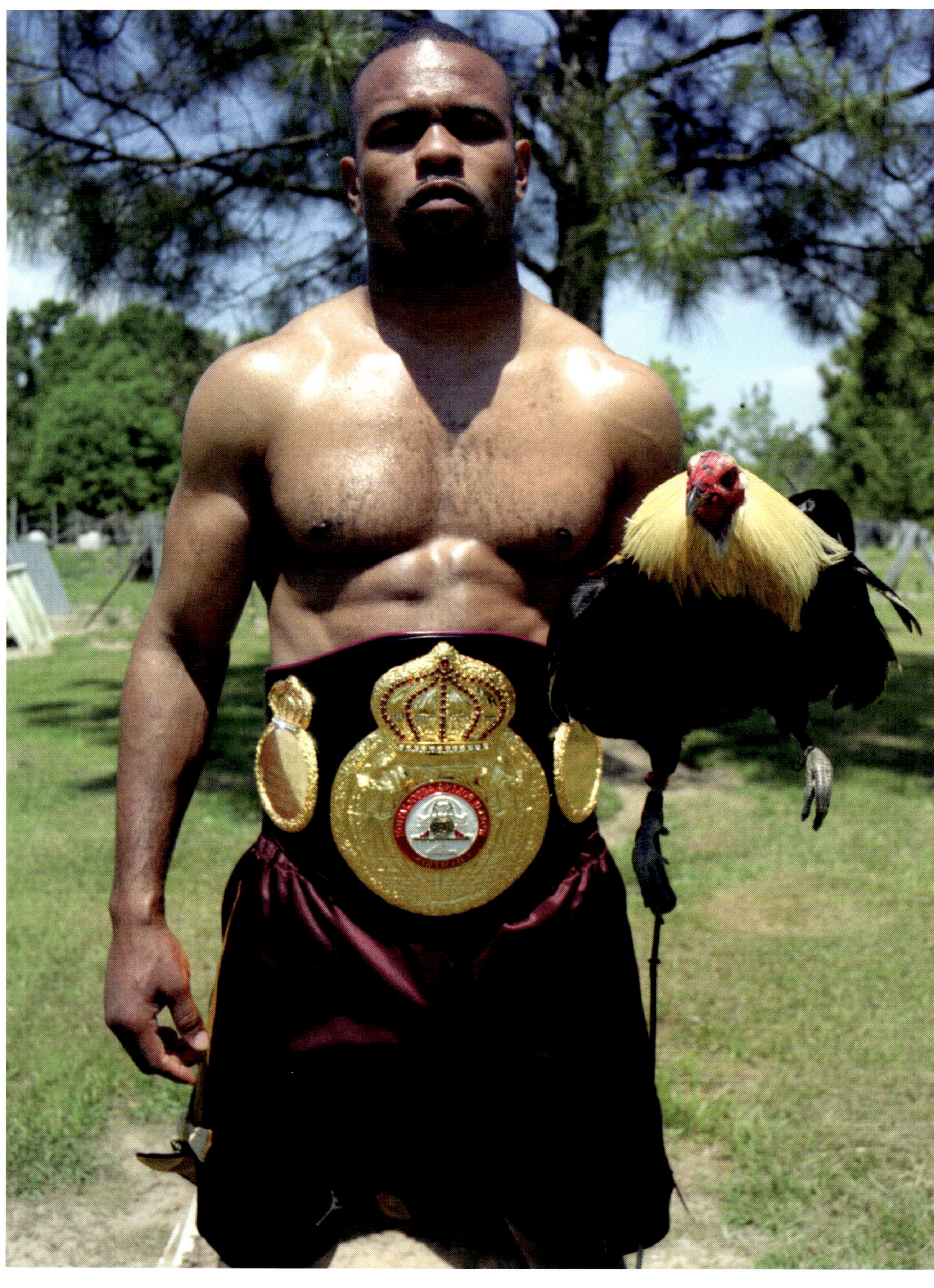

CHERYL DUNN

MERQUI SOSA / MADISON SQUARE GARDEN, 1996 - CHROMOGENIC PRINT / 30 X 34 INCHES

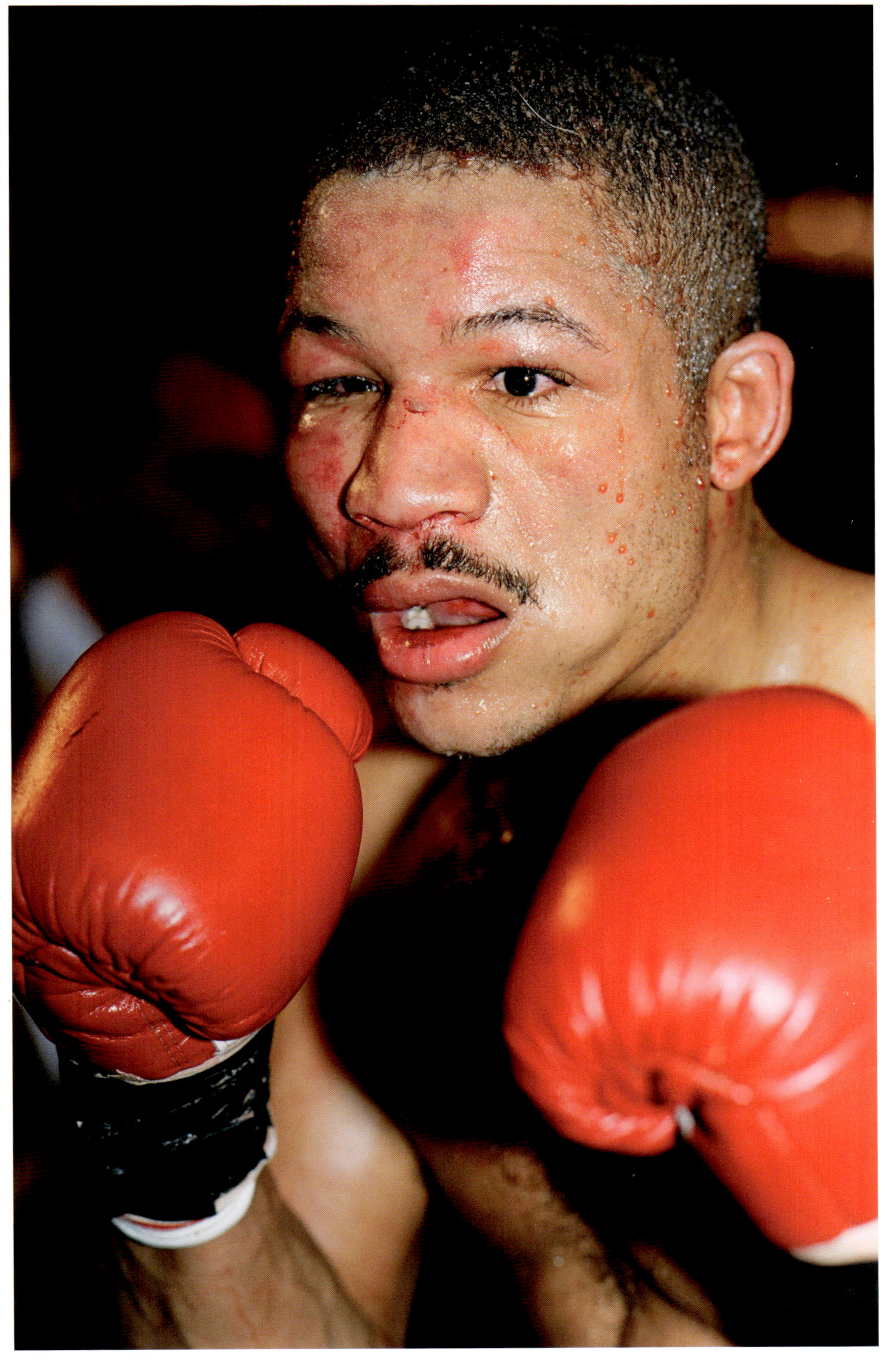

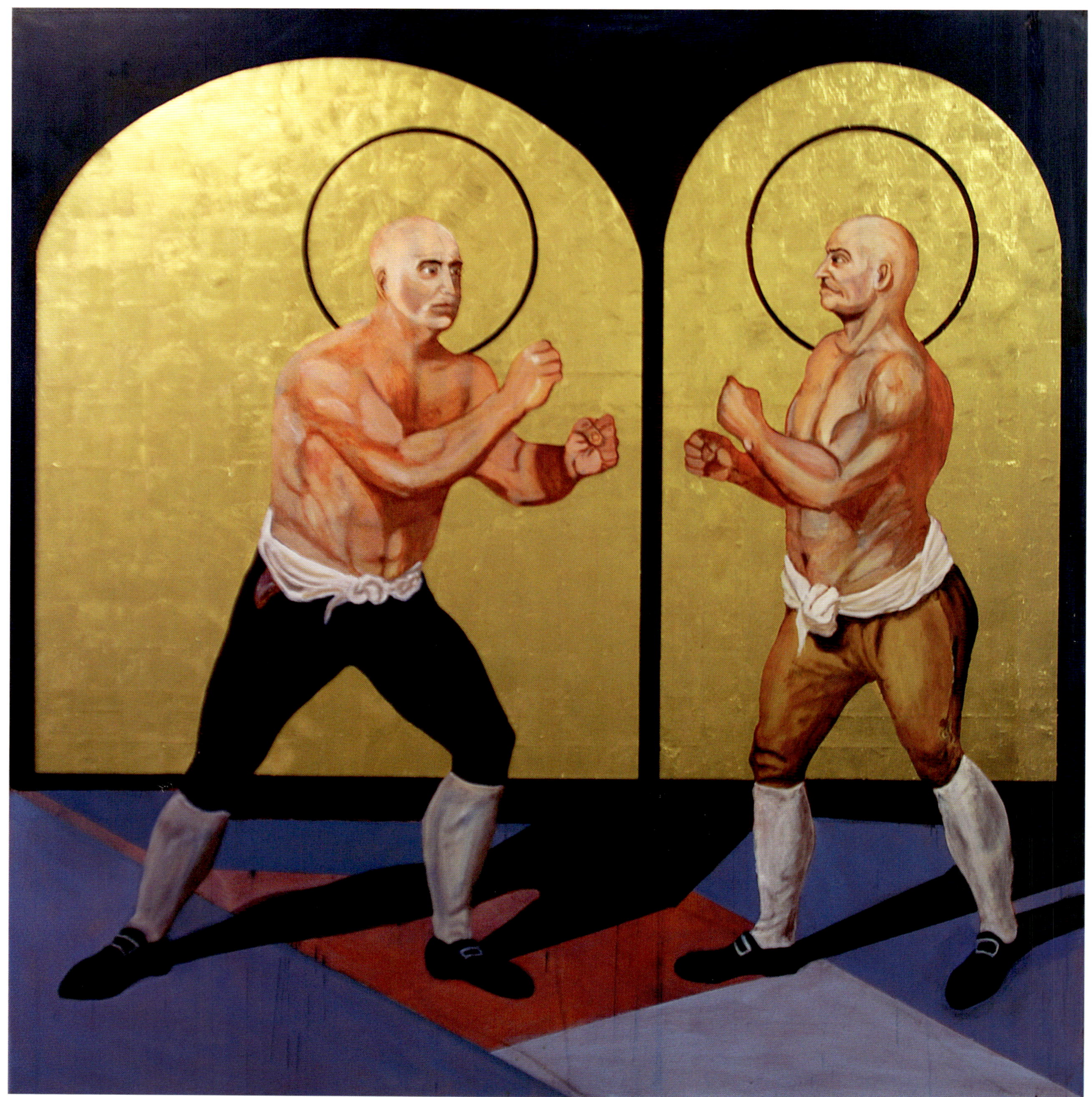

GODFRIED DONKOR

ST TOM MOLINEAUX - UP TO SCRATCH, 2010 - OIL AND GOLD LEAF ON CANVAS / 160 X 200 CM

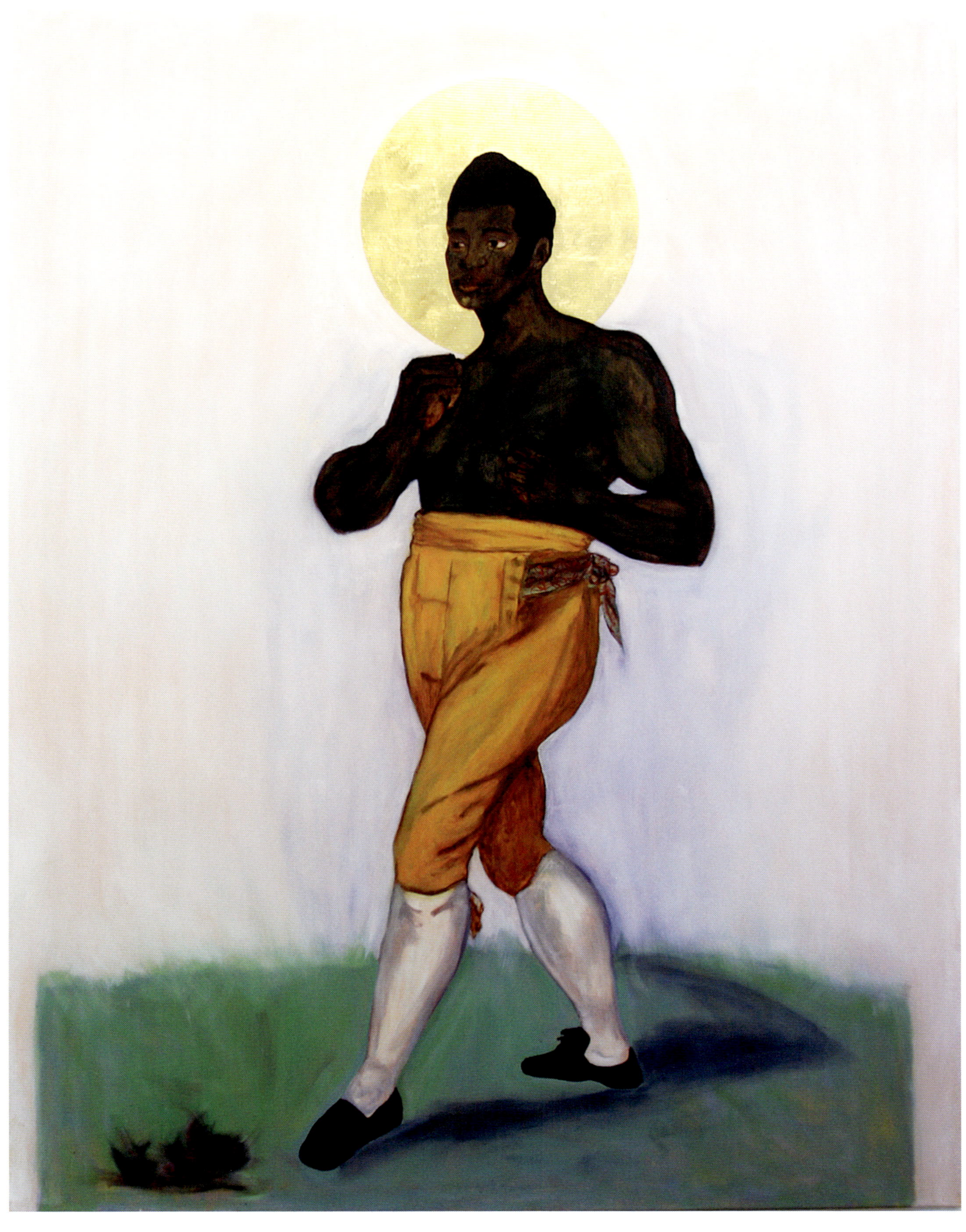

54

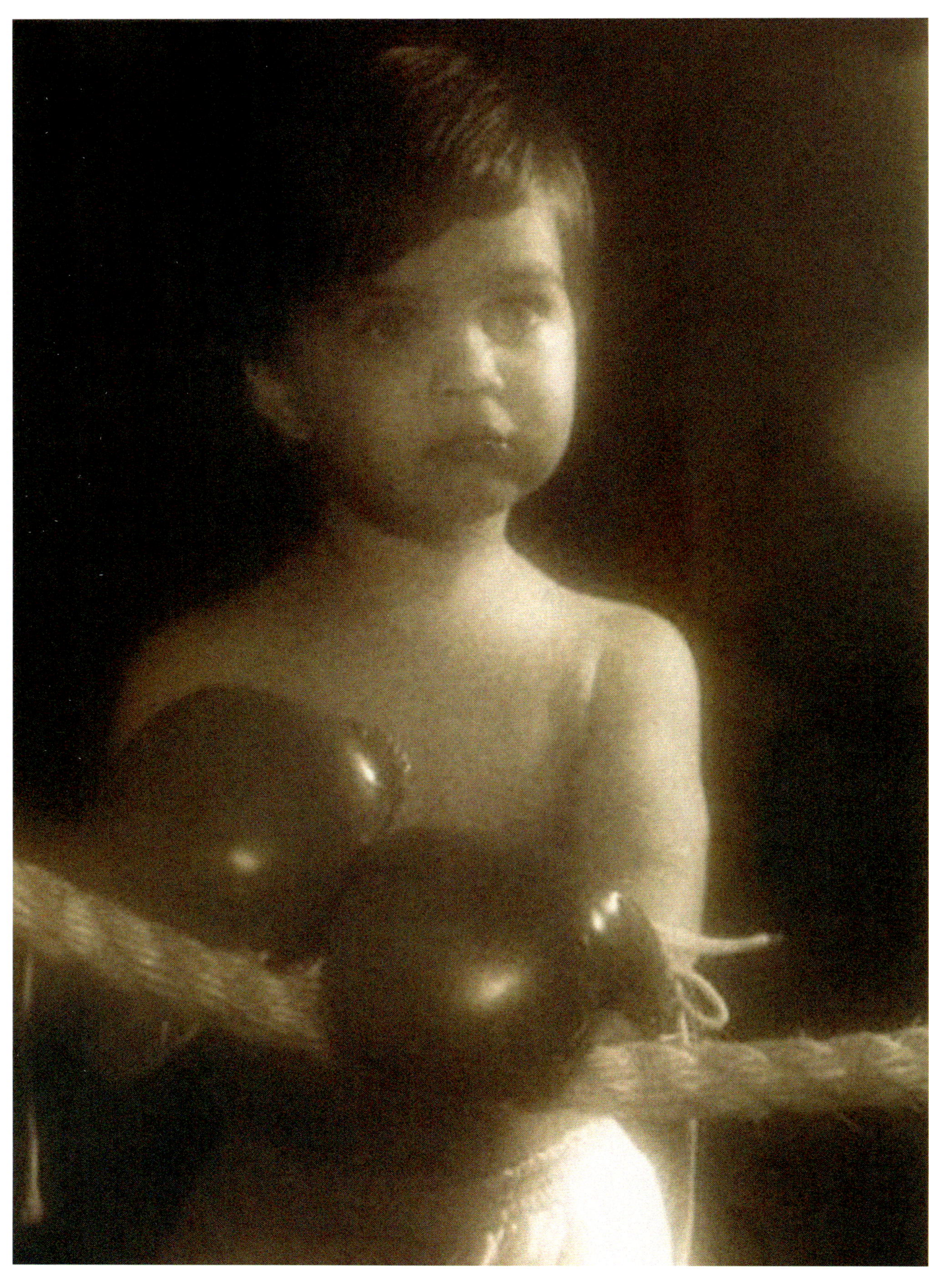

NIR HOD

BRAVO, 2002
ALL COPYRIGHTS NIR HOD

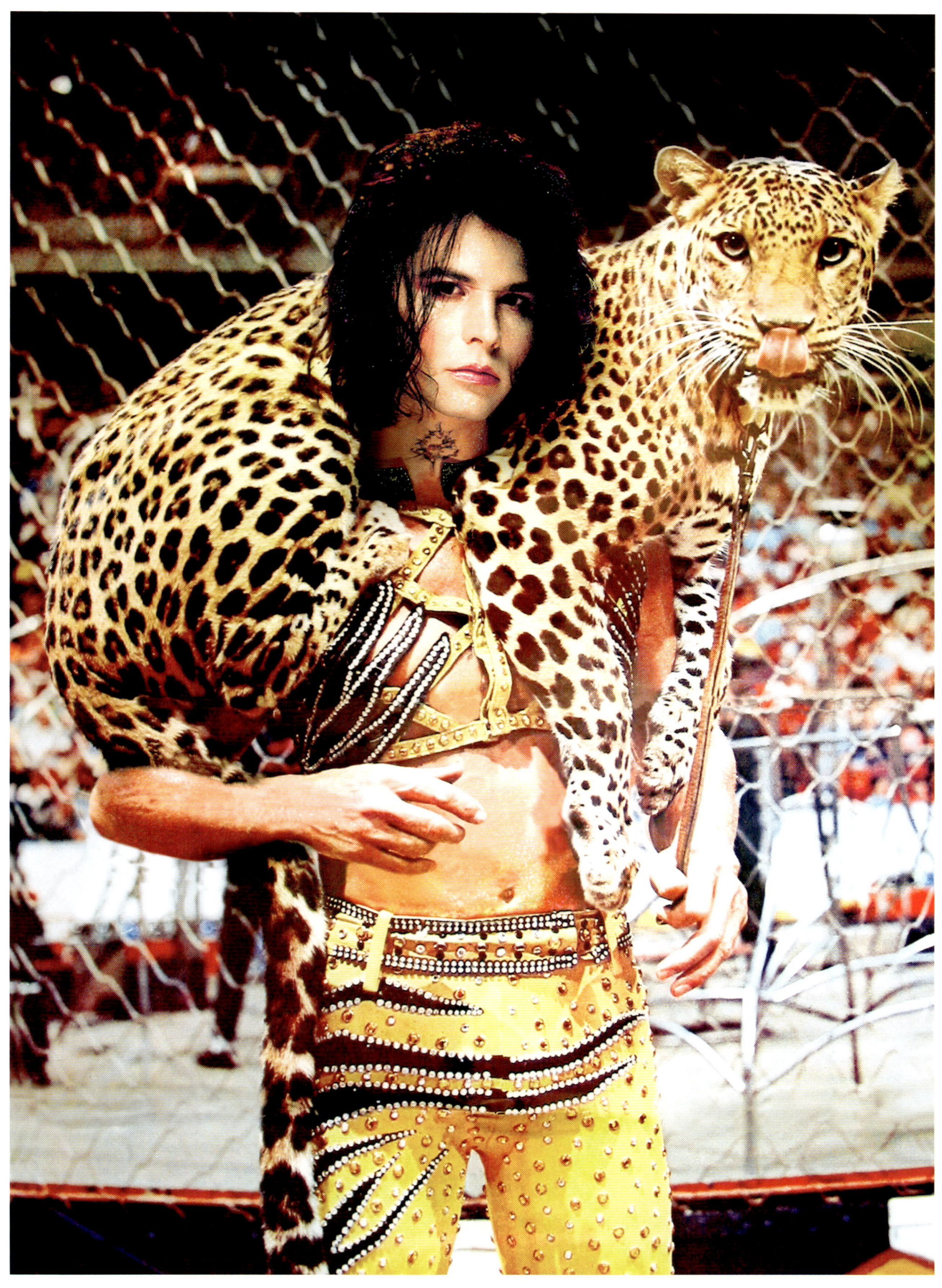

SATCH HOYT

THE DONKINGDOM, IN THE CORNER, 2002 - RED EVERLAST BOXING GLOVES, REINFORCING STEEL, RING AND AUDIO SYSTEM
210 X 120 X 155 CM [BOXER], 147 X 300 X 300 CM [RING], 50 X 50 X 35 CM [AUDIO SYSTEM]

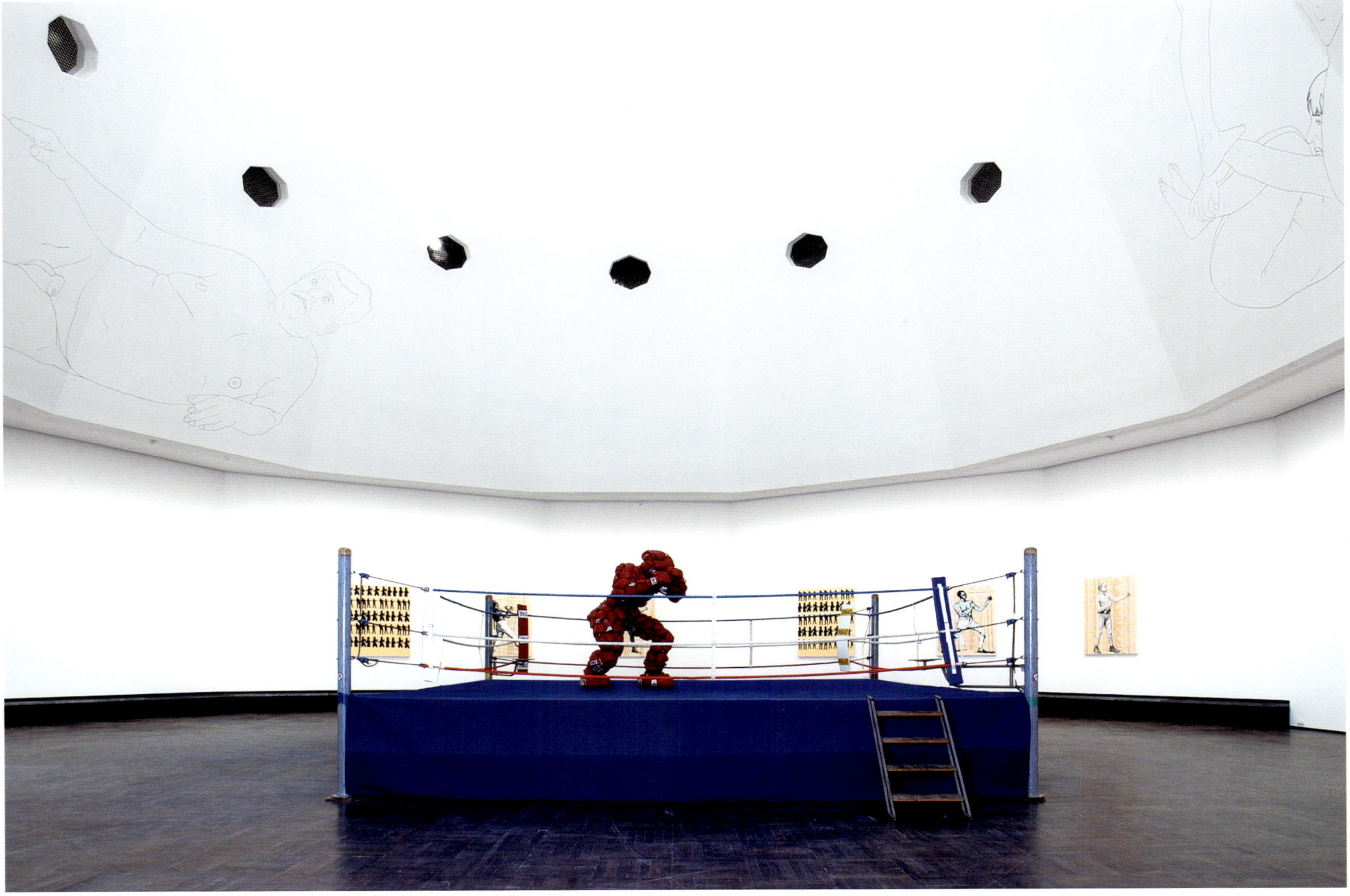

GLENN LIGON

ICE CUBE'S EYES, 1995 - SILKSCREEN INK ON CANVAS PUNCHING BAG / 51 X 14 X 15 INC
COURTESY OF THE ARTIST, LUHRING AUGUSTINE, NEW YORK, & REGEN PROJECTS, LOS ANGELES.

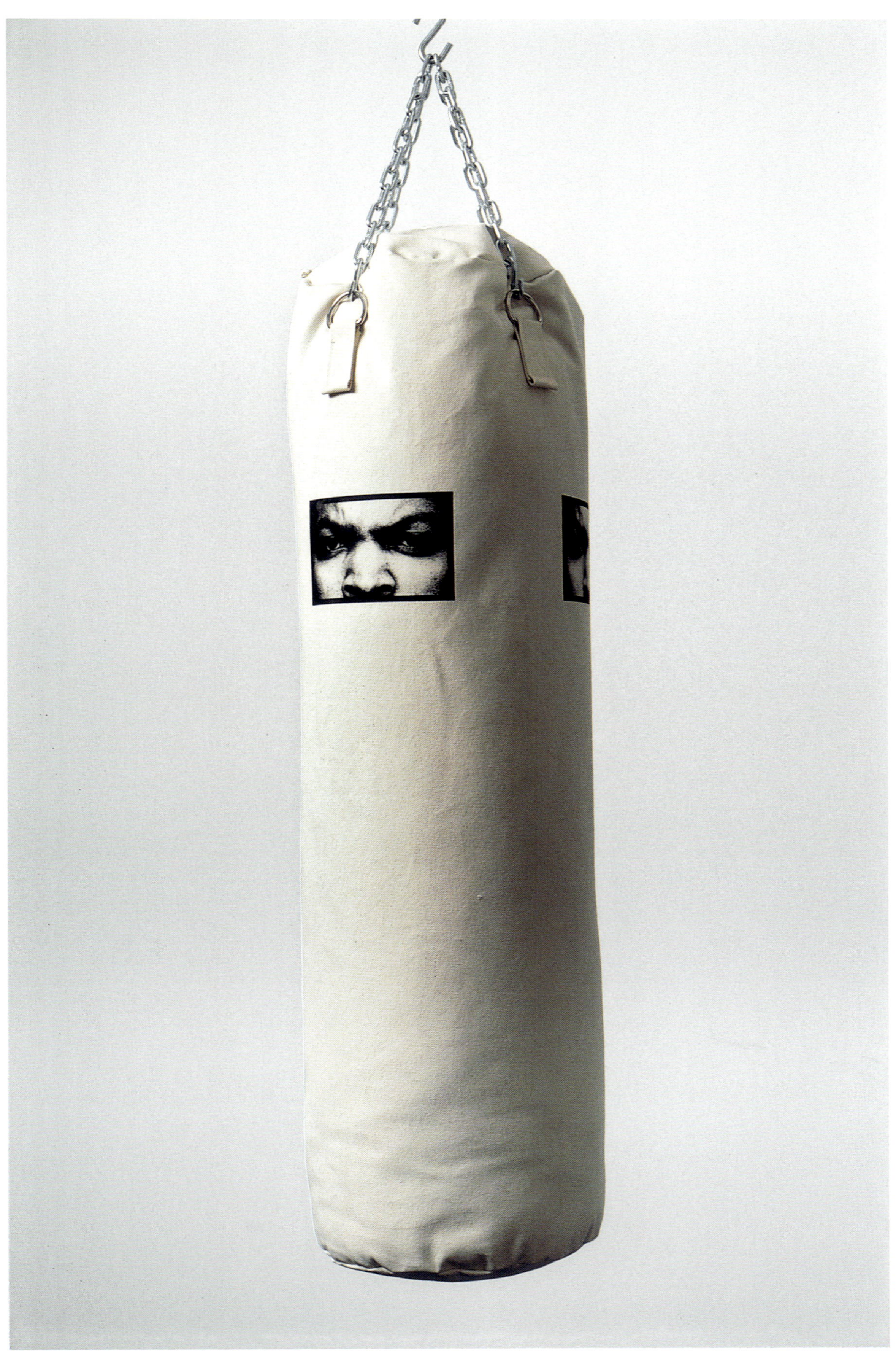

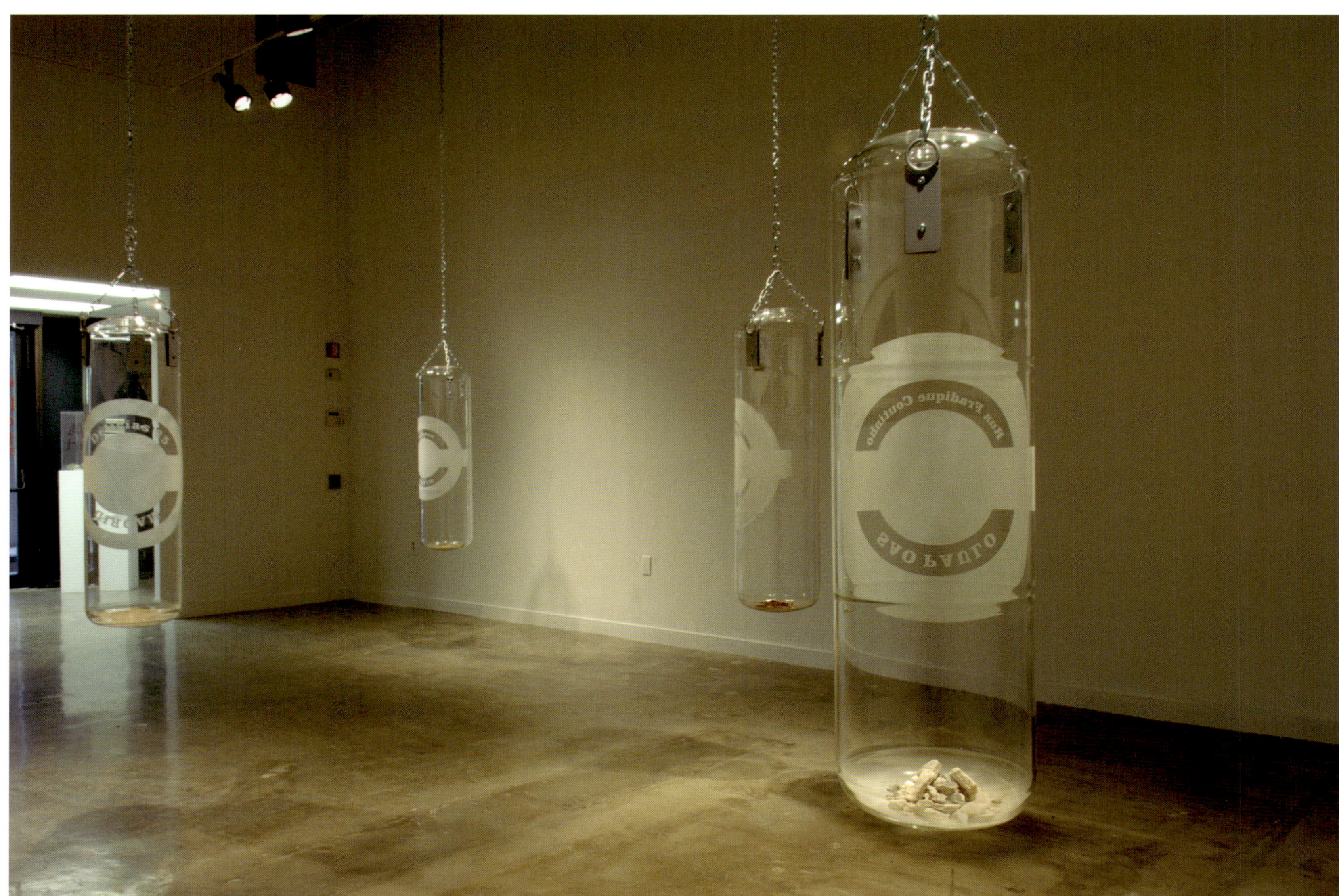
Rue Fradique Coutinho
SÃO PAULO

ALEXANDRE ARRECHEA

DUST, 2006 - BLOWN GLASS, CRUSHED DEBRIS, AND TEXT / 40 X 14 INCHES

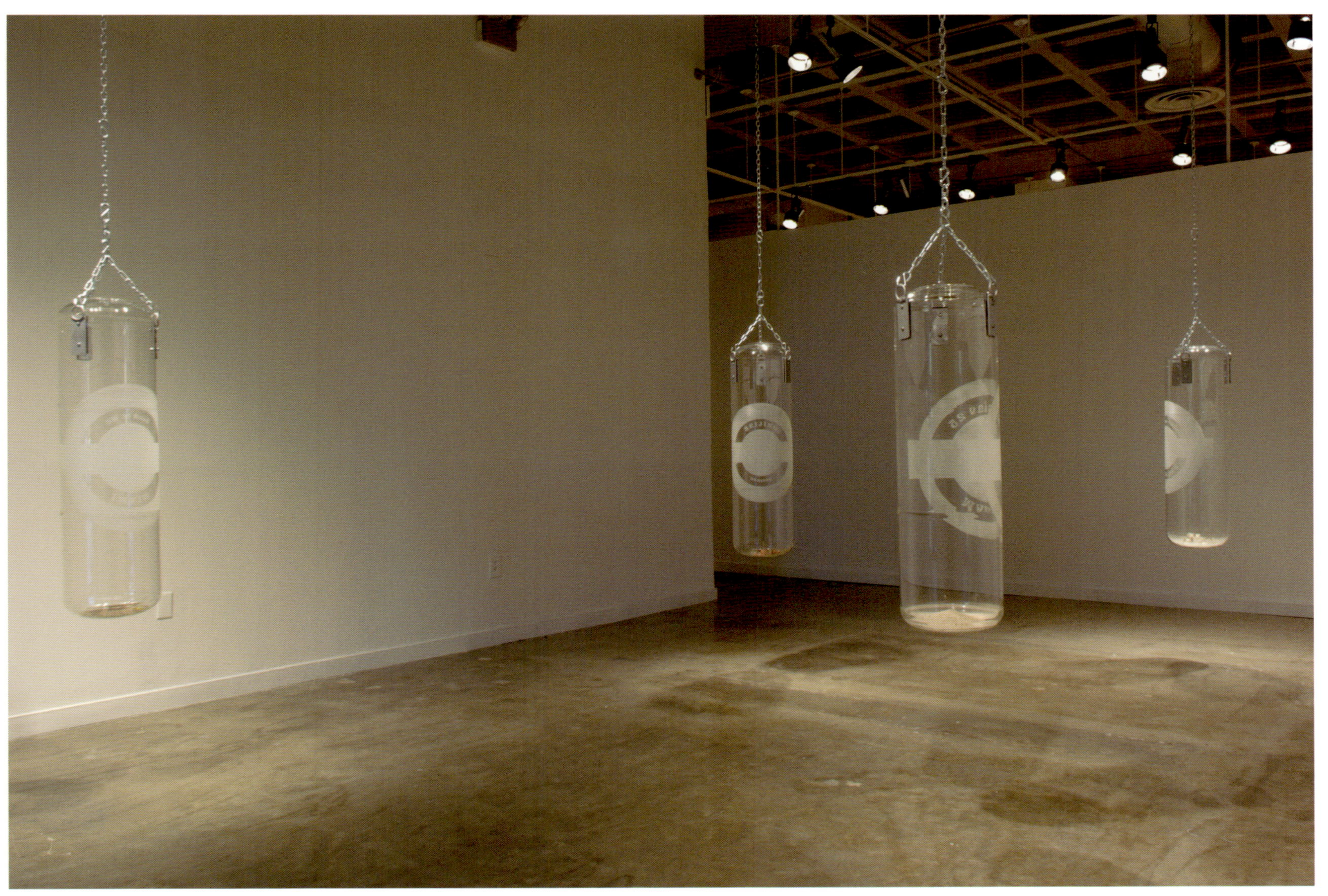

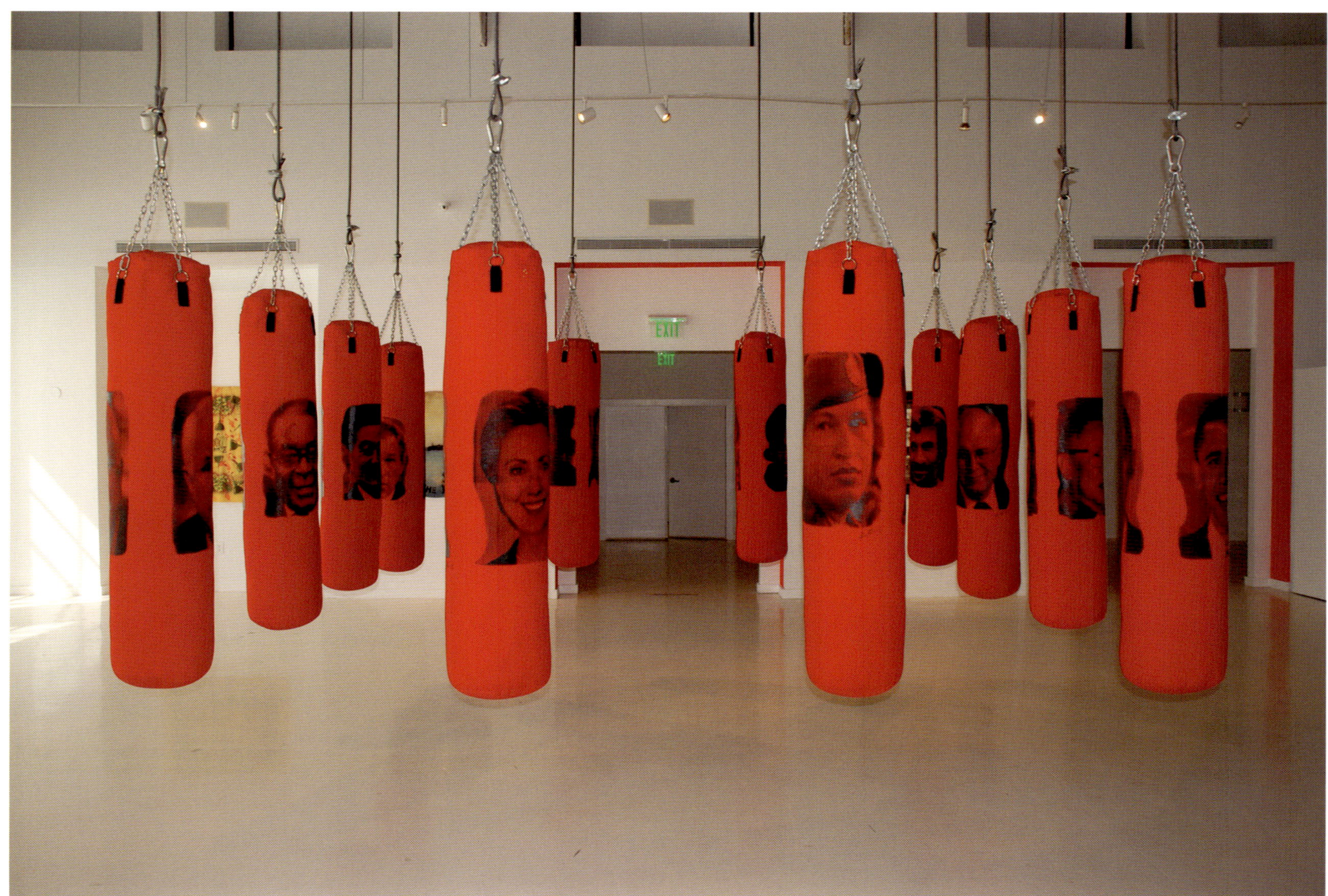
EXIT
Exit

ANTUAN RODRIGUEZ
LEFT OR RIGHT, 2004 - MIXED MEDIA / VARIABLES DIMENSIONS, EDITION 1/6

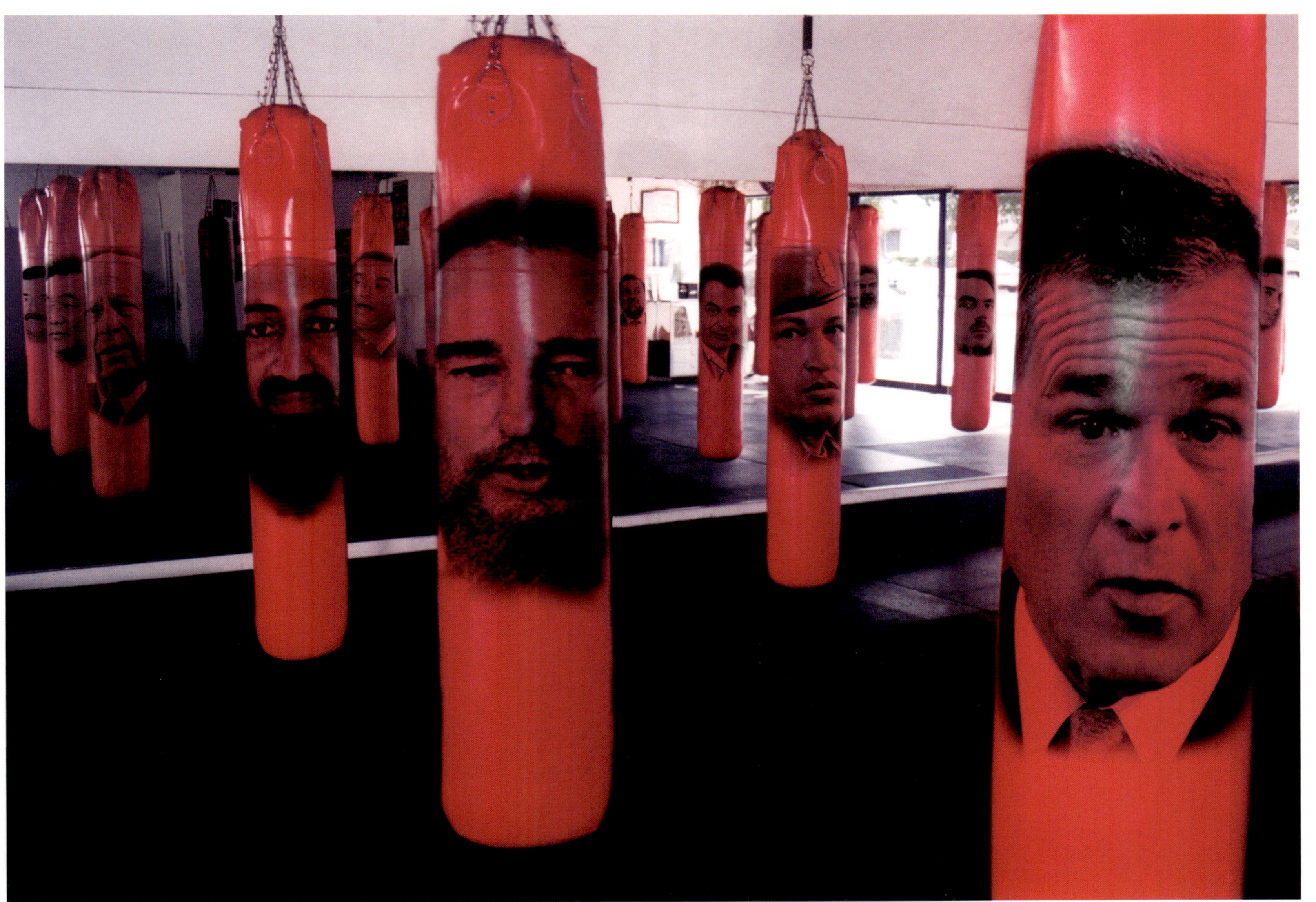

WORK OUT, 2007 - PAPER, ACRYLIC PAINT, HOT GLUE, AND MIRRORS / DIMENSIONS VARIABLE
PHOTO BY JERRY MANN

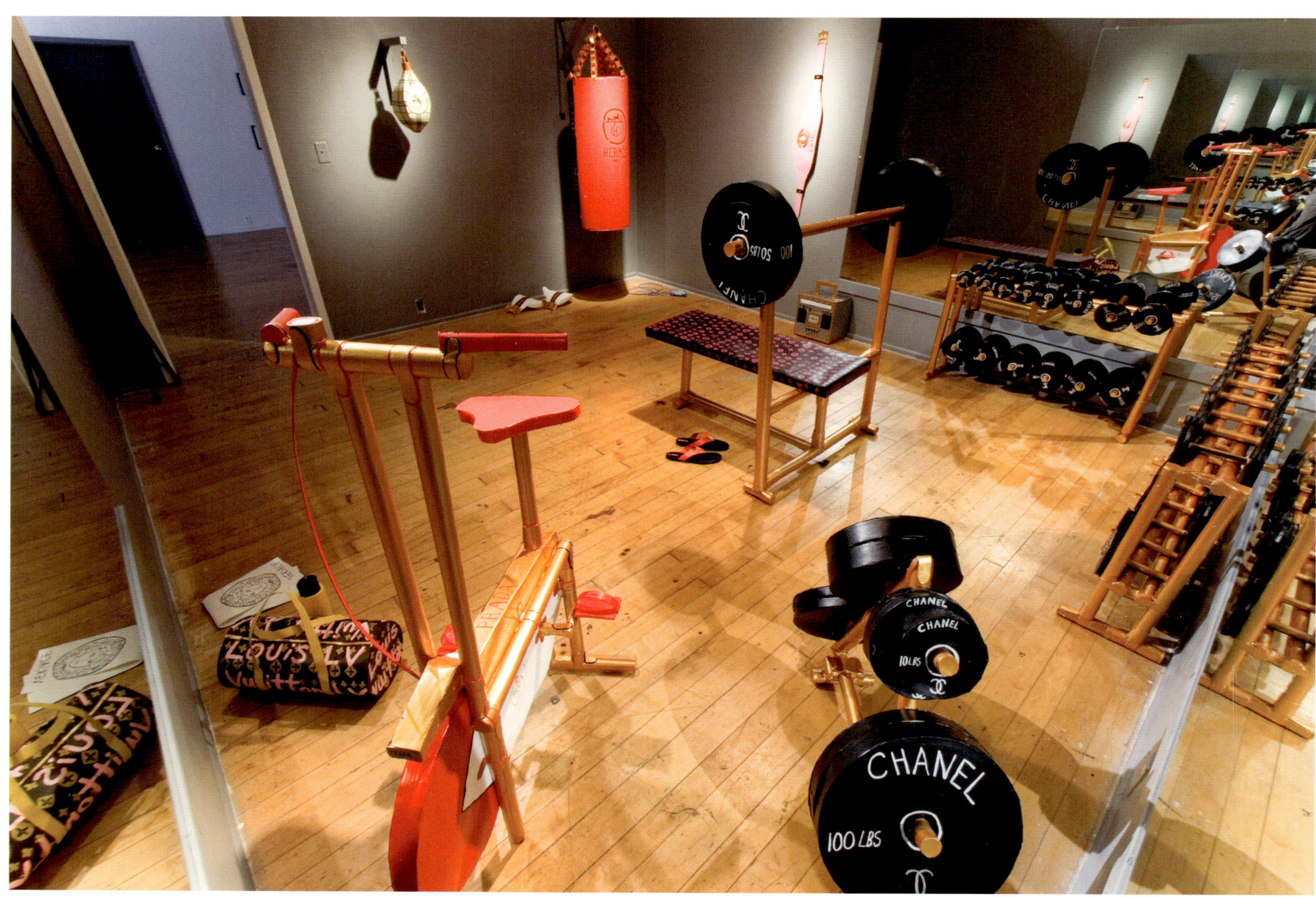

LIBBY BLACK

WORK OUT [DETAIL], 2007 - PAPER, ACRYLIC PAINT, HOT GLUE, AND MIRRORS / DIMENSIONS VARIABLE
PHOTO BY JERRY MANN

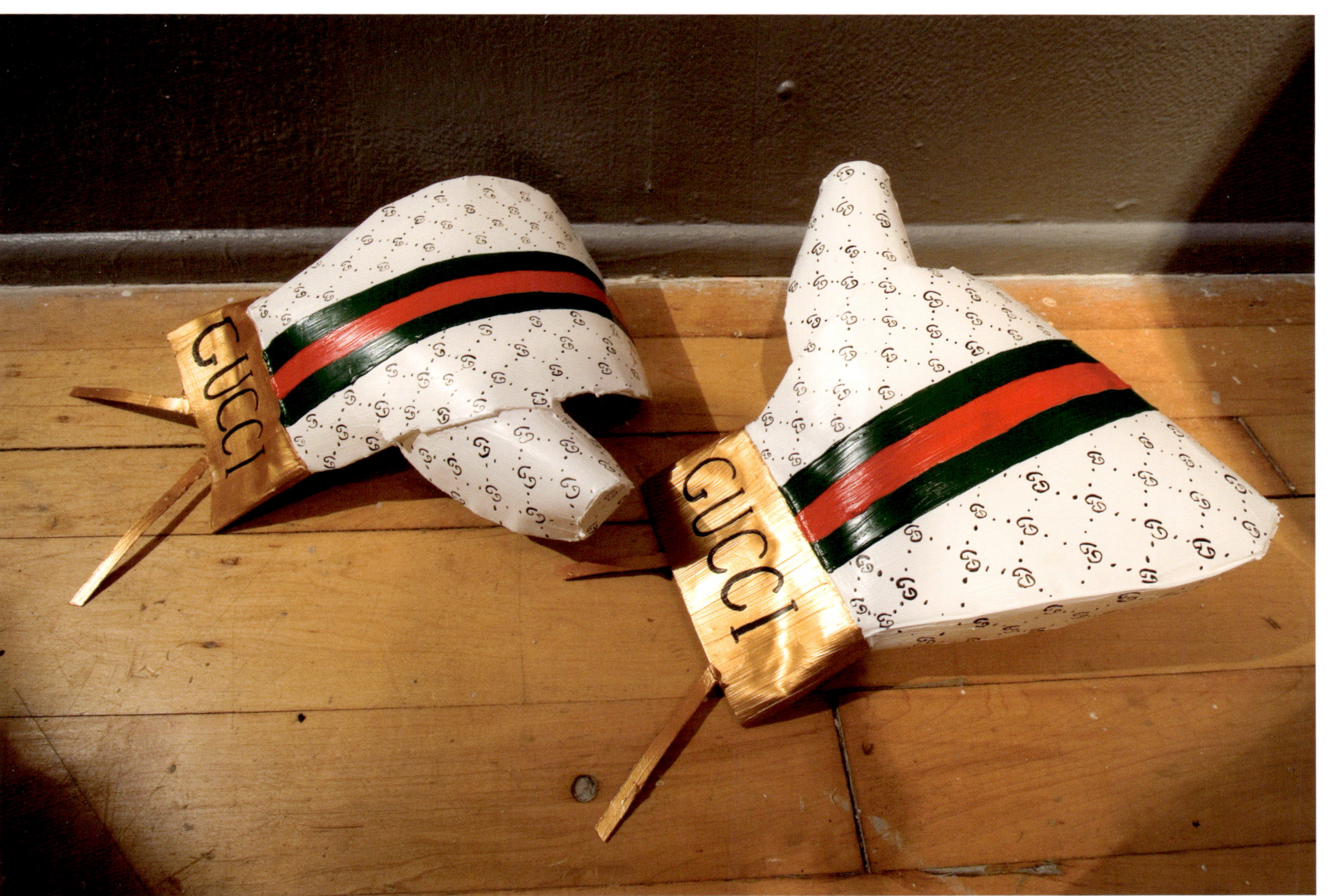

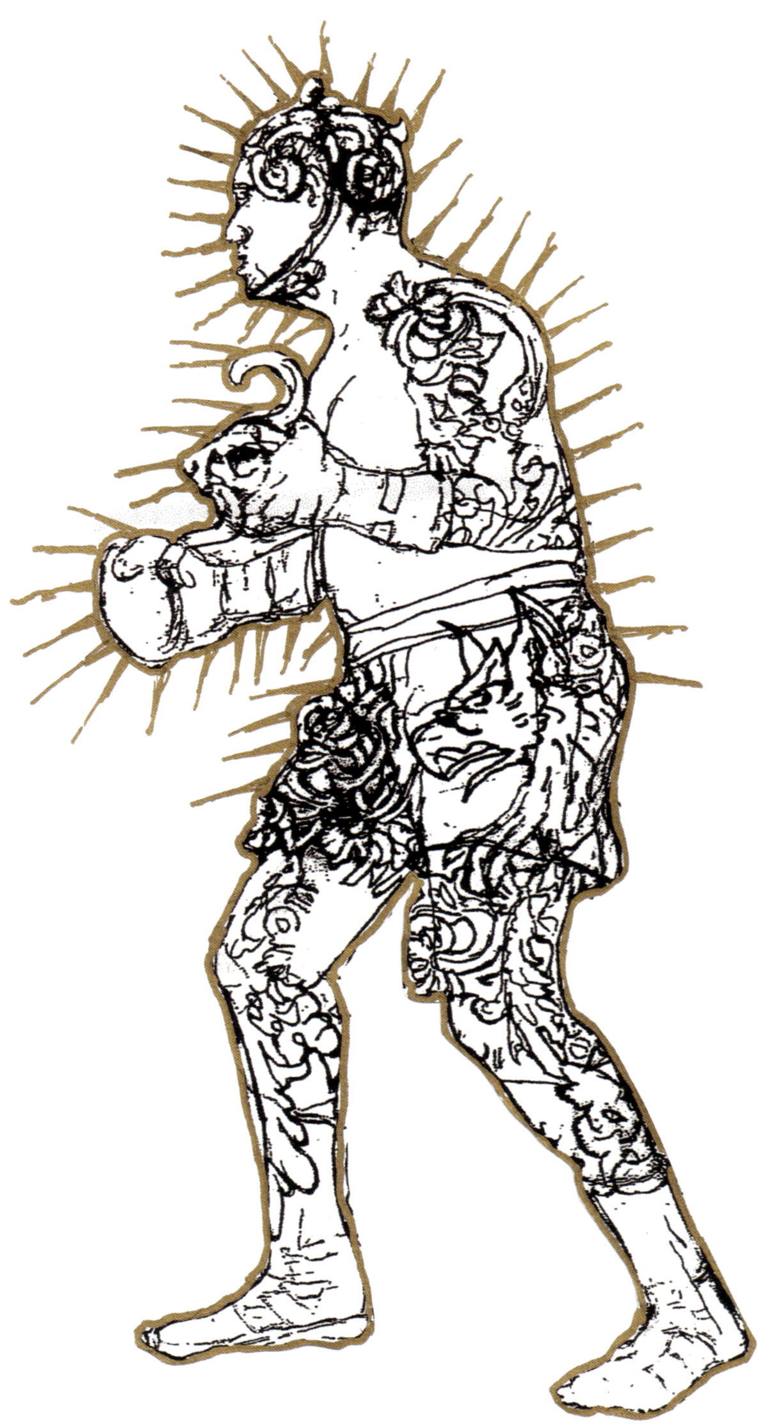

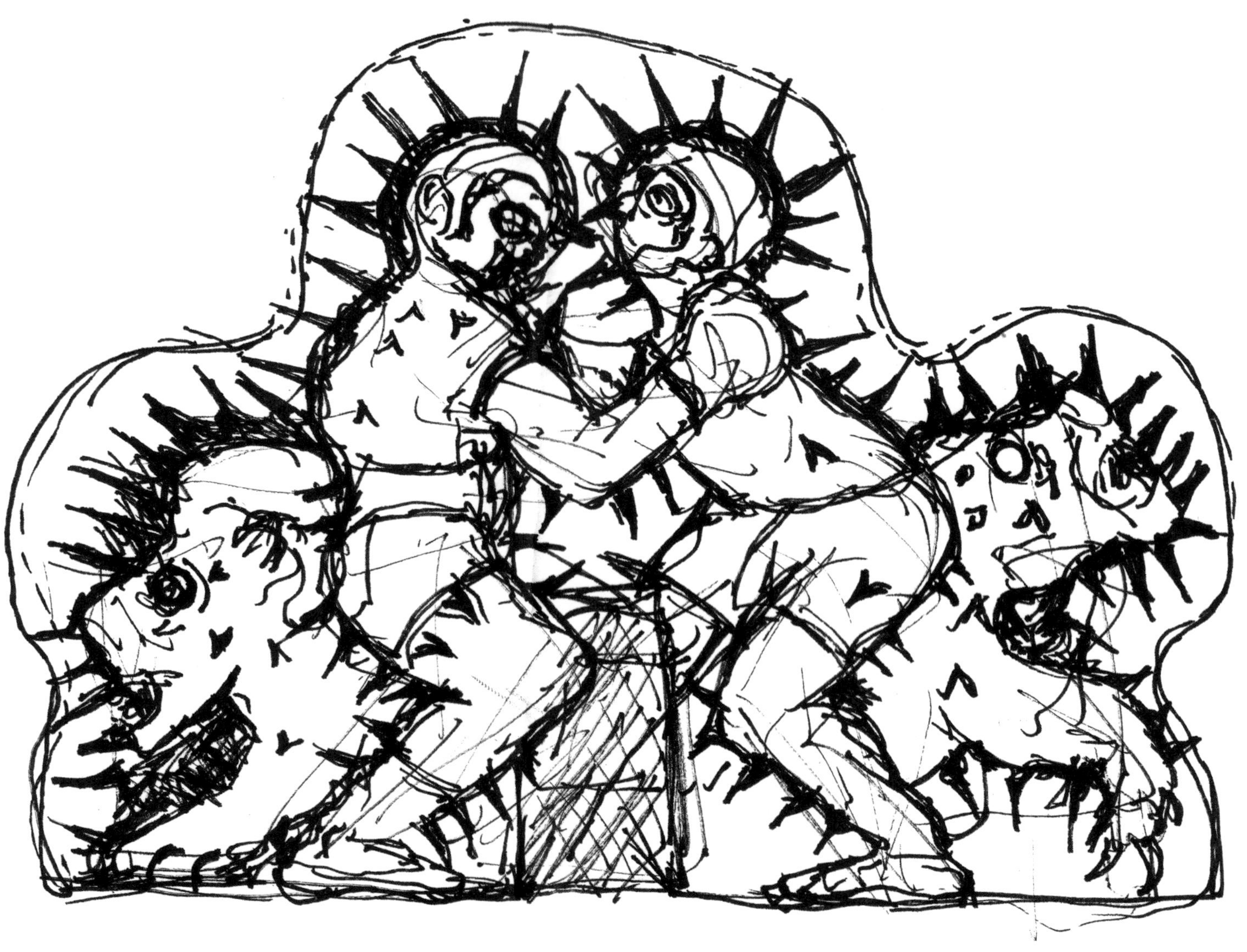

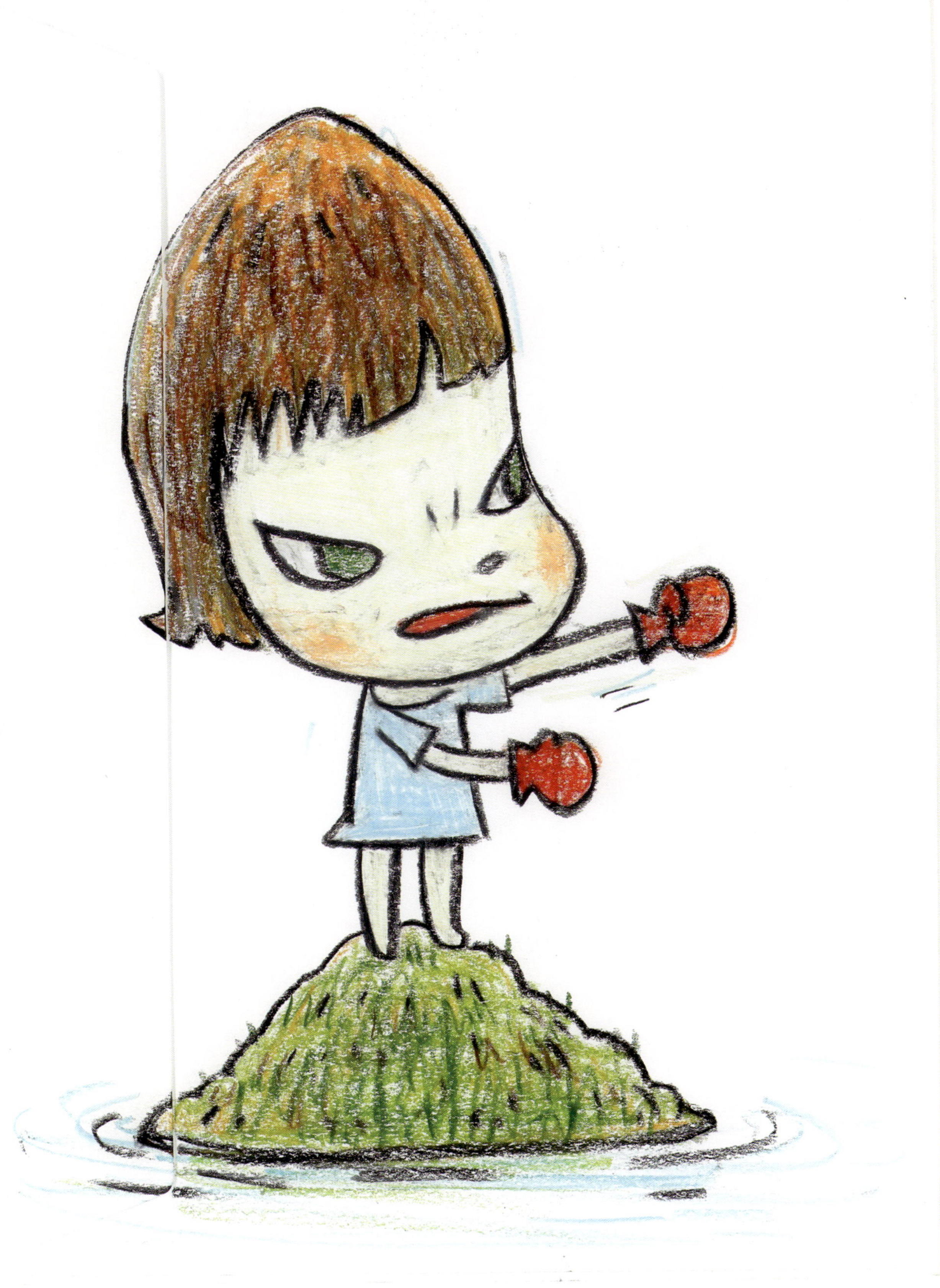
196A PICCADILLY LONDON W1J 9DY

LEROY NEIMAN

ALI VS. FOREMAN, ZAIRE, 1974 - POSTER / 38 X 23 INCHES
COURTESY OF THE LEROY NEIMAN FOUNDATION

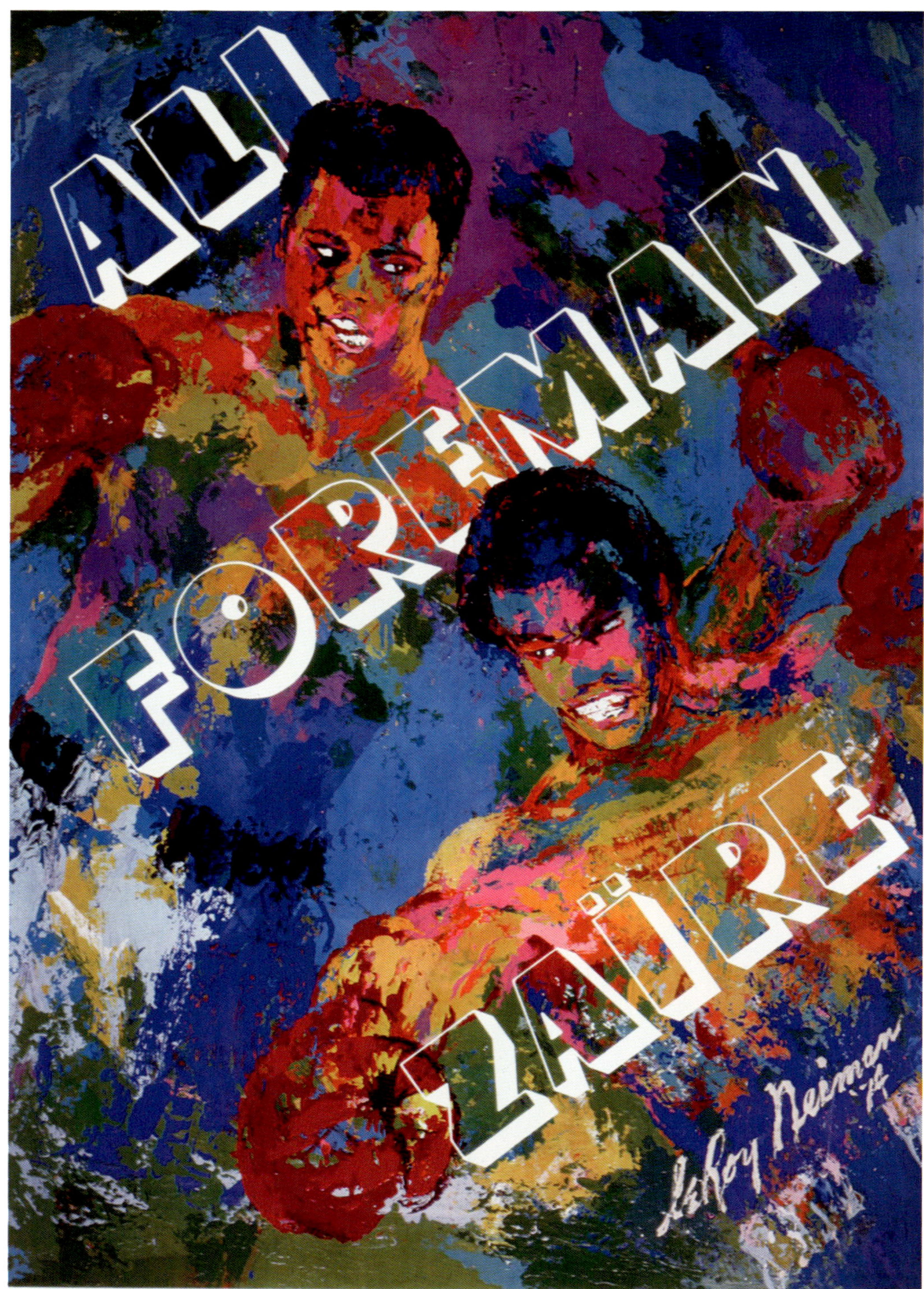

ALI
FOREMAN
FOREMAN
ZAIRE
LeRoy Neiman 74
WORLD HEAVYWEIGHT CHAMPIONSHIP FIGHT · 15 ROUNDS
DIRECT FROM KINSHASA, ZAIRE · TUESDAY · OCTOBER 29
GEORGE FOREMAN VS. MUHAMMAD ALI
PRESENTED BY HEMDALE LEISURE CORPORATION · VIDEO TECHNIQUES, INC. · DON KING PRODUCTIONS
PRODUCED BY JOHN DALY · HENRY A. SCHWARTZ · DON KING/FOR WORLD-WIDE SATELLITE TRANSMISSION

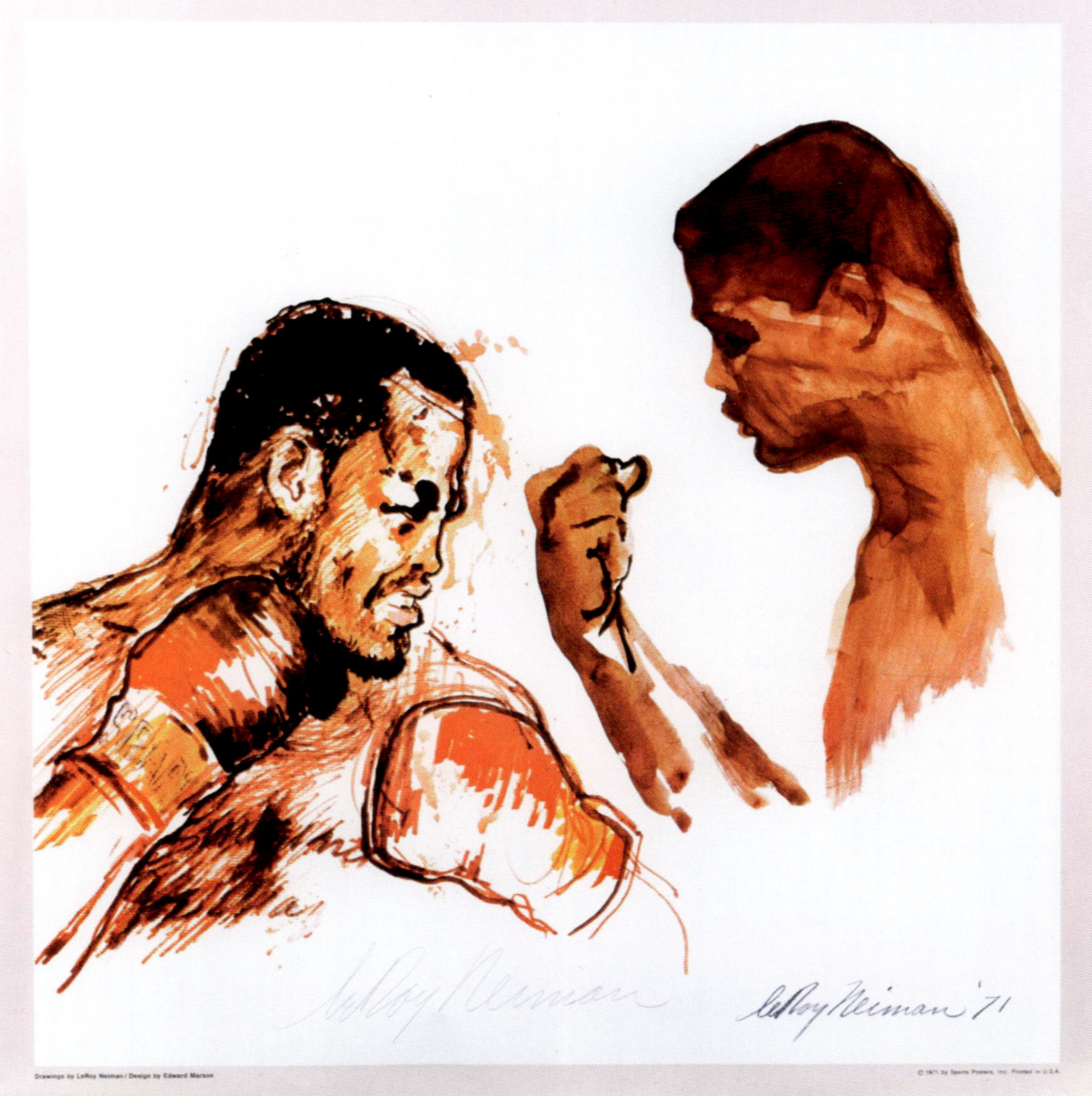
JOE FRAZIER VS.
MUHAMMAD ALI
WORLD HEAVYWEIGHT CHAMPIONSHIP
MADISON SQUARE GARDEN / MAR. 8, 1971
LeRoy Neiman '71
Drawings by LeRoy Neiman / Design by Edward Marlow
© 1971 by Sports Posters, Inc. Printed in U.S.A.

ED RUSCHA

BOXER, 1979 - OIL ON CANVAS / 54 X 60 INCHES
©ED RUSCHA, COURTESY OF THE ARTIST, PHOTO BY PAUL RUSCHA (P1979.20)

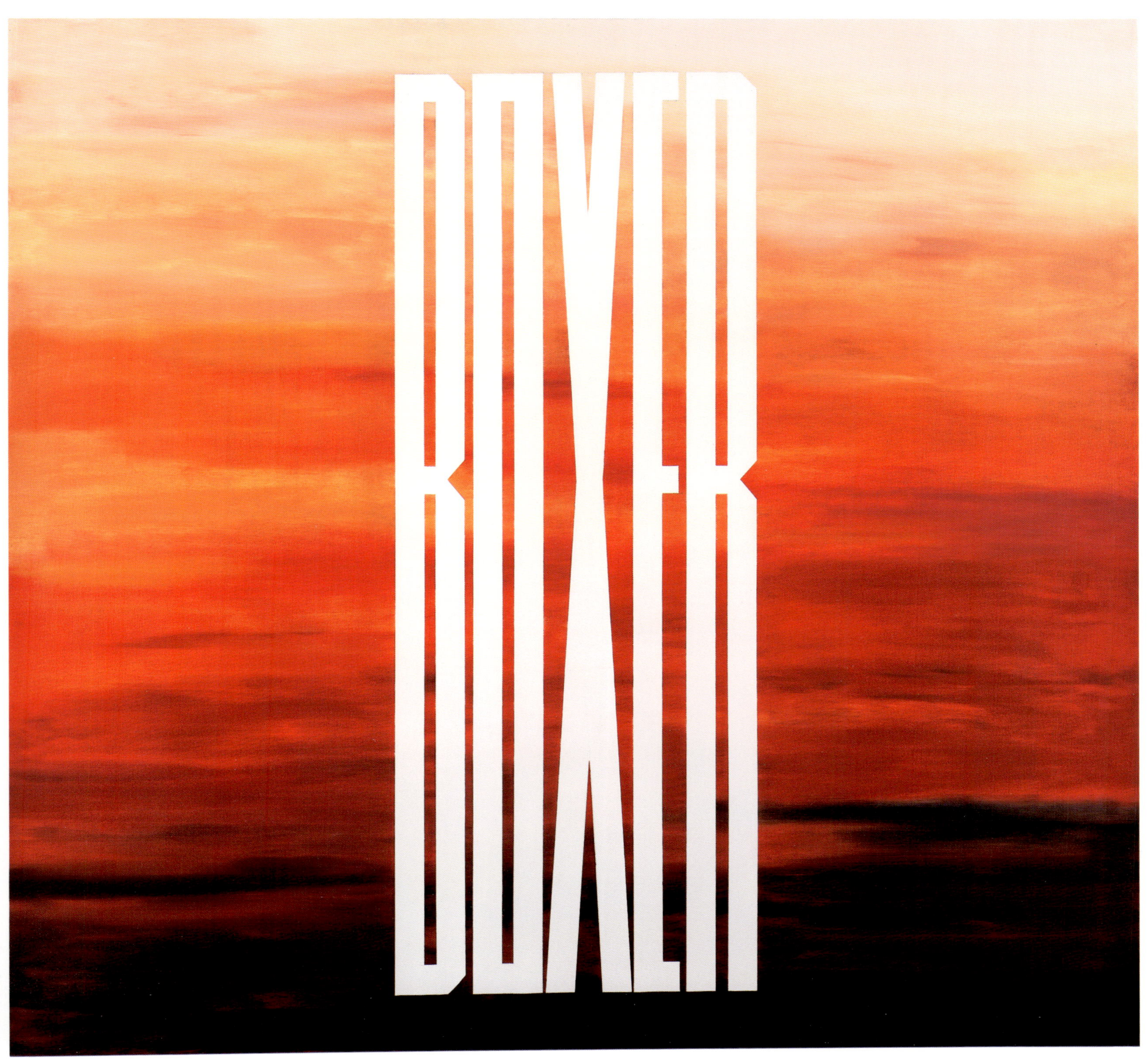

74

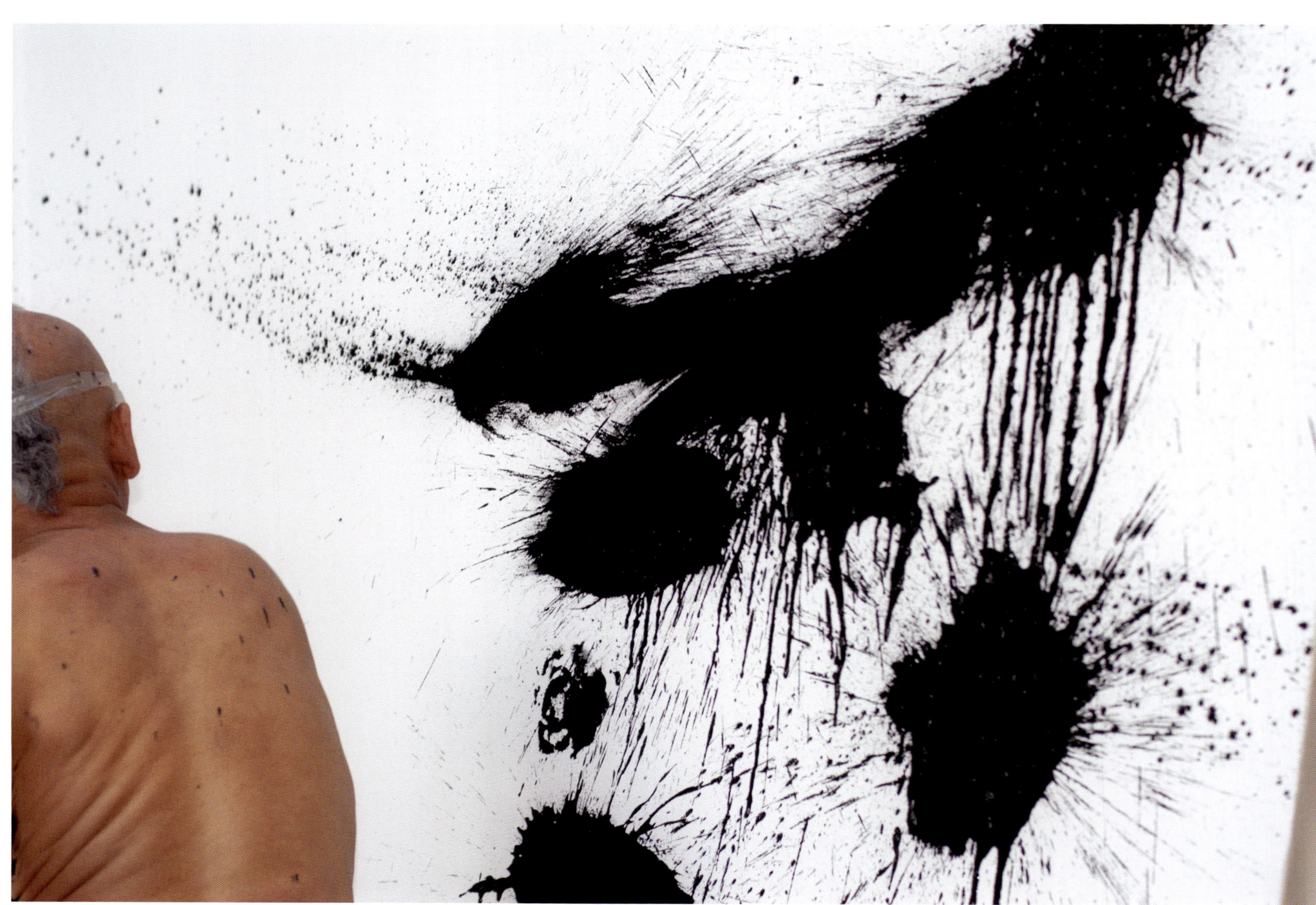

USHIO SHINOHARA

BOXING PAINTING, 2006
COURTESY OF THE ARTIST

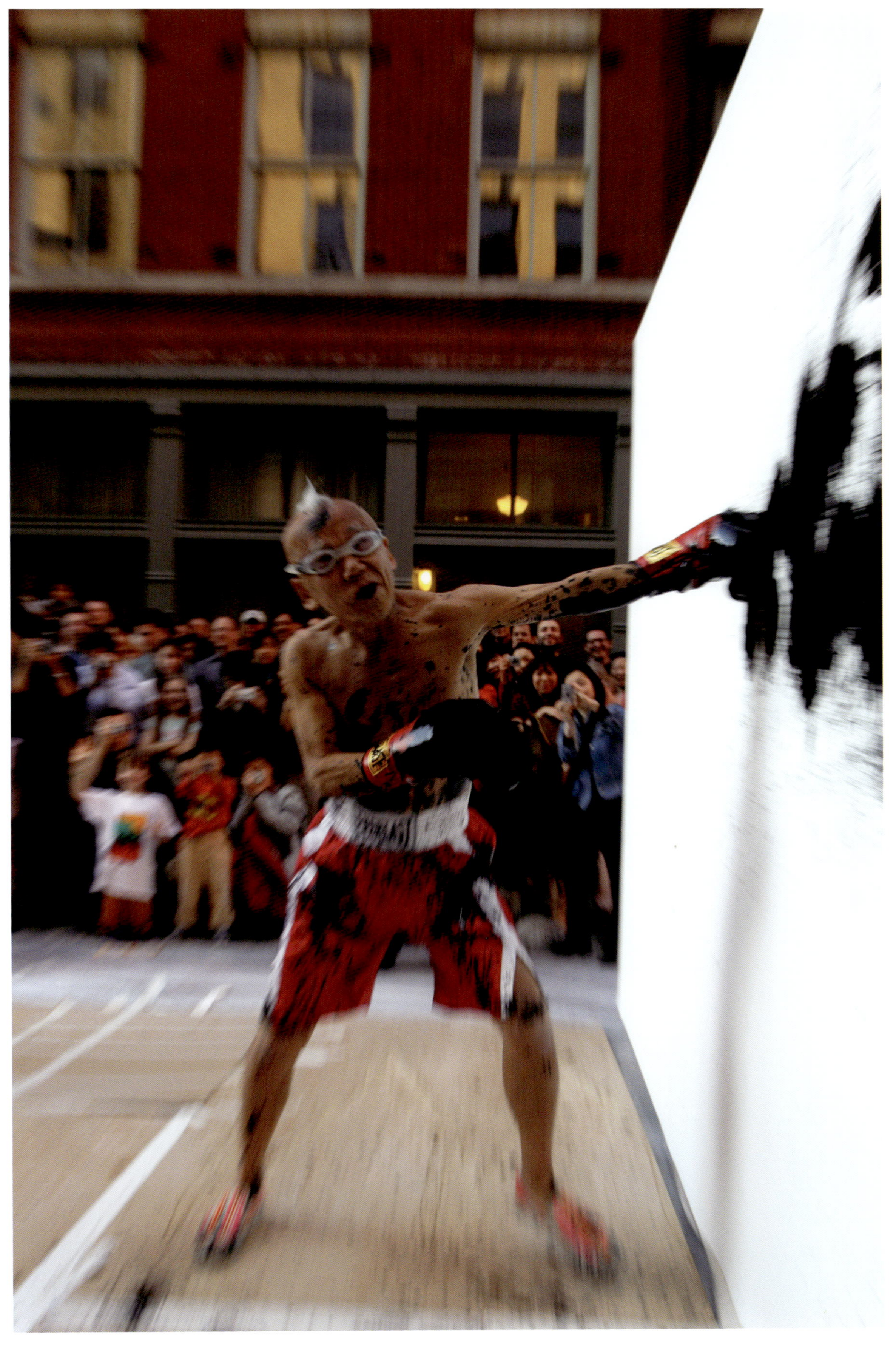

NEWSHA TAVAKOLIAN

TO BE TWENTY IN IRAN, 2010 - C PRINT / 41 X 51 INCHES
© NEWSHA TAVAKOLIA / POLARIS

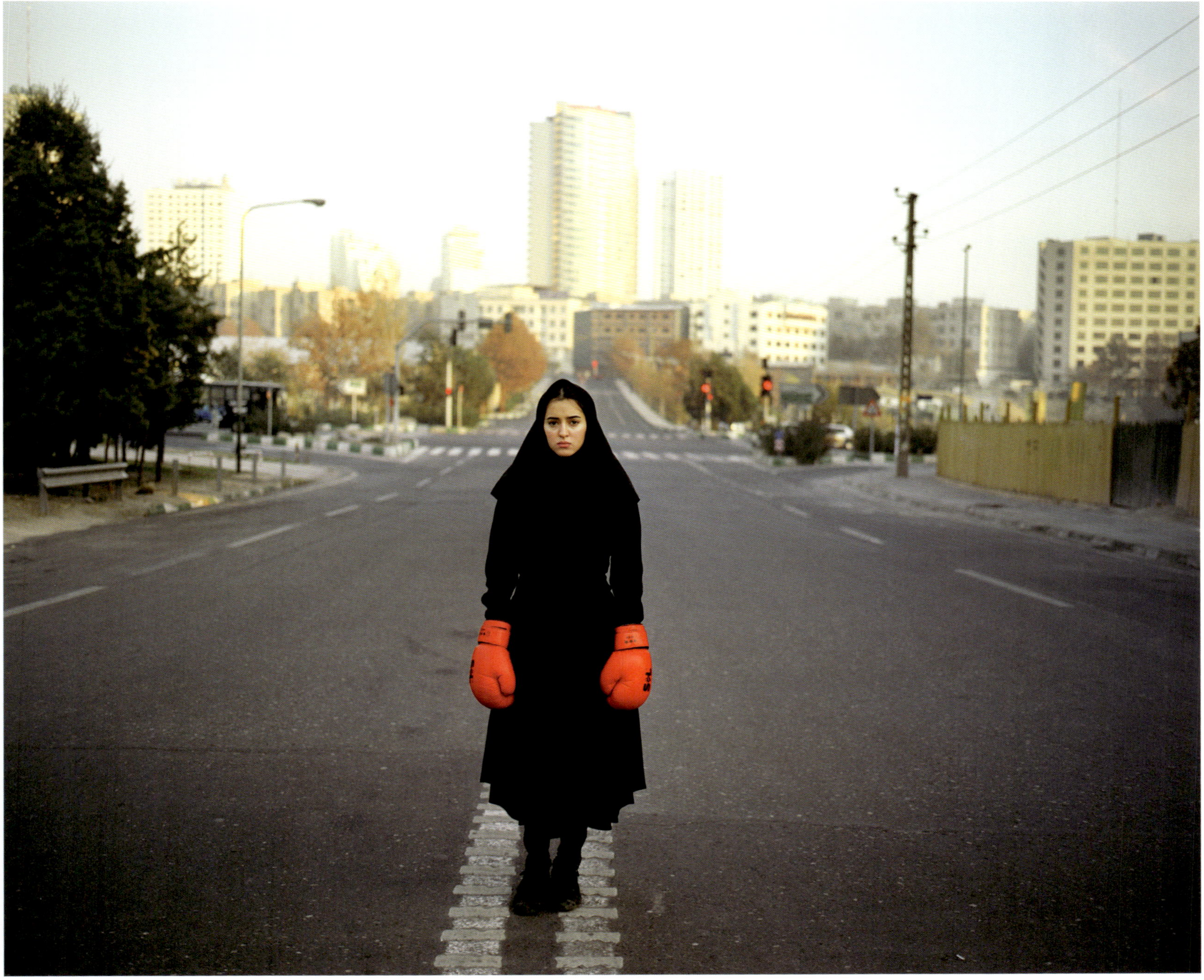

MARTIN WONG

PORTRAIT OF ROBERTO DURAN, 1990 - ACRYLIC ON CANVAS / 16.125 X 13.5 INCHES
COURTESY OF PPOW GALLERY

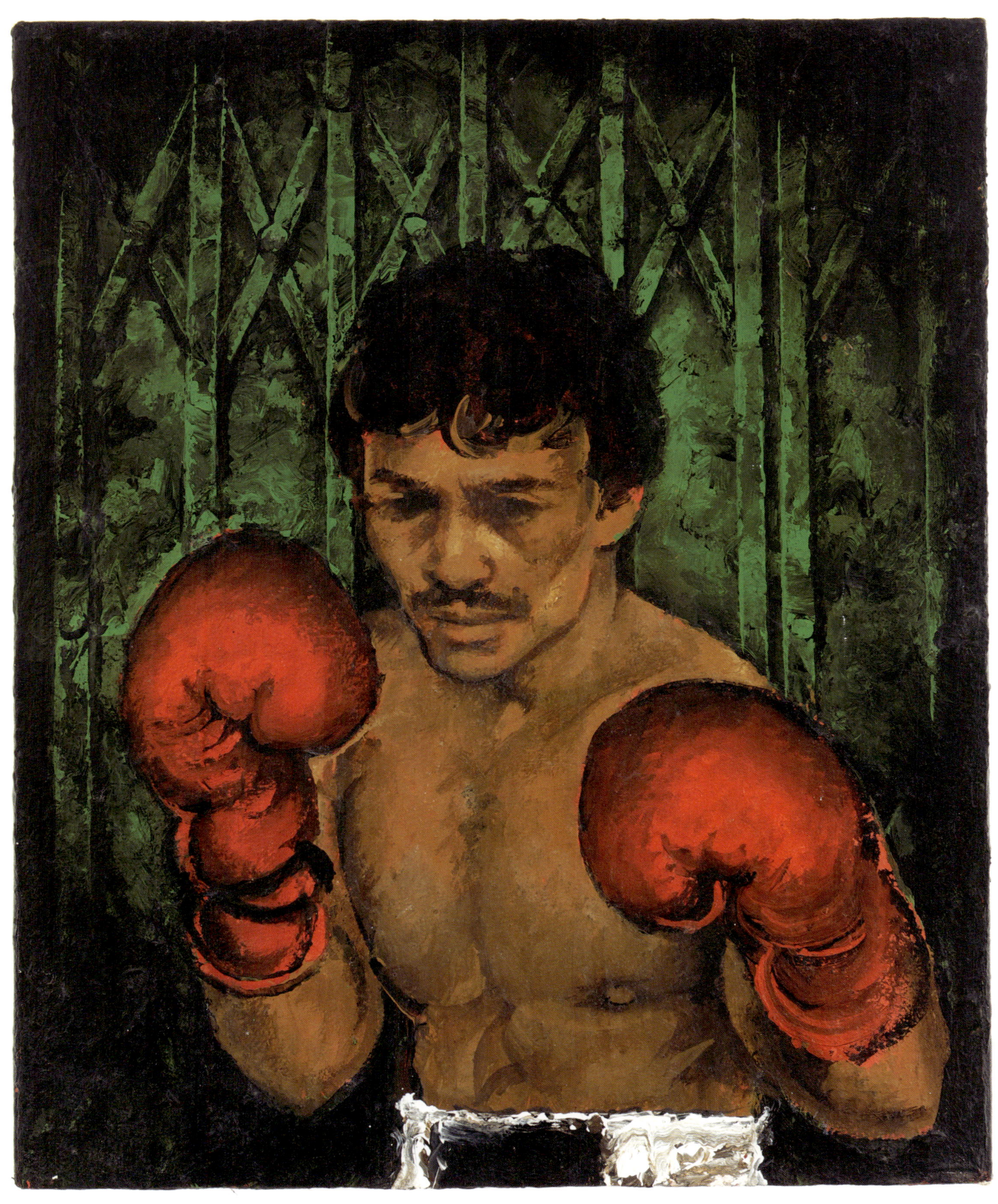

DOUBLE-NOSE/PURSE/PUNCHING BAG/ASHTRAY, 1970 - LITHOGRAPH / 21 X 19 INCHES
© 1970 CLAES OLDENBURG AND GEMINI G.E.L.

80

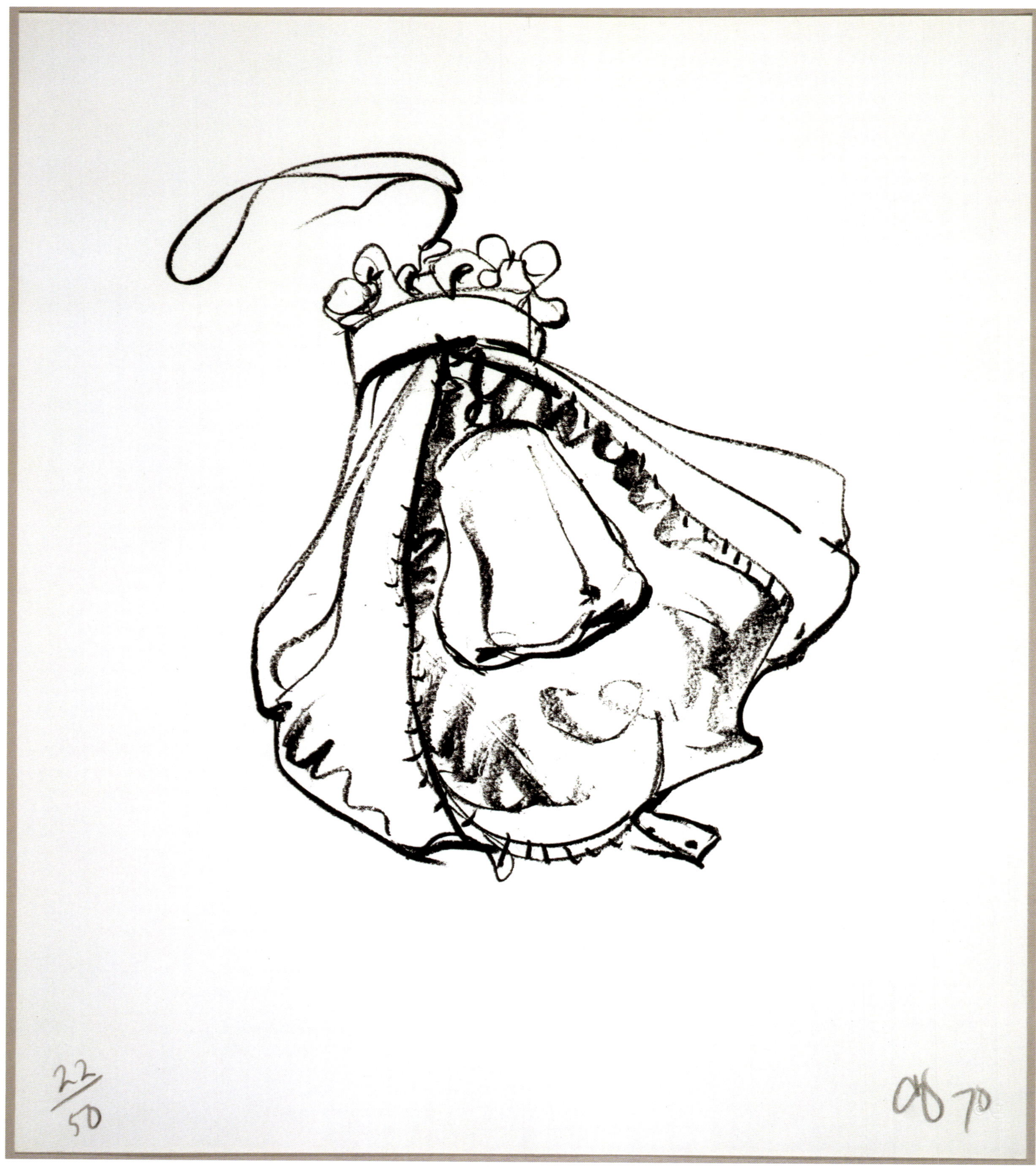

CLAES OLDENBURG

DOUBLE-NOSE/PURSE/PUNCHING BAG/ASHTRAY, 1970 - EDITION SCULPTURE OF LEATHER, BRONZE, AND WOOD / 10.875 X 20.75 X 8.375 INCHES [WEIGHT: 16.25 LBS]
© 1970 CLAES OLDENBURG AND GEMINI G.E.L.

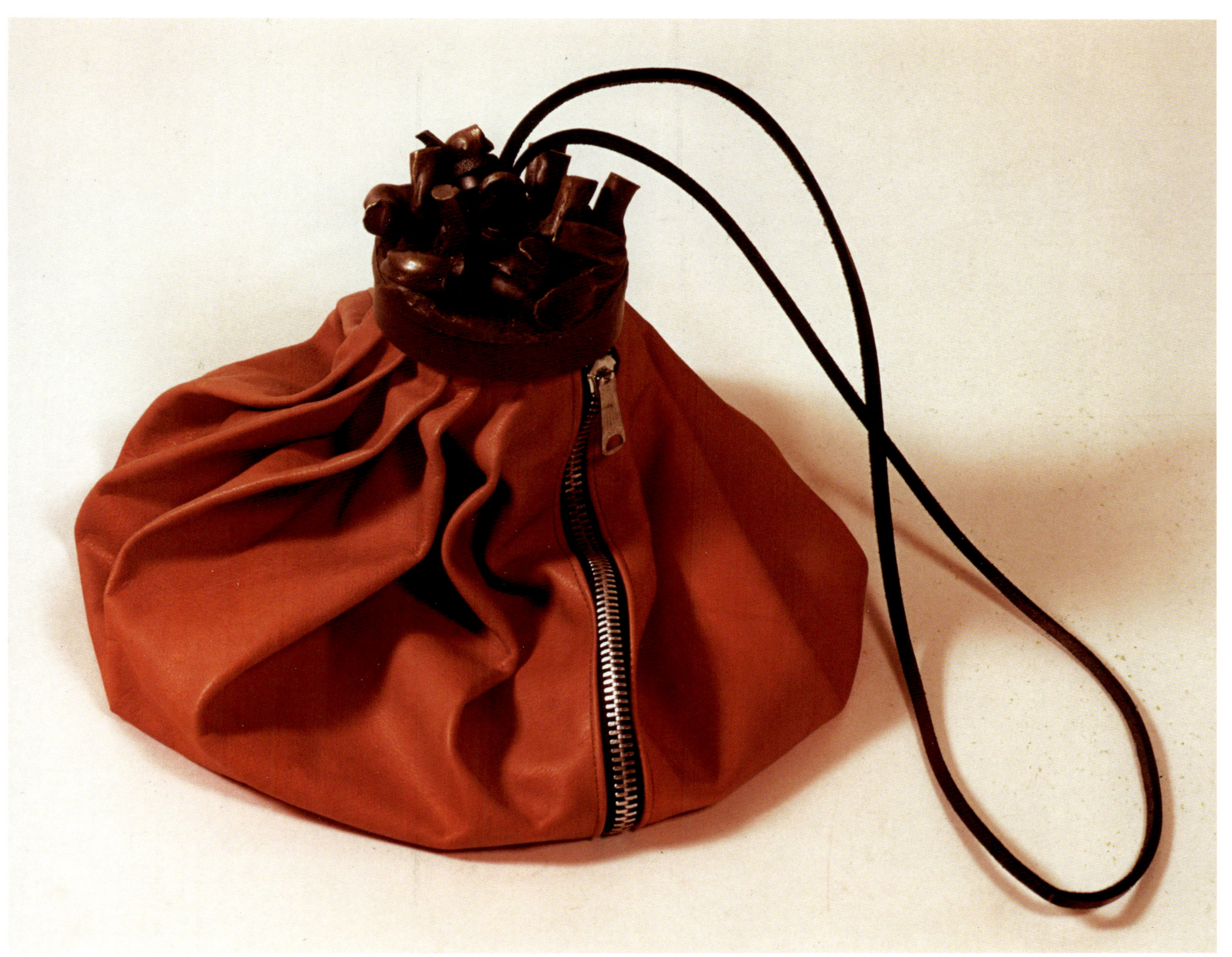

JOSEPH BEUYS

FILZ-TV (FELT TV), 1970 - FELT, PAIR OF BOXING GLOVES, 16MM FILM IN METAL CONTAINER, BLOOD SAUSAGE, INK STAMPS, OIL PAINT / 18.1875 X 3.5625 X 24 INCHES INSTALLED
T. B. WALKER ACQUISITION FUND, 1995
COURTESY WALKER ART CENTER, © 2013 ARTISTS RIGHTS SOCIETY (ARS), NEW YORK / VG BILD-KUNST, BONN

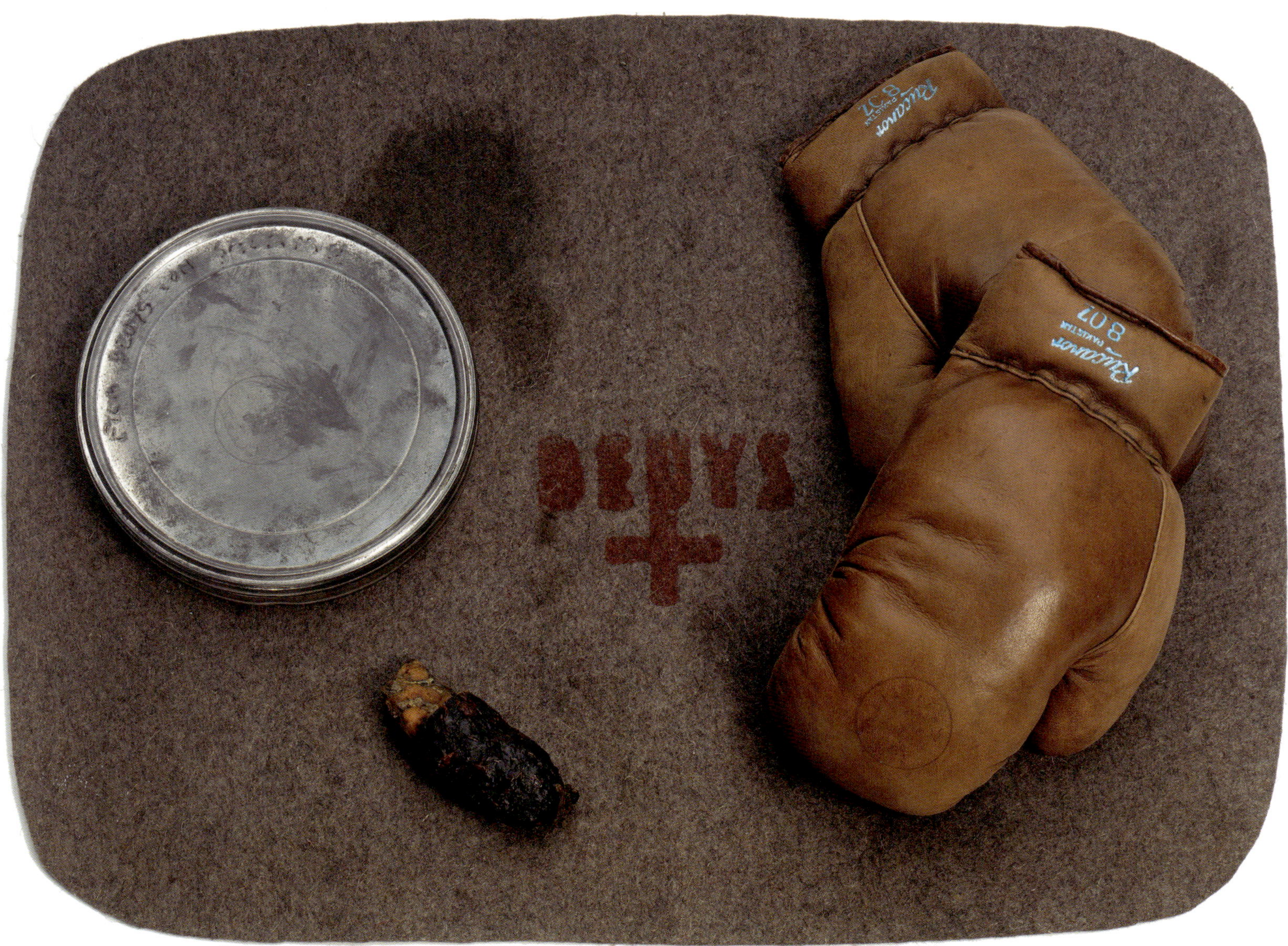

JEANNE SILVERTHORNE

SKELETON WITH BOXING GLOVES AND CRATE, 2012 - PLATINUM SILICONE RUBBER, PHOSPHORESCENT PIGMENT / 9.25 X 2.5 X 2.75 INCHES / EDITION OF 10
COURTESY MCKEE GALLERY, NEW YORK

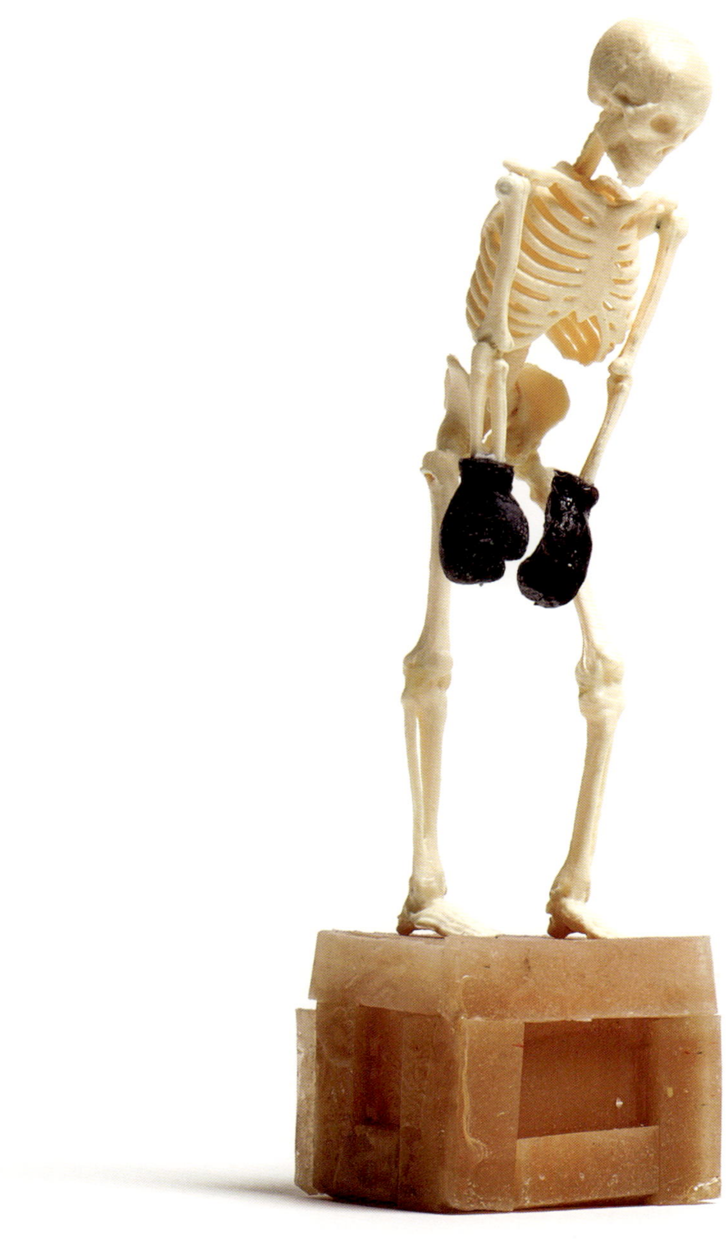

ANONYMOUS ARTIST

PORTRAIT OF MANNY PACQUIAO [COMMISSIONED ON EBAY], 2013 - OIL ON BLACK VELVET / 18 X 24 INCHES
COLLECTION OF CARLOS ROLON
PHOTO BY NATHAN KEAY

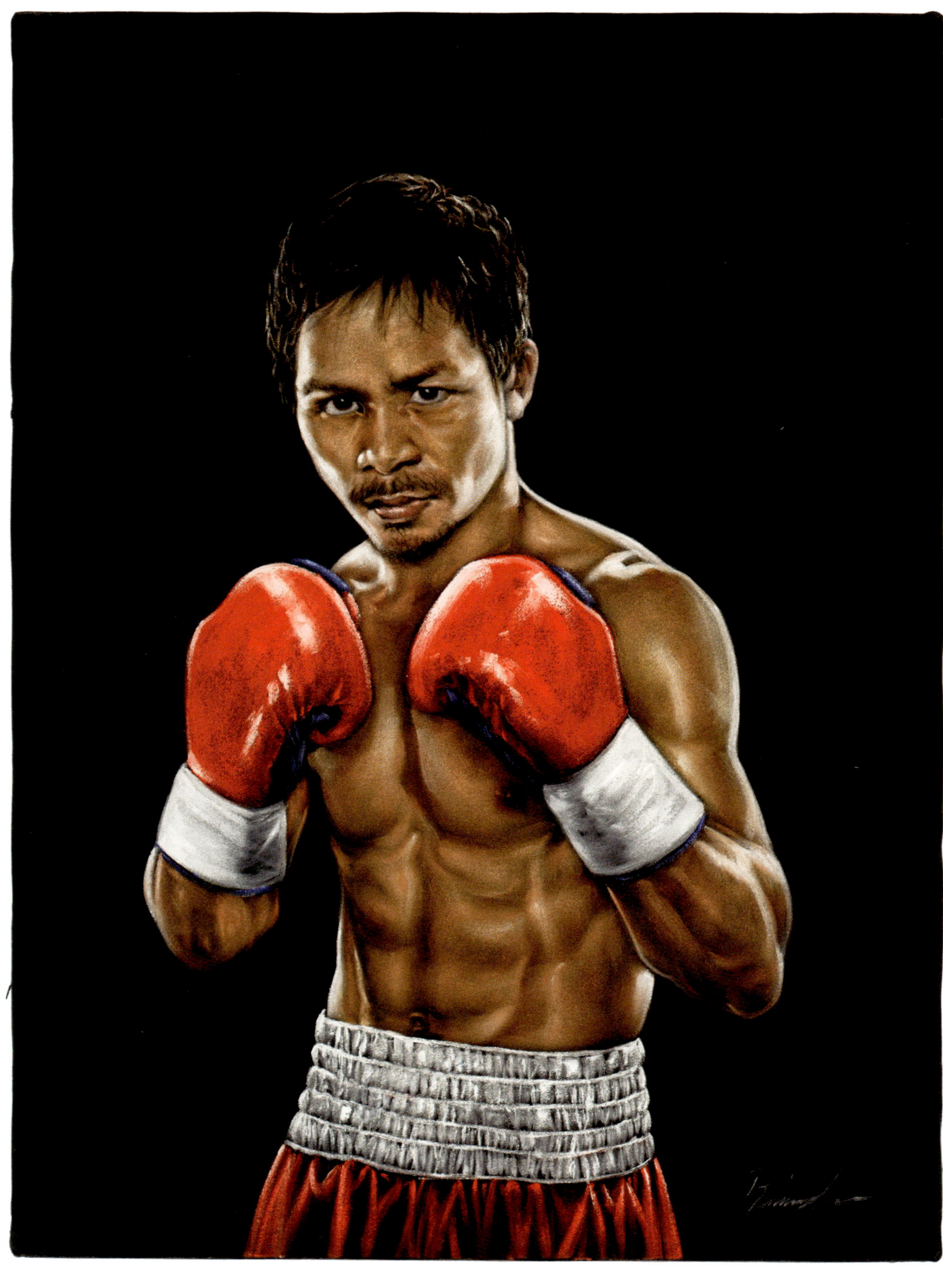

JOE ZUCKER

BOXING PAINTING ROUND #2, 1981 - ACRYLIC, COTTON, RHOPLEX ON CANVAS, ENAMEL ON WOOD
BROOKLYN MUSEUM, GIFT OF MAX MUNN AND TED STEVENS, 1992.272. © JOE ZUCKER

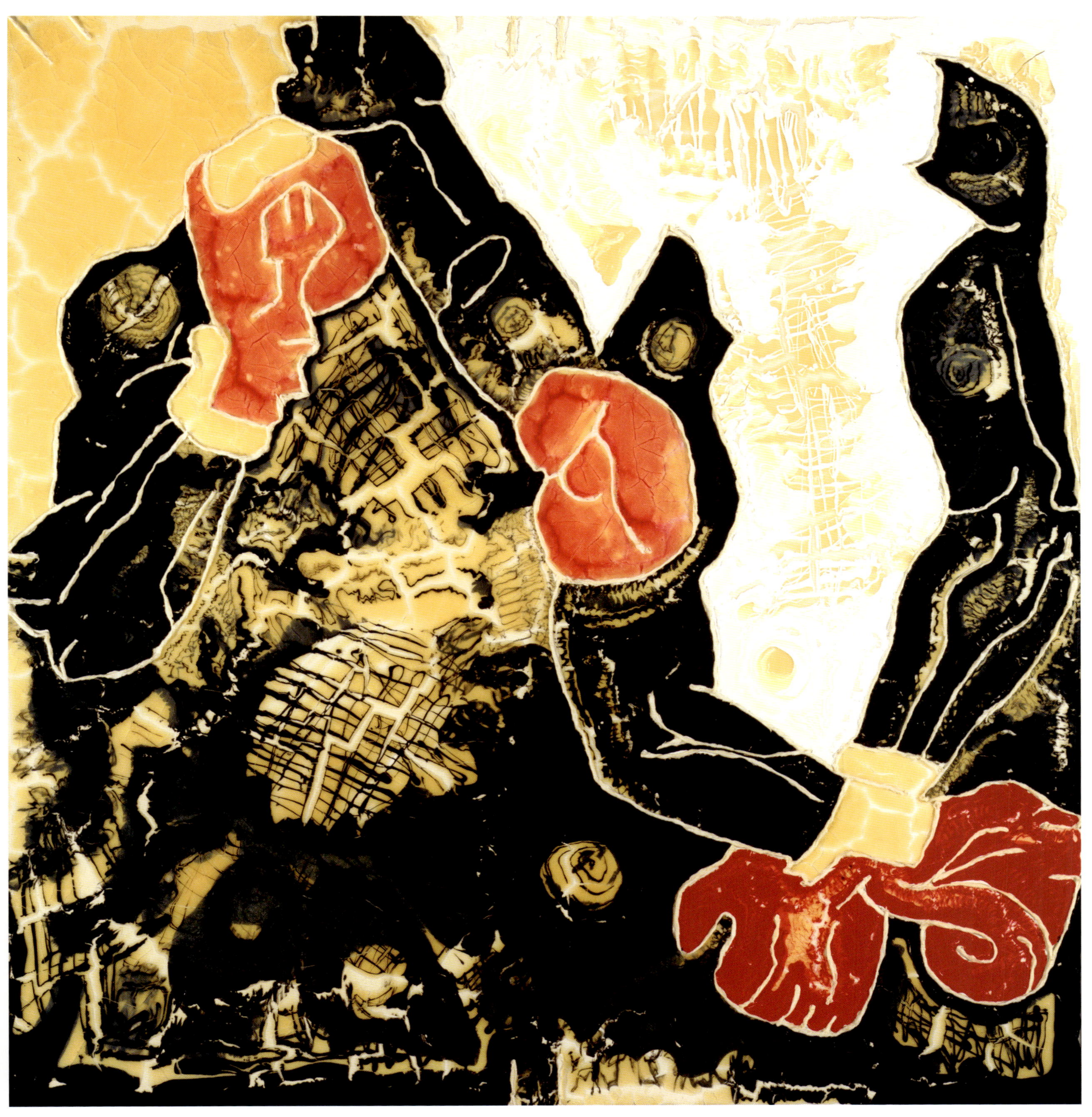

Results **1 - 18** of about **27,000,000** (0.04 seconds)

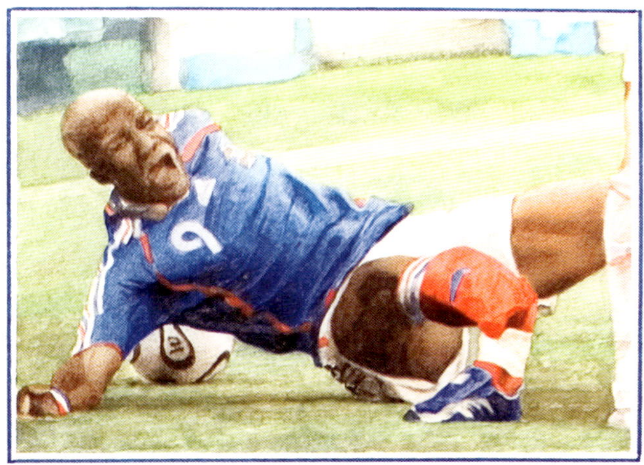

Maybe Not Such a Great **Moment** for HIM!
420 × 462 - 33k - jpg
bblmedia.com

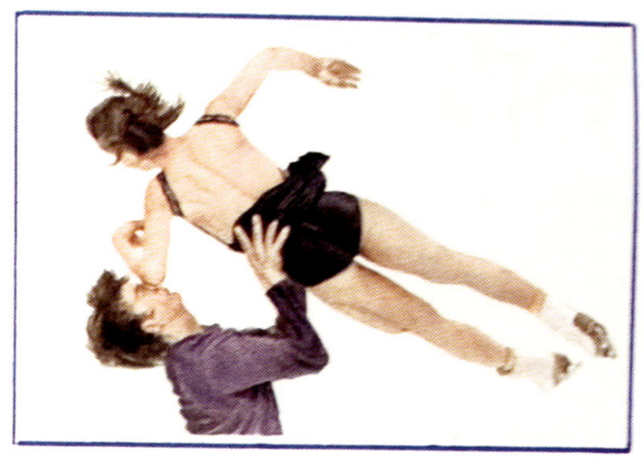

a **moment of**
400 × 267 - 23k - jpg
crazy-picsblog.blogspo...

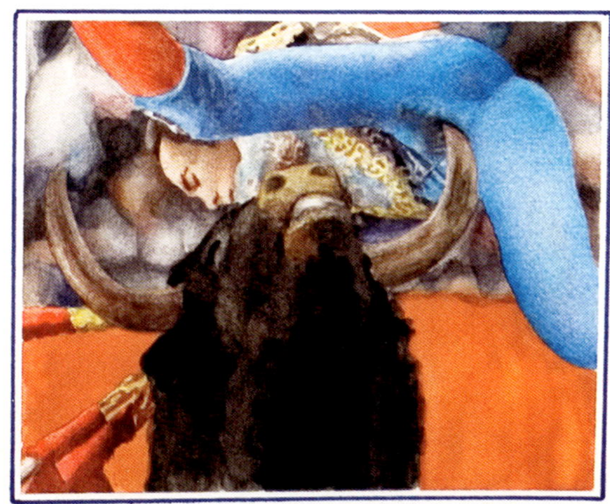

funny **sport moments**-17
410 × 350 - 31k - jpg
druls.com

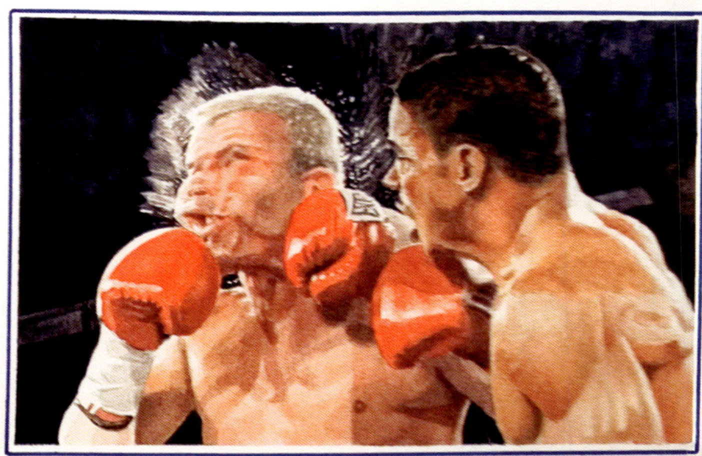

A **Sports Moment**
530 × 331 - 38k - jpg
sarcasticgamer.com

JEFF WALL

BOXING, 2011 - COLOUR PHOTOGRAPH / 215 X 295 CM
COURTESY OF THE ARTIST

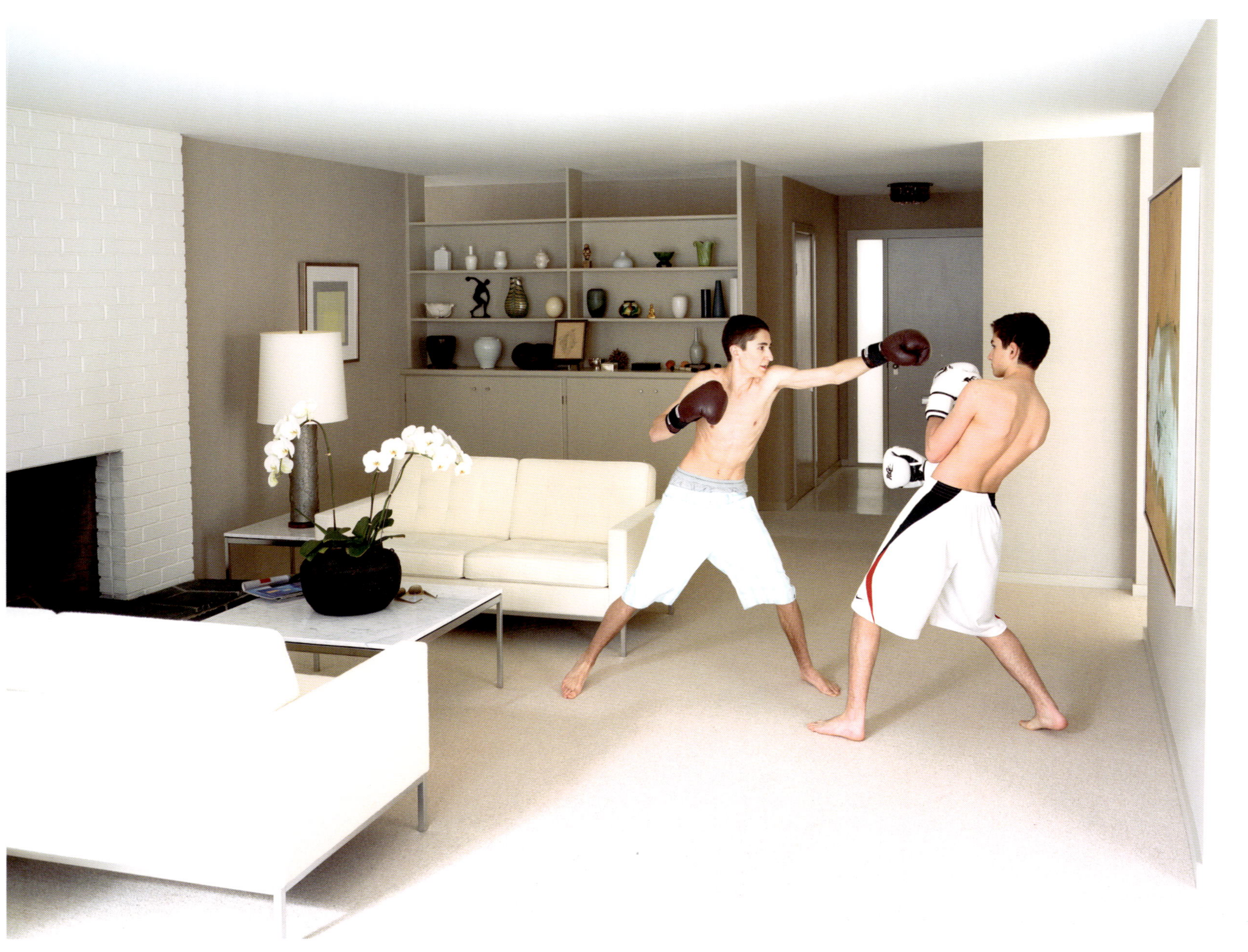

REBECCA HORN

FIGHT FOR ART, 1998 - BOXING GLOVES, ARM APPARATUS [2], MOTOR, BOOKS, BLACK PAINT / DIMENSIONS VARIABLE
COLLECTION OF NANCY AND BOB MAGOON, ASPEN
PHOTO BY JASON DEWEY

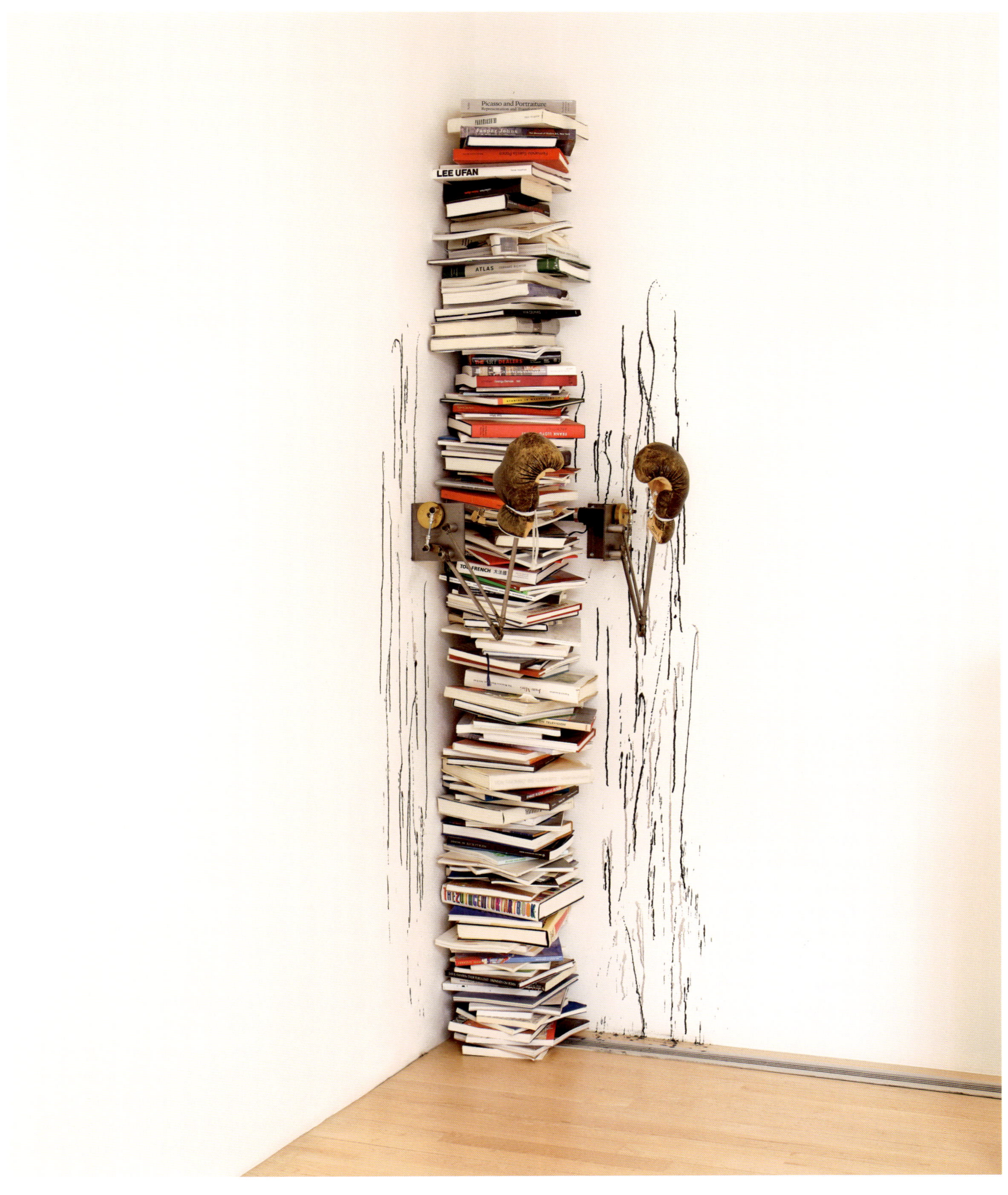

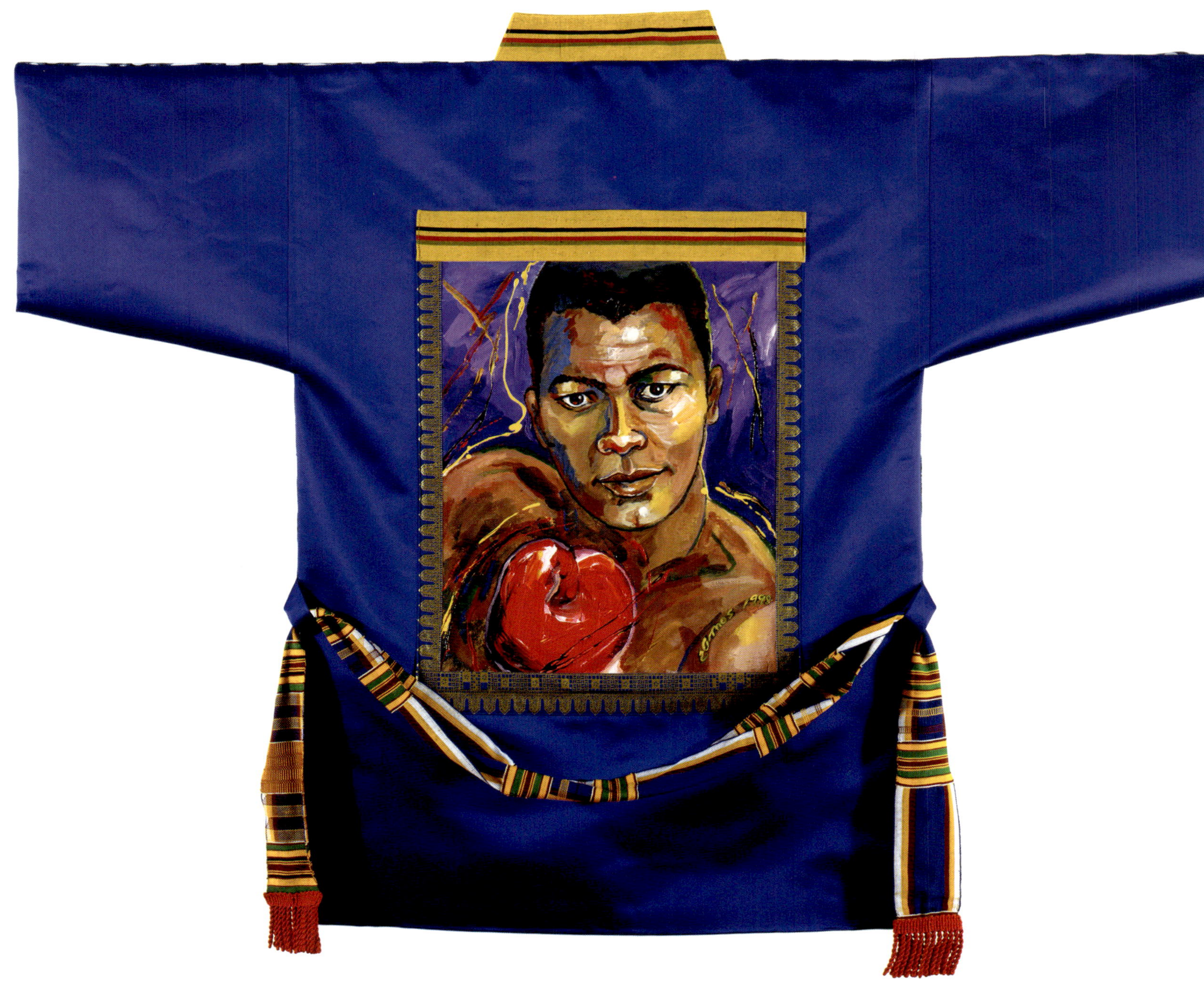

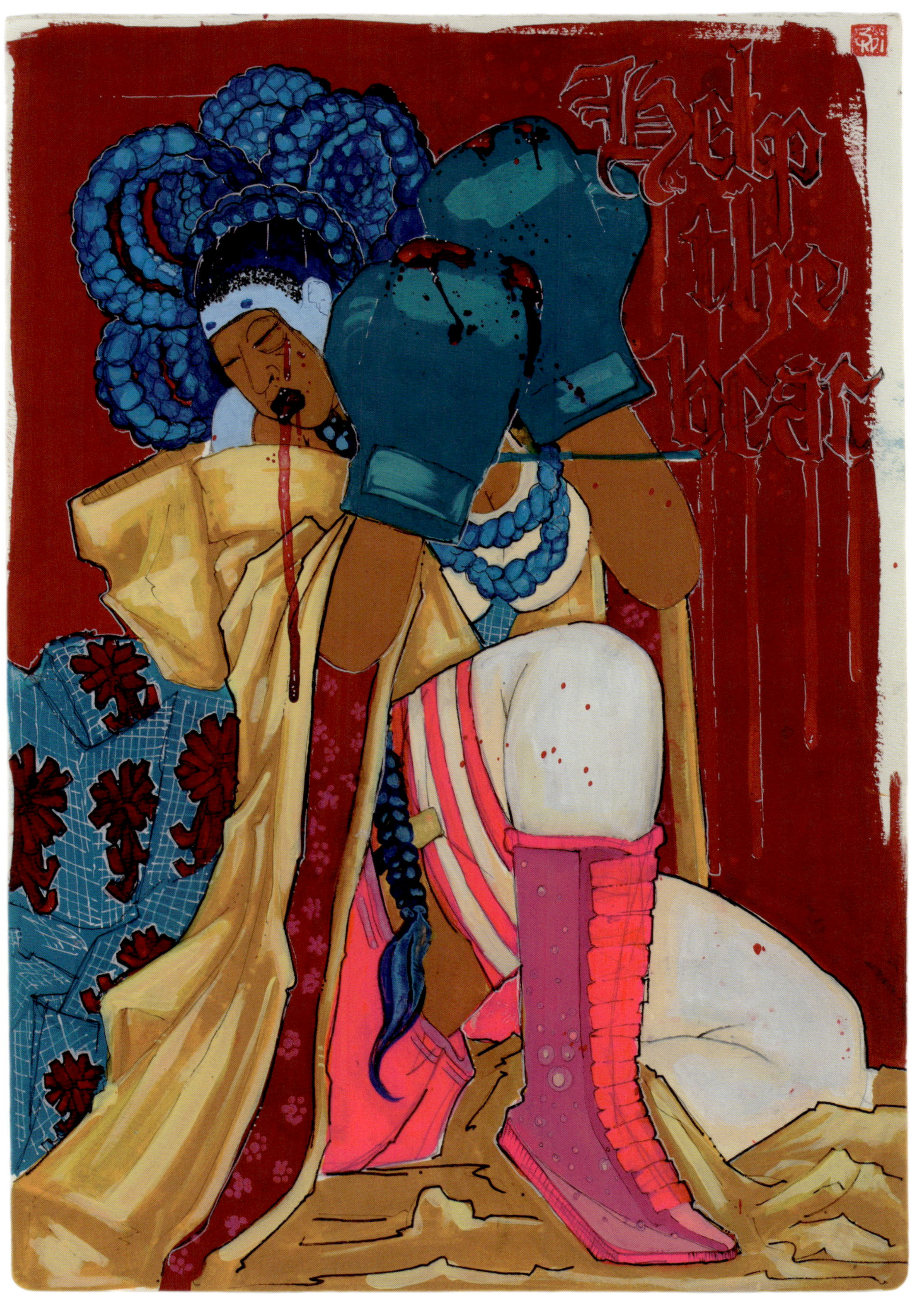
Help
the
bear

92

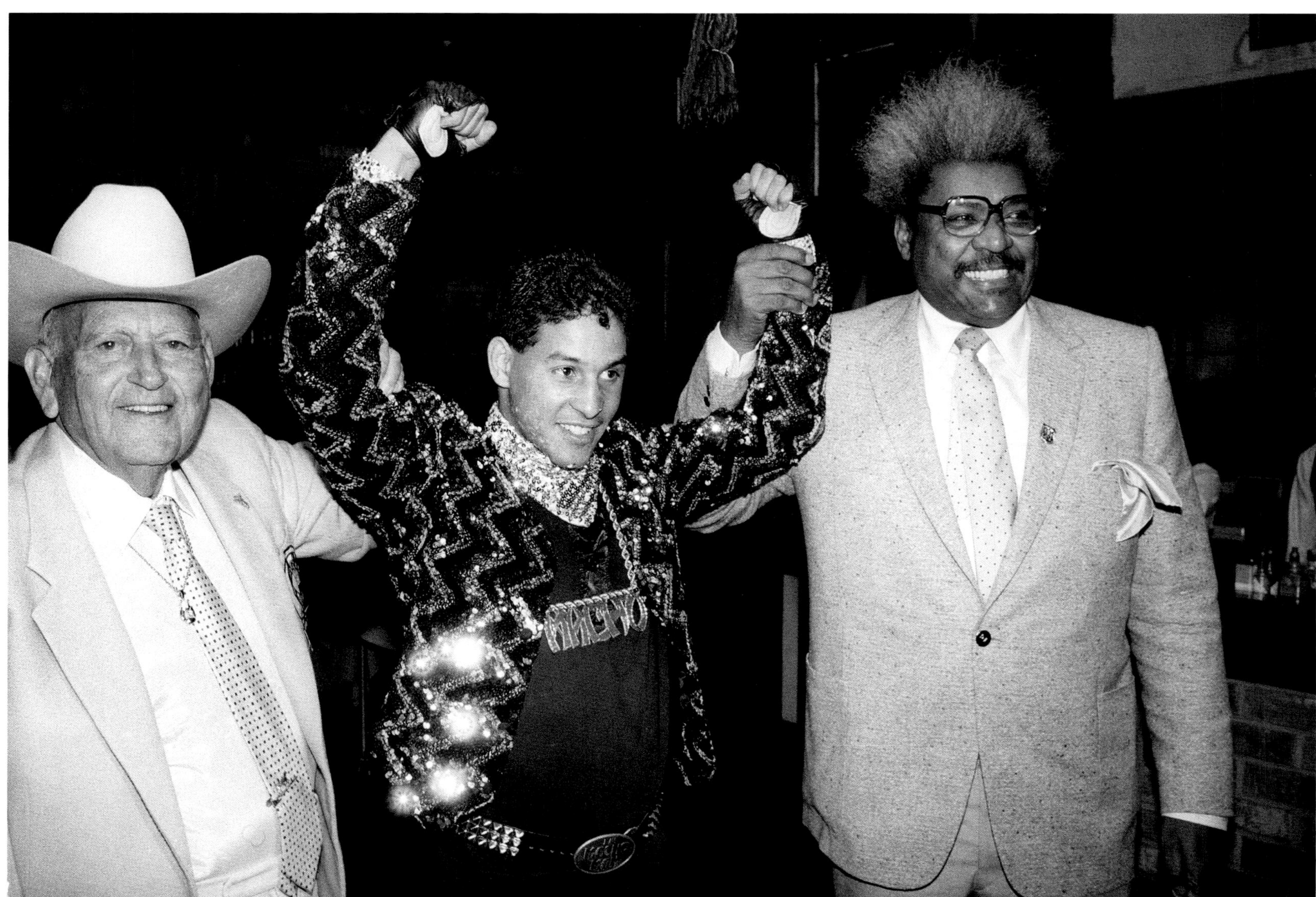

AHN YOUNG-JOON

UNTITLED [WOMEN'S LIGHT FLYWEIGHT, SOUTH KOREA], 2010 - C-PRINT / VARIOUS
PHOTO © DAVID AHN YOUNG-JOON / AP / CORBIS

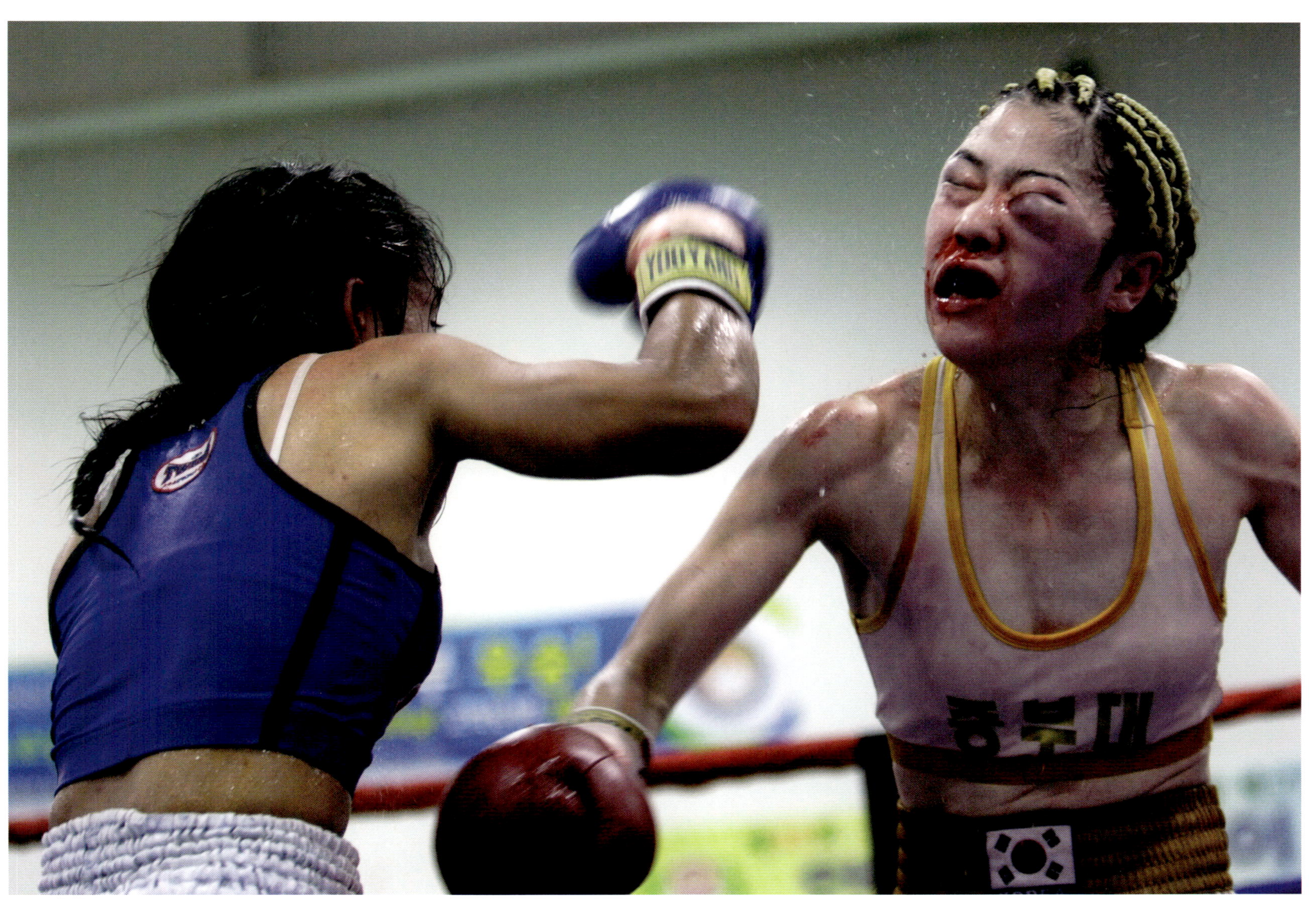

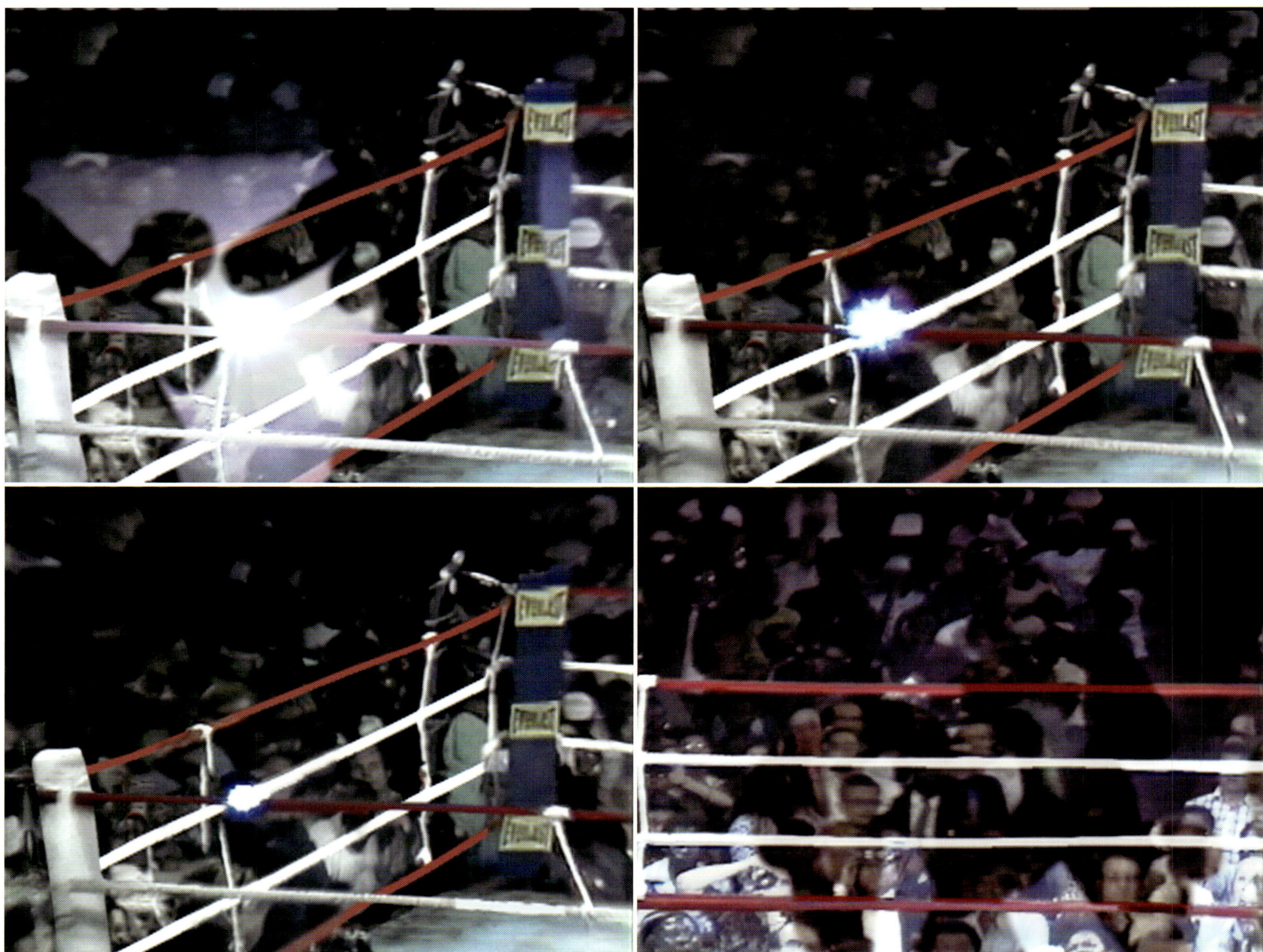
EVERLAST
EVERLAST
EVERLAST

SAM TAYLOR-WOOD

VIEW OF *3 MINUTE ROUND*, 2008 - TWO-CHANNEL VIDEO, 3 MINUTES / DIMENSIONS VARIABLE
PINCHUKARTCENTRE © 2008, PHOTOS BY SERGEI ILLIN

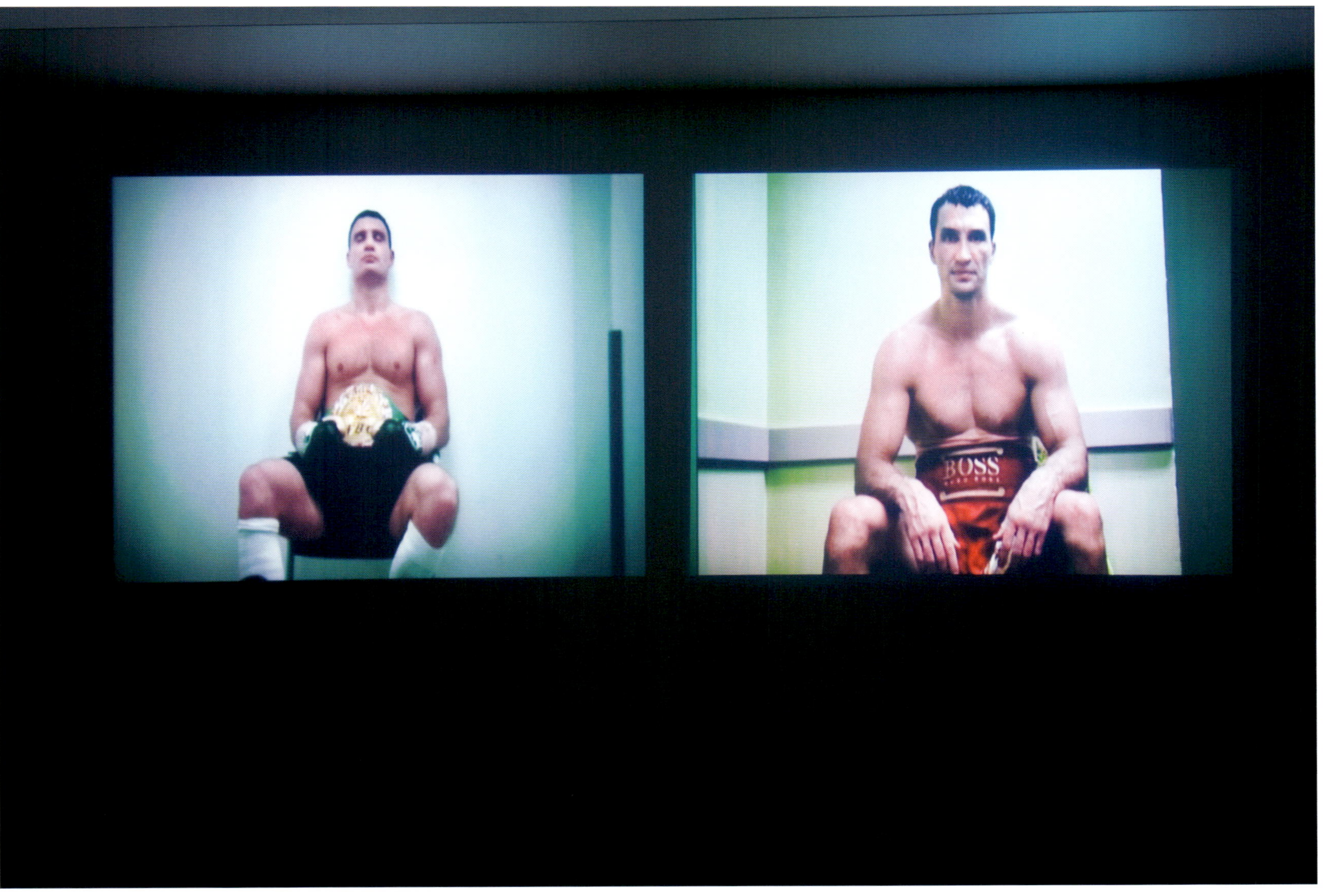

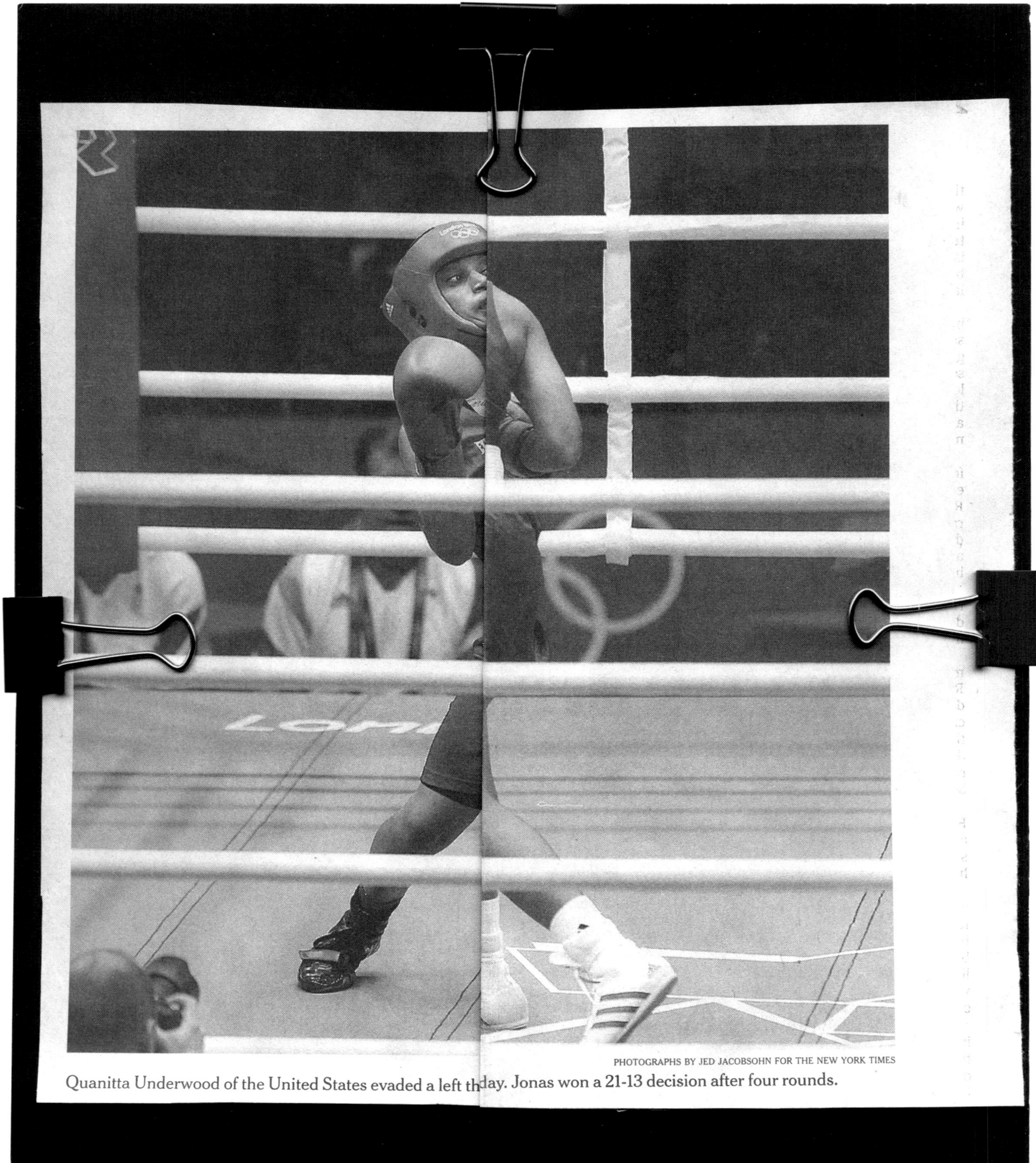

PHOTOGRAPHS BY JED JACOBSOHN FOR THE NEW YORK TIMES

Quanitta Underwood of the United States evaded a left th day. Jonas won a 21-13 decision after four rounds.

ANDREAS GURSKY

KLITSCHKO, 1999 - C-PRINT / 207 X 261 X 6.2 CM
© 2013 ANDREAS GURSKY / ARTISTS RIGHTS SOCIETY (ARS), NEW YORK / VG BILD-KUNST, BONN
COURTESY SPRÜTH MAGERS BERLIN LONDON

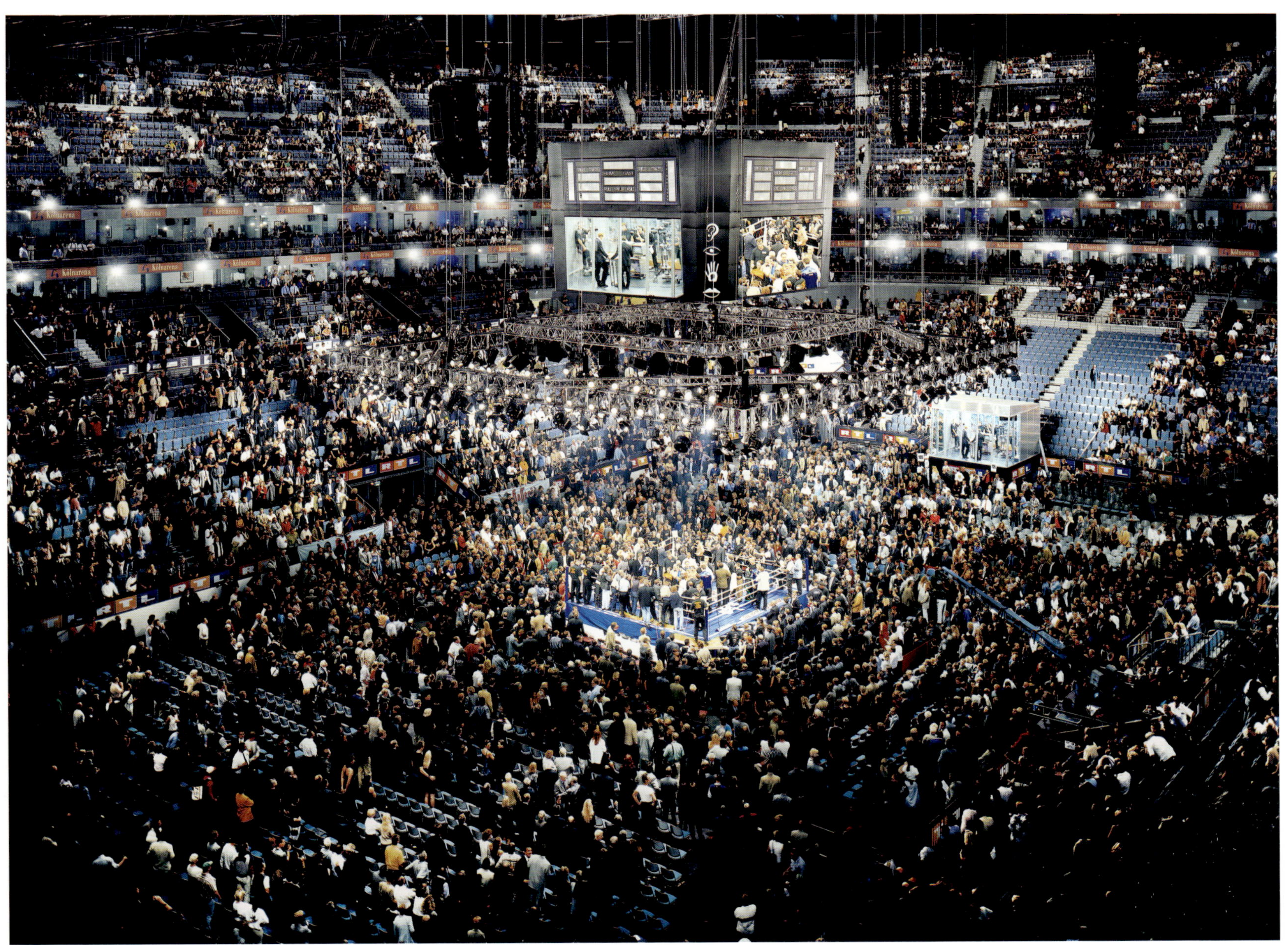

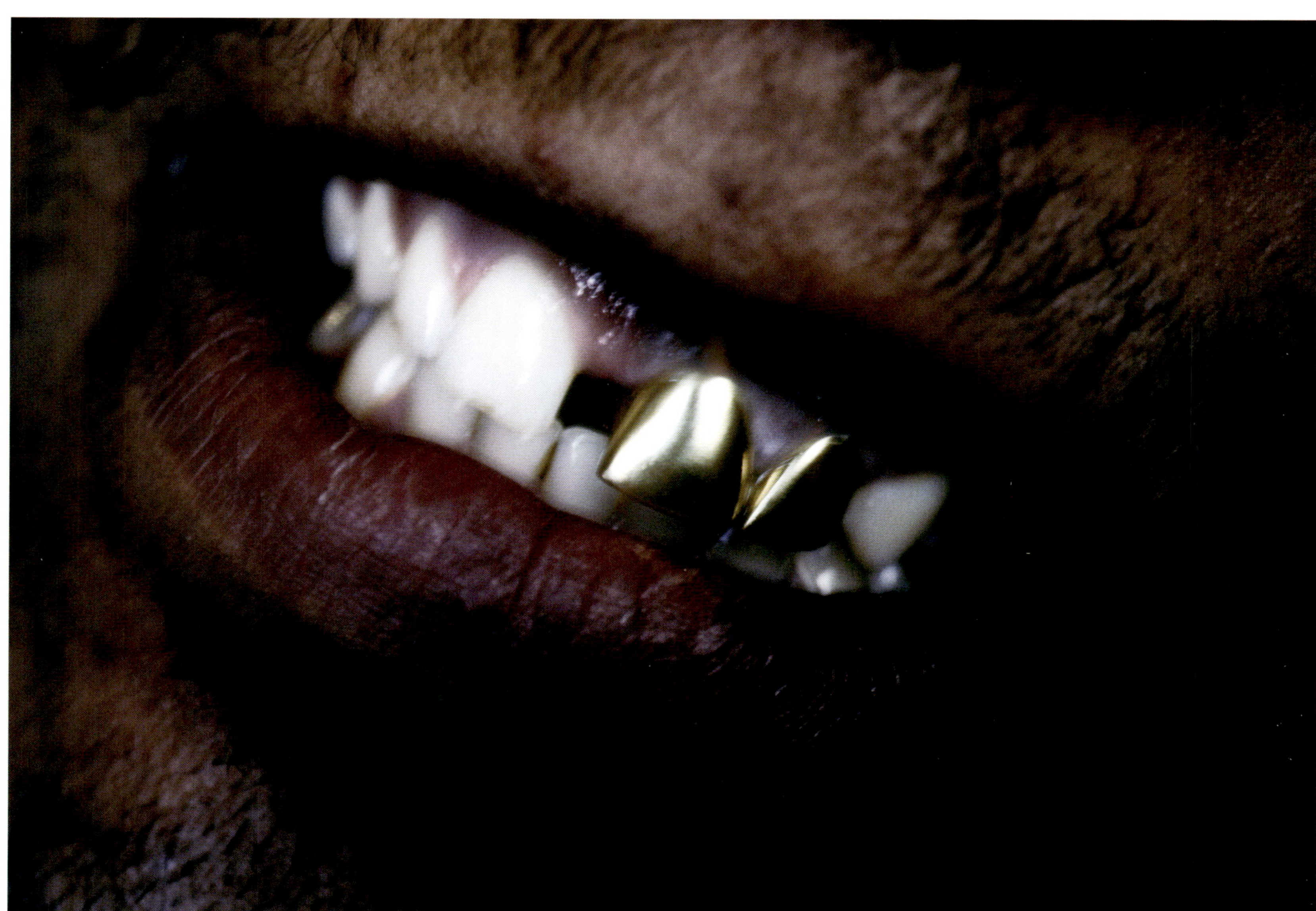

GOLD TEETH [MIKE TYSON ON PLANE TO JAPAN], 1988 - C-PRINT / VARIOUS

LORI GRINKER

CUS AD MIKE [MIKE TYSON, AGE 14, TRAINING AT CUS D'AMATO'S GYM, NYC], 1981 - C-PRINT / VARIOUS

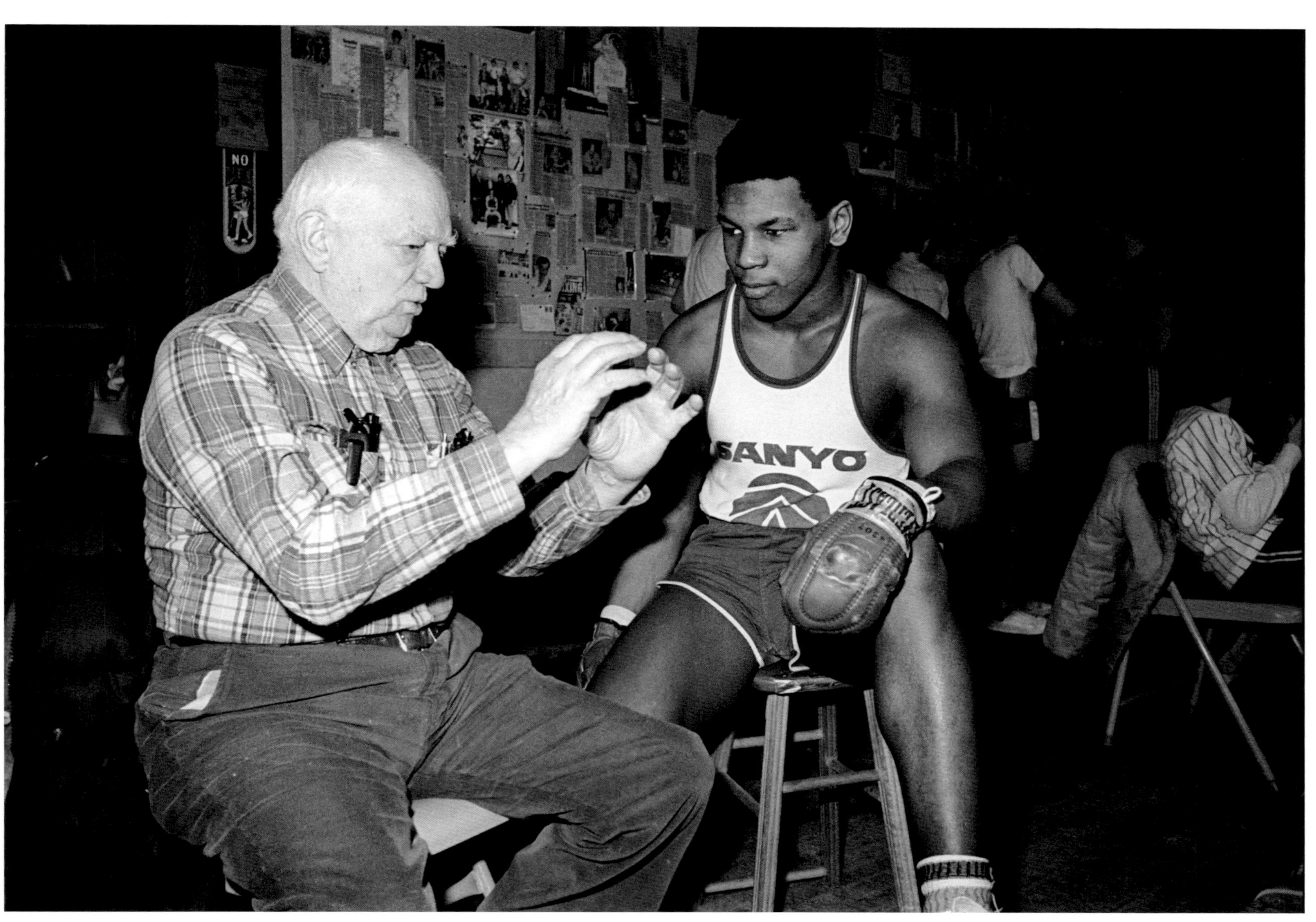

DAVID HAMMONS

CHAMP. 1989 - RUBBER INNER TUBE AND BOXING GLOVES / 66 X 19 X 27 INCHES
COLLECTION MUSEUM OF CONTEMPORARY ART SAN DIEGO MUSEUM PURCHASE WITH FUNDS FROM THE AWARDS IN THE VISUAL ARTS PROGRAM
PABLO MASON © DAVID HAMMONS 2013

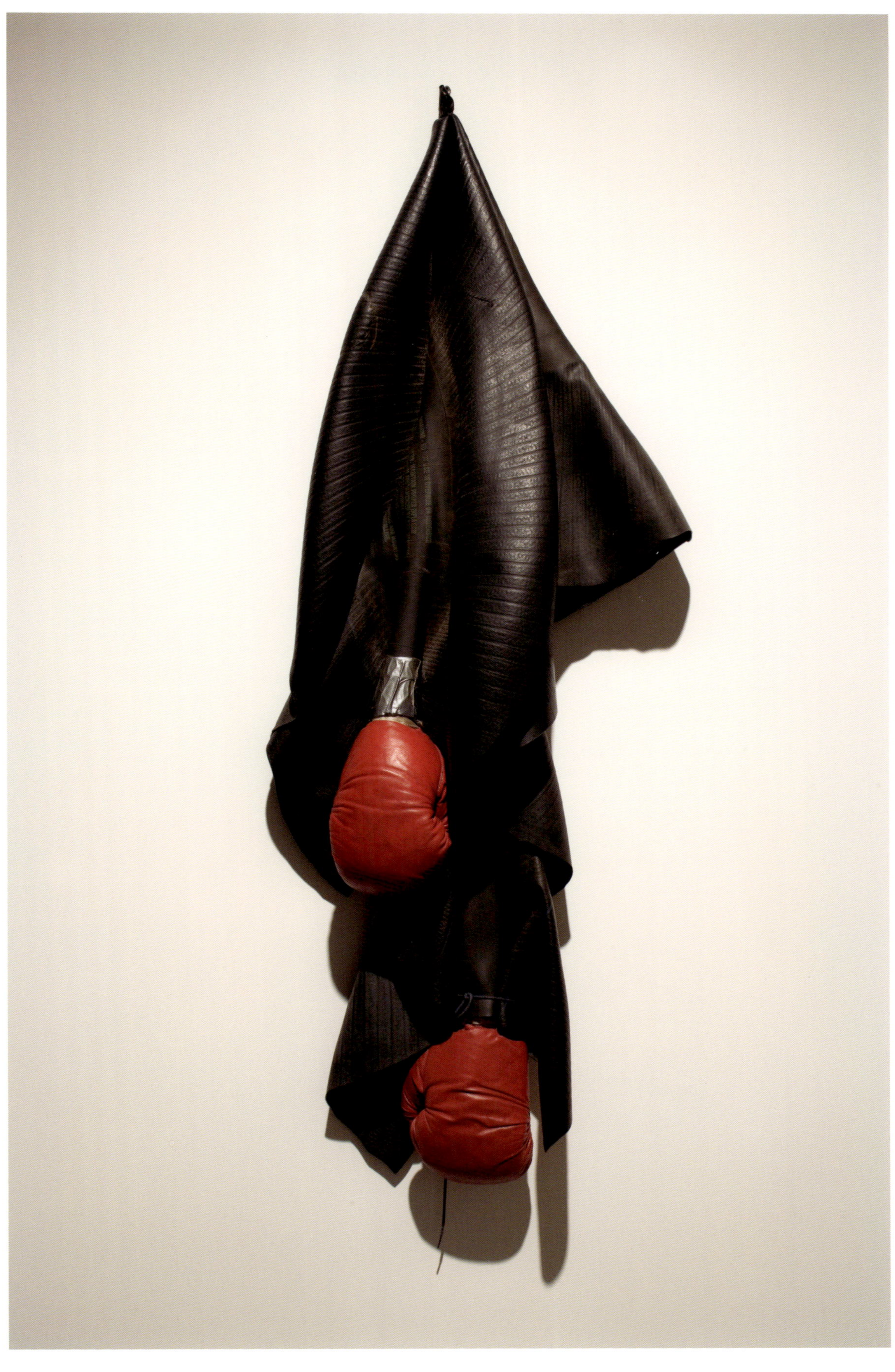

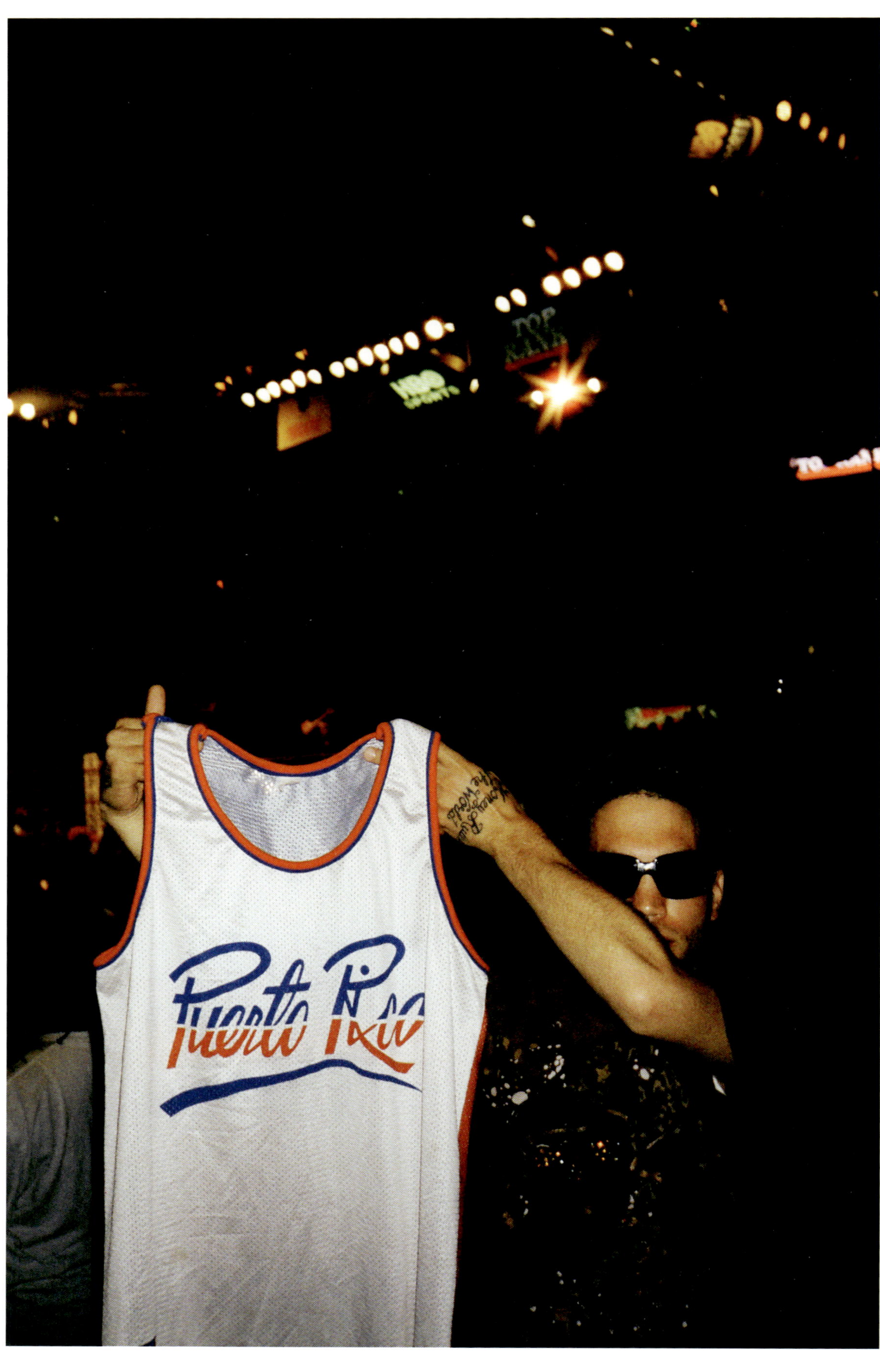
Puerto Ric

ROBERT BENAVIDES

COTTO, 2009 - 35MM COLOR TRANSPARENCY / 11 X 14 INCHES

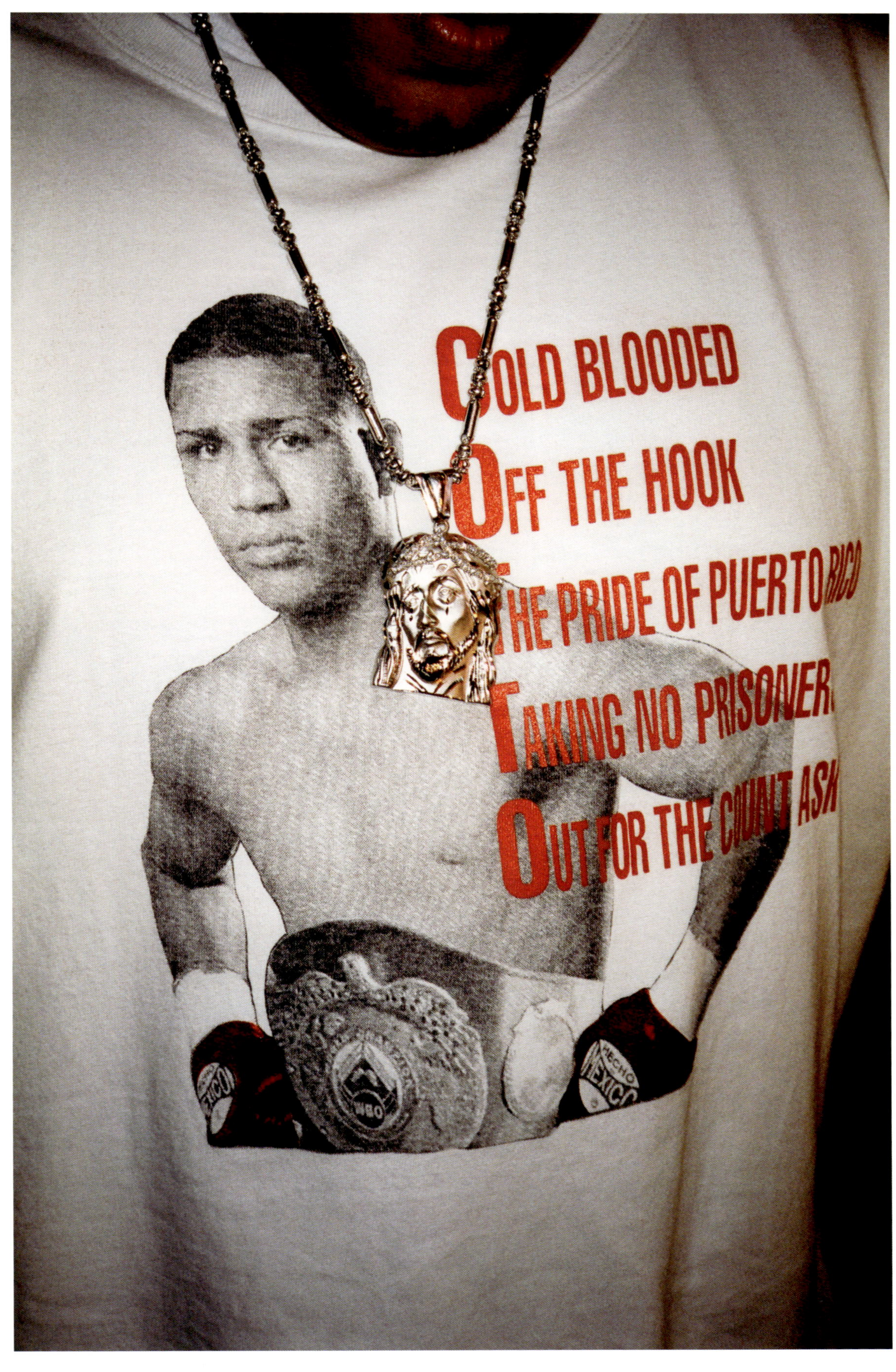

NICK CAVE
IN COLLABORATION WITH BOB FAUST

SECOND SKIN, 2013 - MIXED MEDIA / DIMENSIONS VARIABLE
DENVER ART MUSEUM

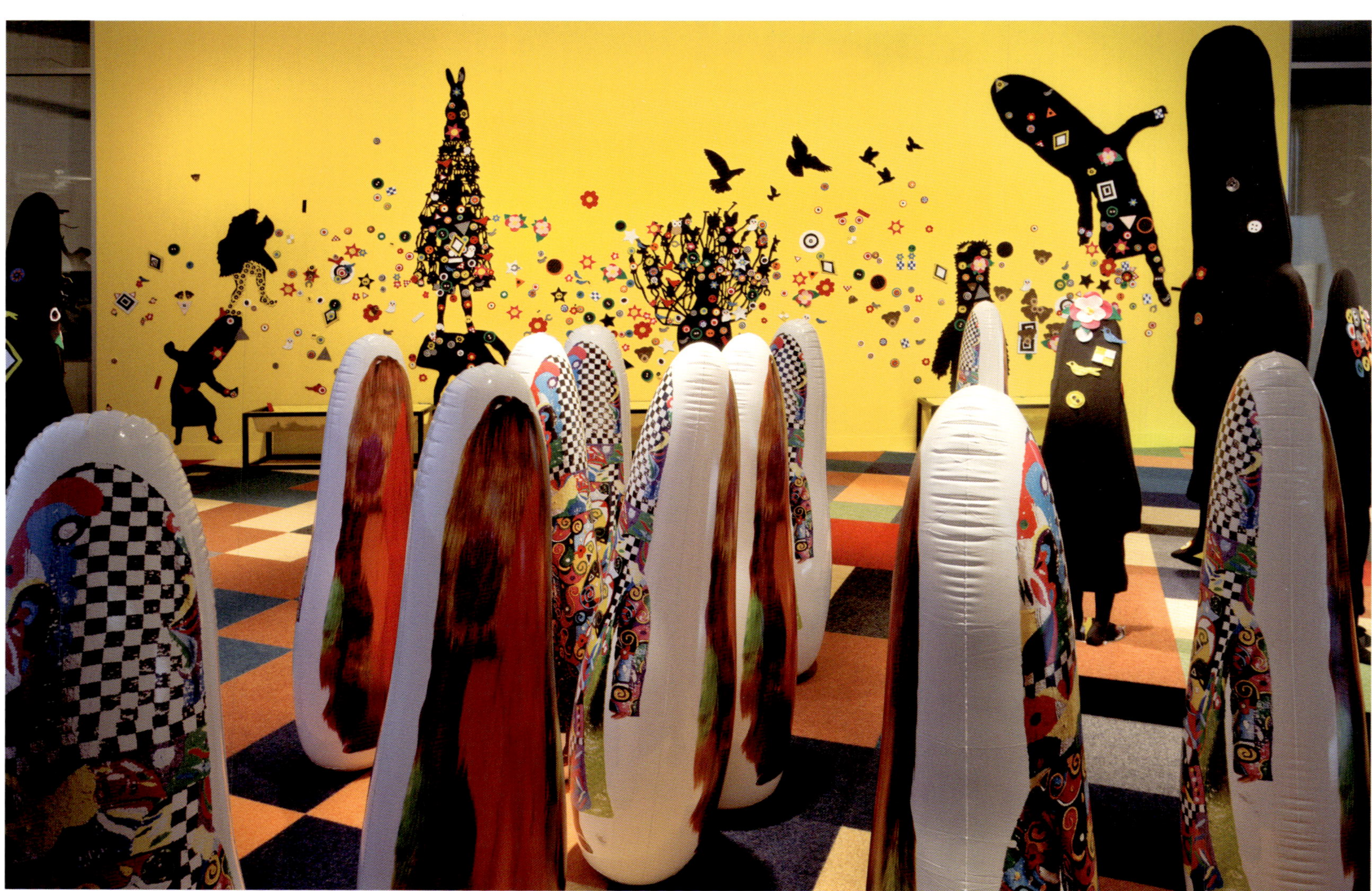

NICK CAVE
IN COLLABORATION WITH BOB FAUST

PUNCHING BAG, 2013 - MIXED MEDIA / DIMENSIONS VARIABLE

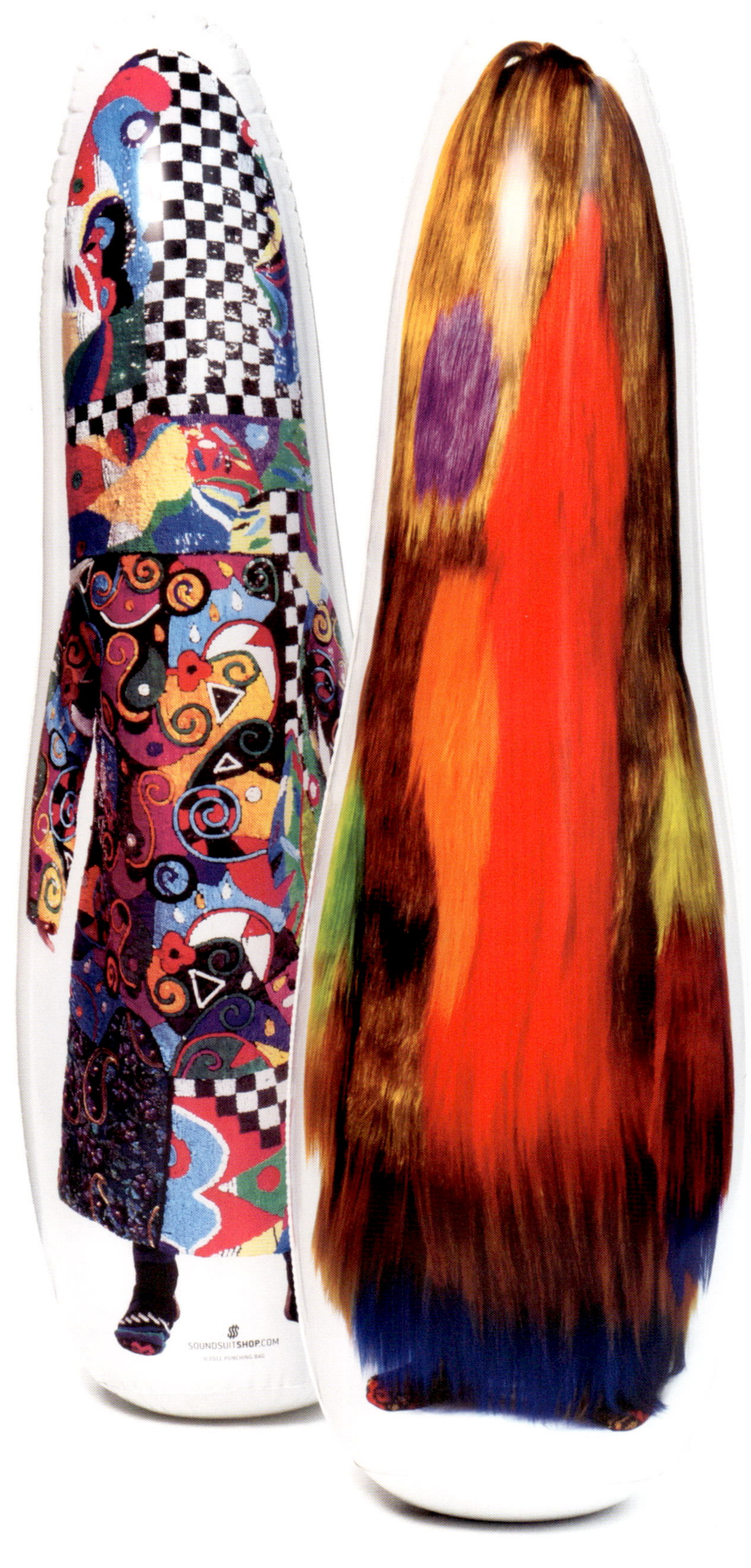

THE ILLUSTRIOUS KITES MADE IN BOXING STYLES, 2004 - GOLDEN FLUID ACRYLIC PAINT, FLAG BUNTING, COTTON/POLYESTER THREAD / 600 X 180 X 96 INCHES
MINT MUSEUM OF ART IN CHARLOTTE, NORTH CAROLINA

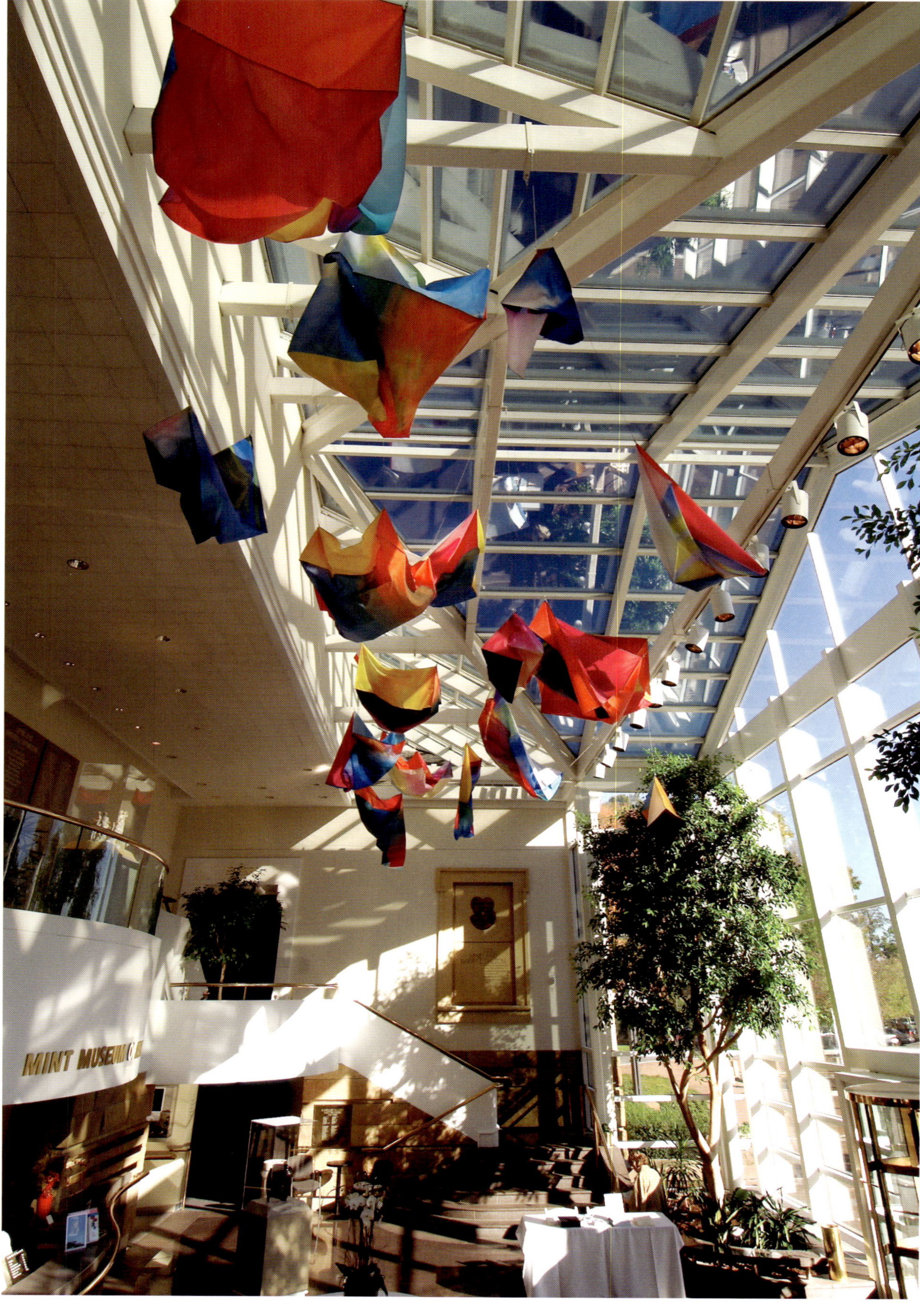

SAM GILLIAM

THE ILLUSTRIOUS KITES MADE IN BOXING STYLES, 2004 - GOLDEN FLUID ACRYLIC PAINT, FLAG BUNTING, COTTON/POLYESTER THREAD / 600 X 180 X 96 INCHES
MINT MUSEUM OF ART IN CHARLOTTE, NORTH CAROLINA

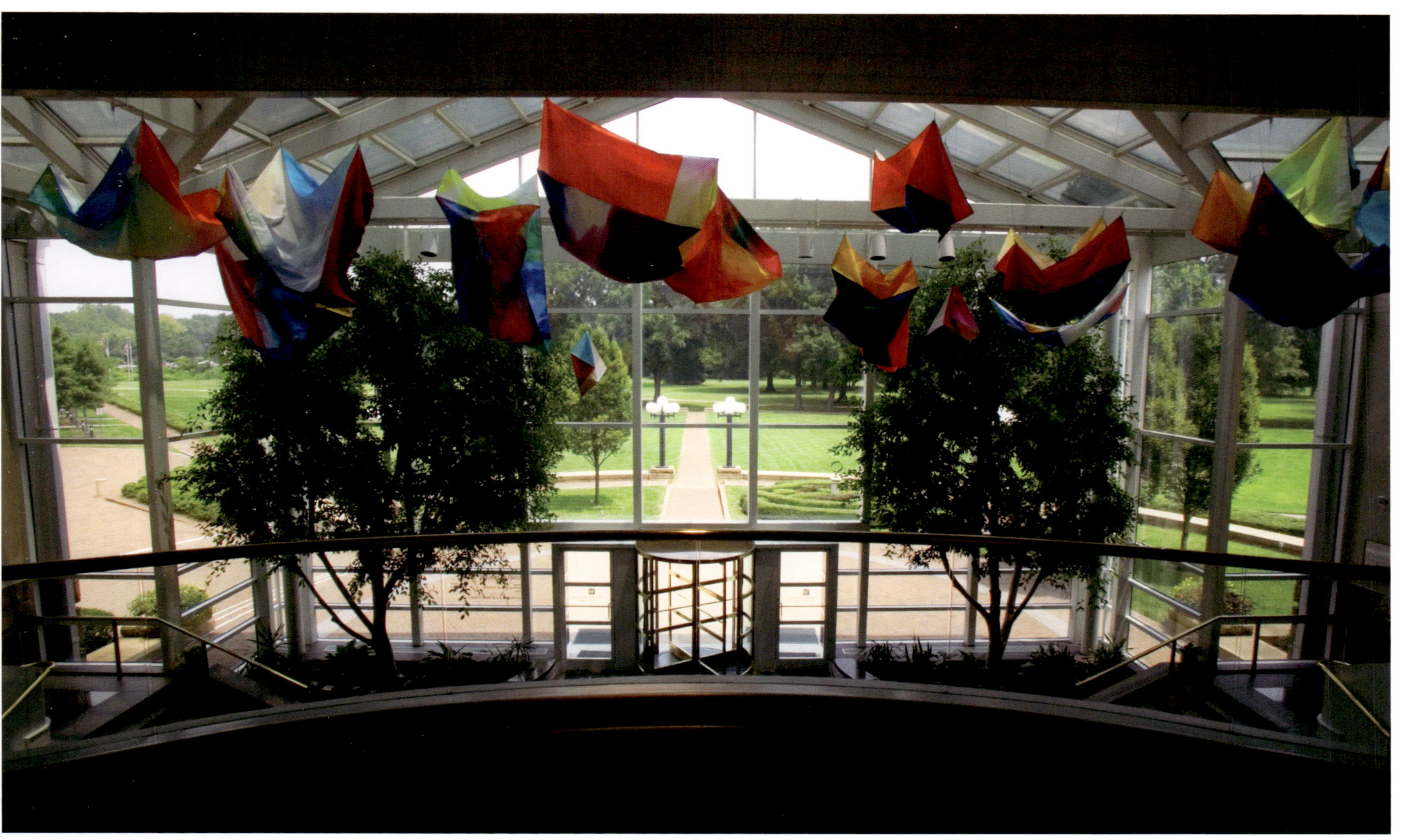

JULES DE BALINCOURT

BOXING YOUR SUBCONSCIOUS, 2005 - OIL AND ENAMEL ON PANEL / 61 X 122 CM
COURTESY OF SALON 94 AND THE ARTIST, NEW YORK, NY

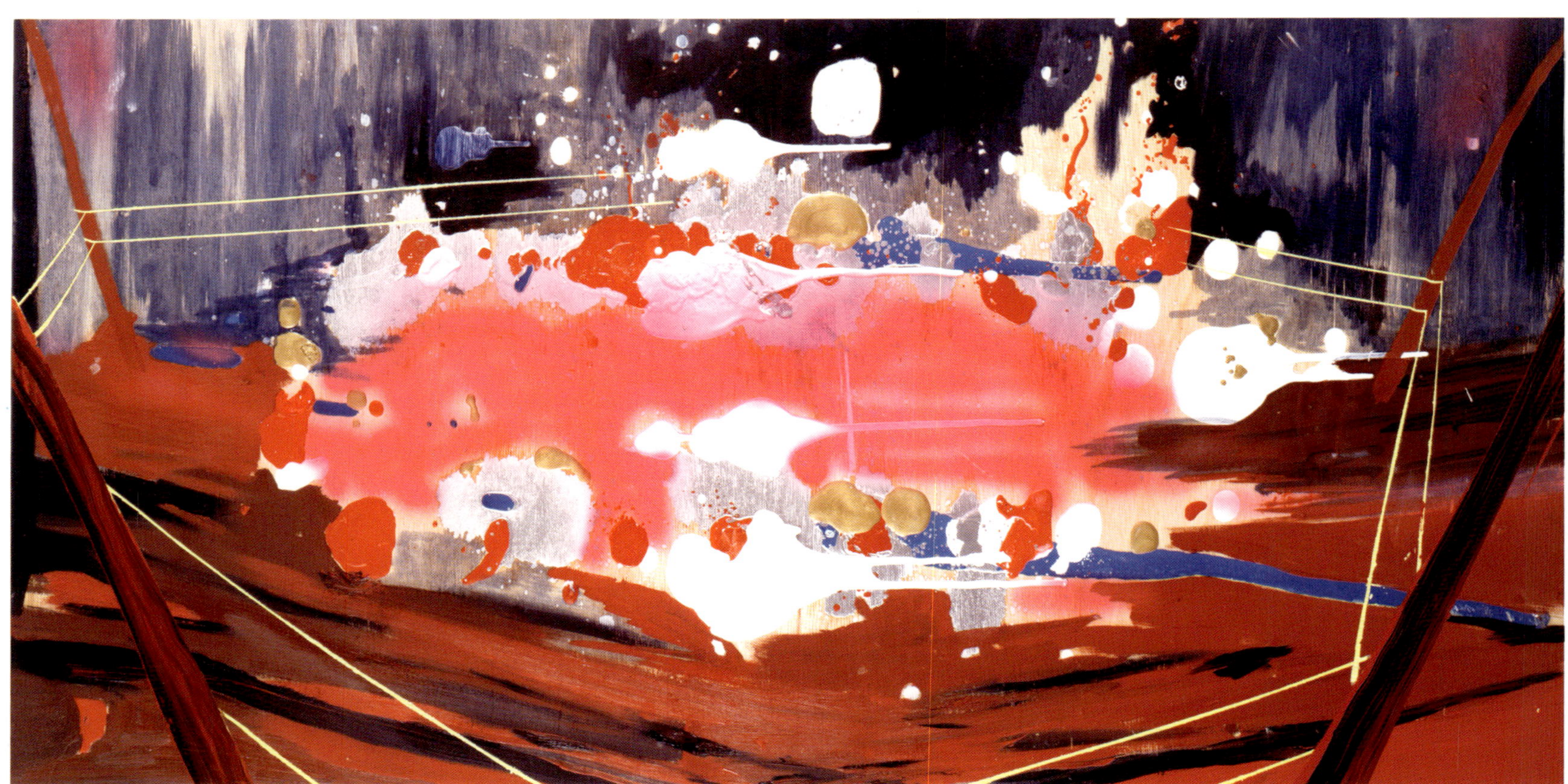

RASHID JOHNSON

SELF PORTRAIT LAYING ON JACK JOHNSON'S GRAVE, 2006 - LAMBDA PRINT / 40.5 X 49.5 INCHES
COURTESY OF THE ARTIST AND HAUSER & WIRTH

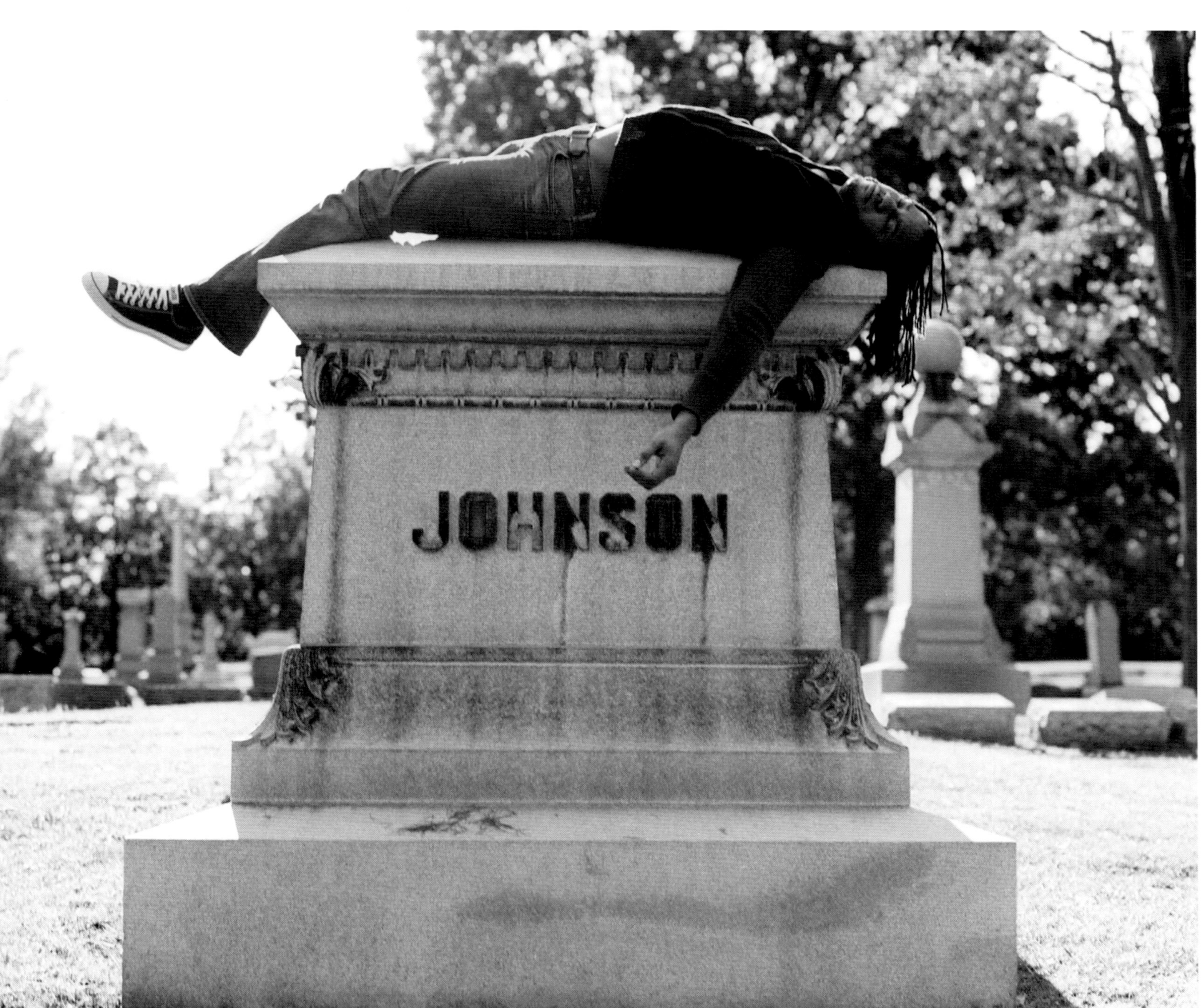

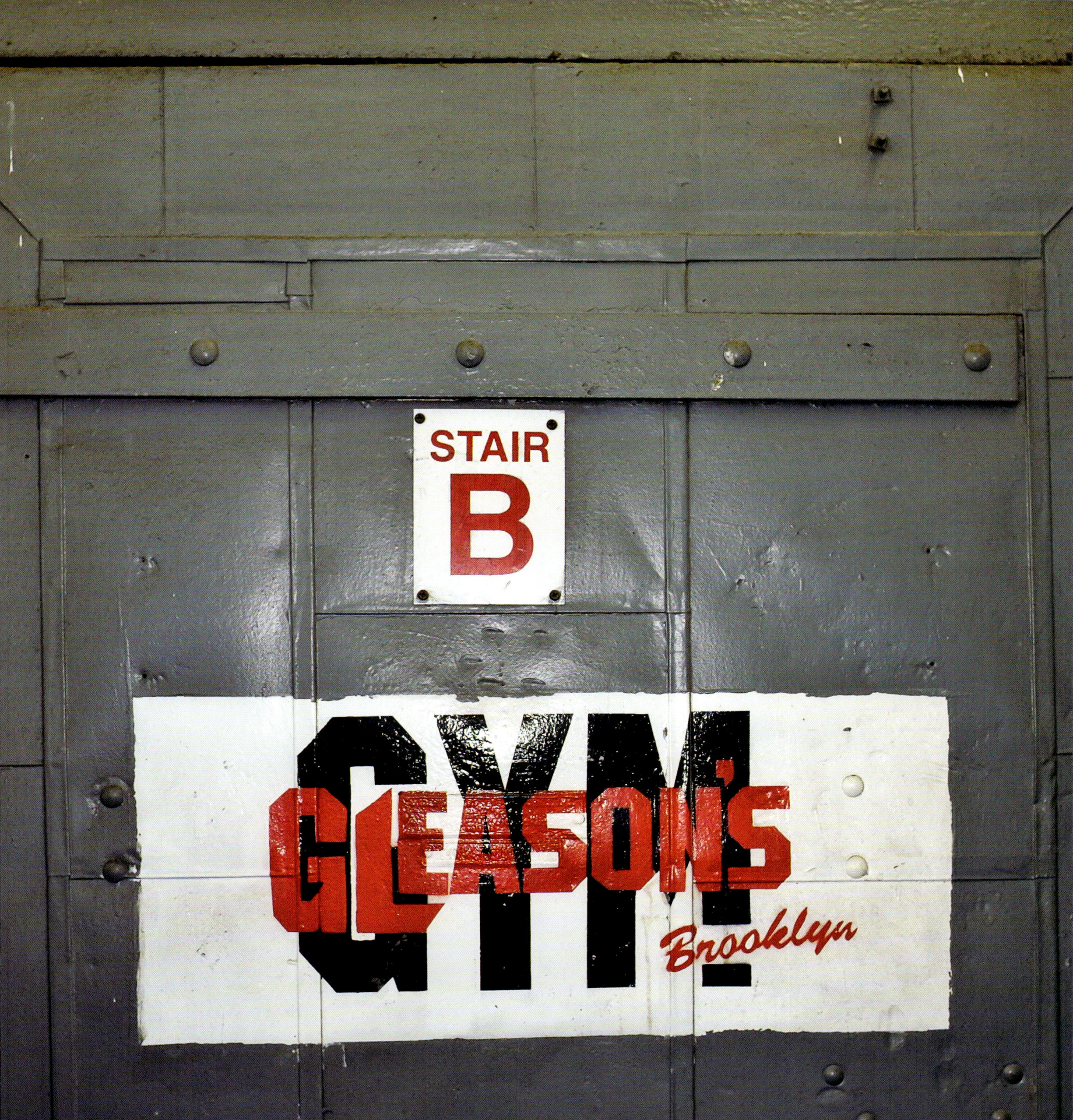

STAIR
B
GYM
GLEASON'S
Brooklyn

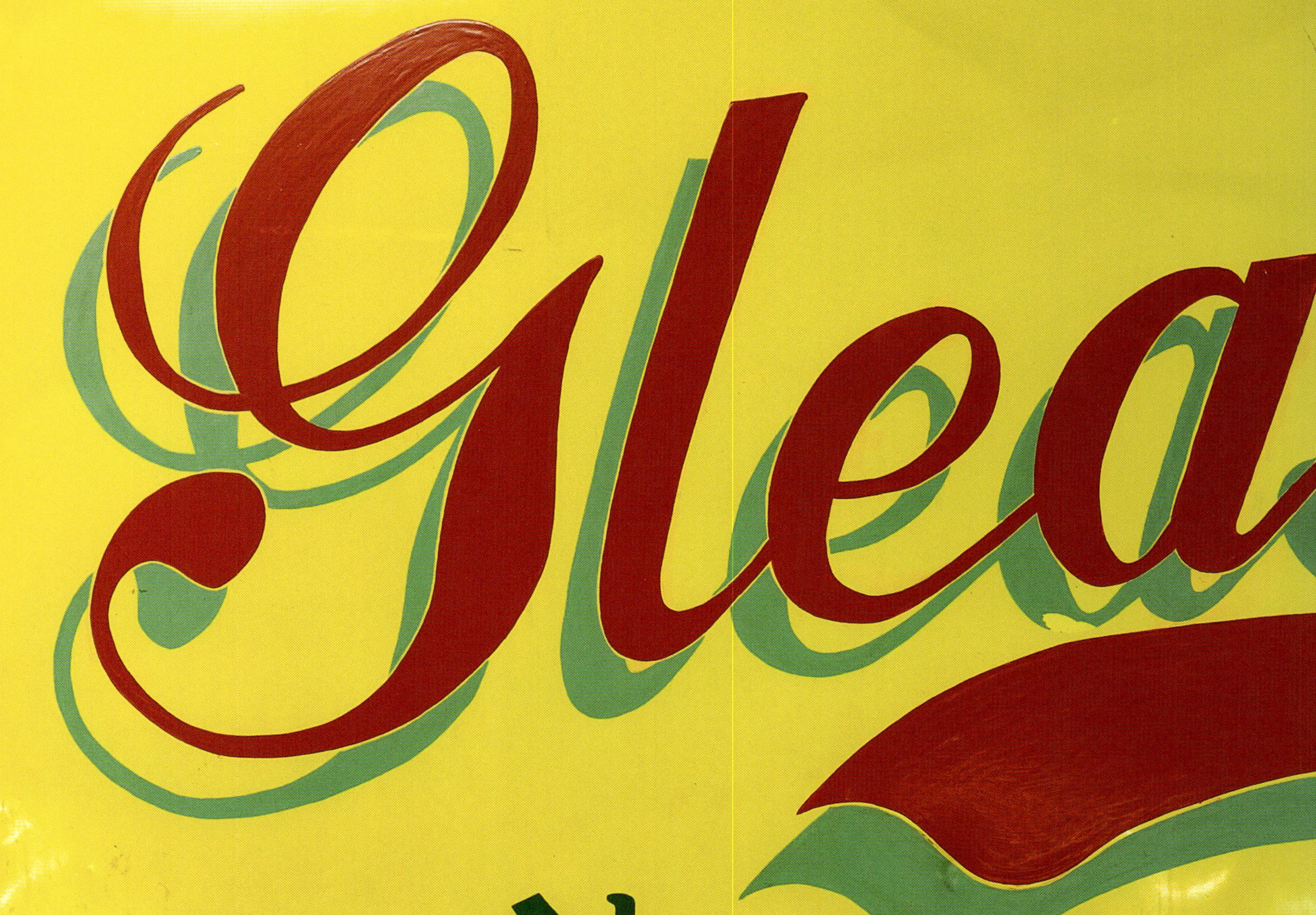
Glea
Now, whoeu
a strong and collect
let him come forwa
and put up his ha

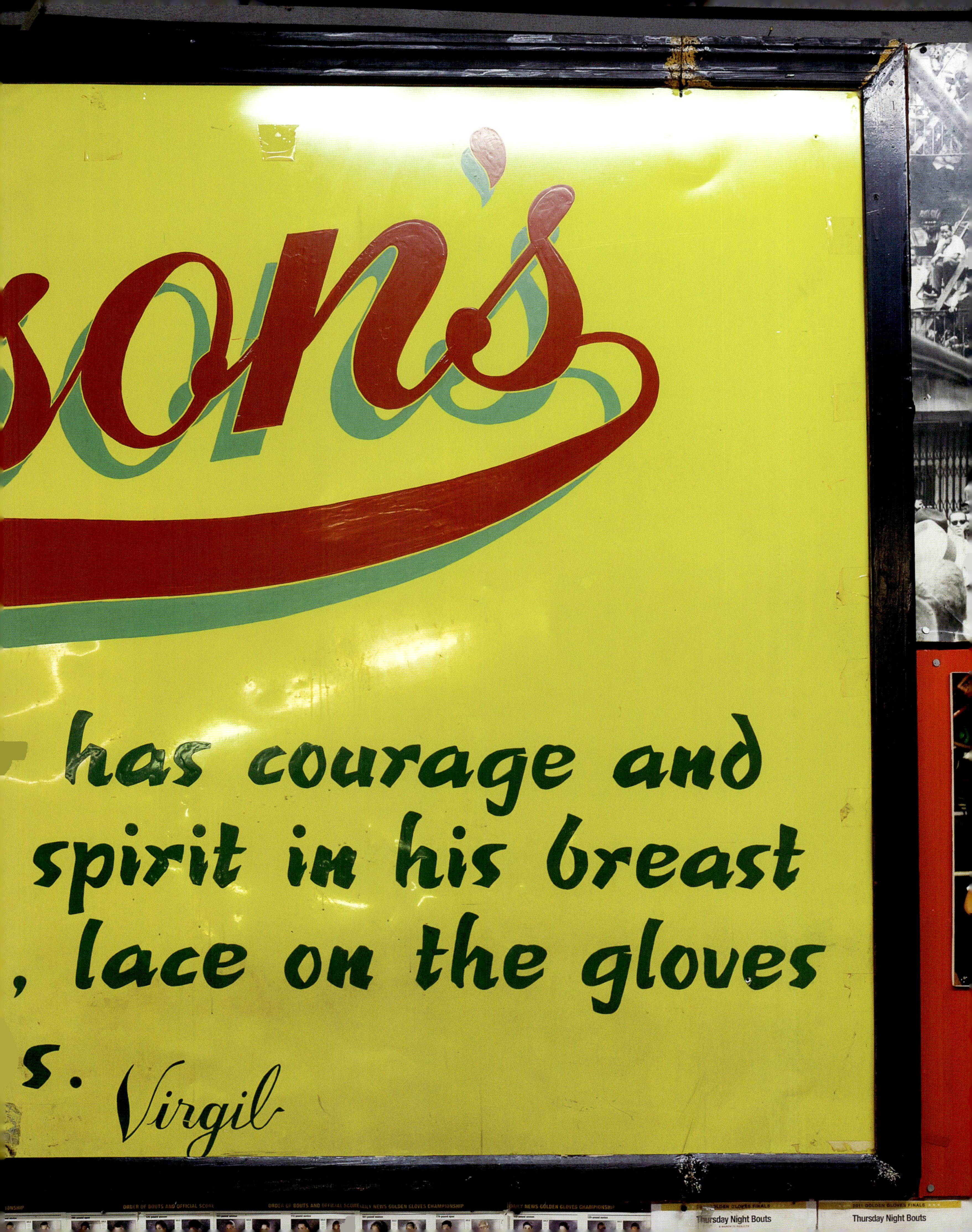

son's

has courage and
spirit in his breast
, lace on the gloves
s.   *Virgil*

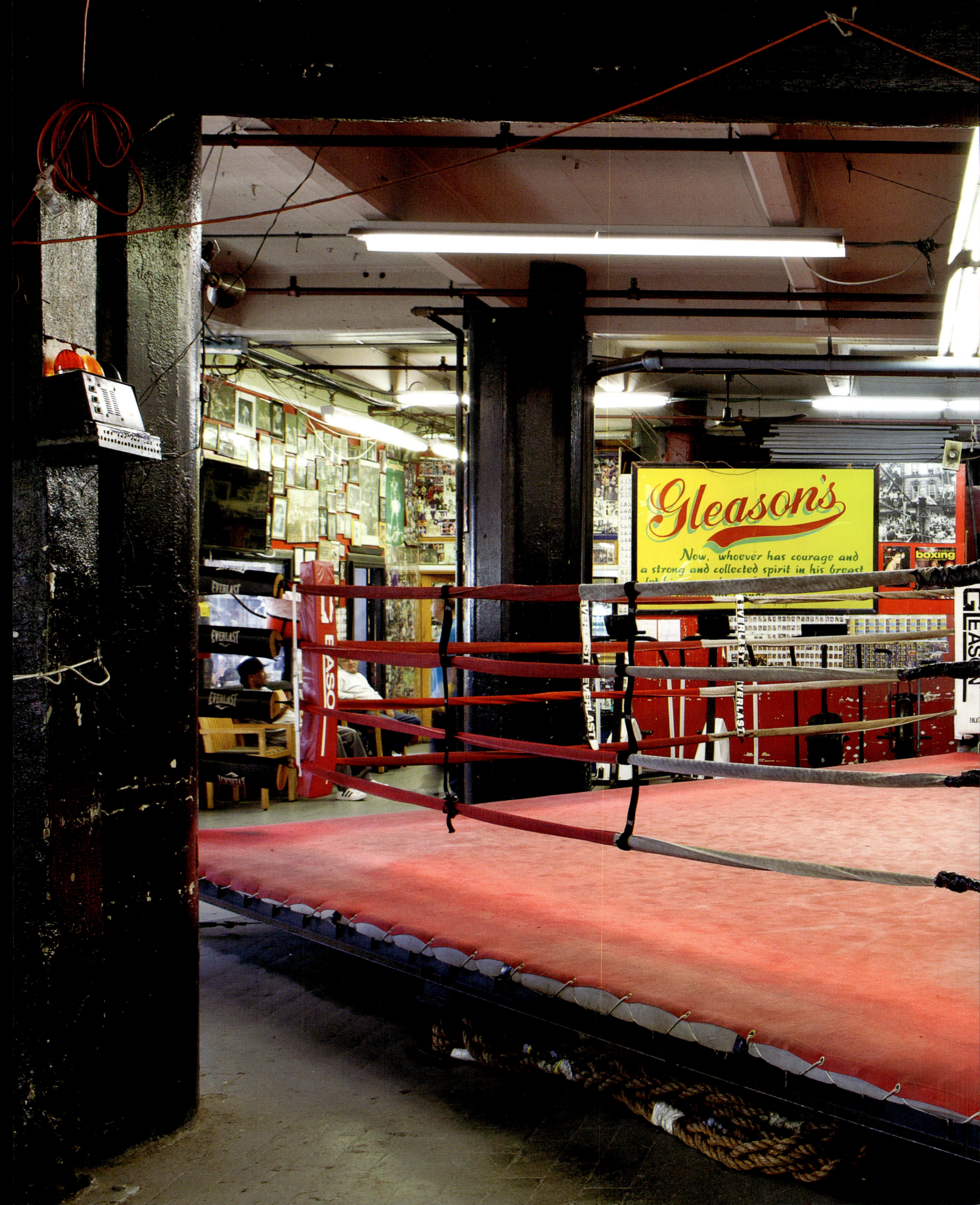
Gleason's
Now, whoever has courage and
a strong and collected spirit in his breast

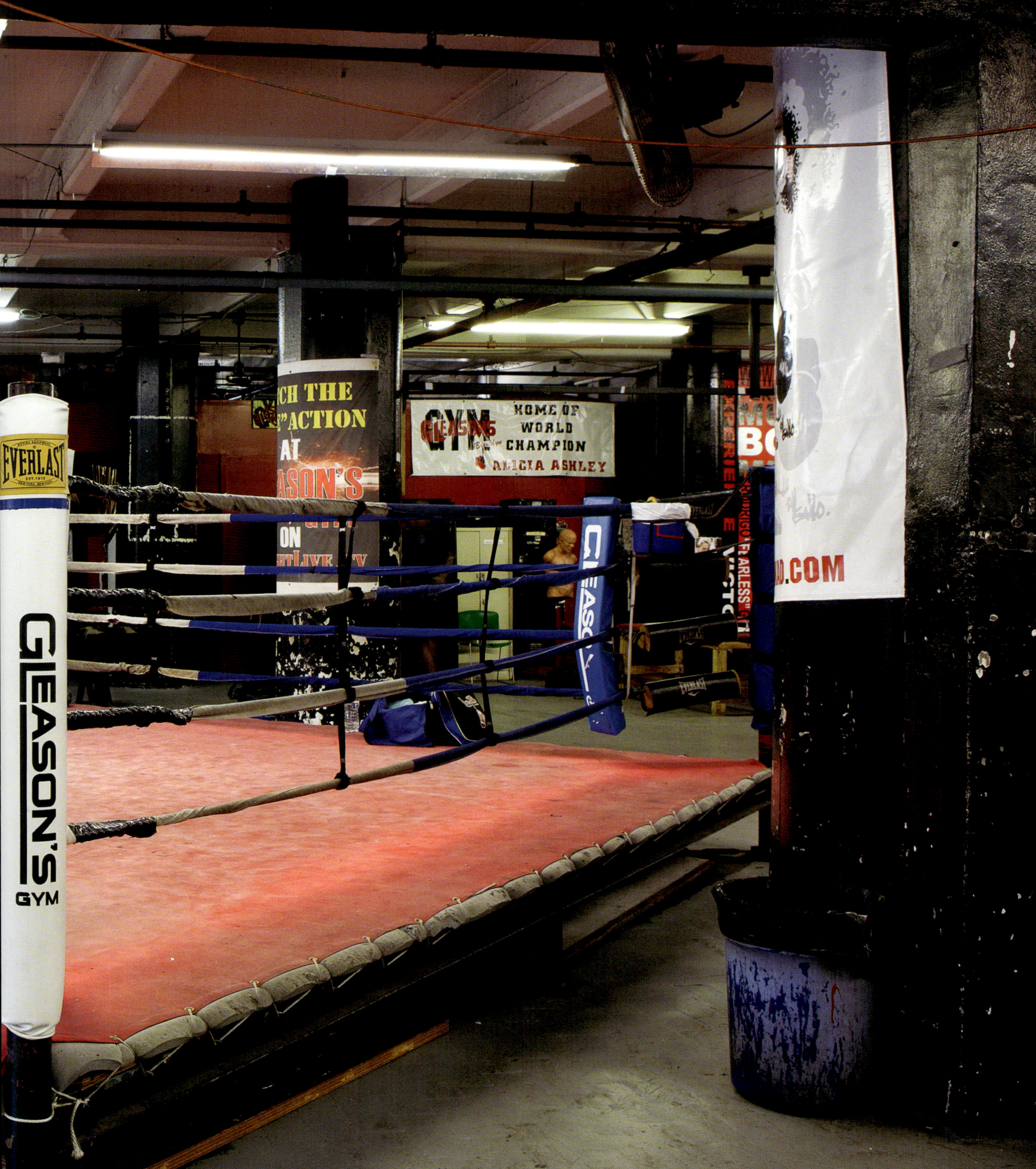
EVERLAST
GLEASON'S
GYM
ICH THE
"ACTION
AT
EASON'S
ON
HOME OF
WORLD
CHAMPION
ALICIA ASHLEY
GLEASON'S
GYM
.COM

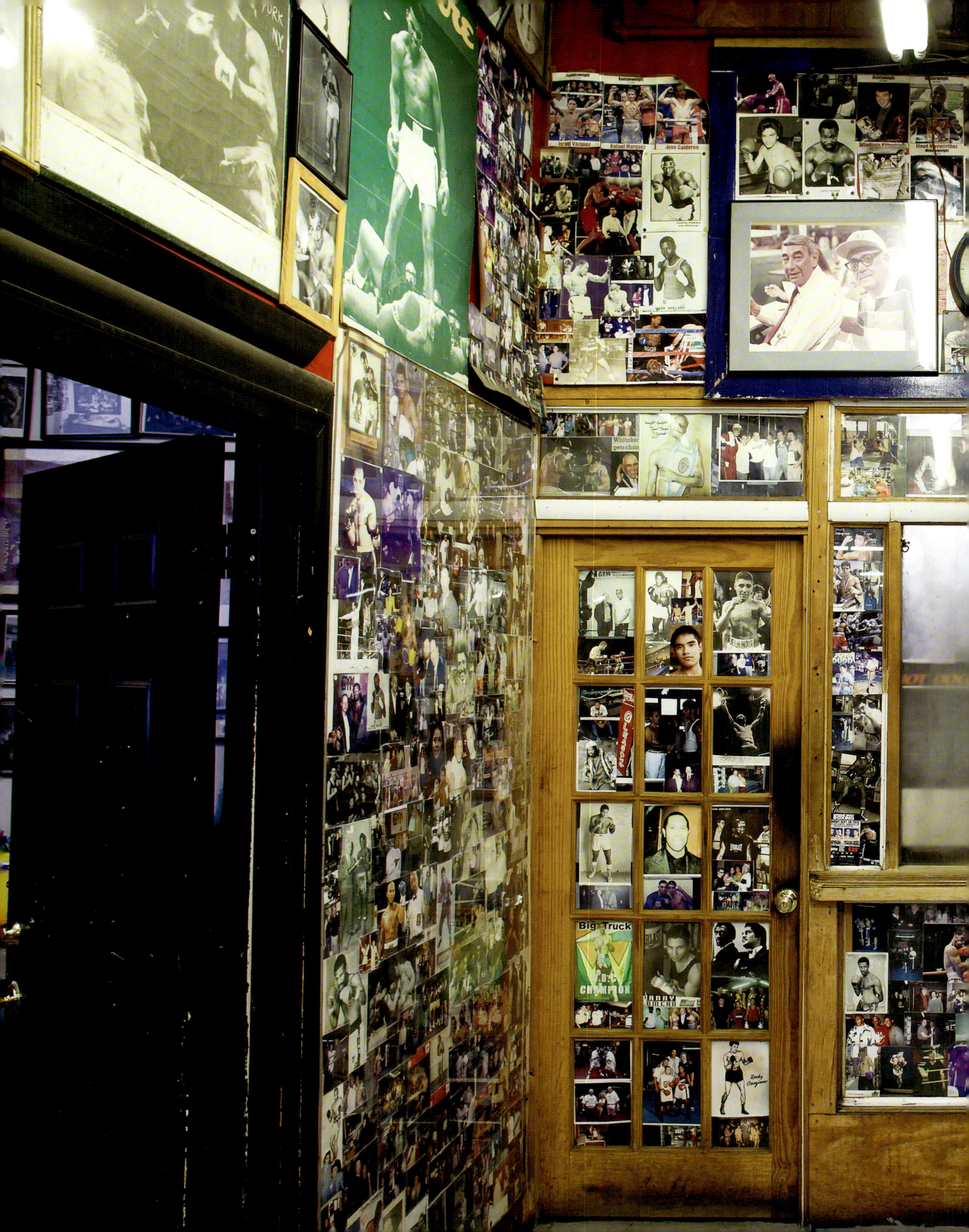

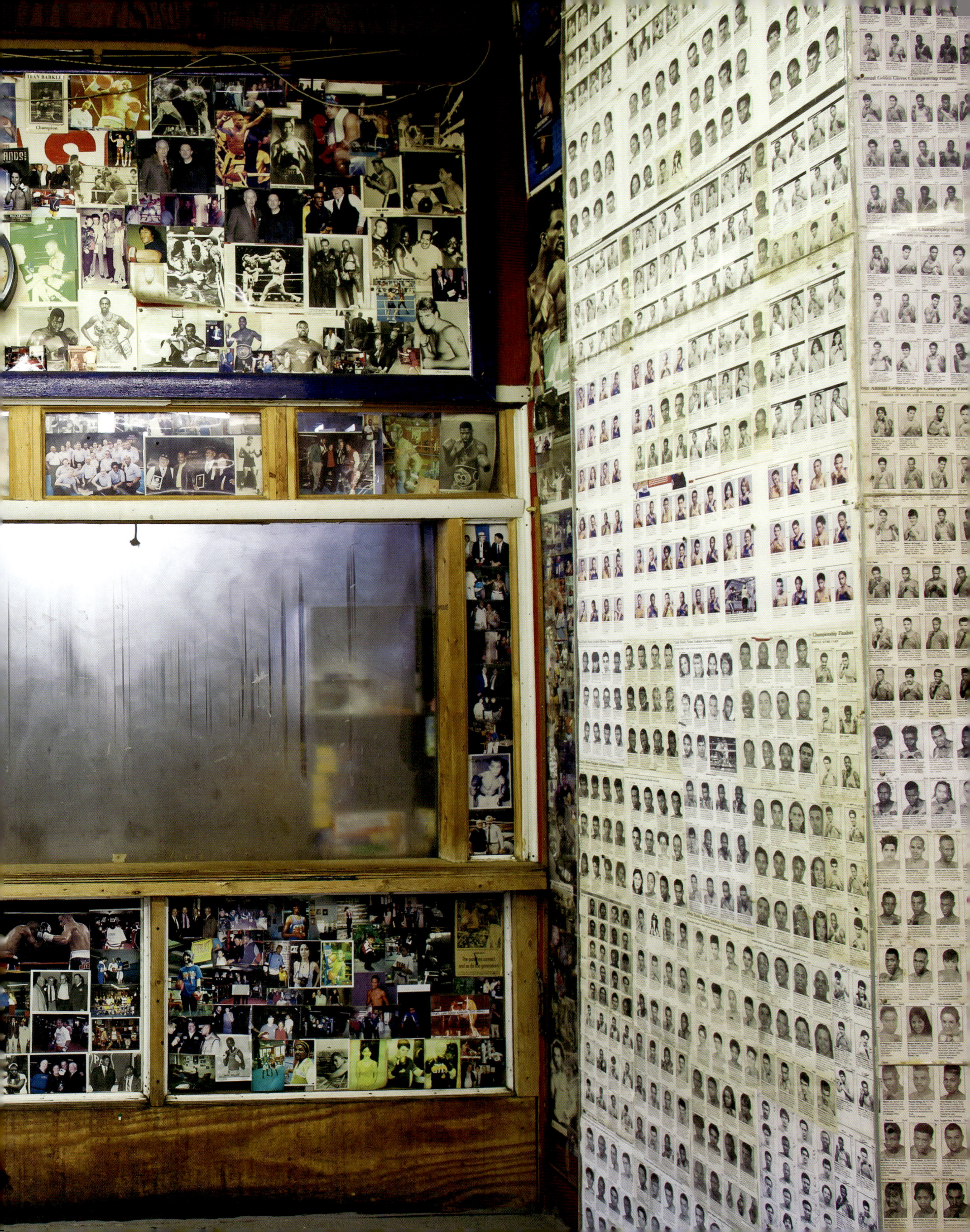

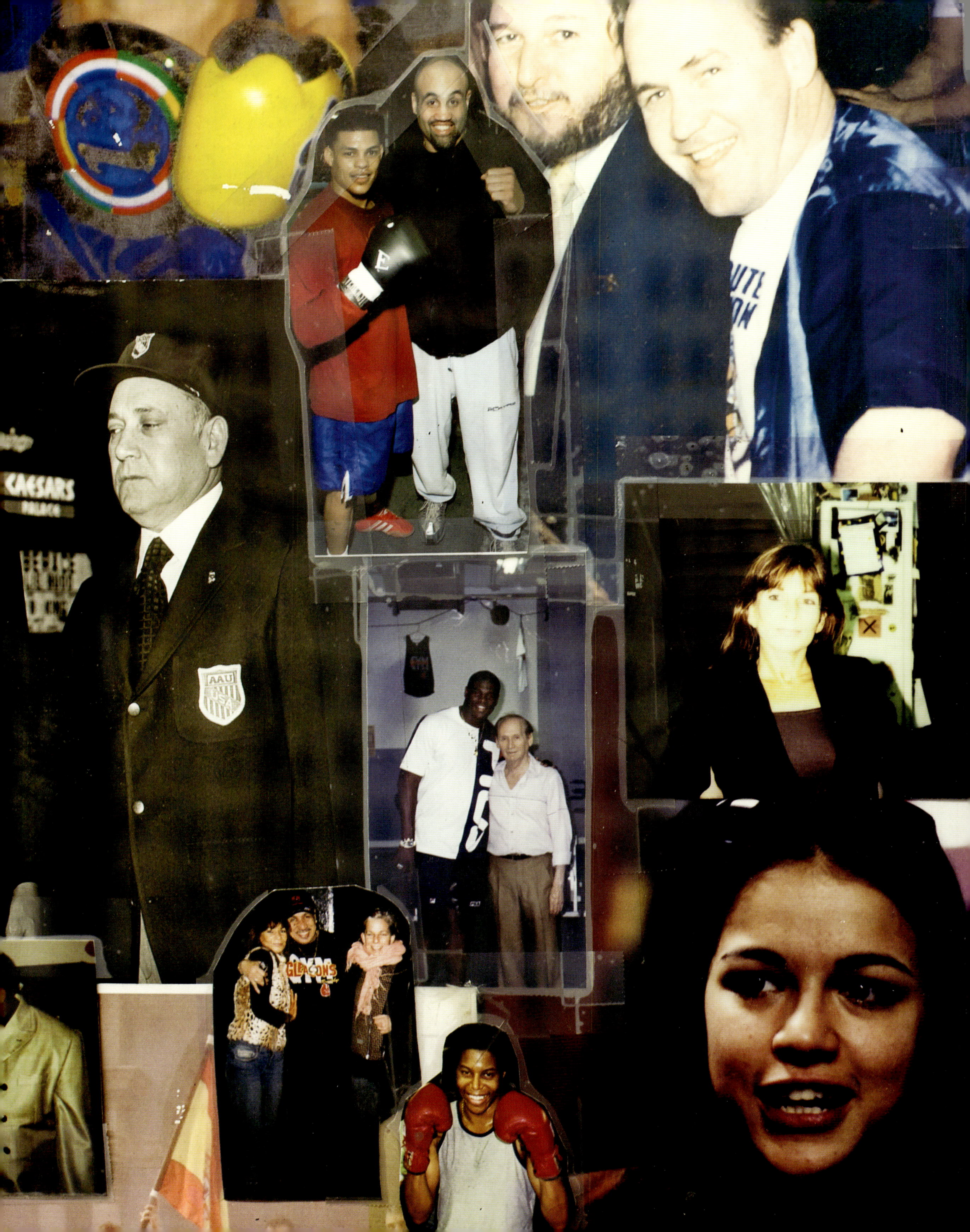

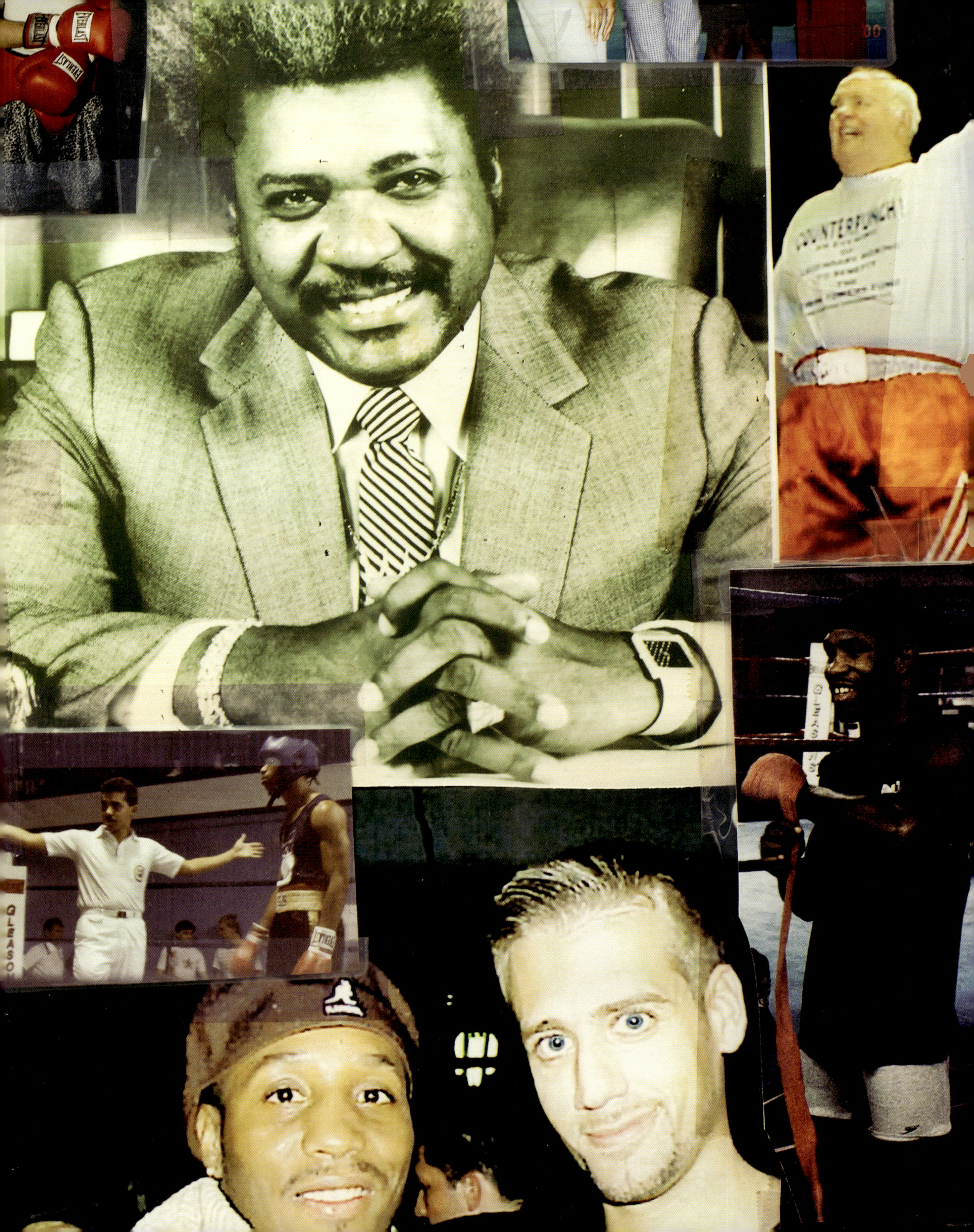

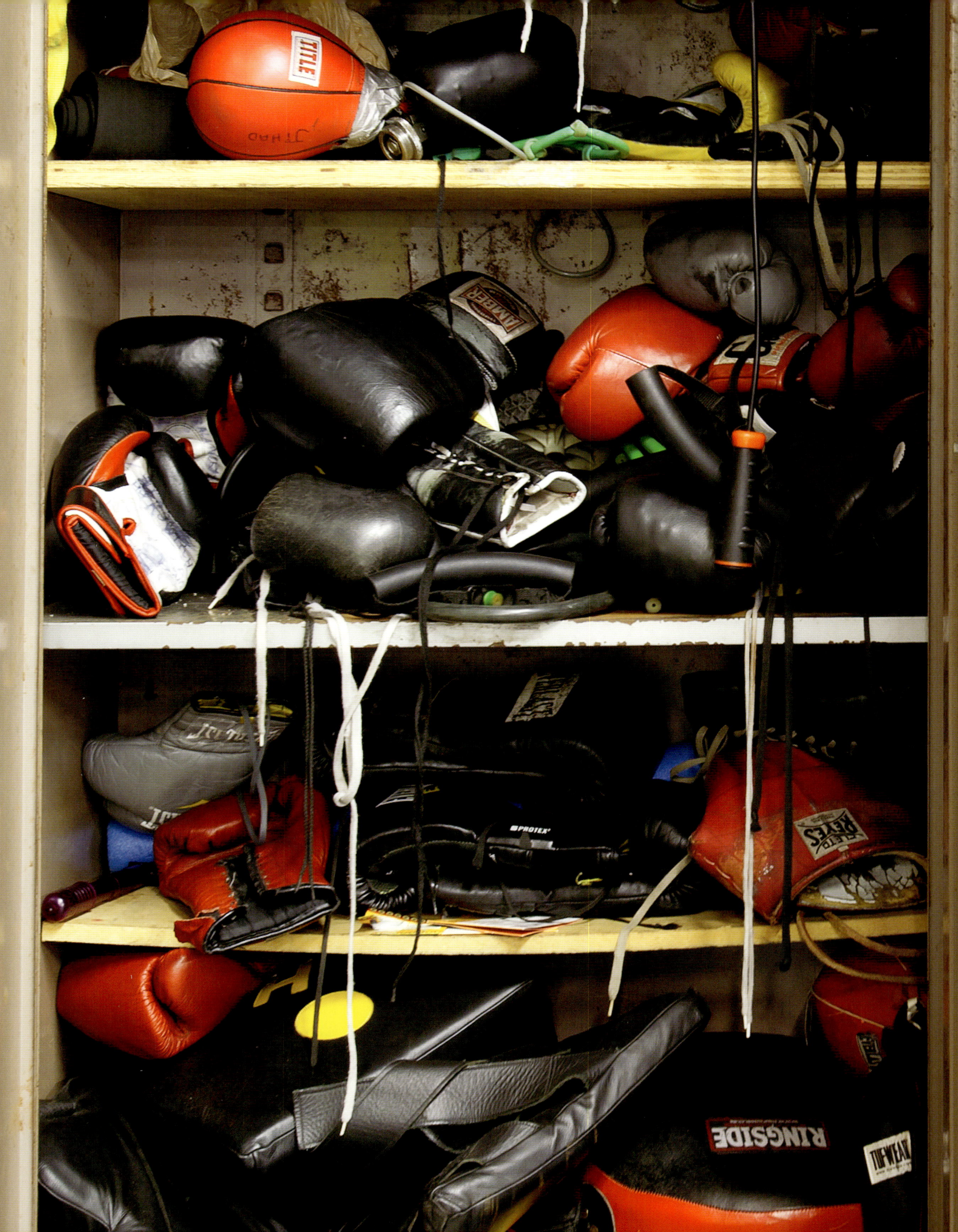

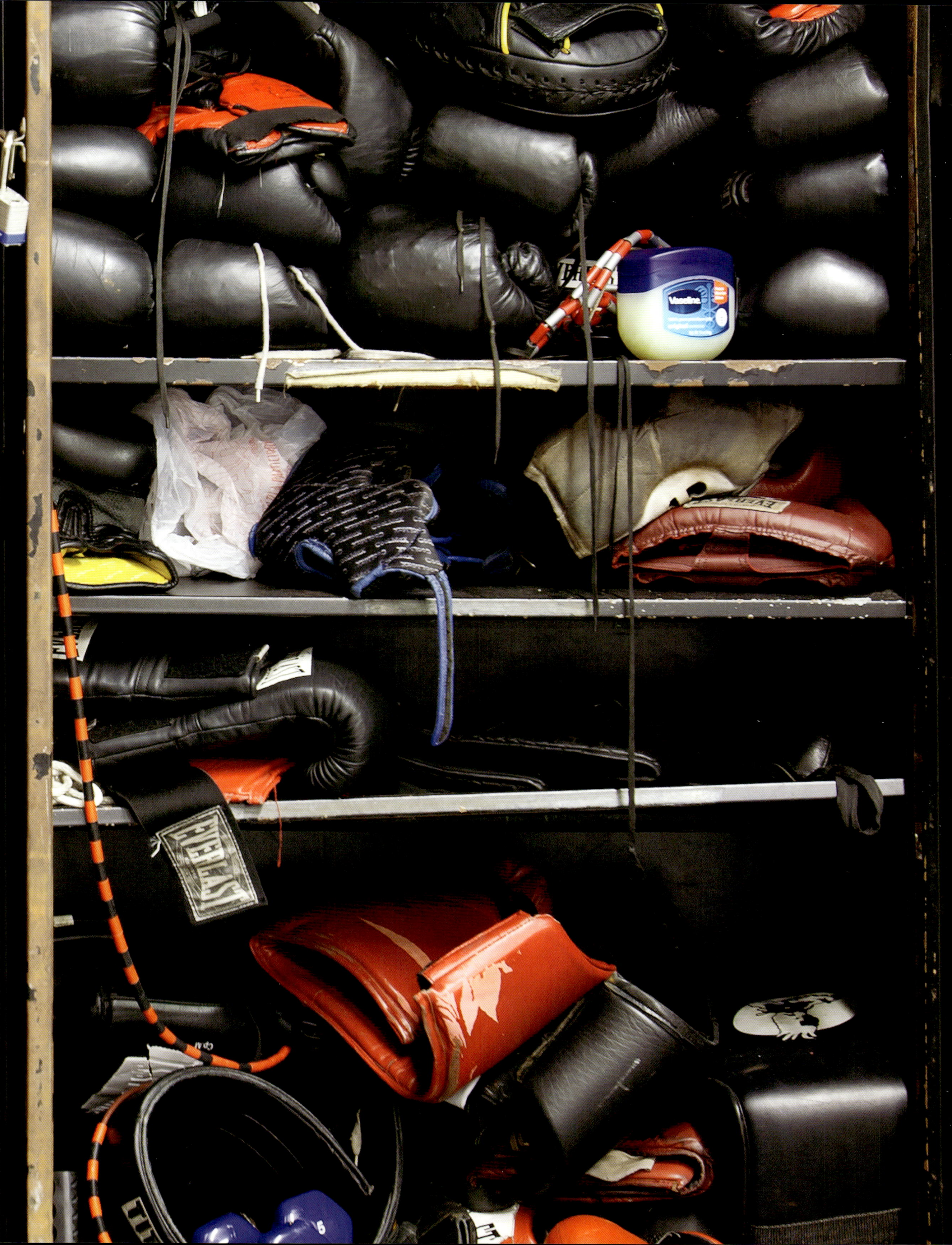

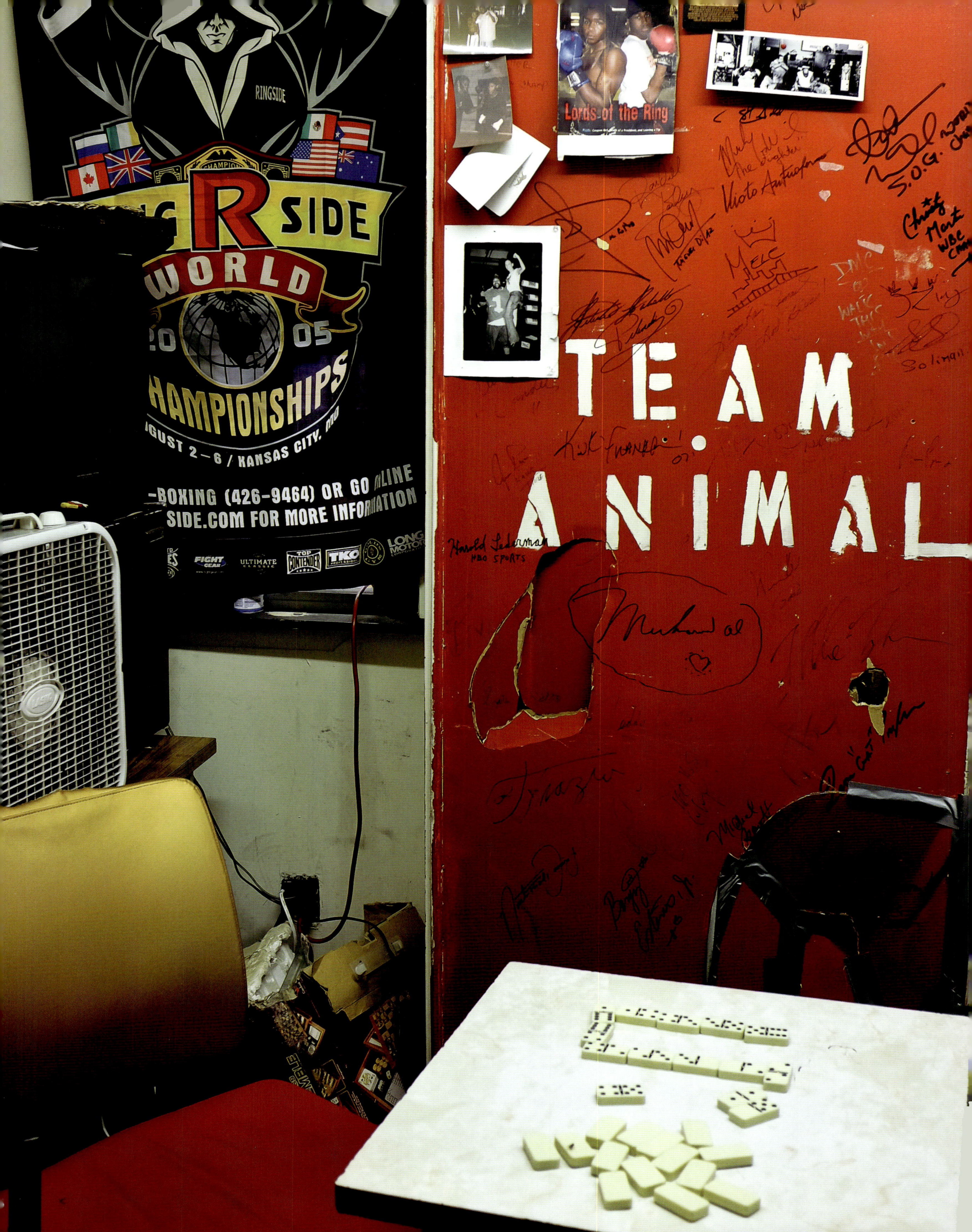
RINGSIDE
RING SIDE
WORLD
20 05
CHAMPIONSHIPS
AUGUST 2 - 6 / KANSAS CITY, MO
BOXING (426-9464) OR GO ONLINE
SIDE.COM FOR MORE INFORMATION
FIGHT GEAR
ULTIMATE
TOP CONTENDER
TKO
LONG MOTORS
Lords of the Ring
TEAM
ANIMAL
Harold Lederman
HBO SPORTS

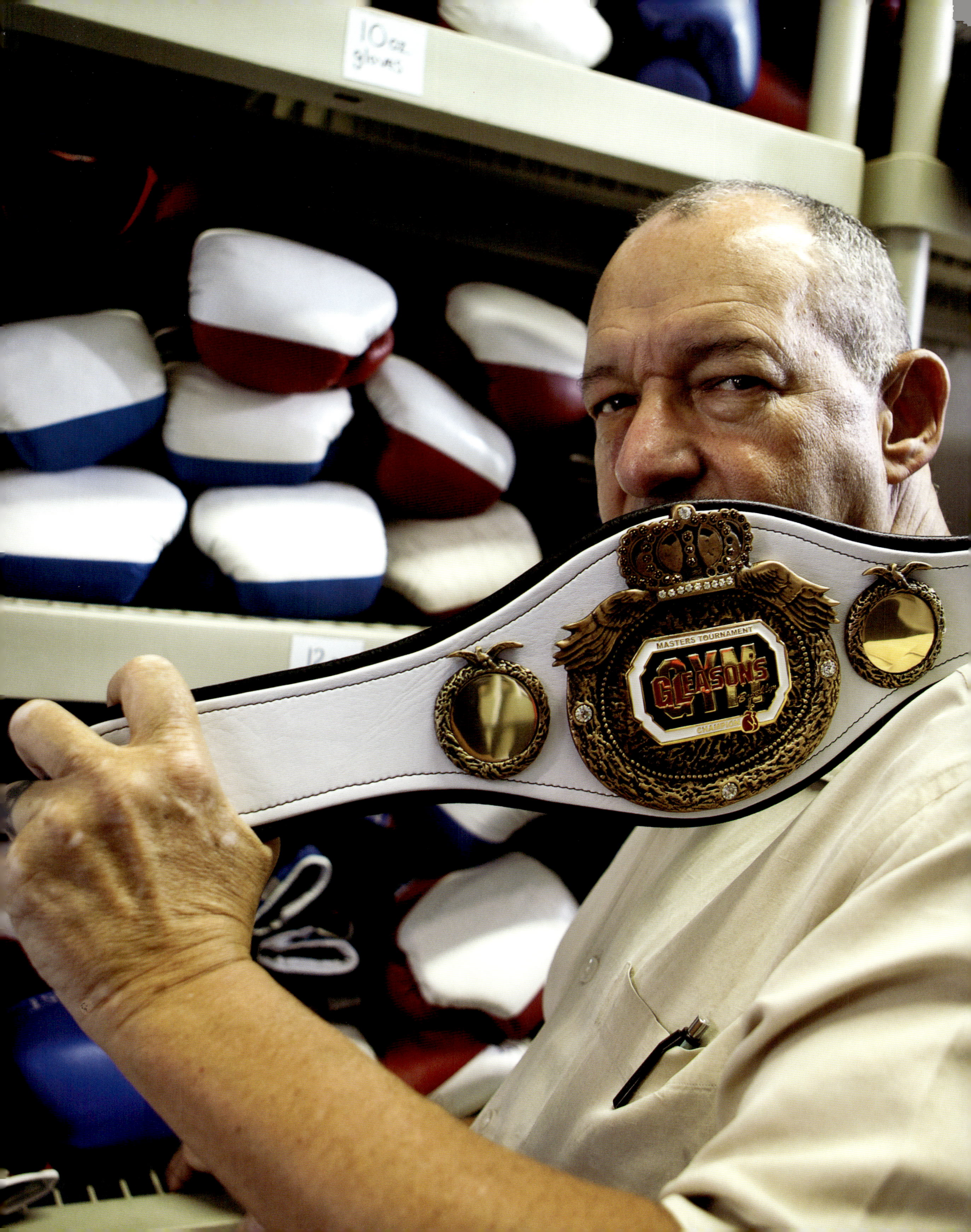

10 oz.
gloves
12
MASTERS TOURNAMENT
GLEASONS
GYM
CHAMPION

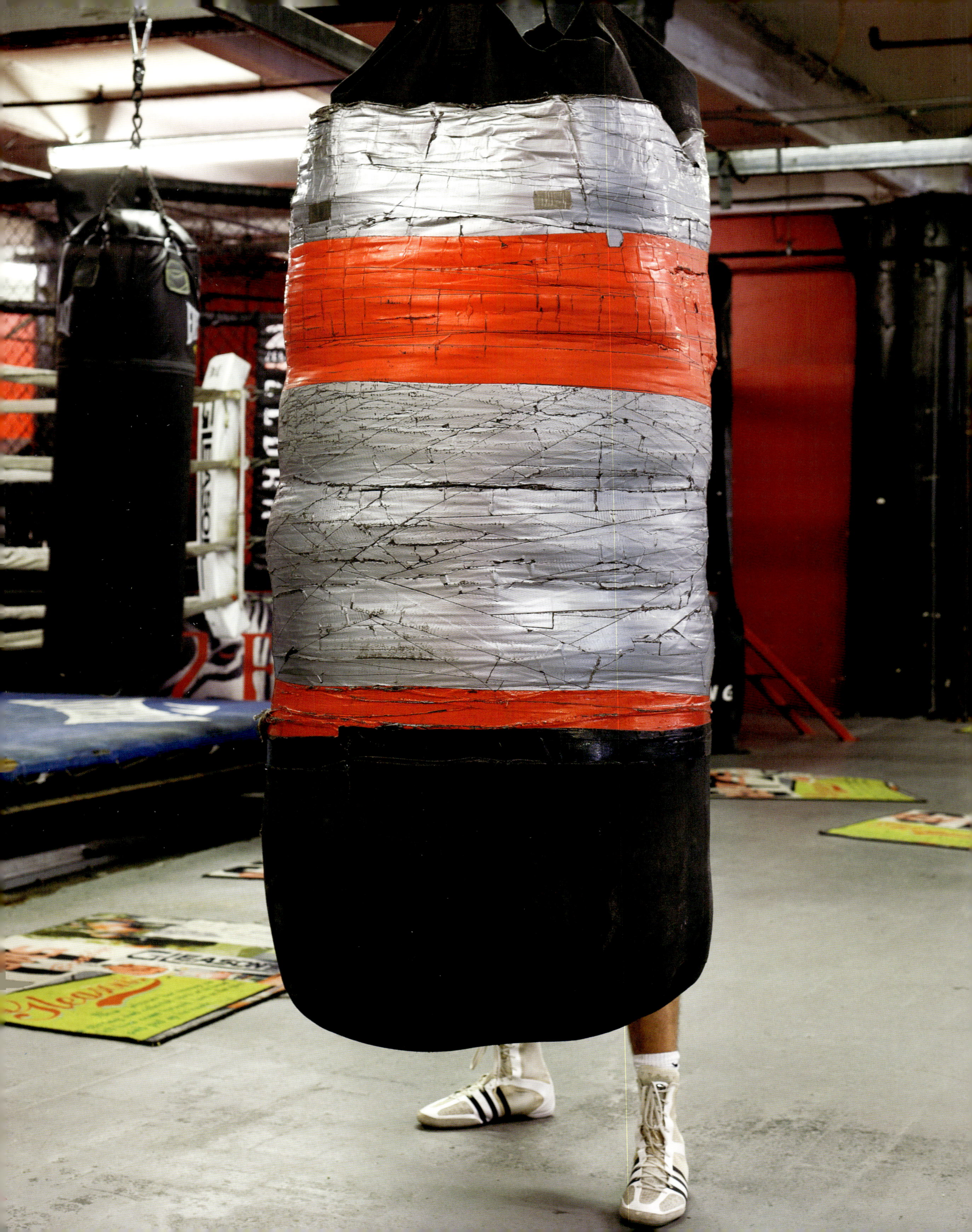

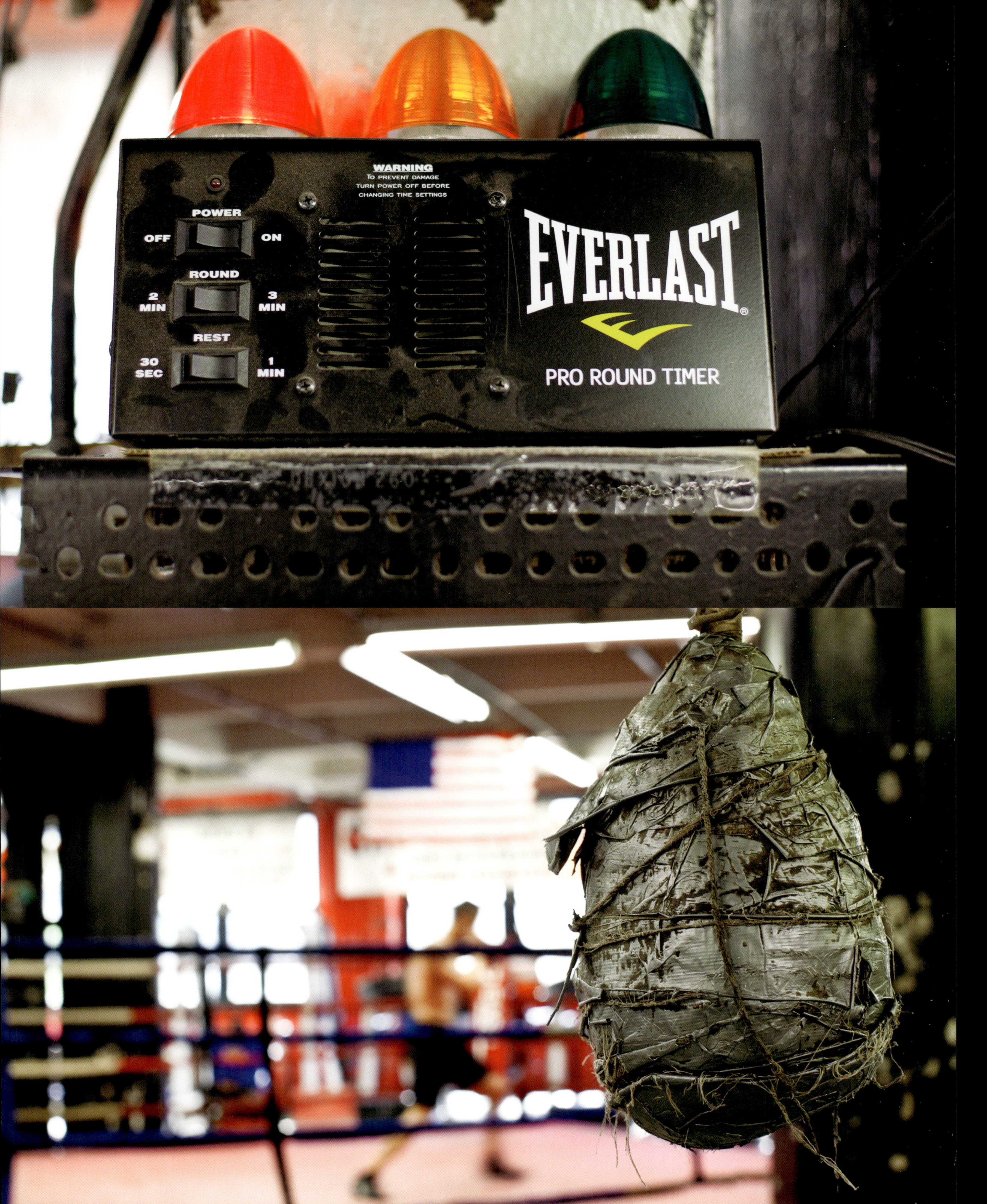

WARNING
To PREVENT DAMAGE
TURN POWER OFF BEFORE
CHANGING TIME SETTINGS
POWER
OFF
ON
ROUND
2
MIN
3
MIN
REST
30
SEC
1
MIN
EVERLAST
PRO ROUND TIMER

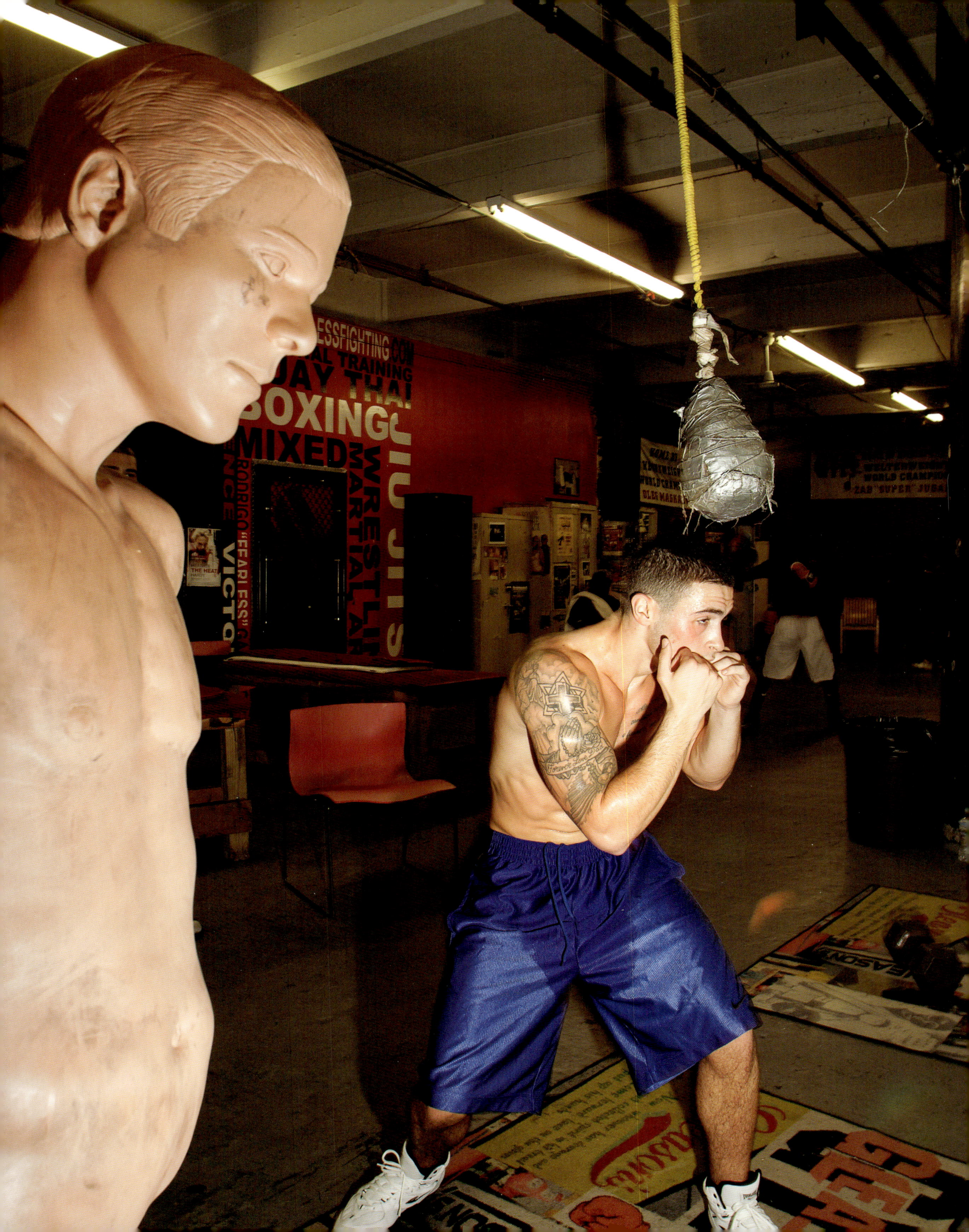

LESSFIGHTING.COM
AL TRAINING
DAY THAI
BOXING
MIXED
WRESTLI
MARTIAL
JIU JITSU
RODRIGO "FEARLESS" GR
NCE VICTO

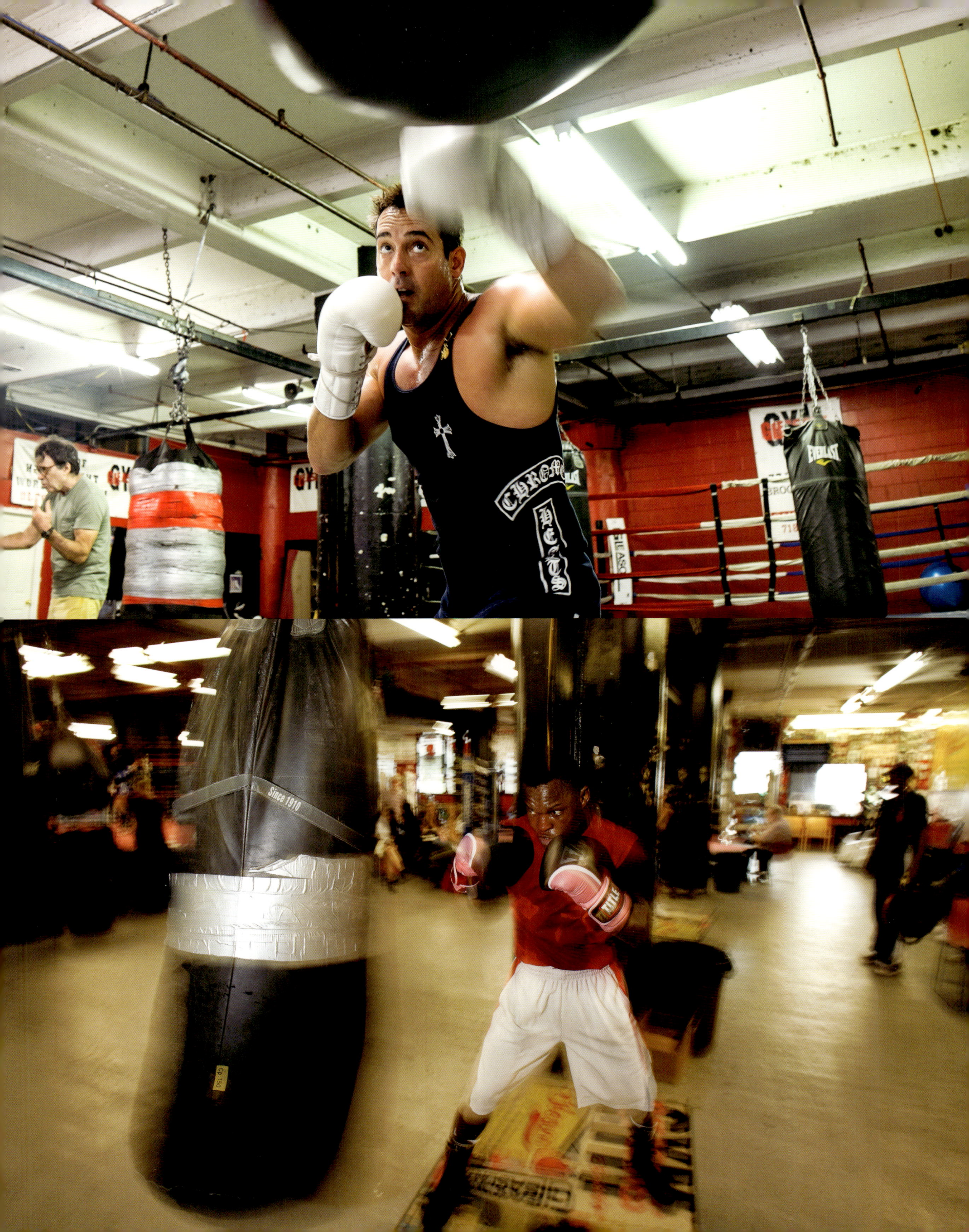

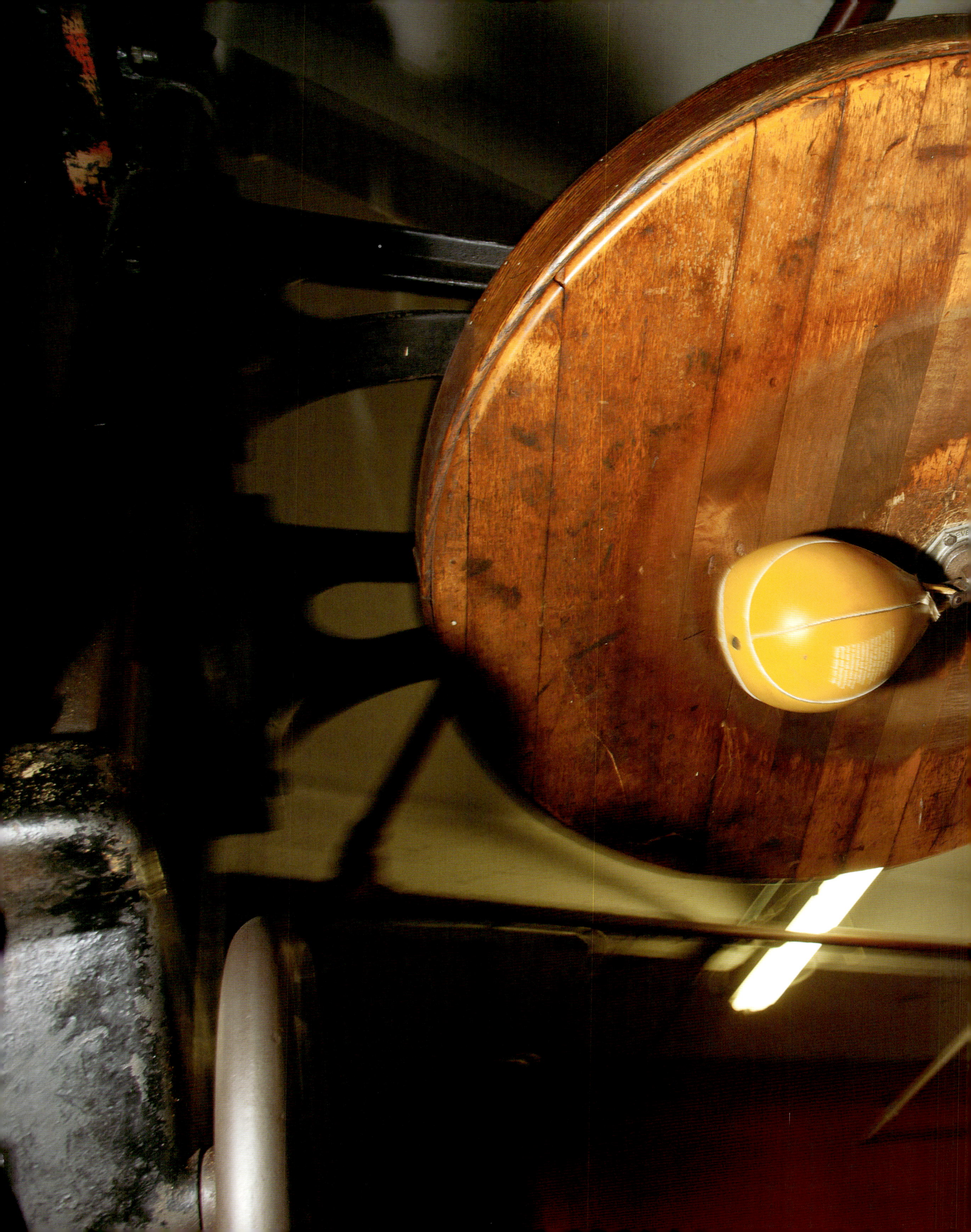

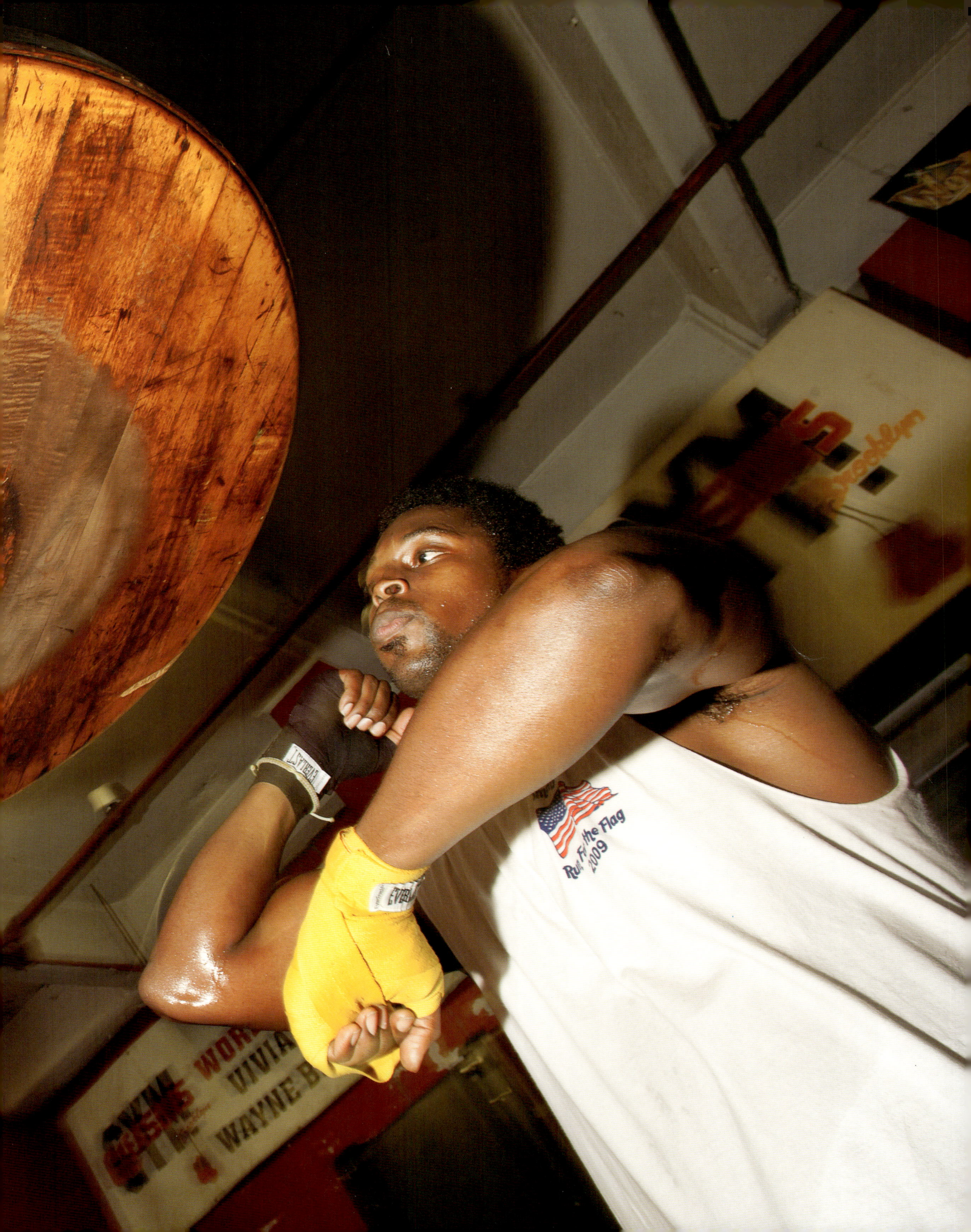

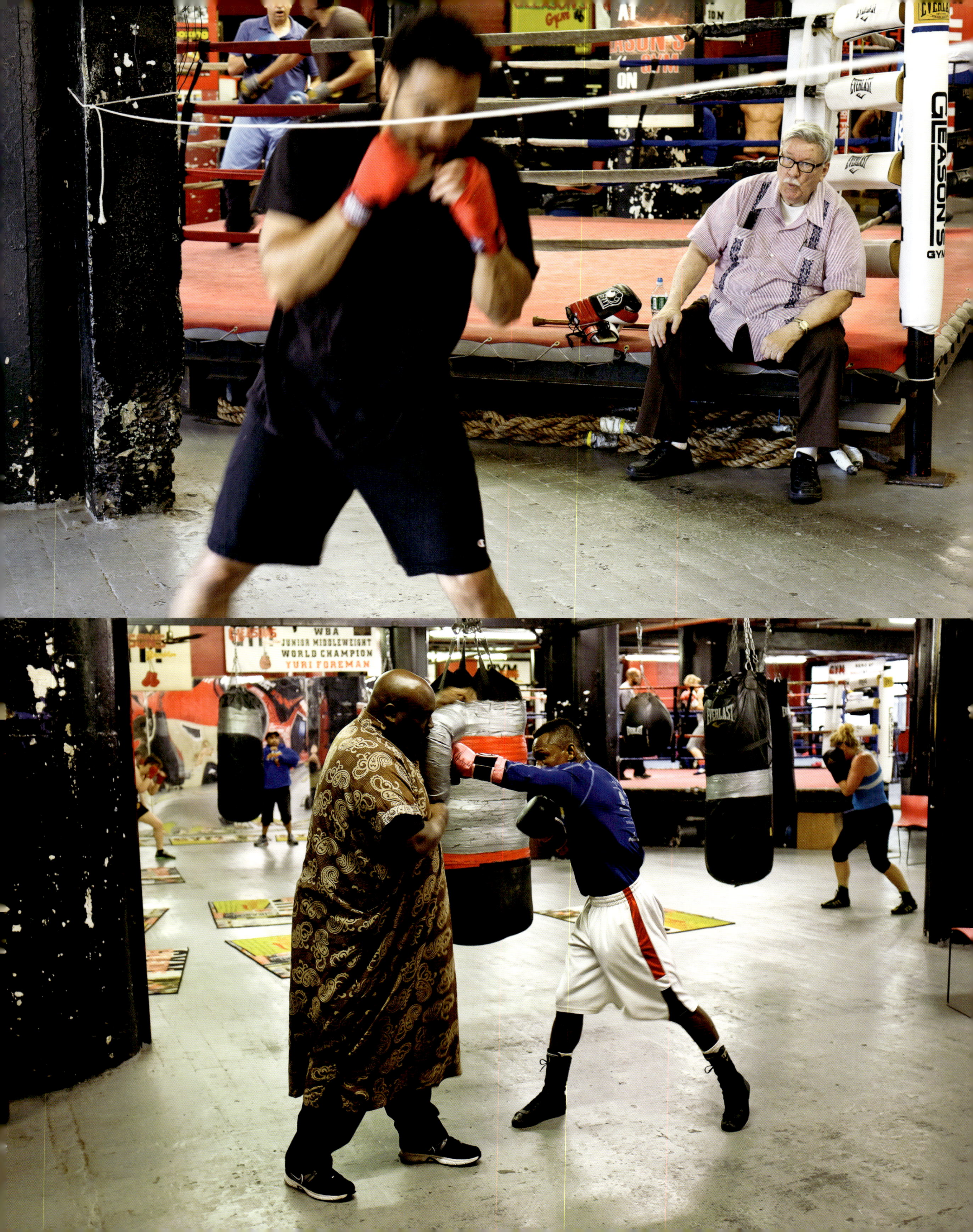

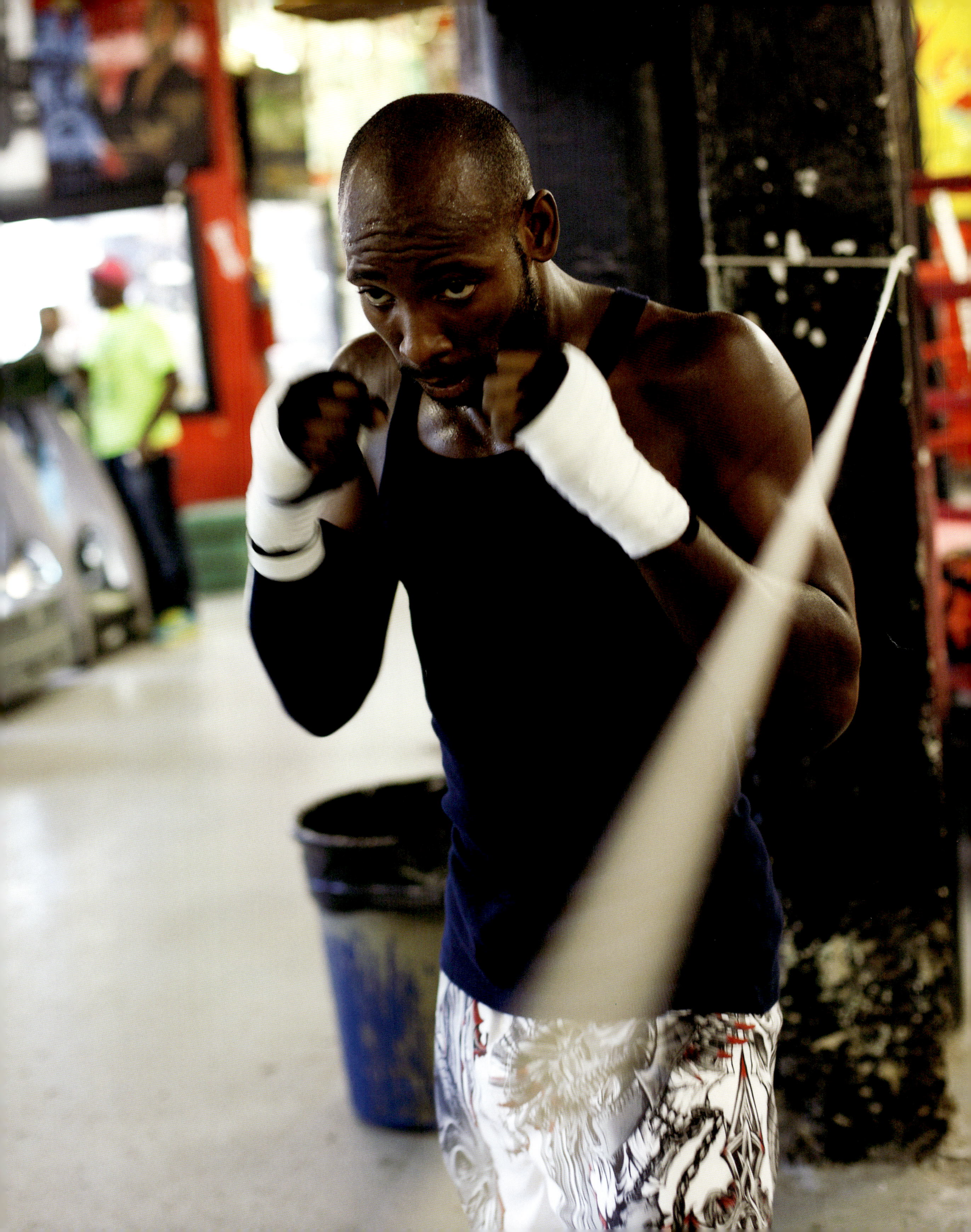

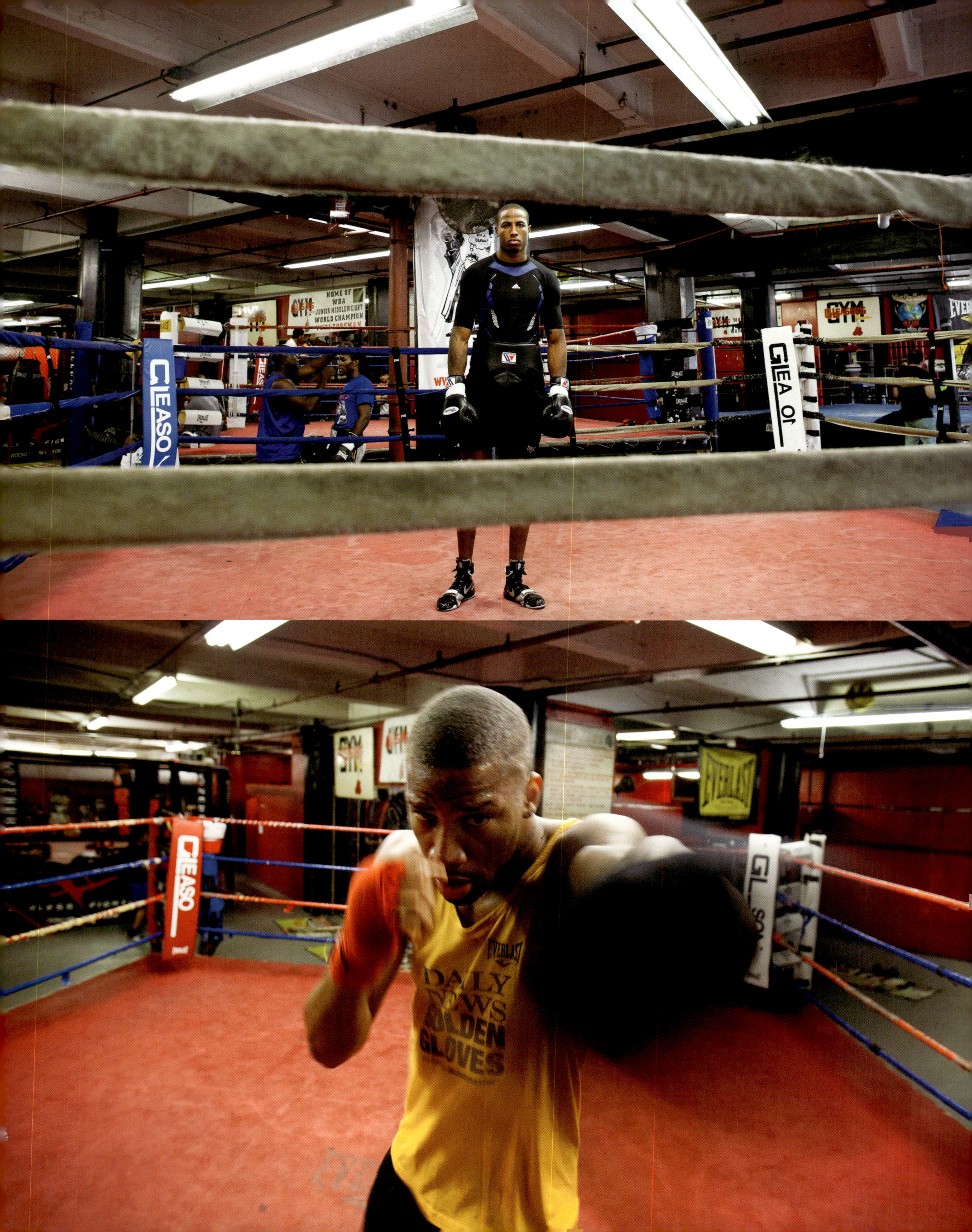

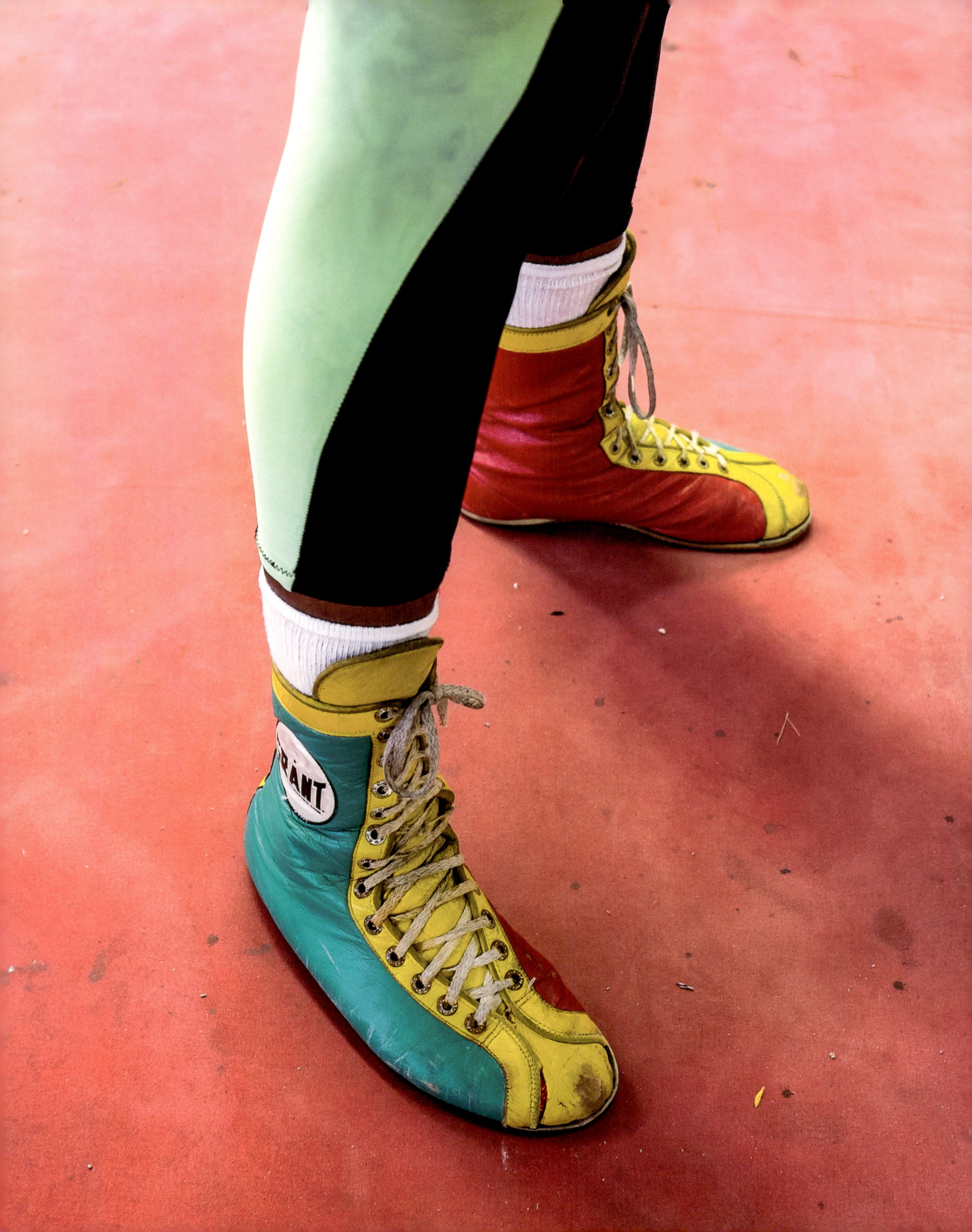

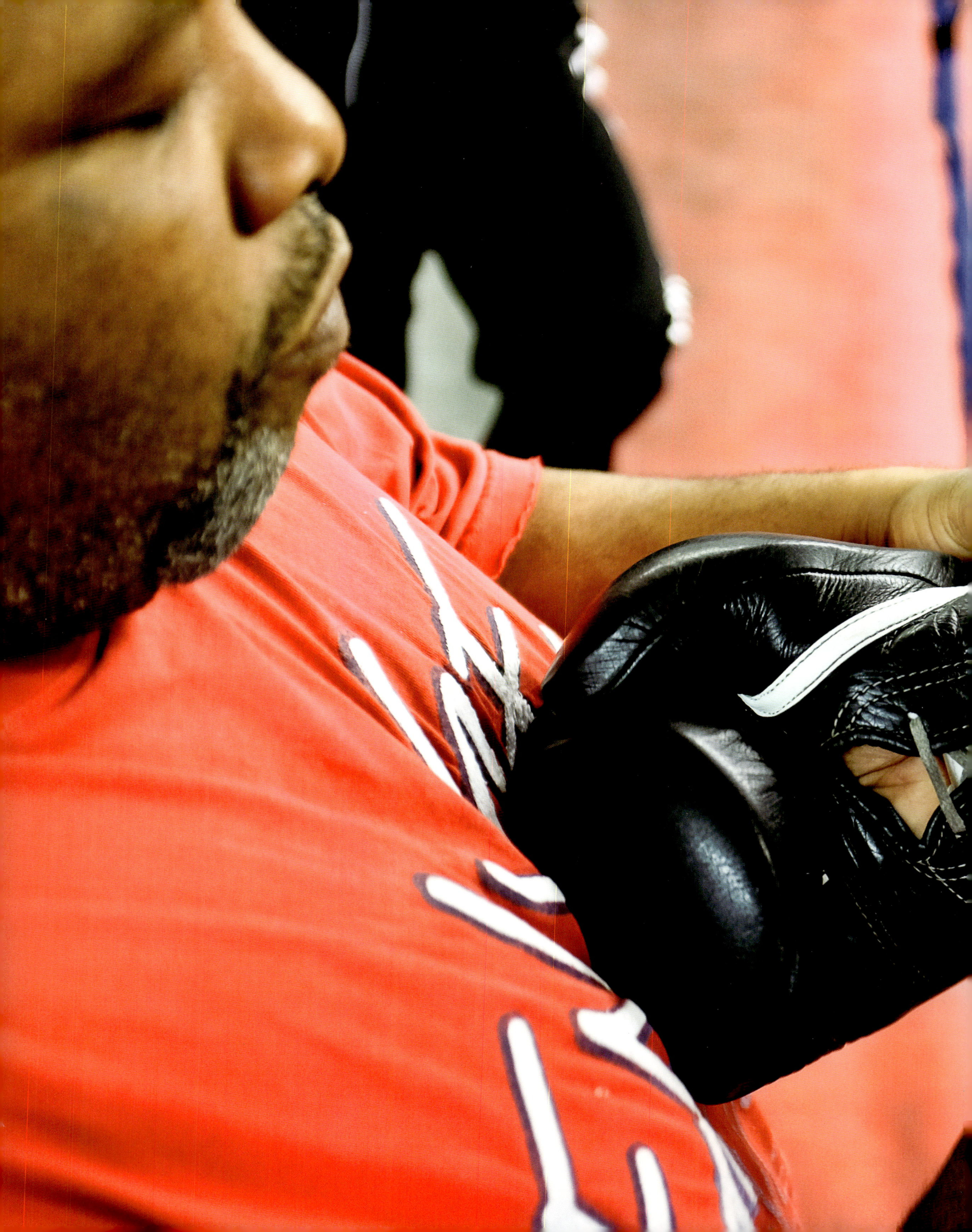

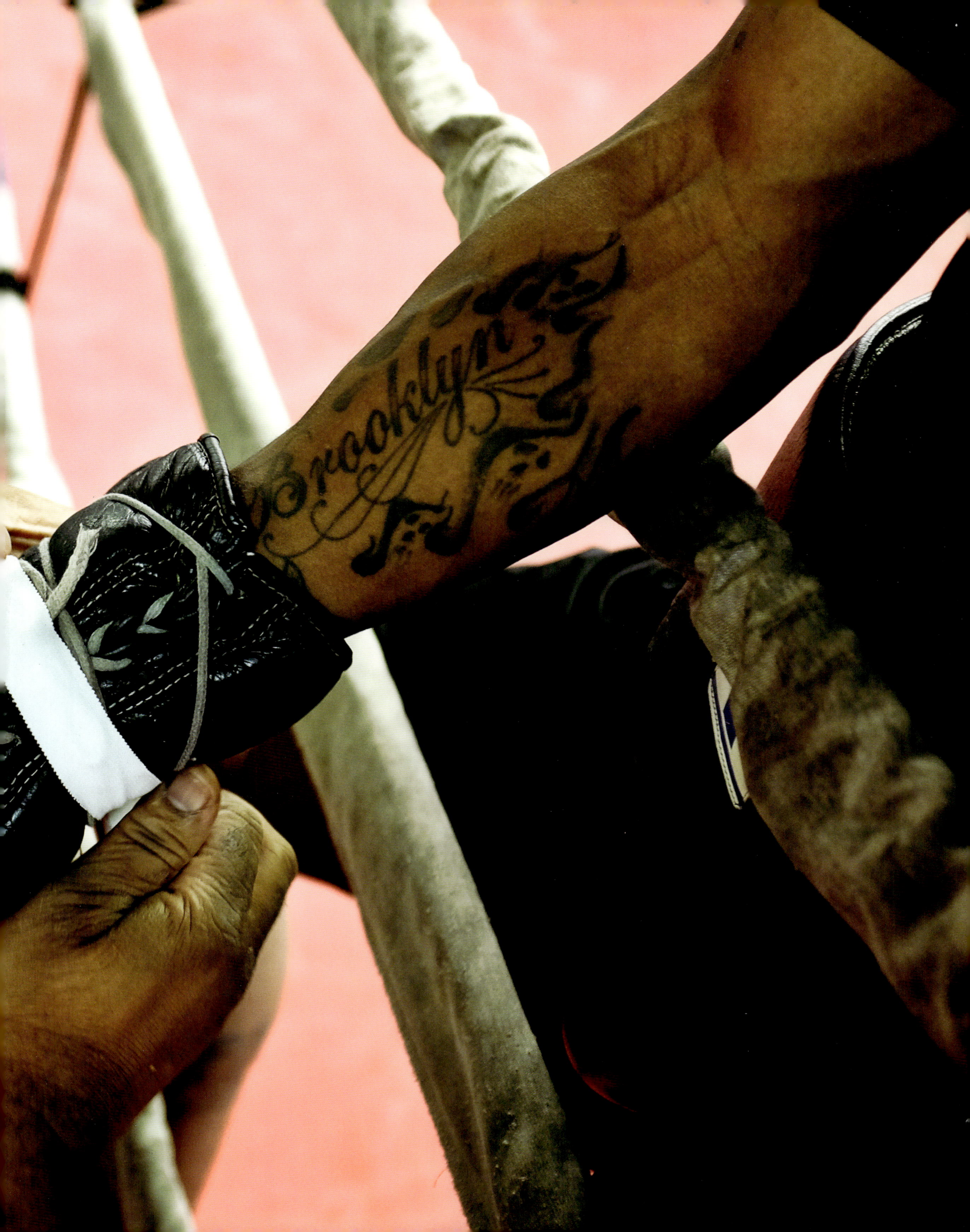

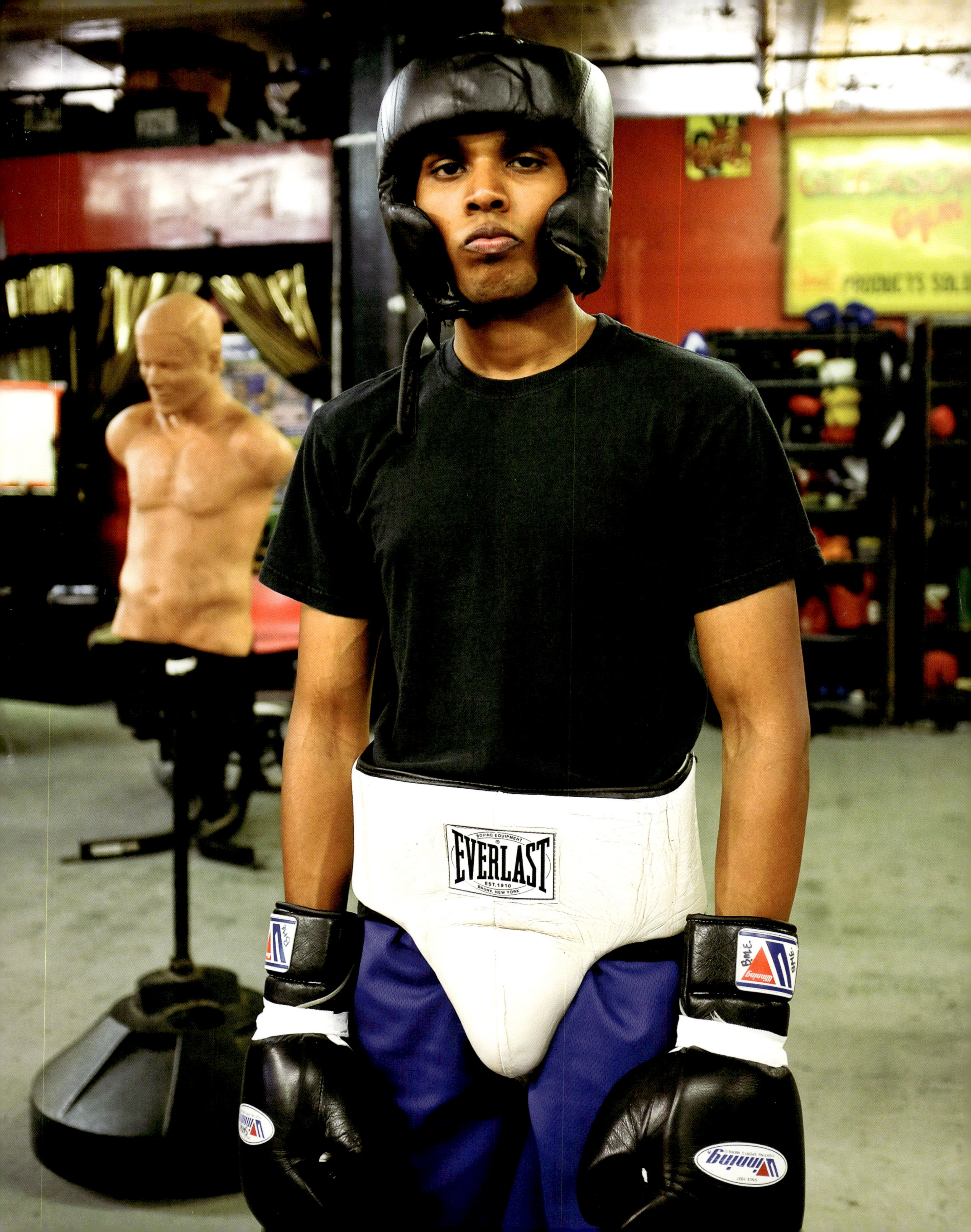

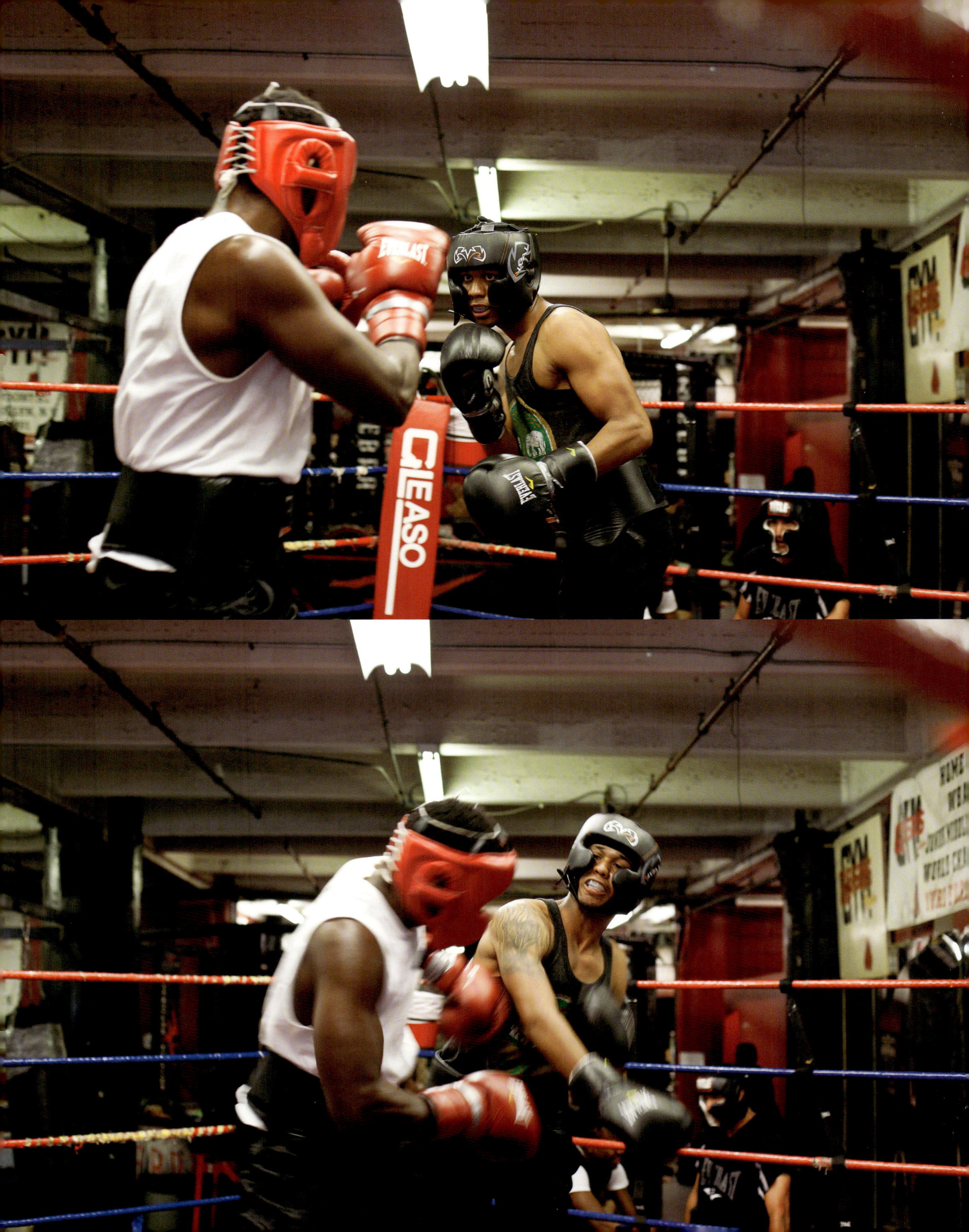

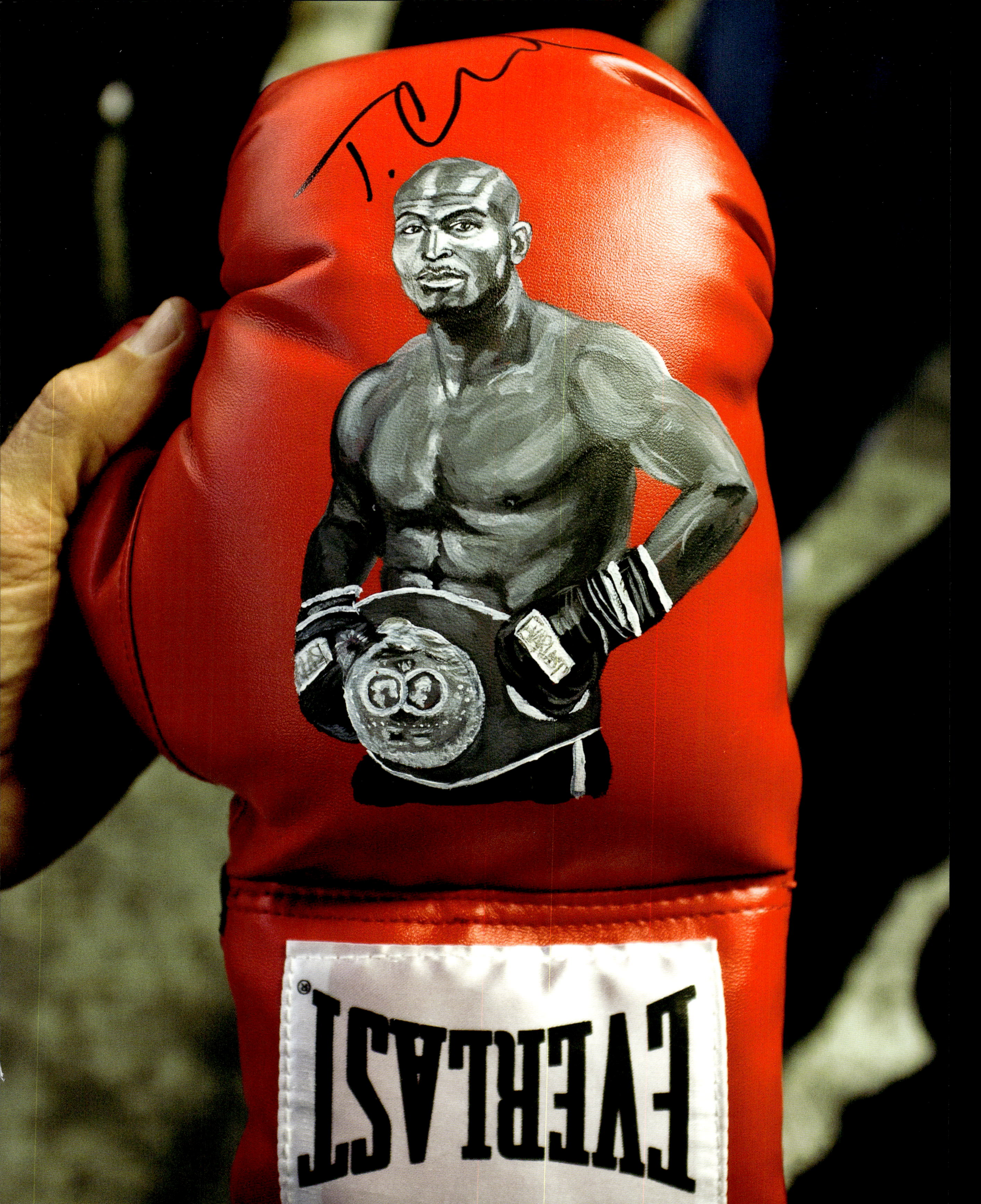

EVERLAST

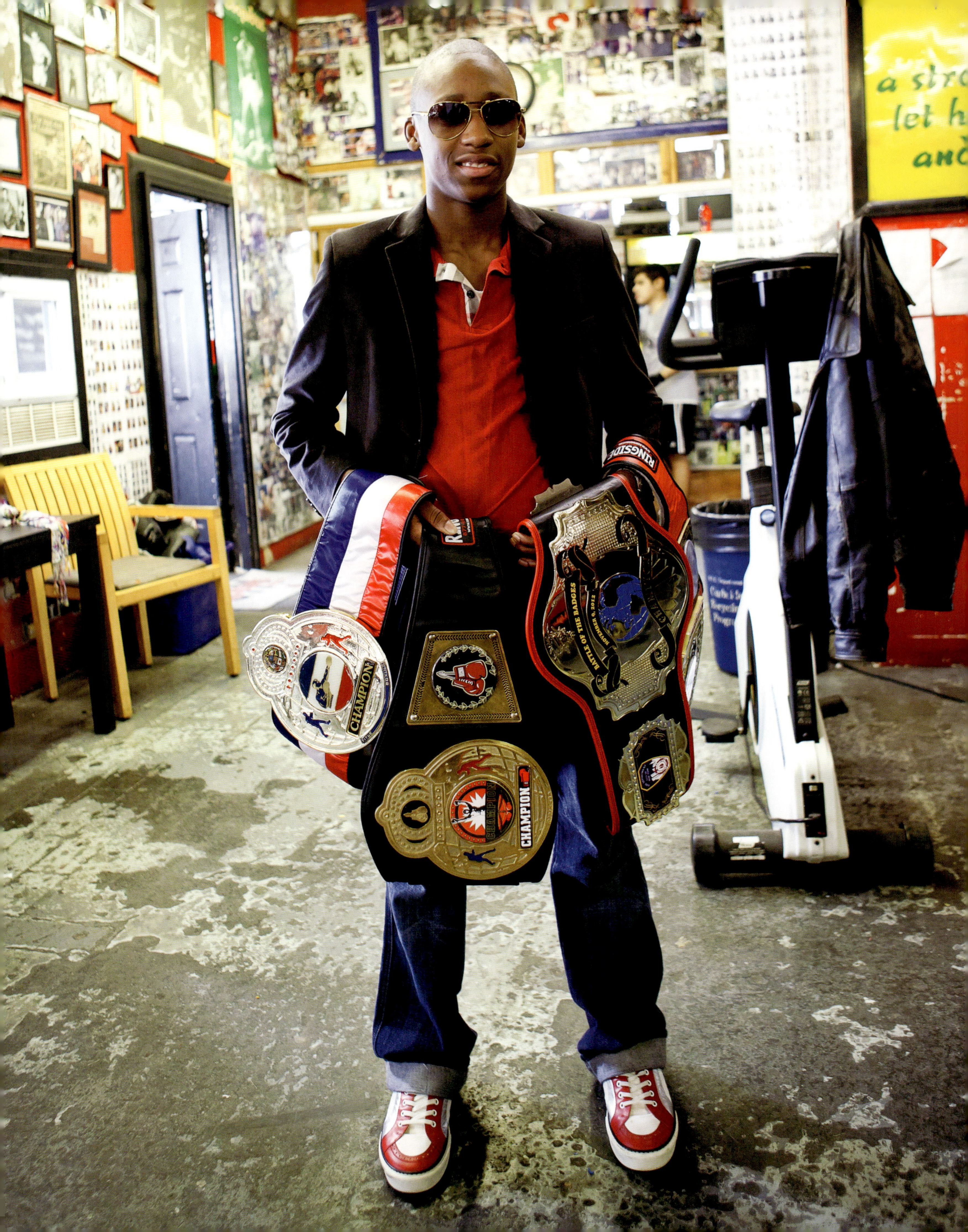

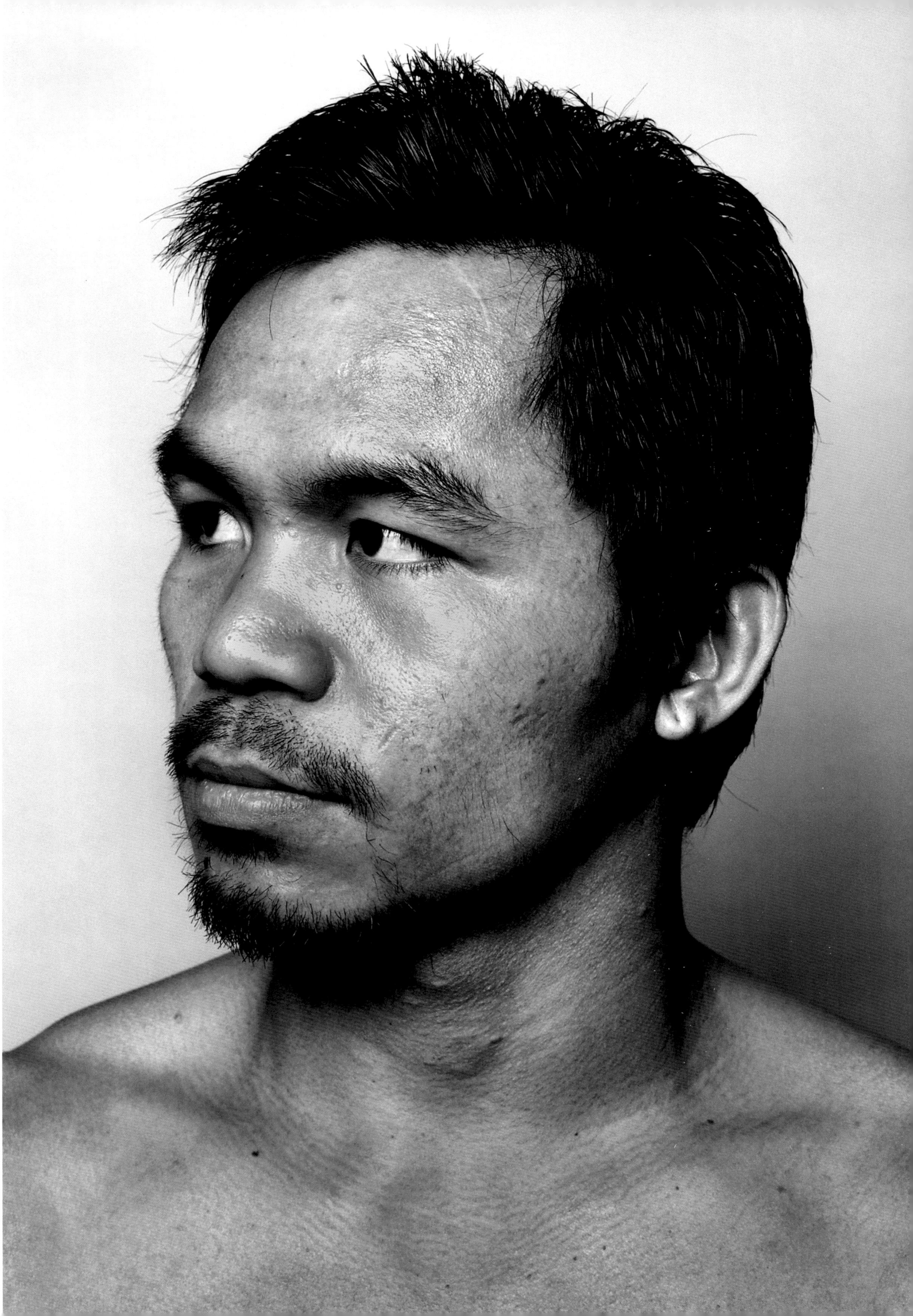

MANNY PACQUIAO, 'PAC - MAN' / LOS ANGELES, 2008

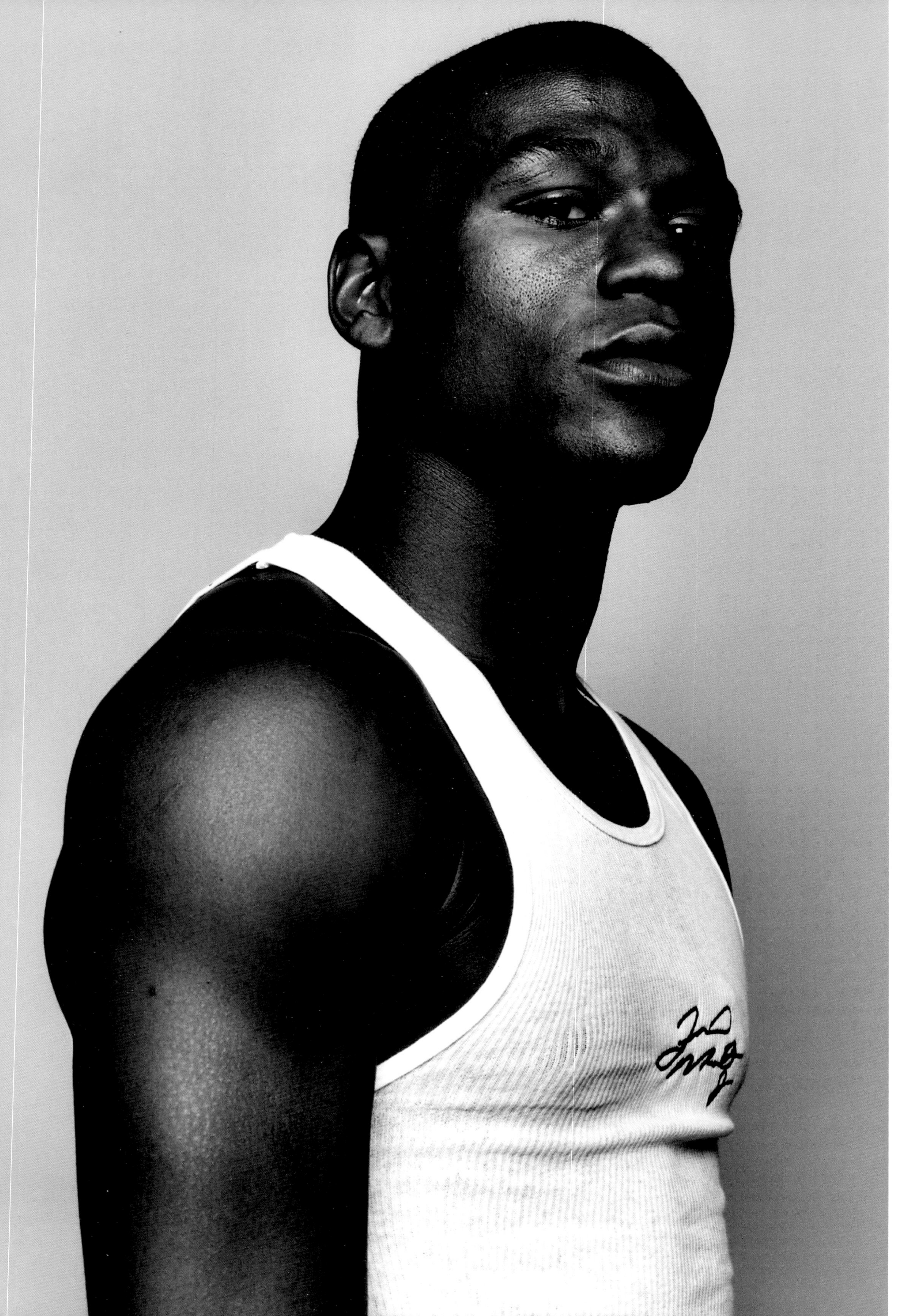

FLOYD MAYWEATHER JR., 'POUND - FOR - POUND' / NEW YORK, 2005

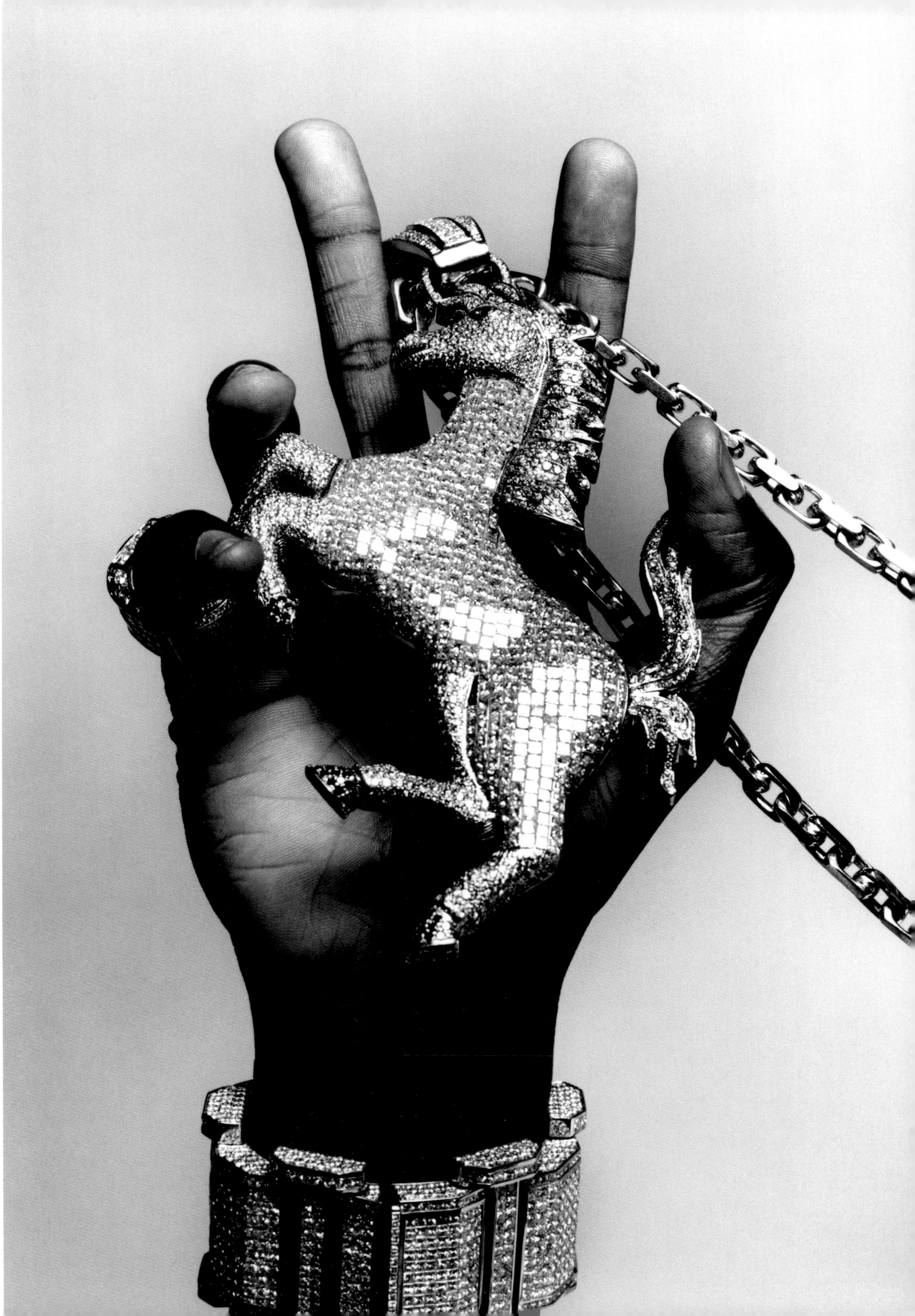

FLOYD MAYWEATHER JR., 'BLING - BLING' / NEW YORK, 2004

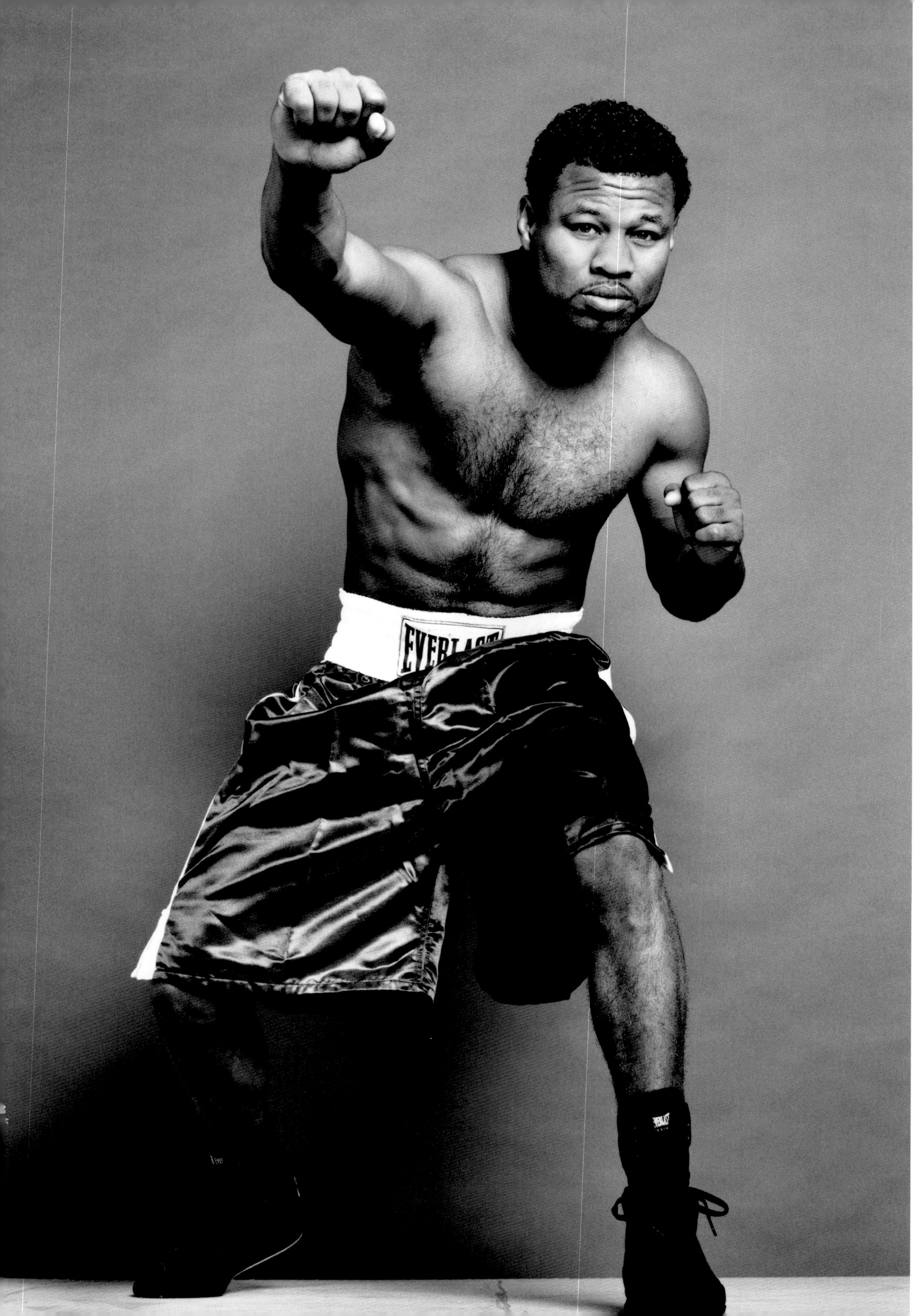

SHANE MOSLEY, 'SUGAR SHANE MOSLEY' / NEW YORK, 2004

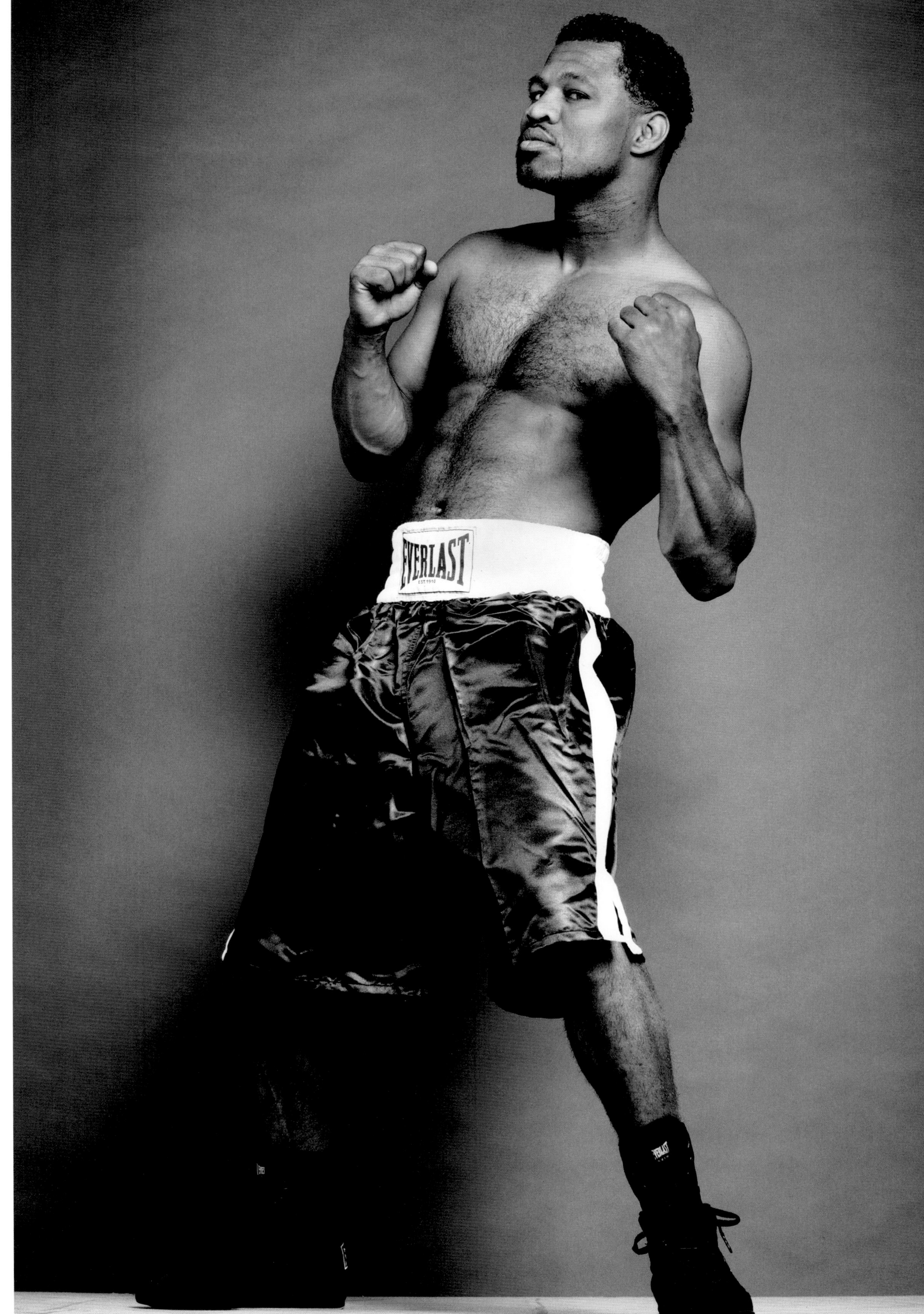

SHANE MOSLEY, 'SUGAR SHANE MOSLEY' / NEW YORK, 2004

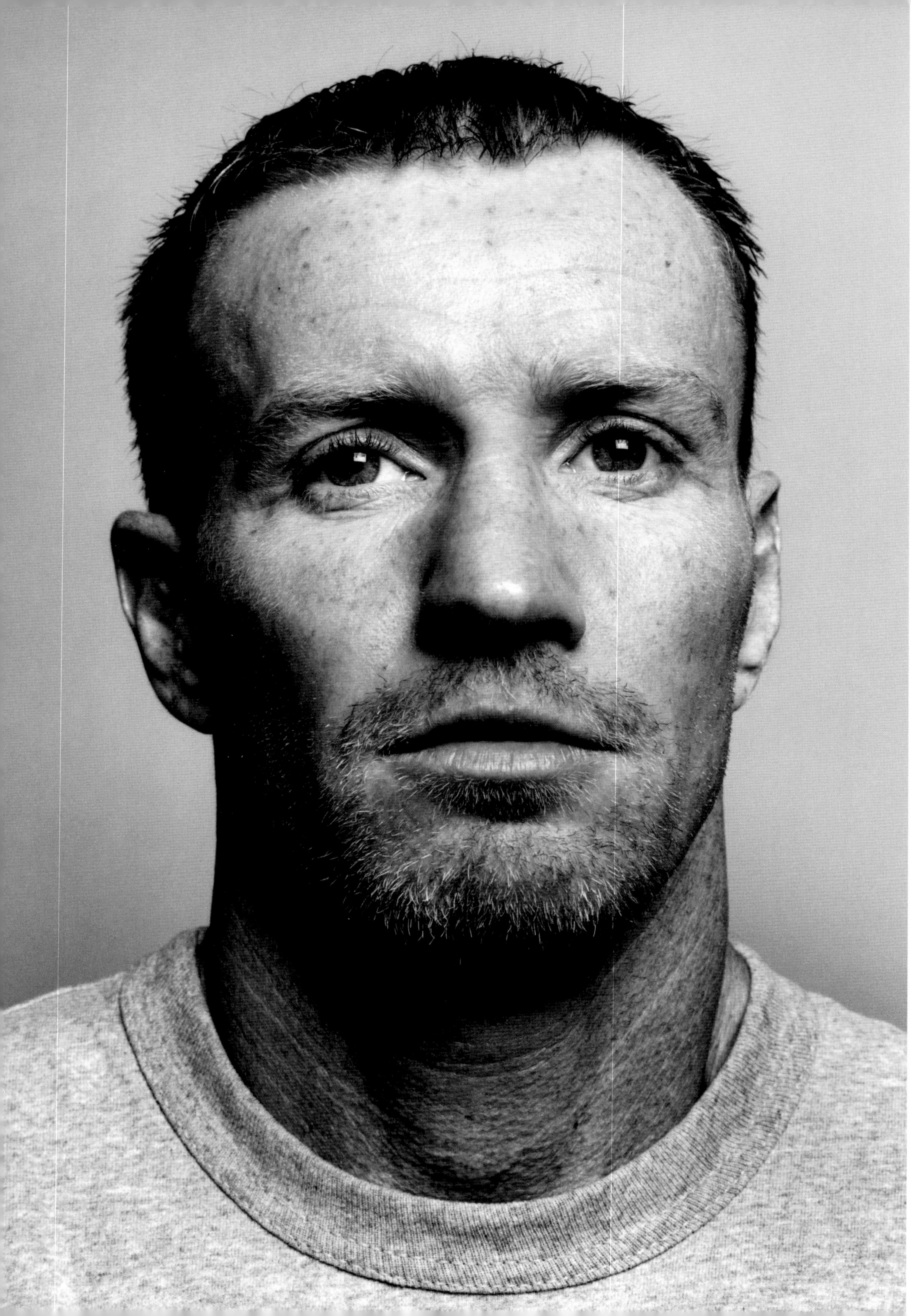

MICKY WARD. 'IRISH MICKY WARD' / ATLANTIC CITY, 2003

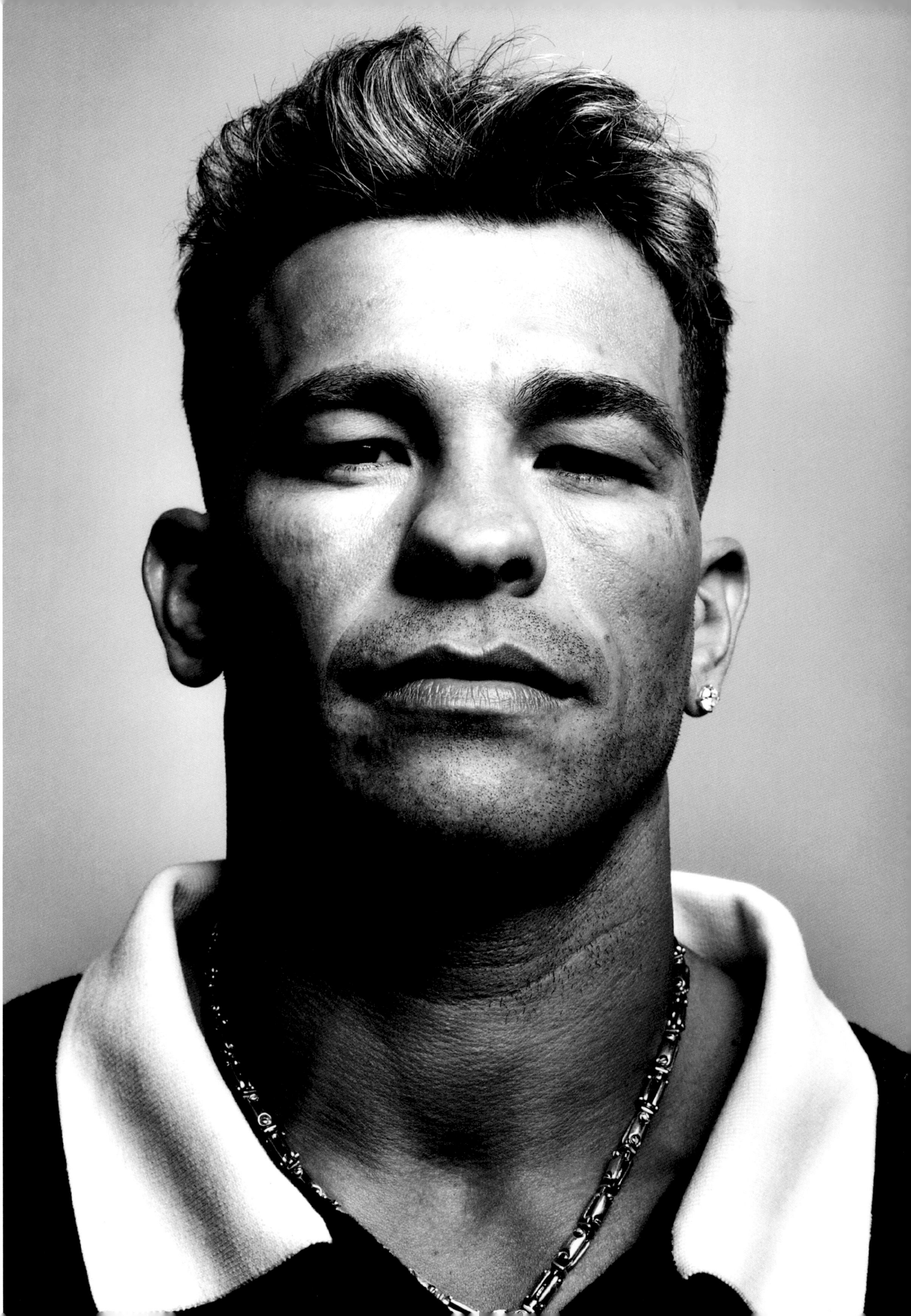

ARTURO GATTI, 'THUNDER' / ATLANTIC CITY, 2003

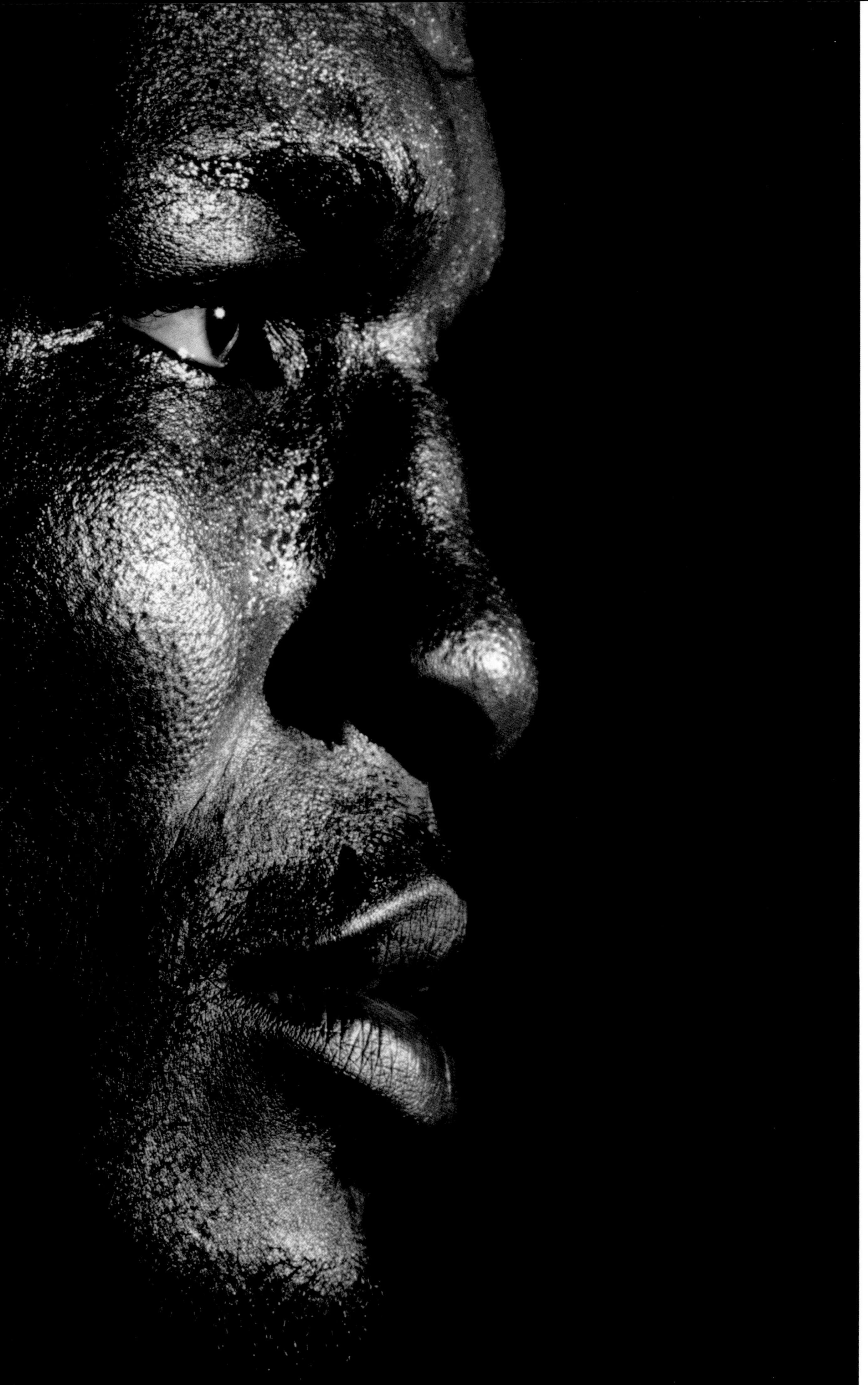

BERNARD HOPKINS, 'THE EXCECUTIONER' / PHILADELPHIA, 2004

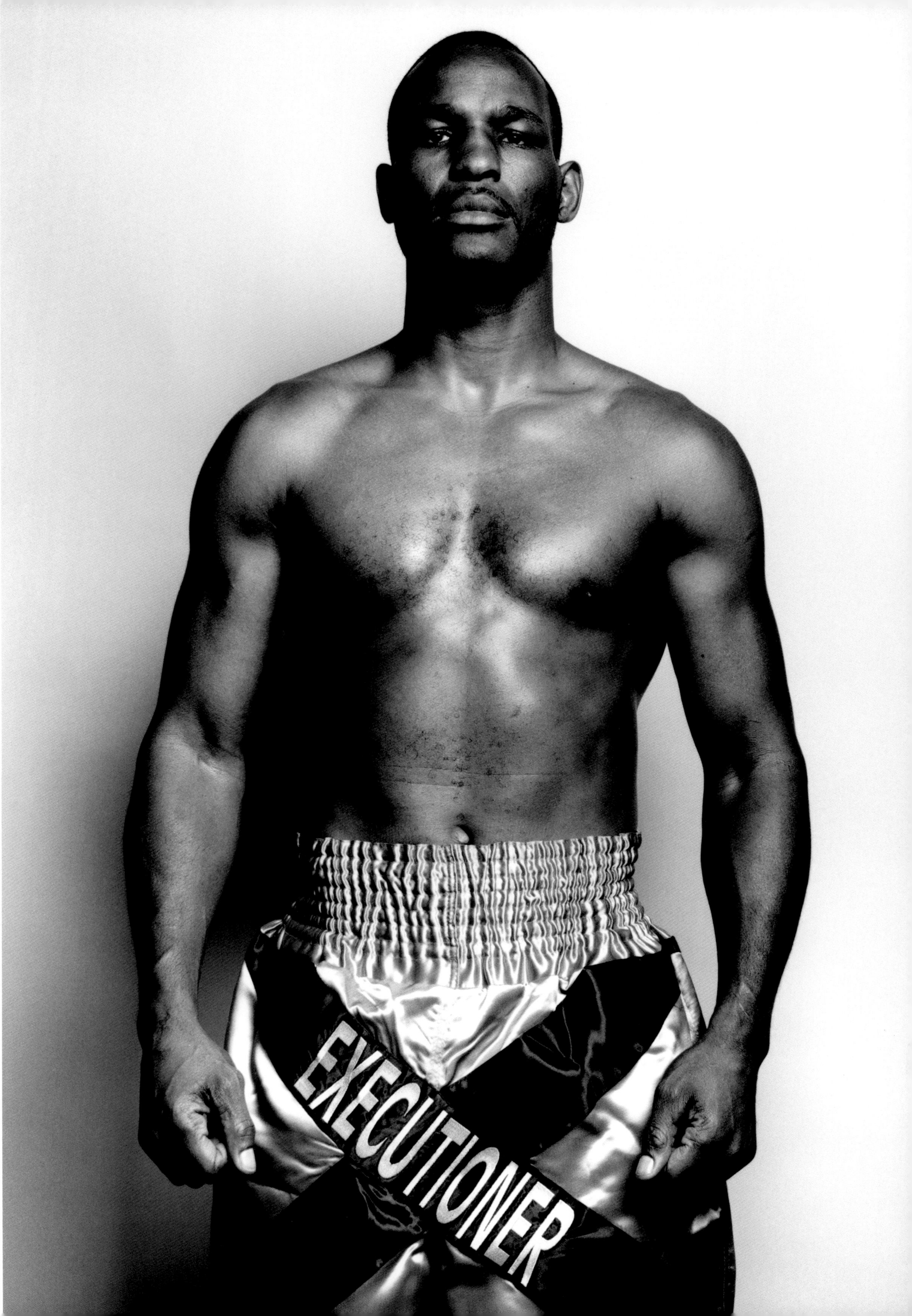

BERNARD HOPKINS, 'THE EXCECUTIONER' / NEW YORK, 2003

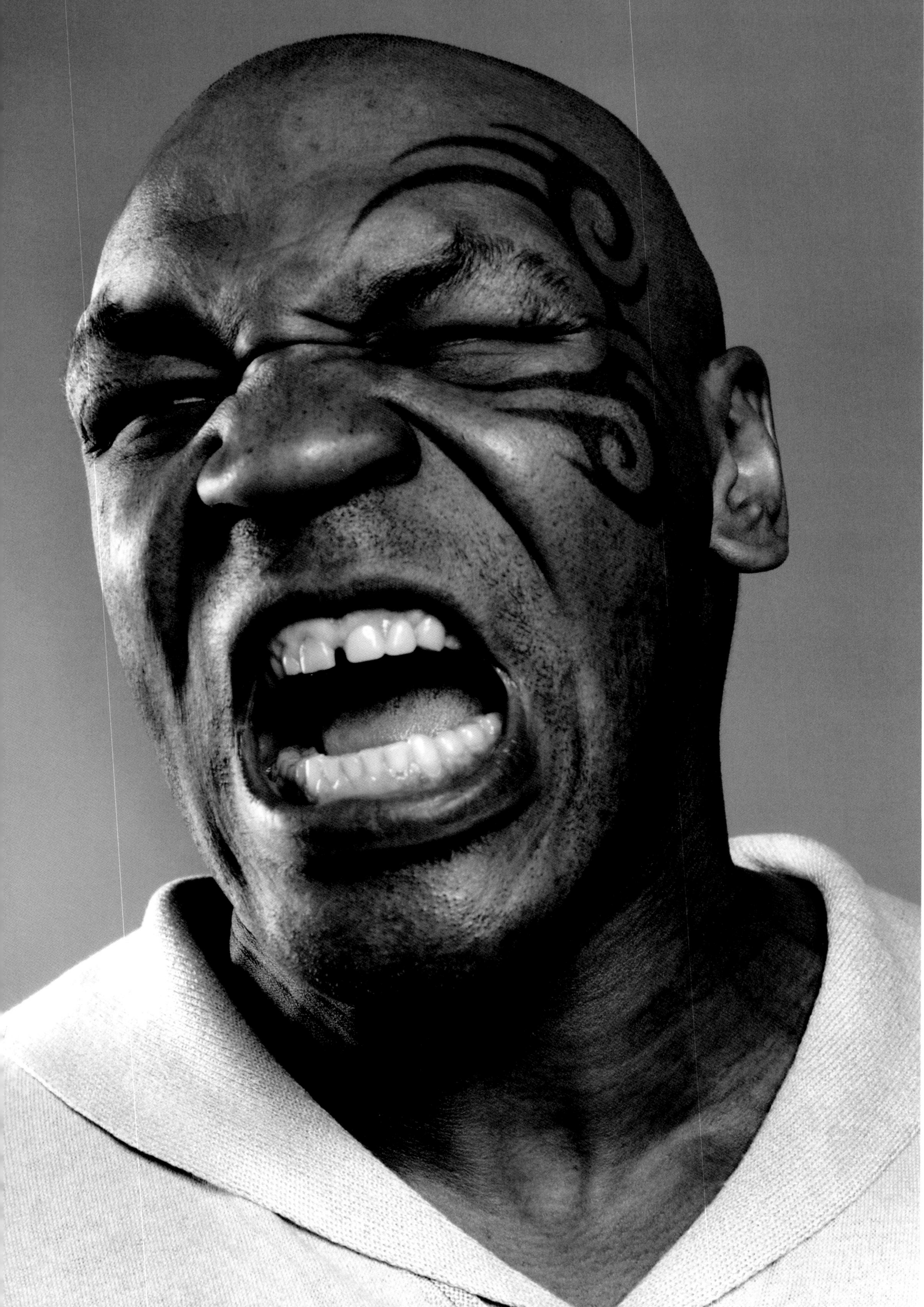

MIKE TYSON / LAS VEGAS. 2010

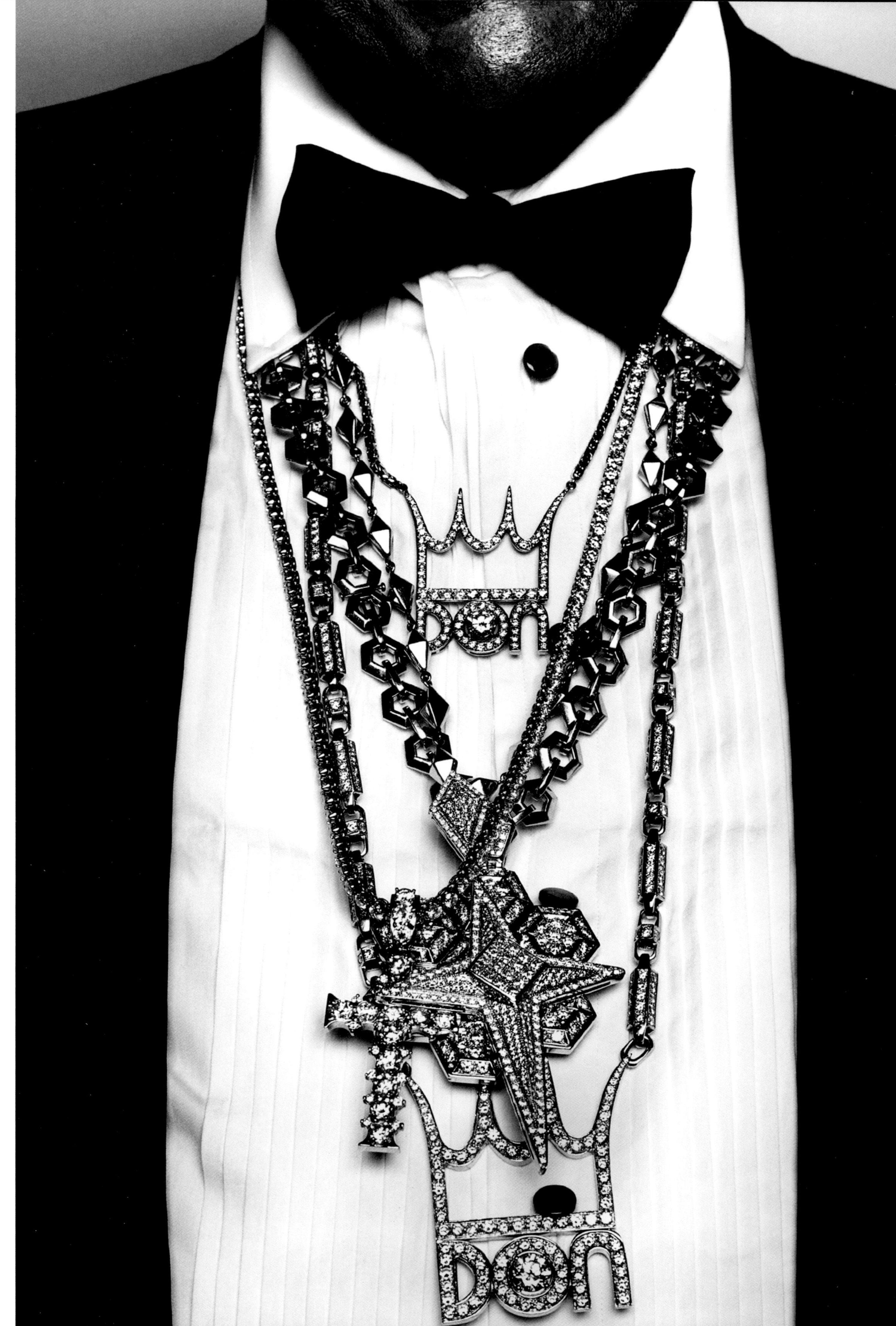

DON KING, 'BLING' / NEW YORK 2005

CHERYL DUNN
['RING CARD GIRLS' 1991-1997]

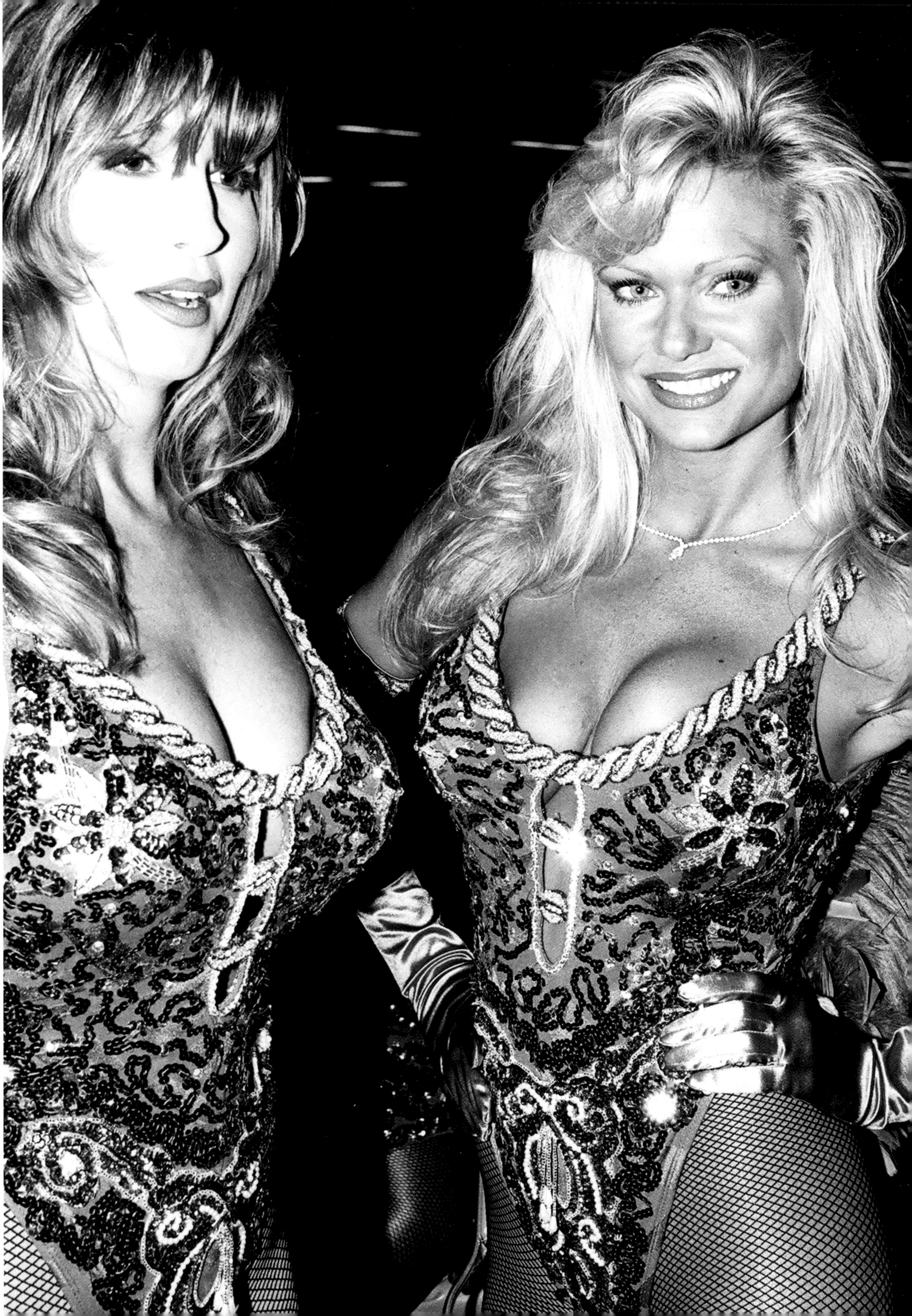

TRUMP GIRLS / ATLANTIC CITY, 1994

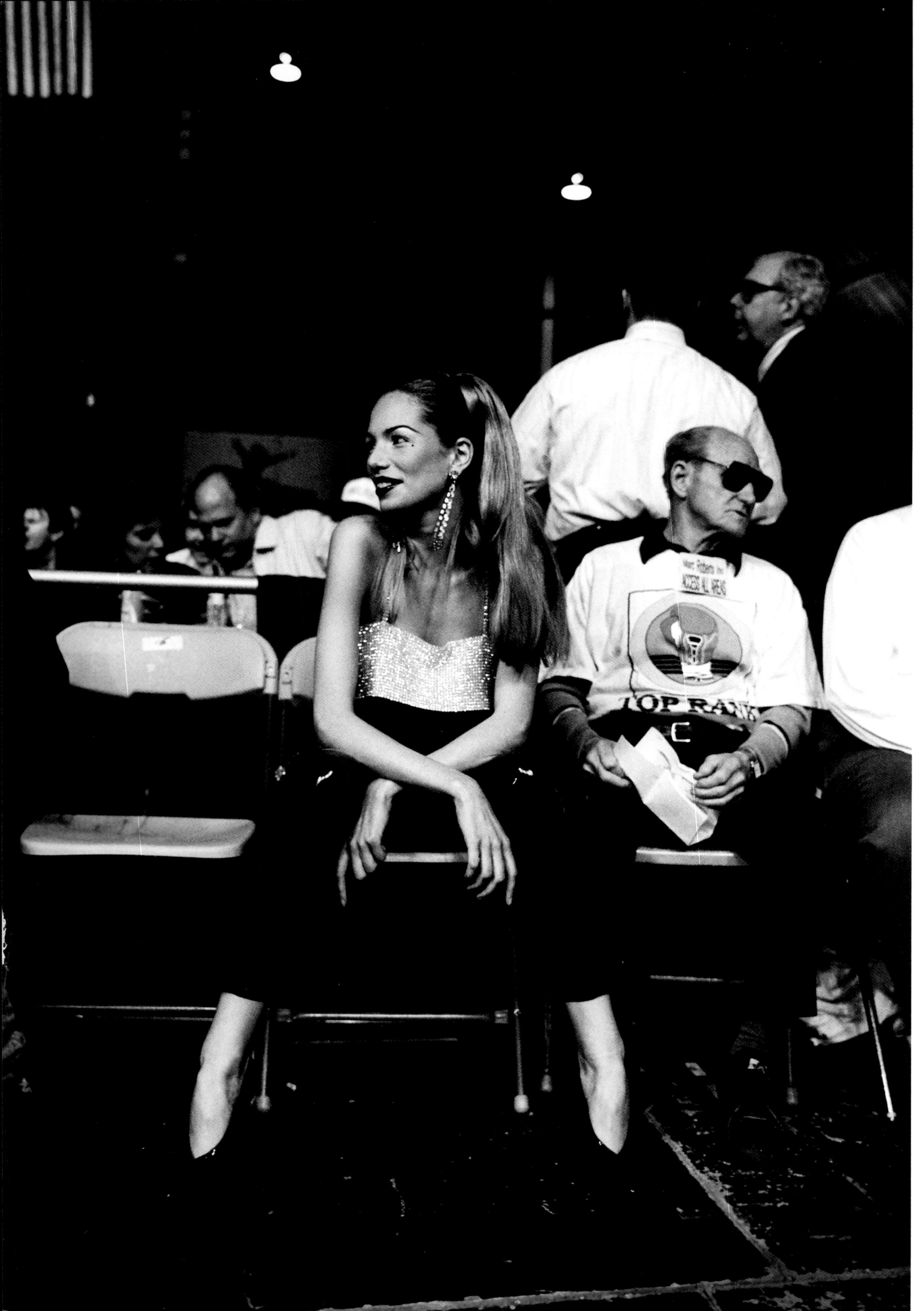

RESTING RING CARD GIRL / NEW JERSEY, 1997

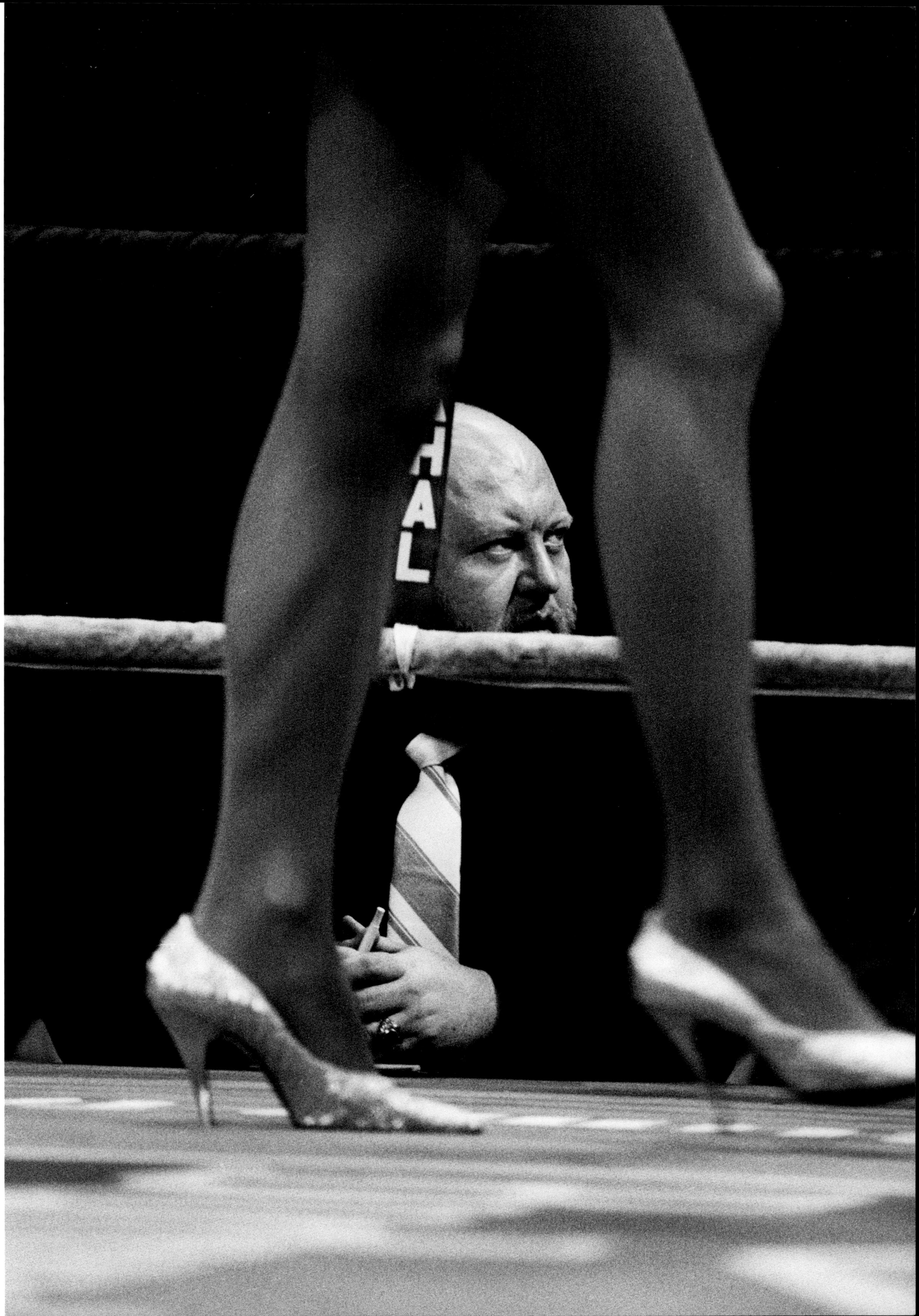

JUDGE AND LEGS / NEW JERSEY, 1991

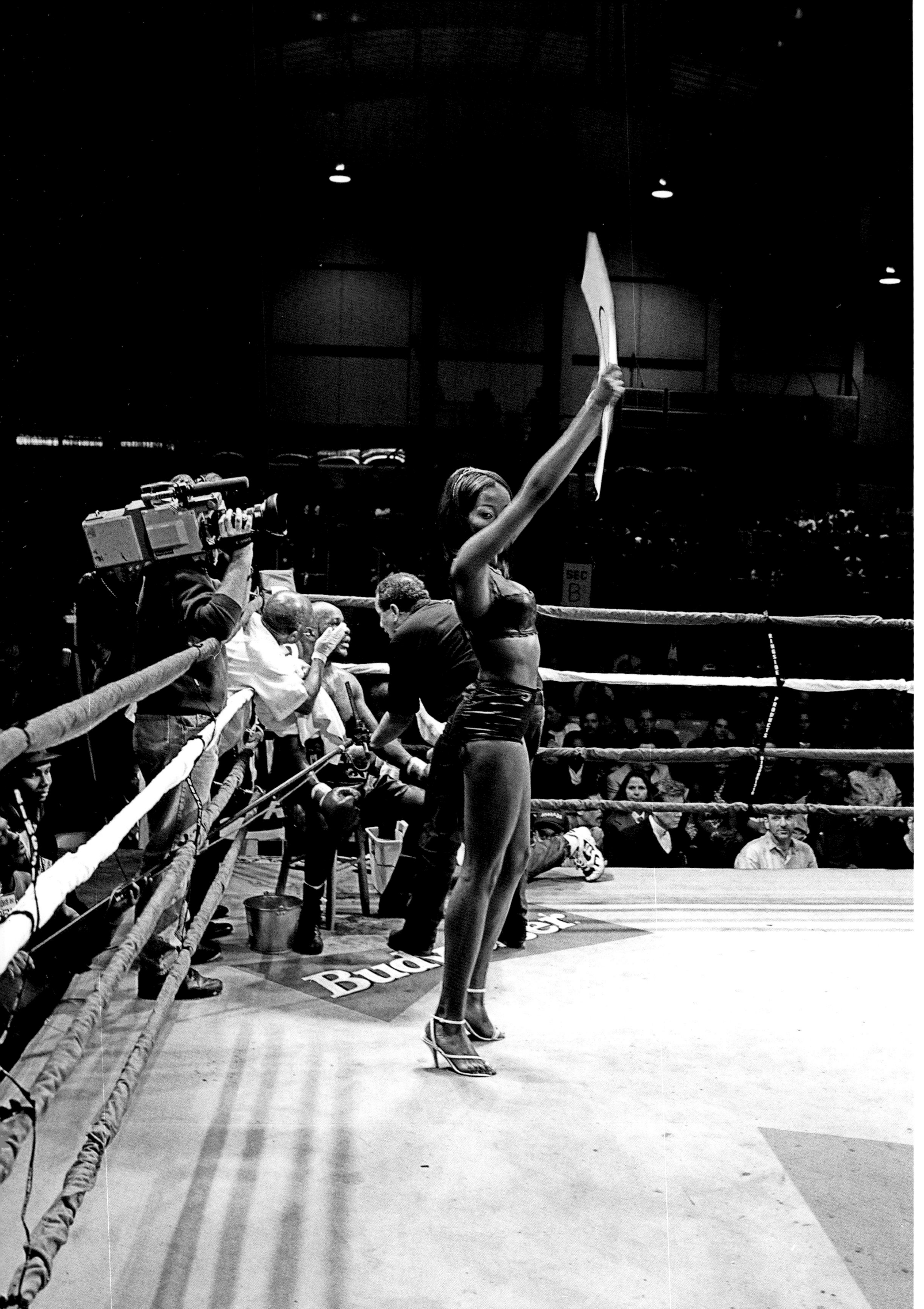

RING CARD GIRL. SHANNON BRIGGS FIGHT / NEWJERSEY. 1996

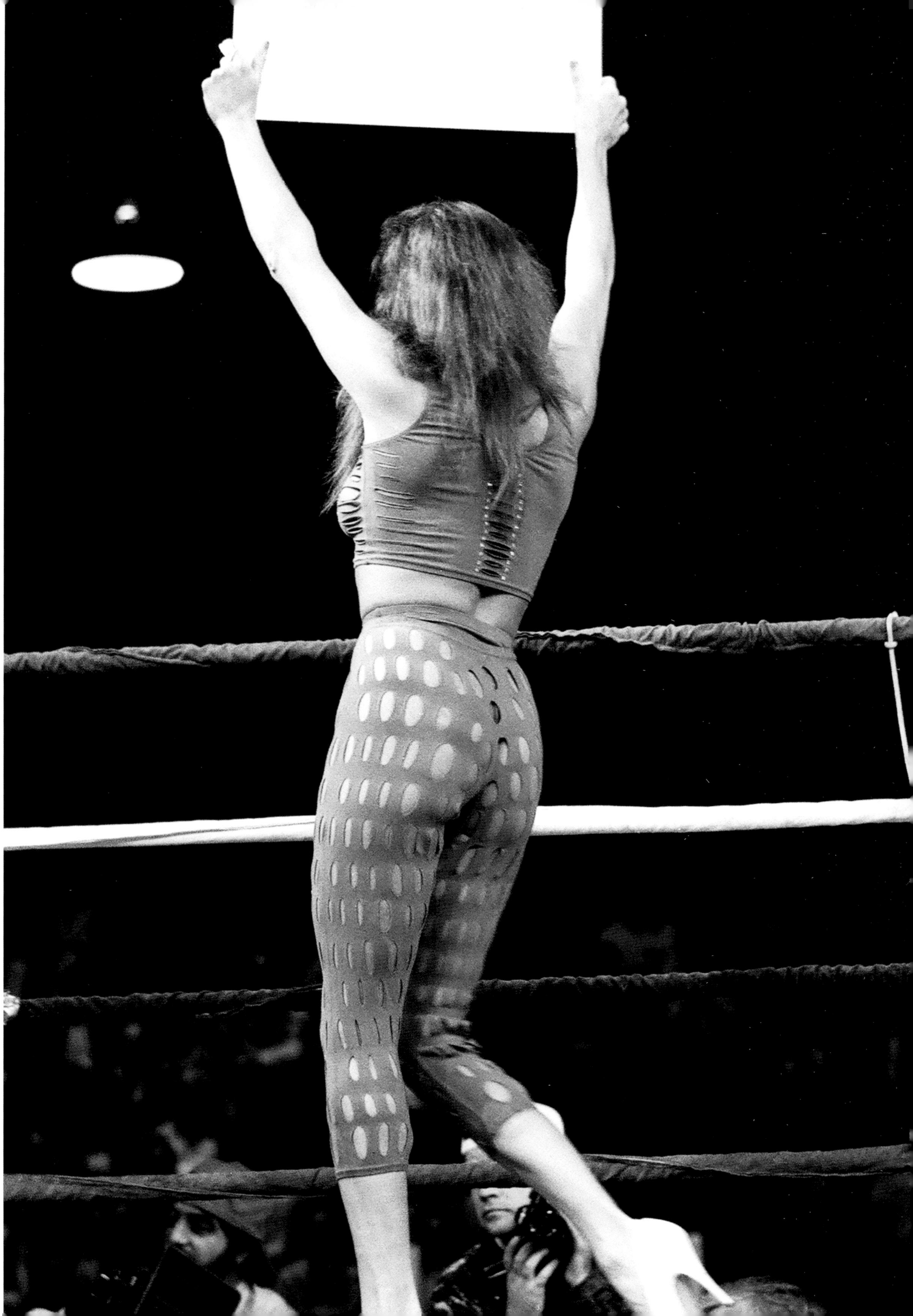

PEKA BOO RING CARD GIRL / ATLANTIC CITY, 1993

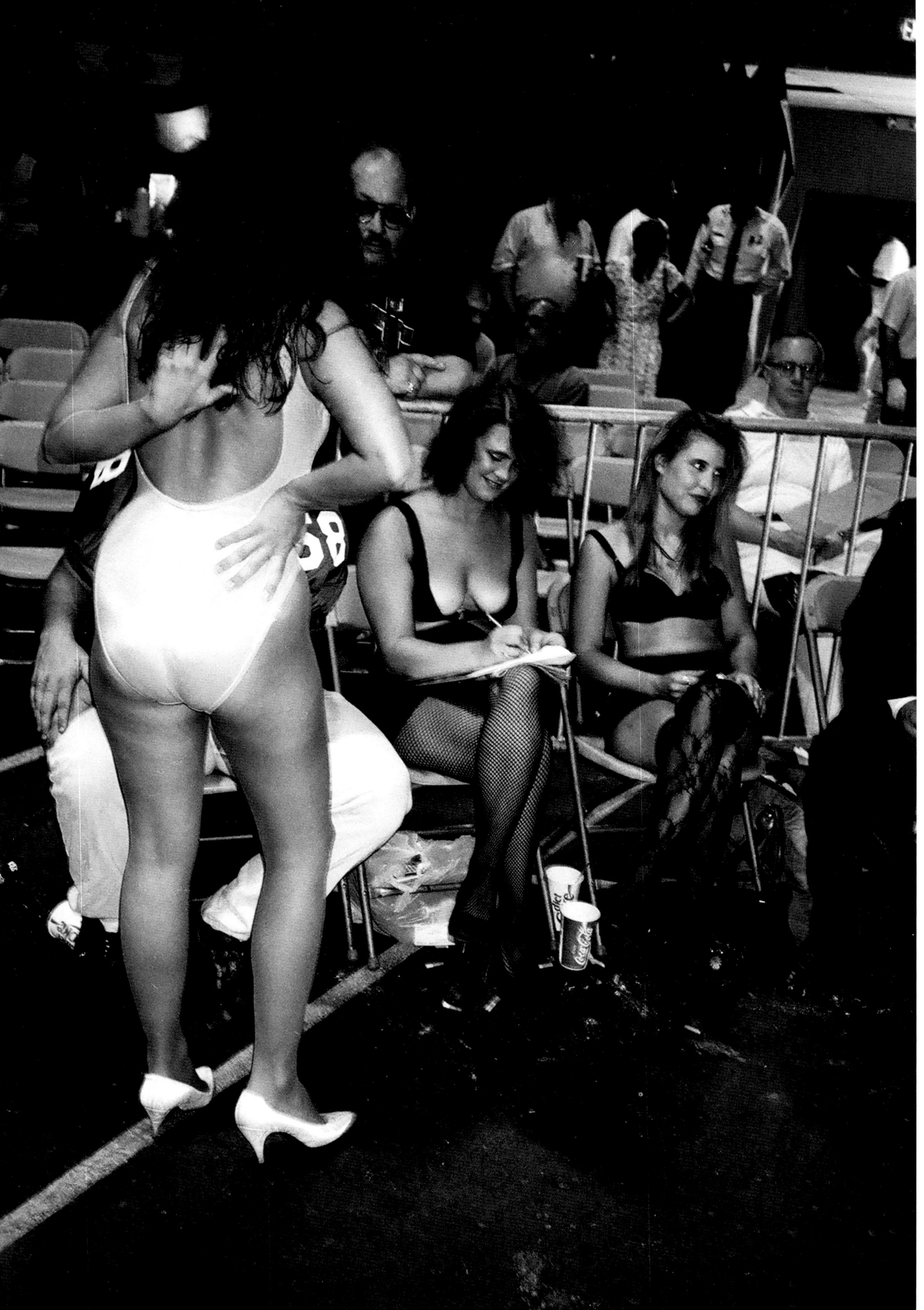

RING CARD GIRLS GROUP / ATLANTIC CITY, 1992

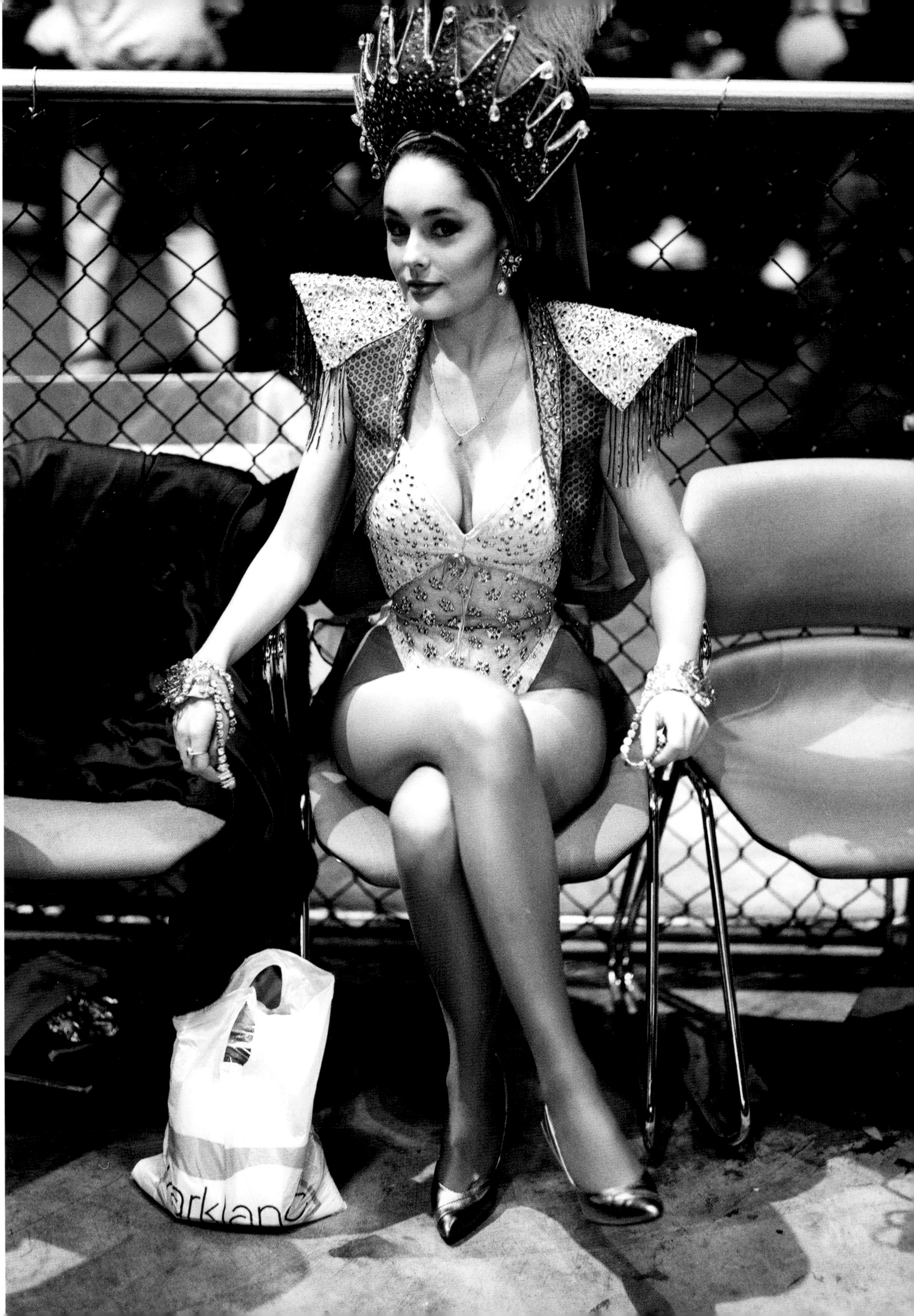

SITTING TRUMP GIRL / ATLANTIC CITY, 1994

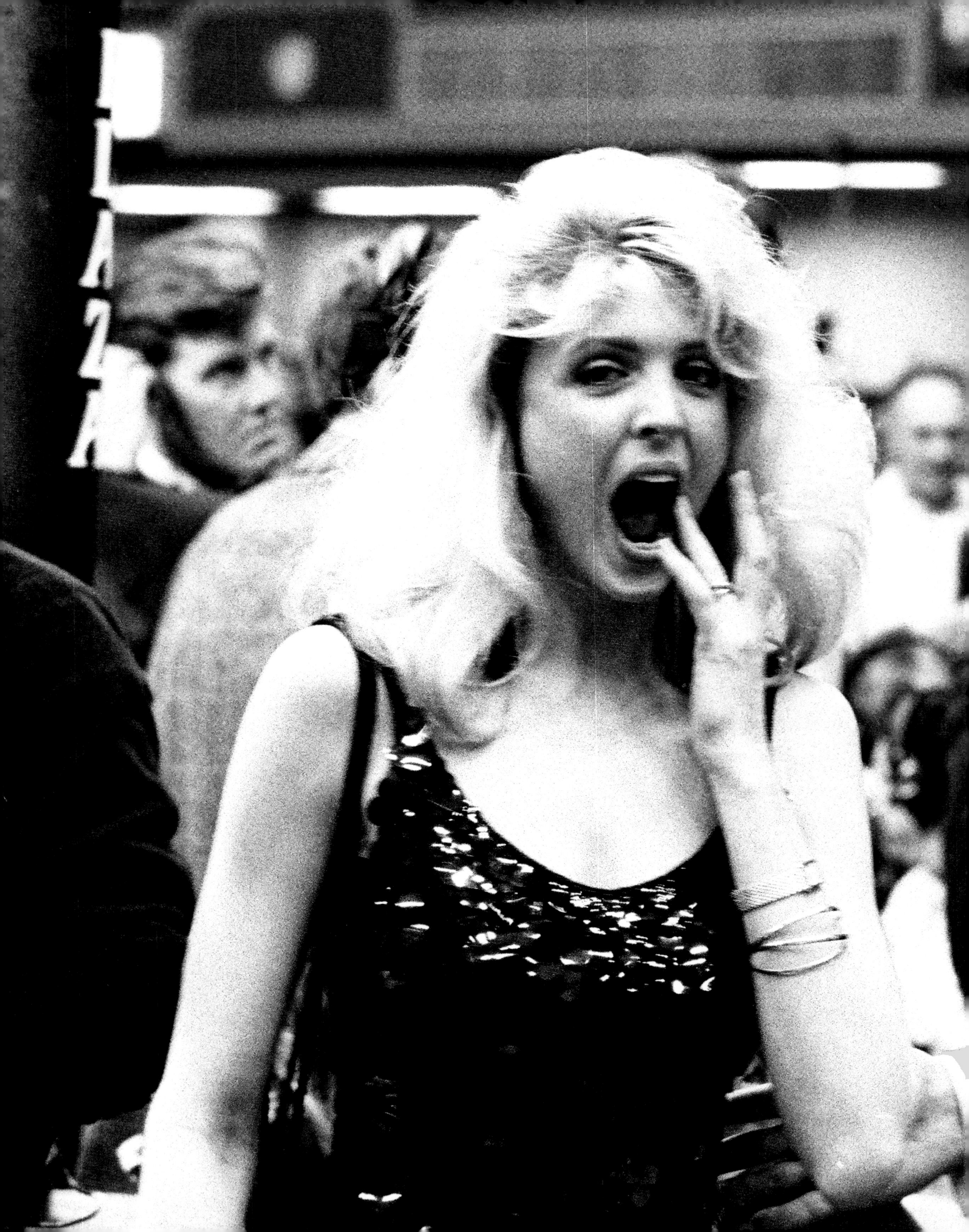

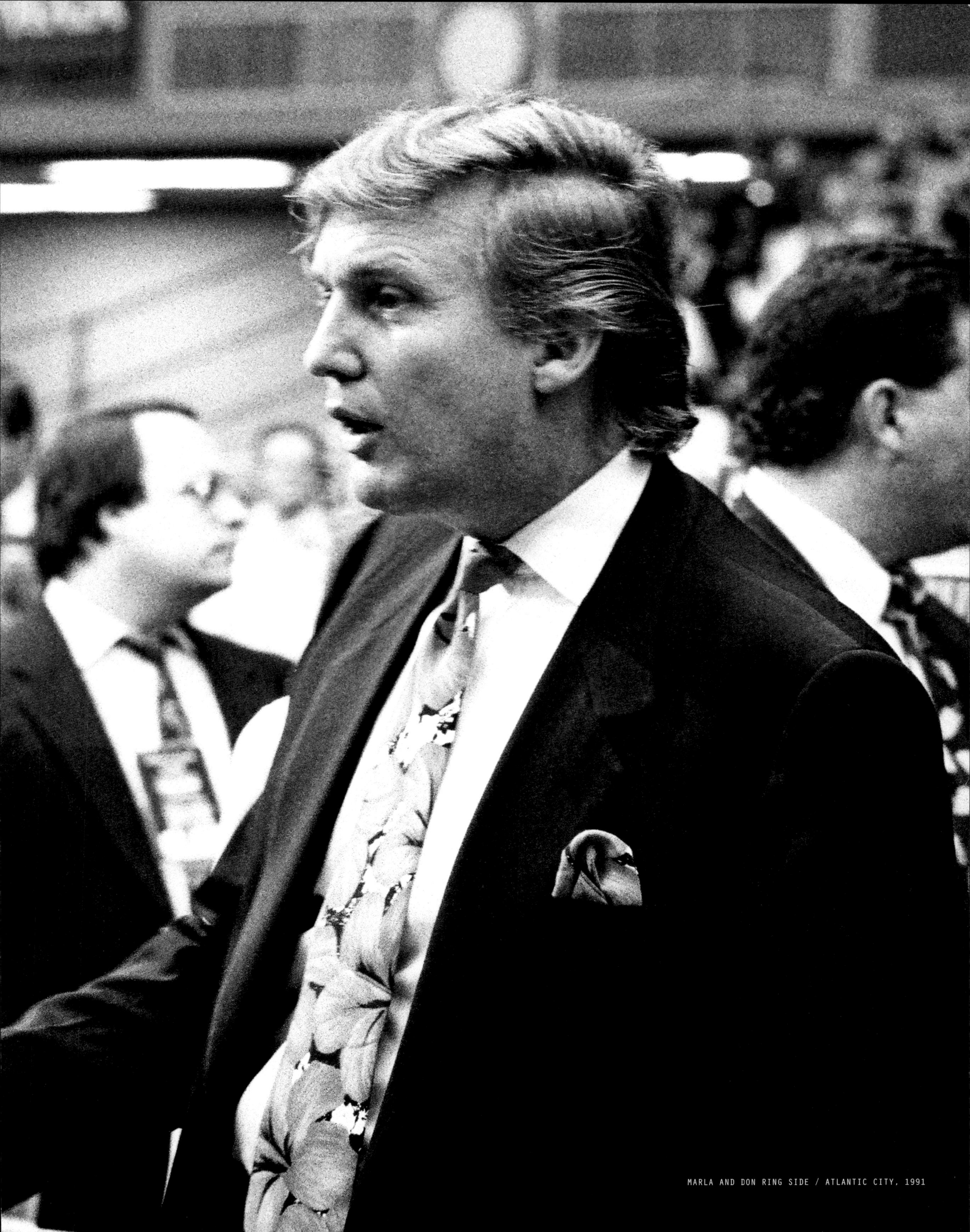

MARLA AND DON RING SIDE / ATLANTIC CITY, 1991

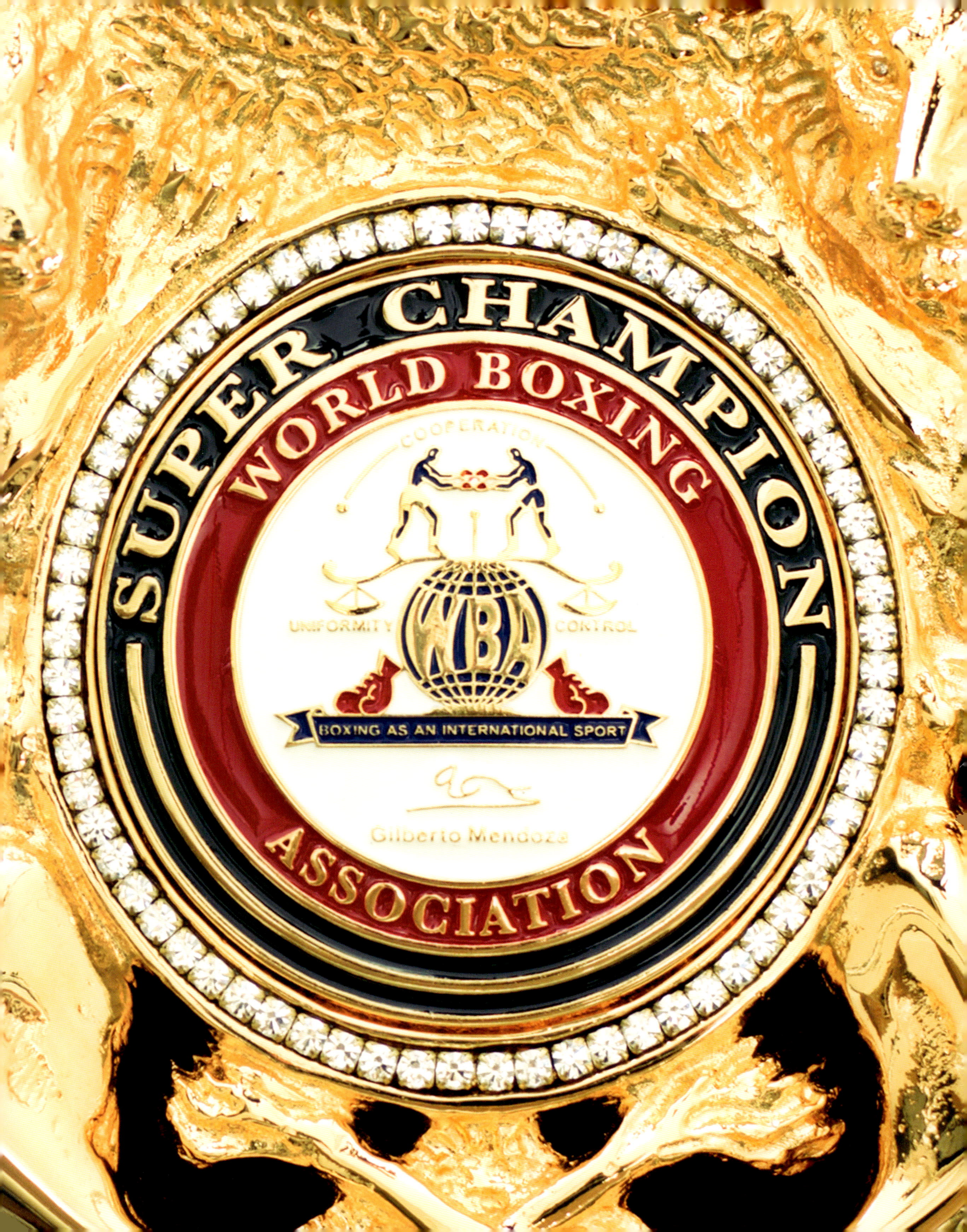

SUPER CHAMPION
WORLD BOXING
ASSOCIATION
COOPERATION
UNIFORMITY
CONTROL
WBA
BOXING AS AN INTERNATIONAL SPORT
Gilberto Mendoza

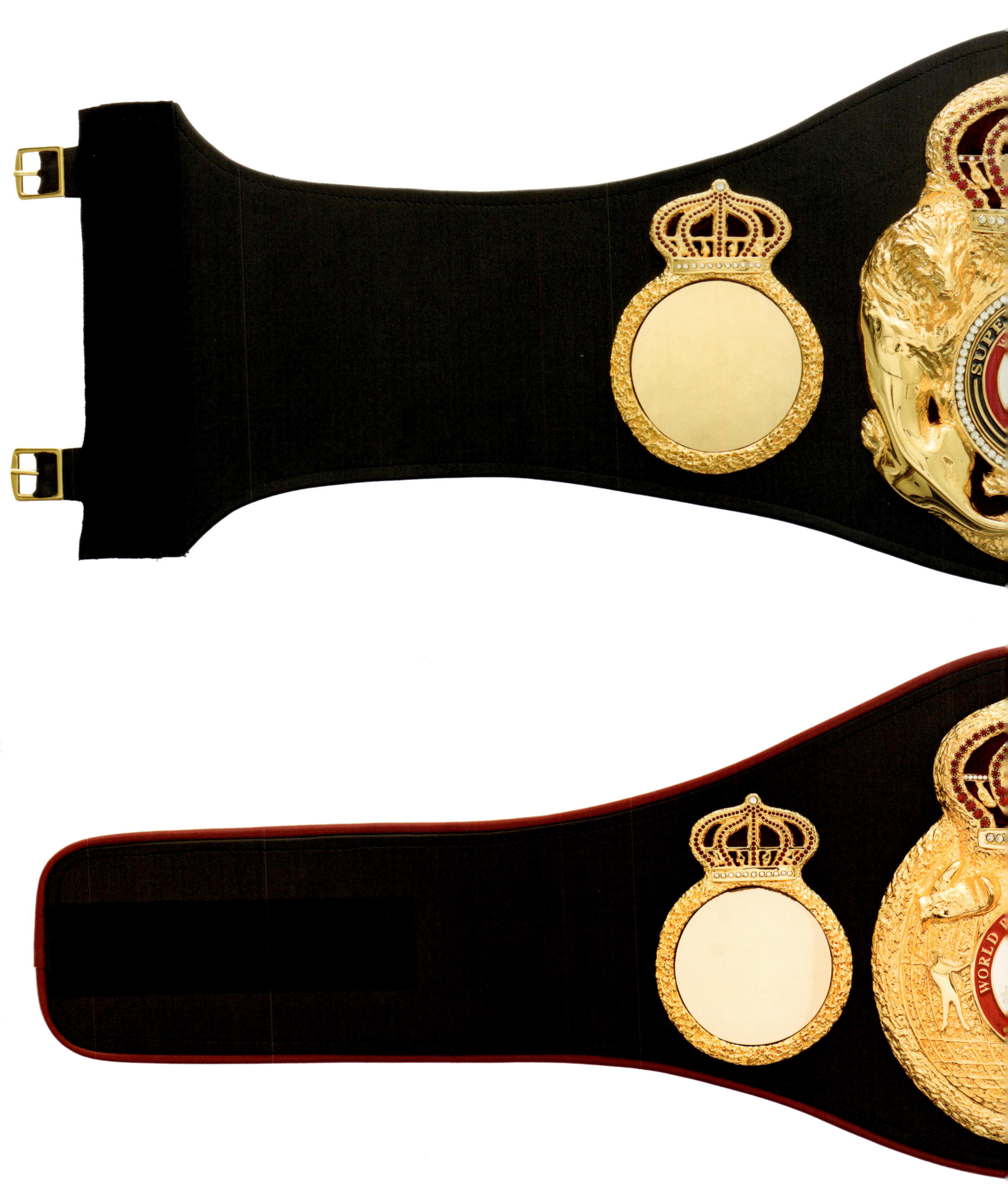

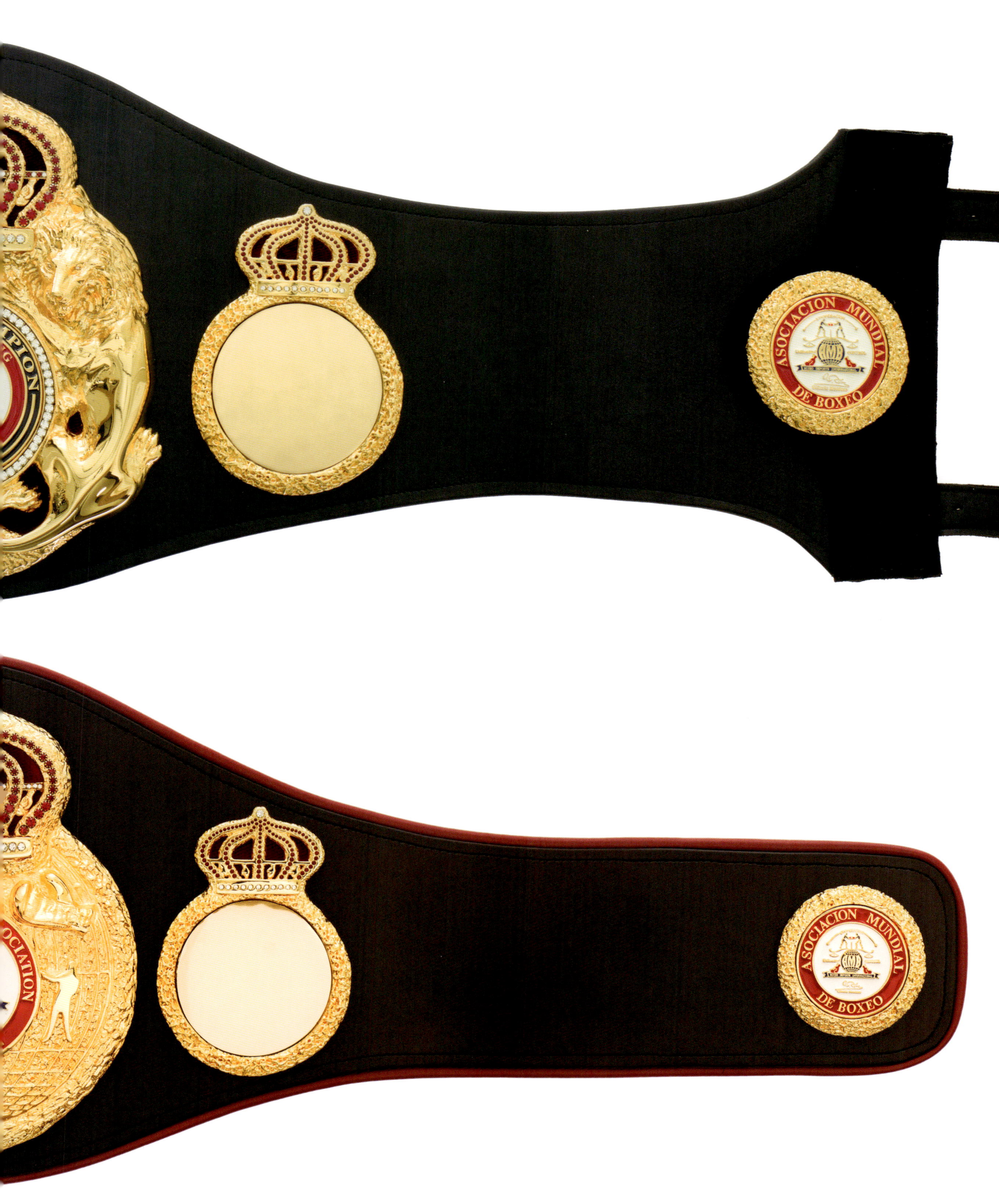

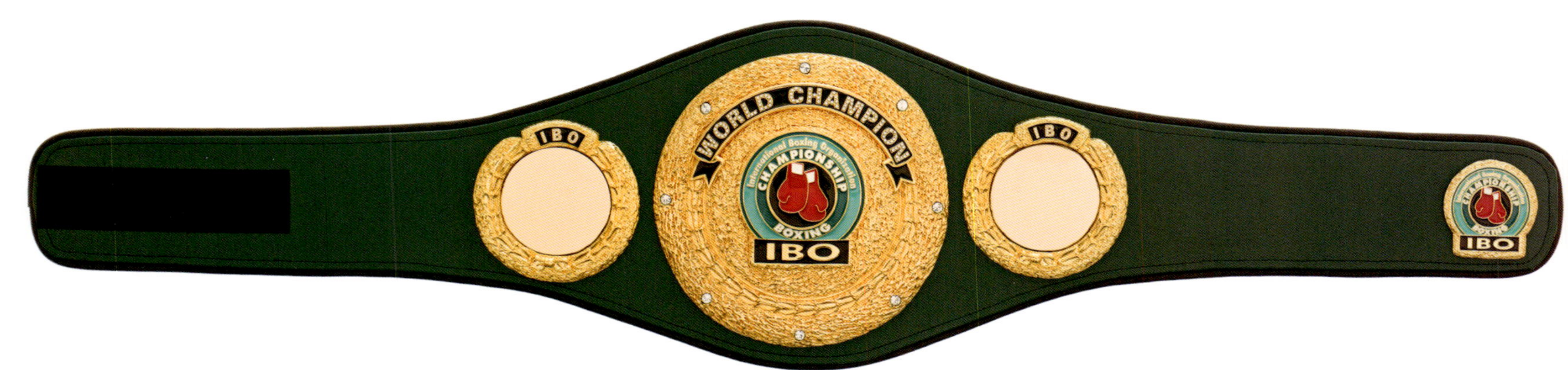

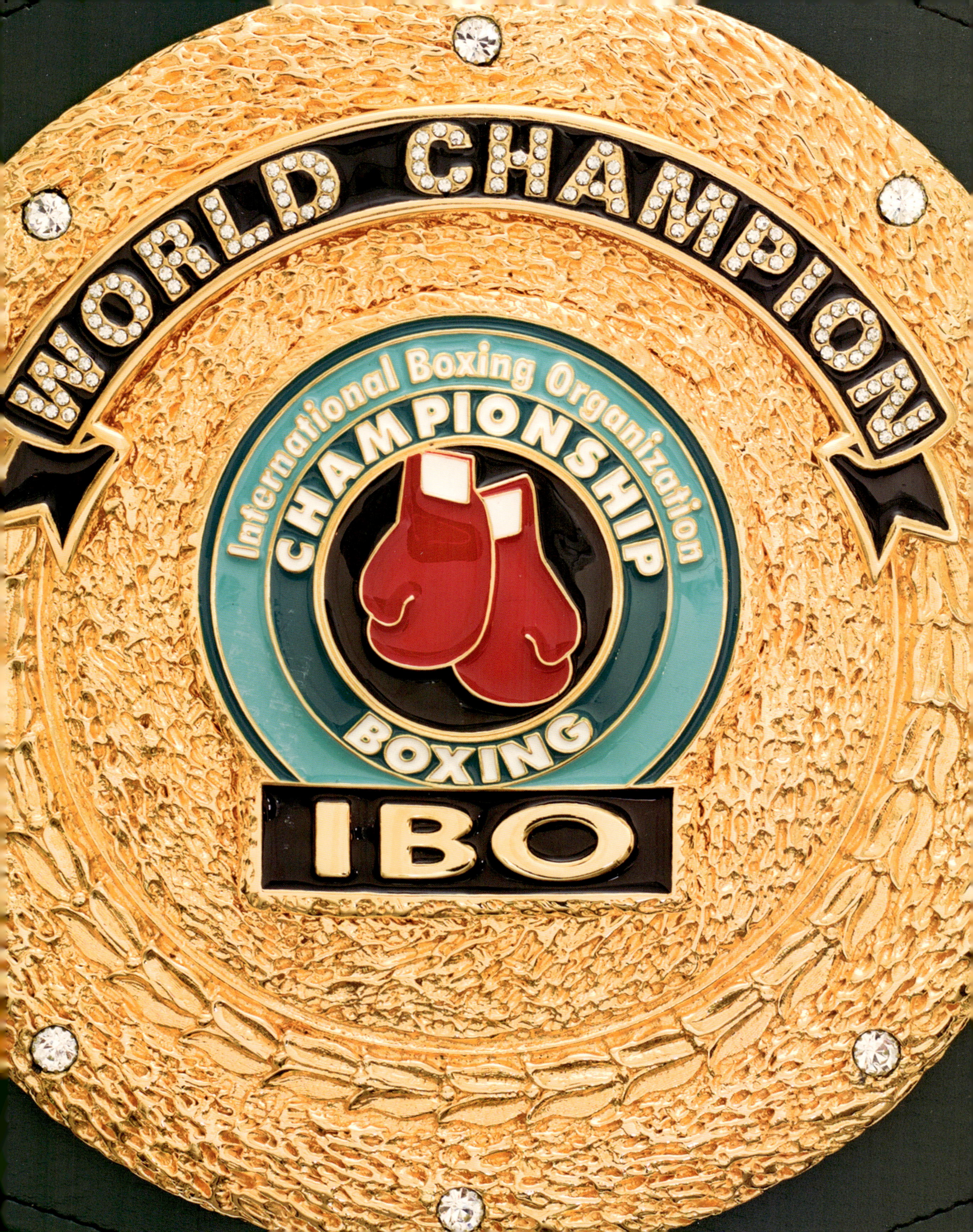

WORLD CHAMPION
International Boxing Organization
CHAMPIONSHIP
BOXING
IBO

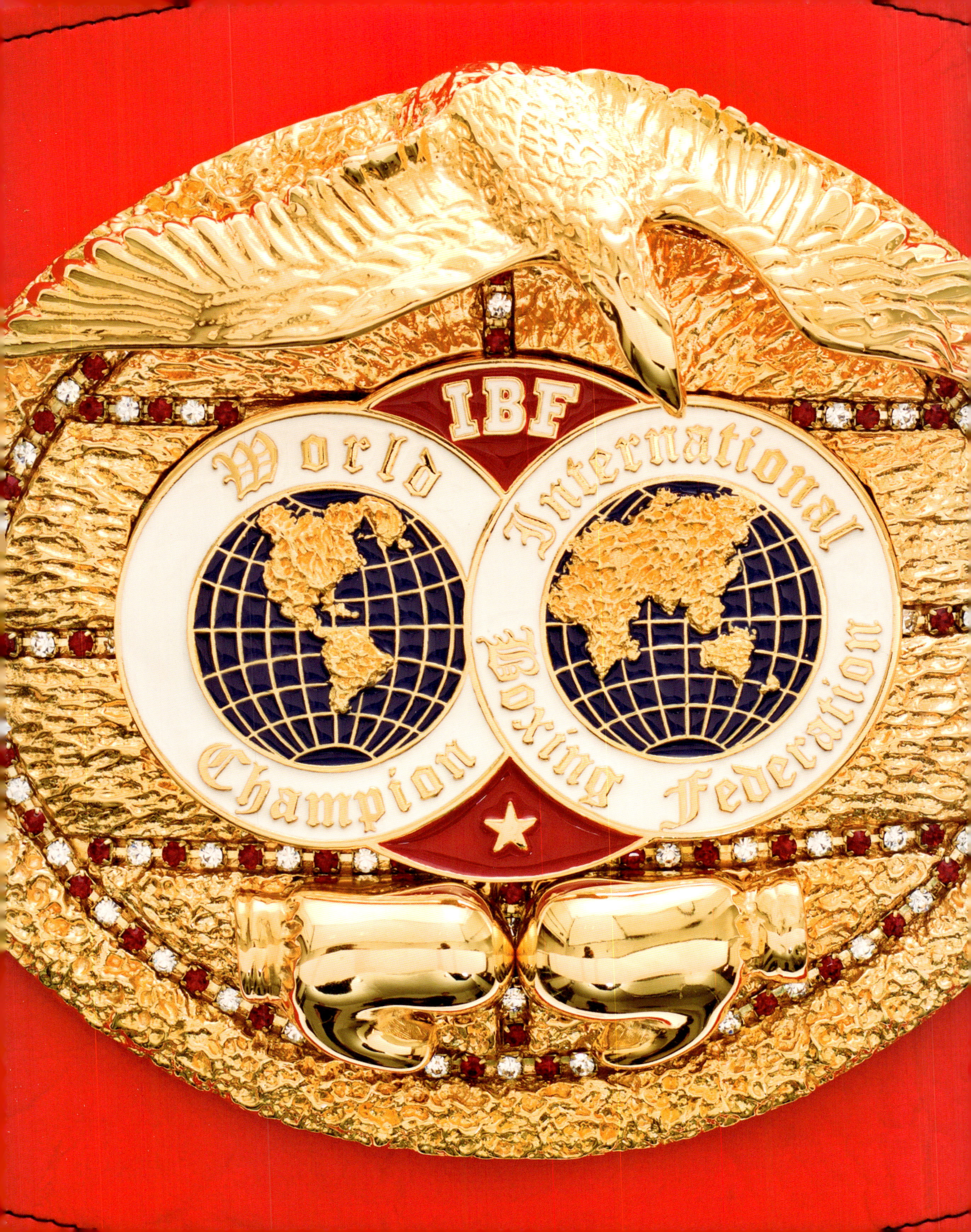

IBF
World
International
Champion
Boxing
Federation

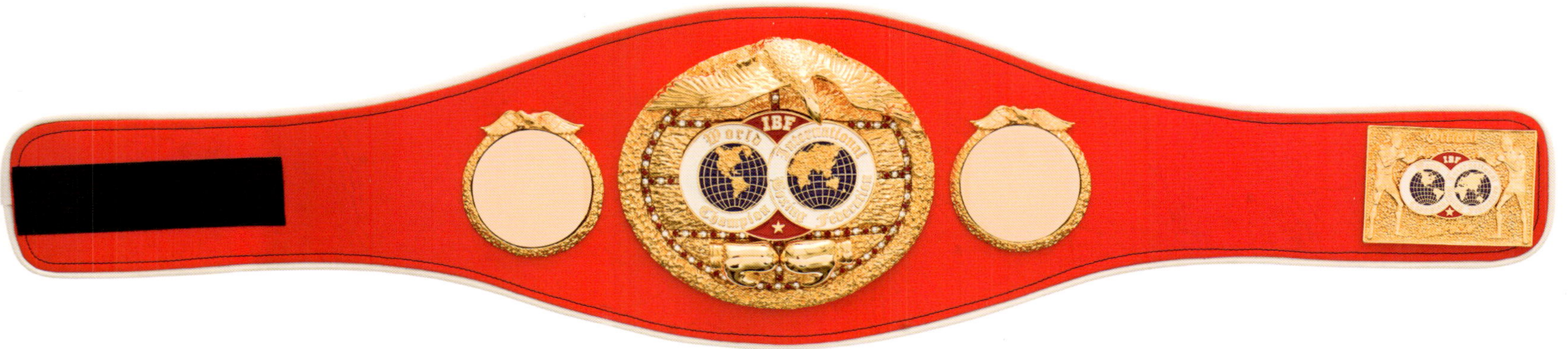

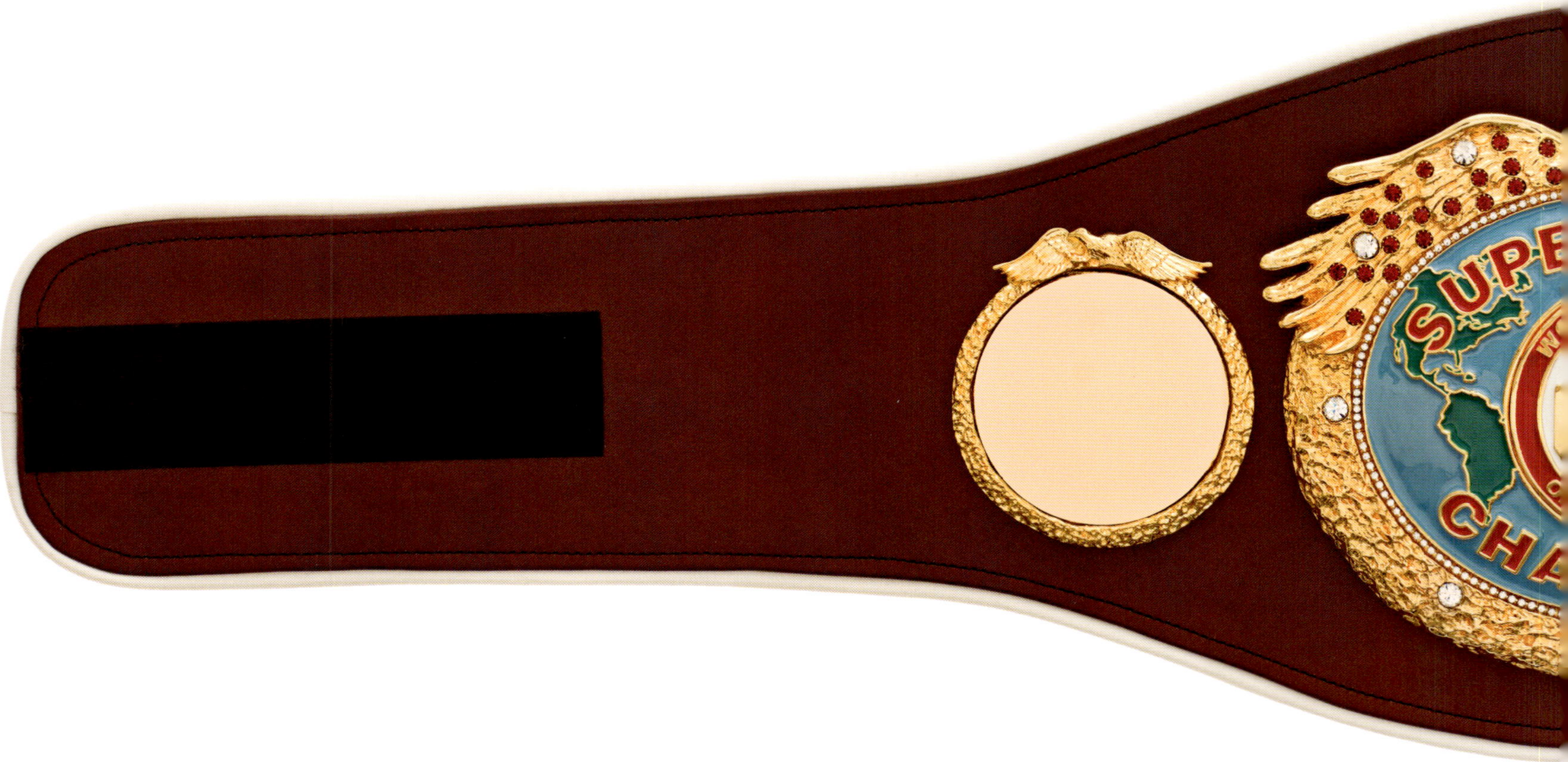

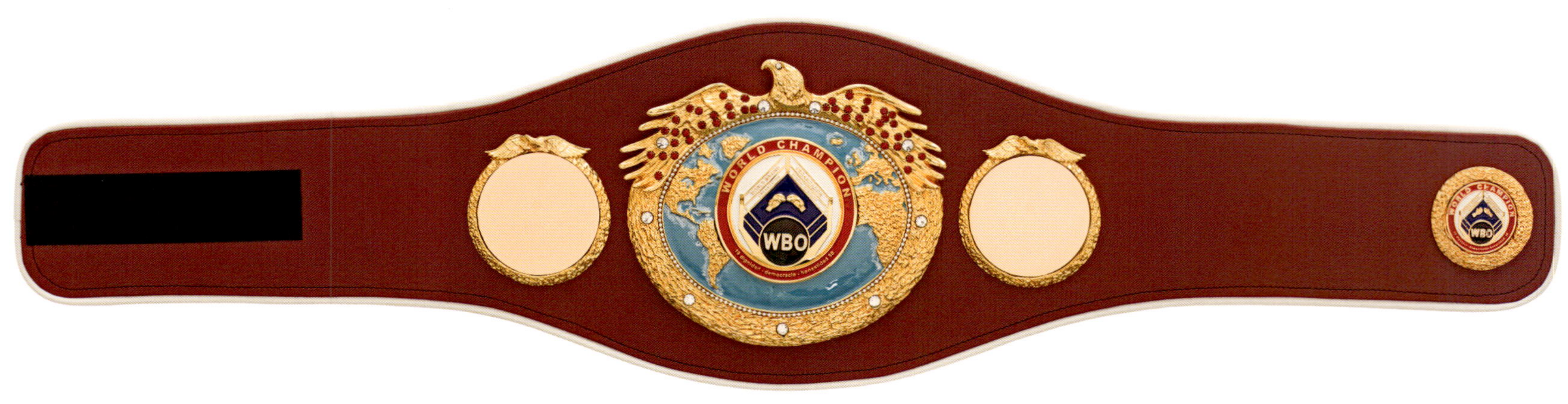

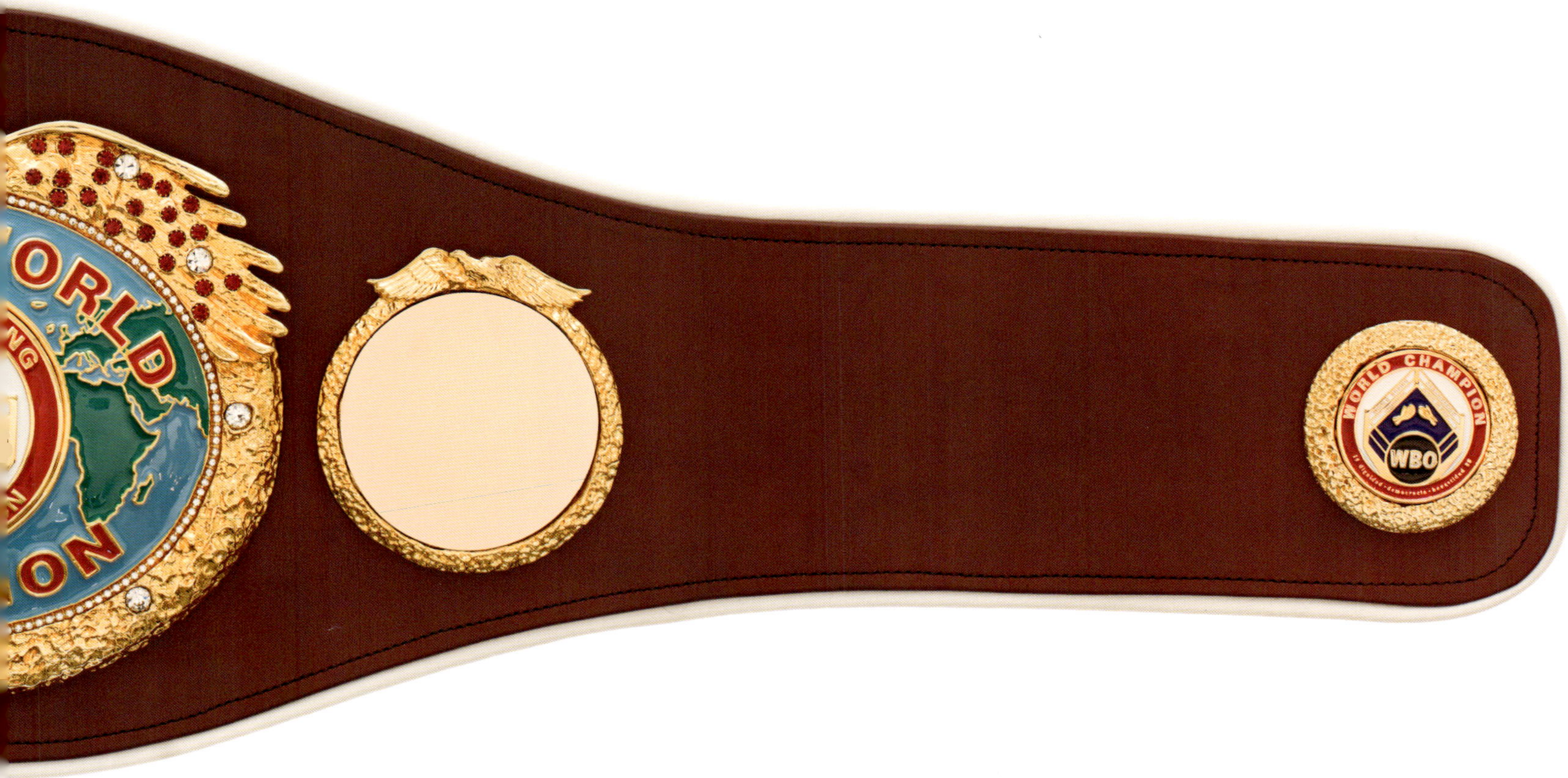

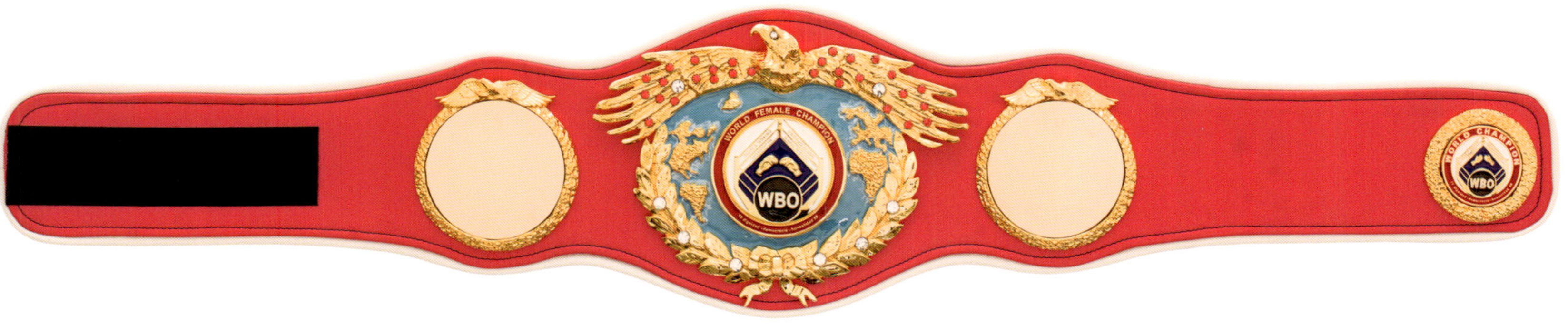

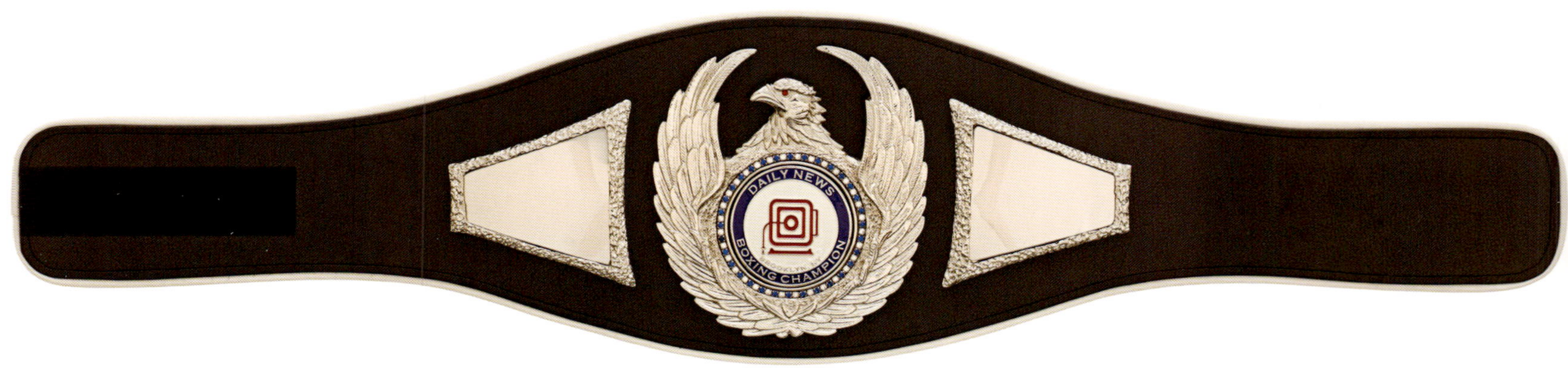

DAILY NEWS
BOXING CHAMPION

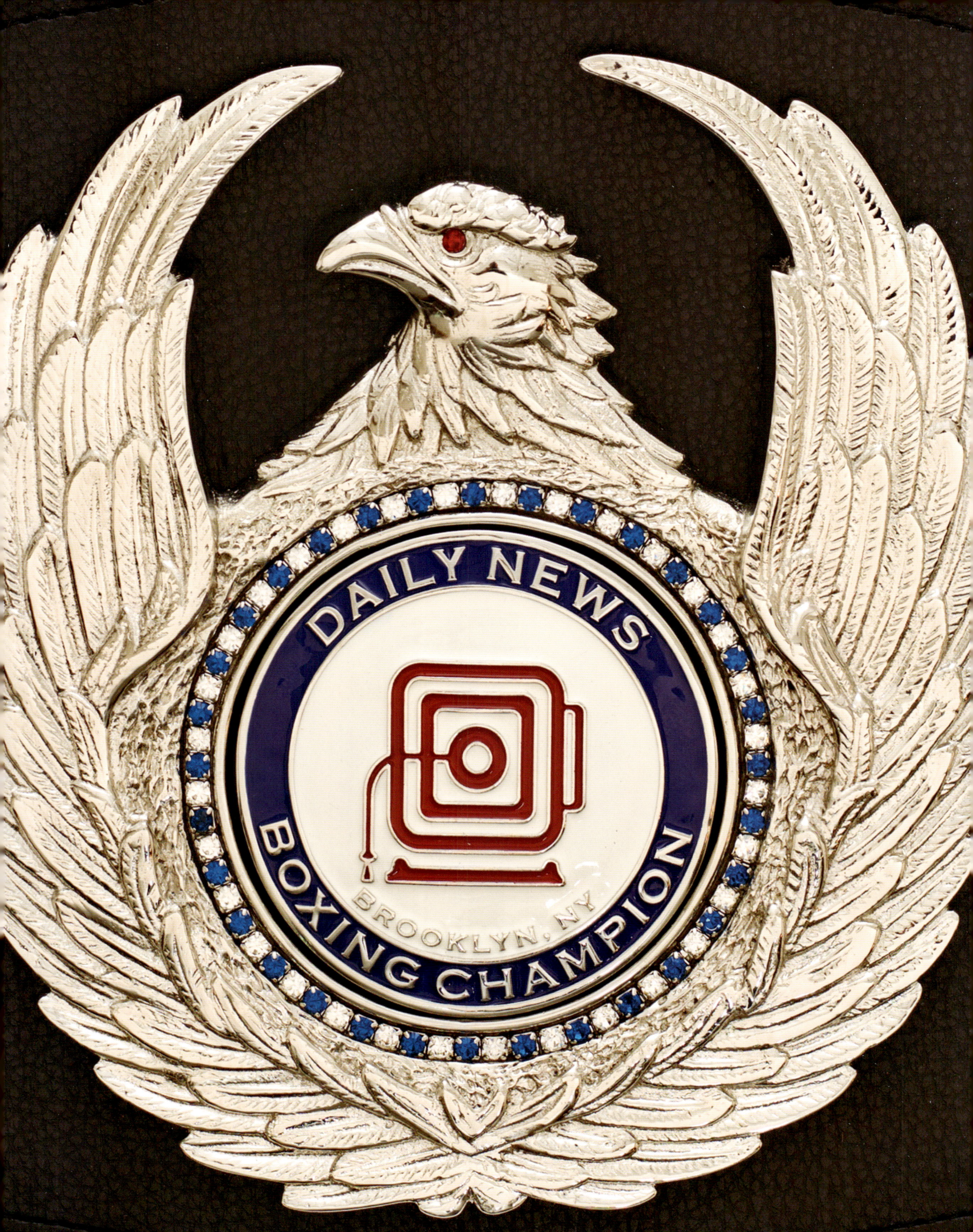

DAILY NEWS
BOXING CHAMPION
BROOKLYN, NY

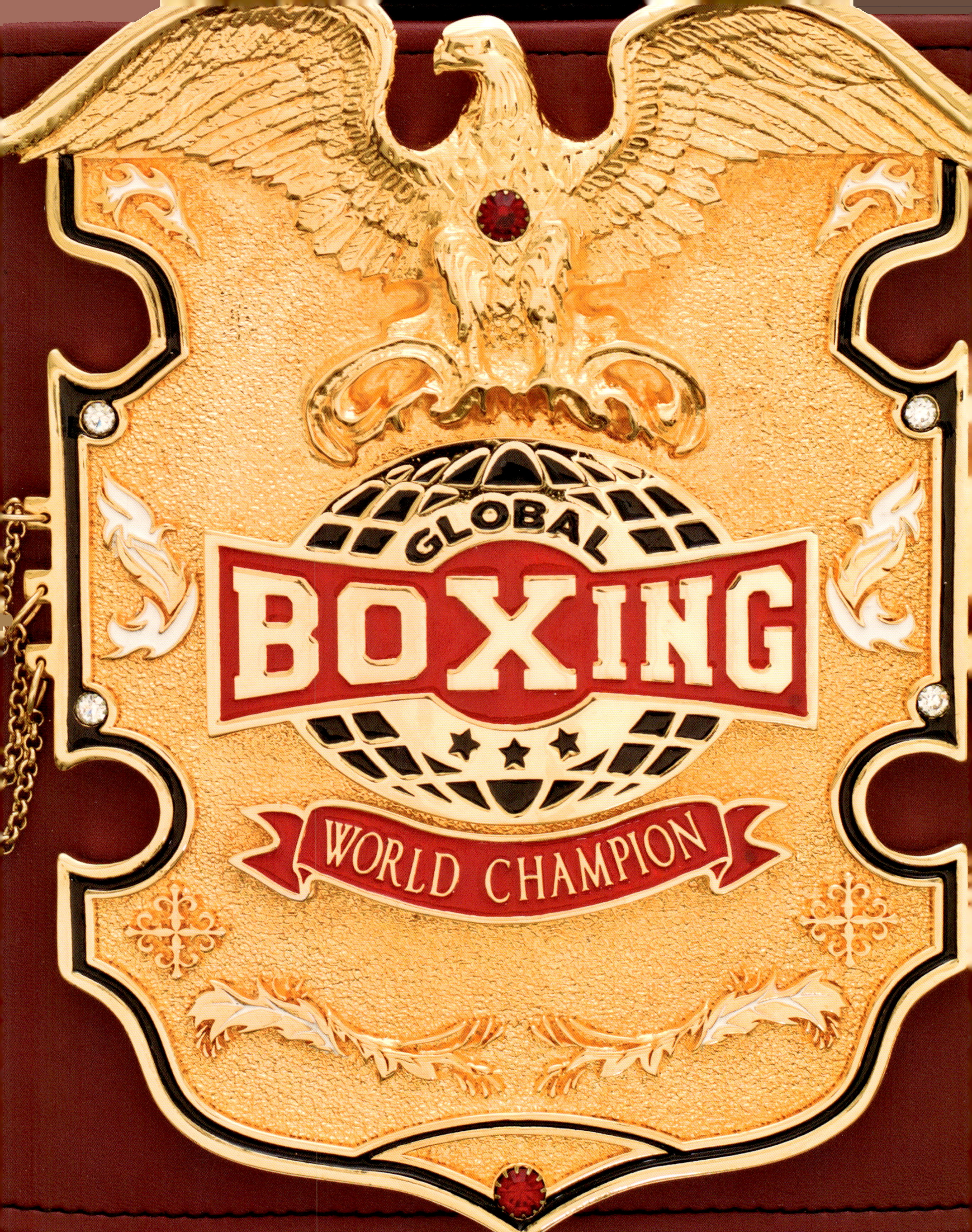

GLOBAL
BOXING
WORLD CHAMPION

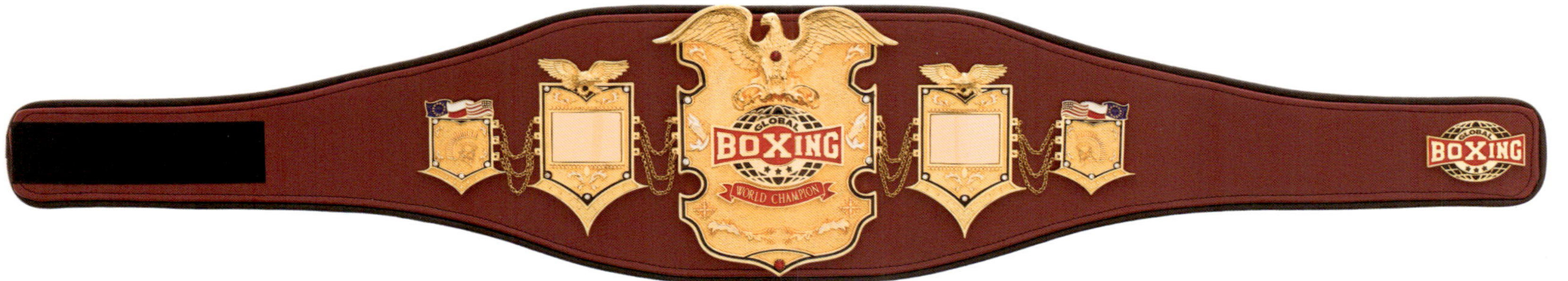

Boxing has always had a rich and colorful history. However, the sweet science is now as much a platform for entertainment as it is an athletic sport; the prizefight has transformed into a type of performance art - complete with costumes, visuals and audio. Entrance outfits are more structured to reflect the boxer's identity and fighters enter the ring with, at times, outlandish behavior, music and custom light shows. Flashes of colors and sequined costumes are now a product of the fighter's vivid imagination.

The following work created is not only a homage to boxing culture, but also to Puerto Rican immigration to America. Inspired by the boxers' use of fabric works, this new imagery is exuberant with color, texture, and patterns. It experiments with surfaces that create a visual dialogue between the physical charge of boxing (the garments worn by the fighters), themes of victory, craft-making and my own childhood upbringing as a first generation immigrant.

Along with these new works is a series of custom-made trophies that occupy the blue-collar trophy den space. These pieces are created for people like my father and mother who came to the U.S for a better life; they arrived with certain dreams and aspirations that never quite materialized but still achieved success in other aspects of their life.   CARLOS ROLON/DZINE

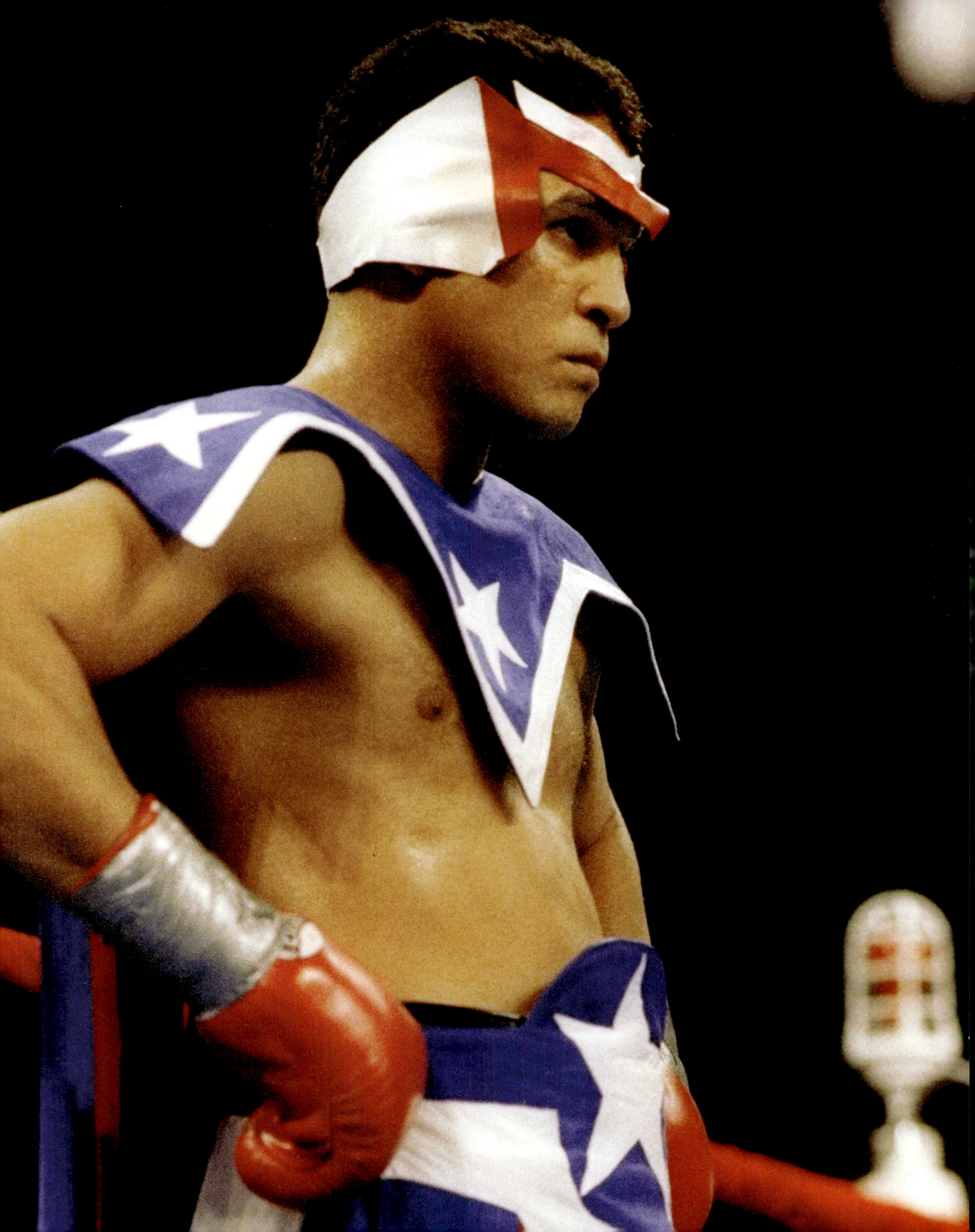

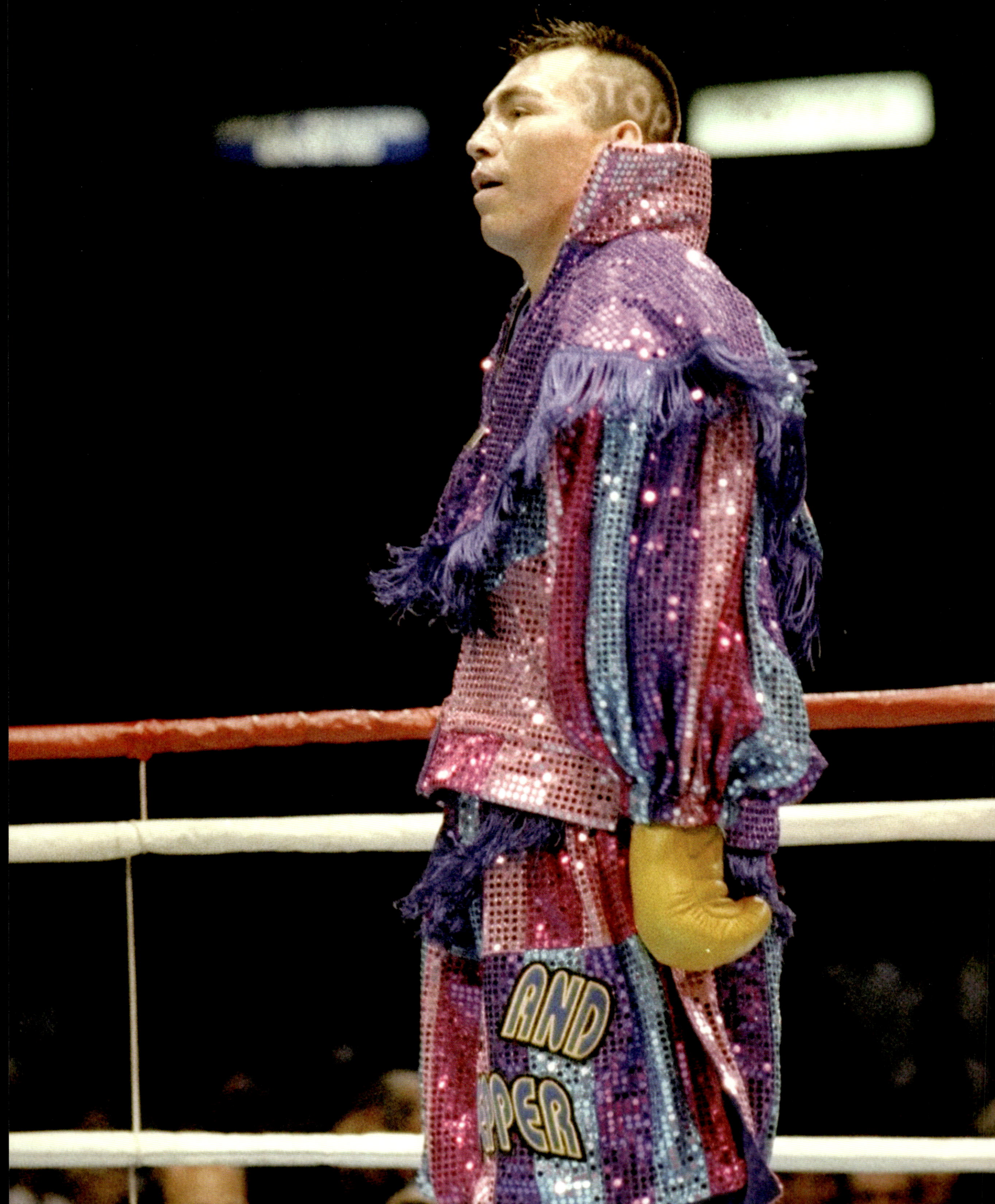
AND
PPER

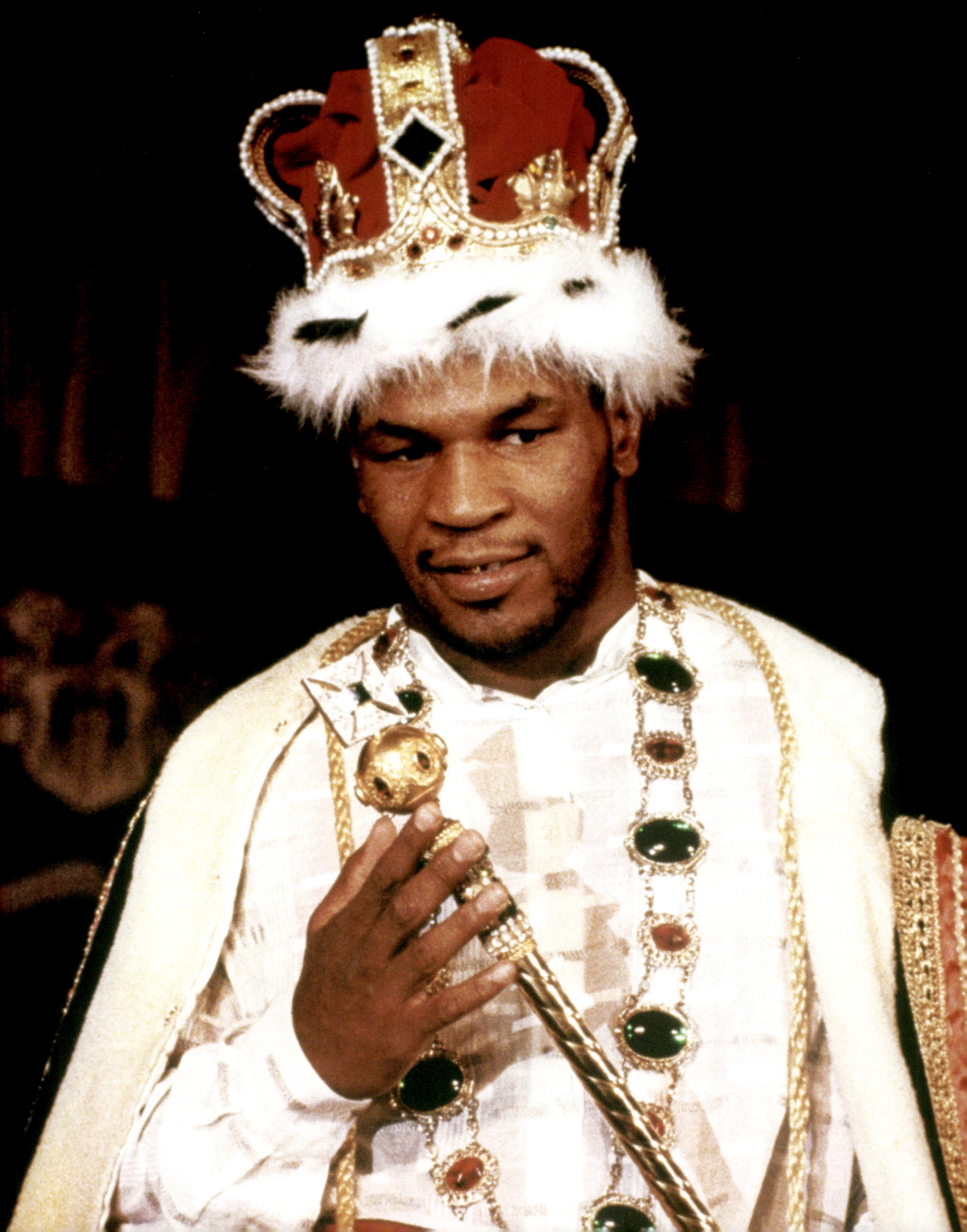

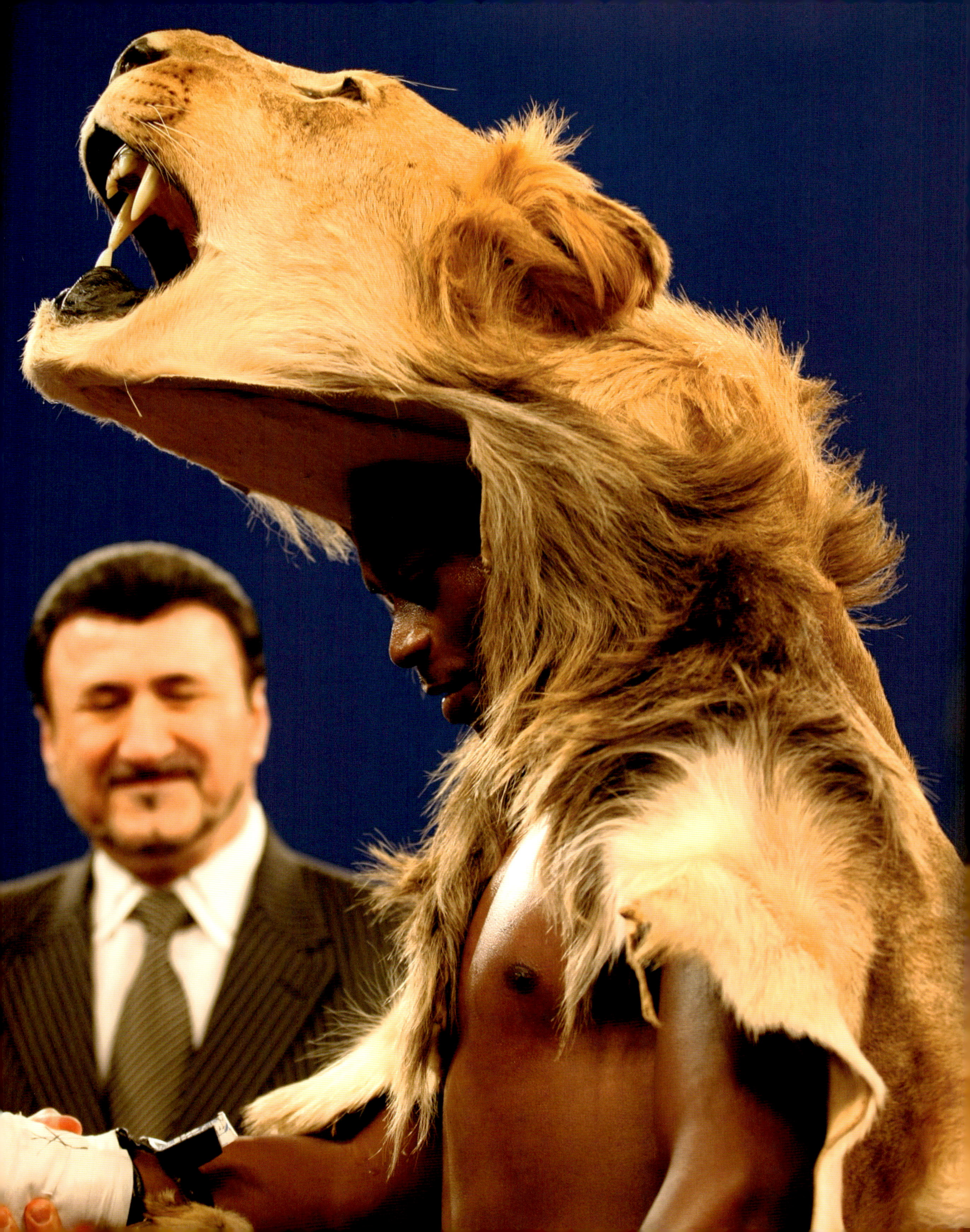

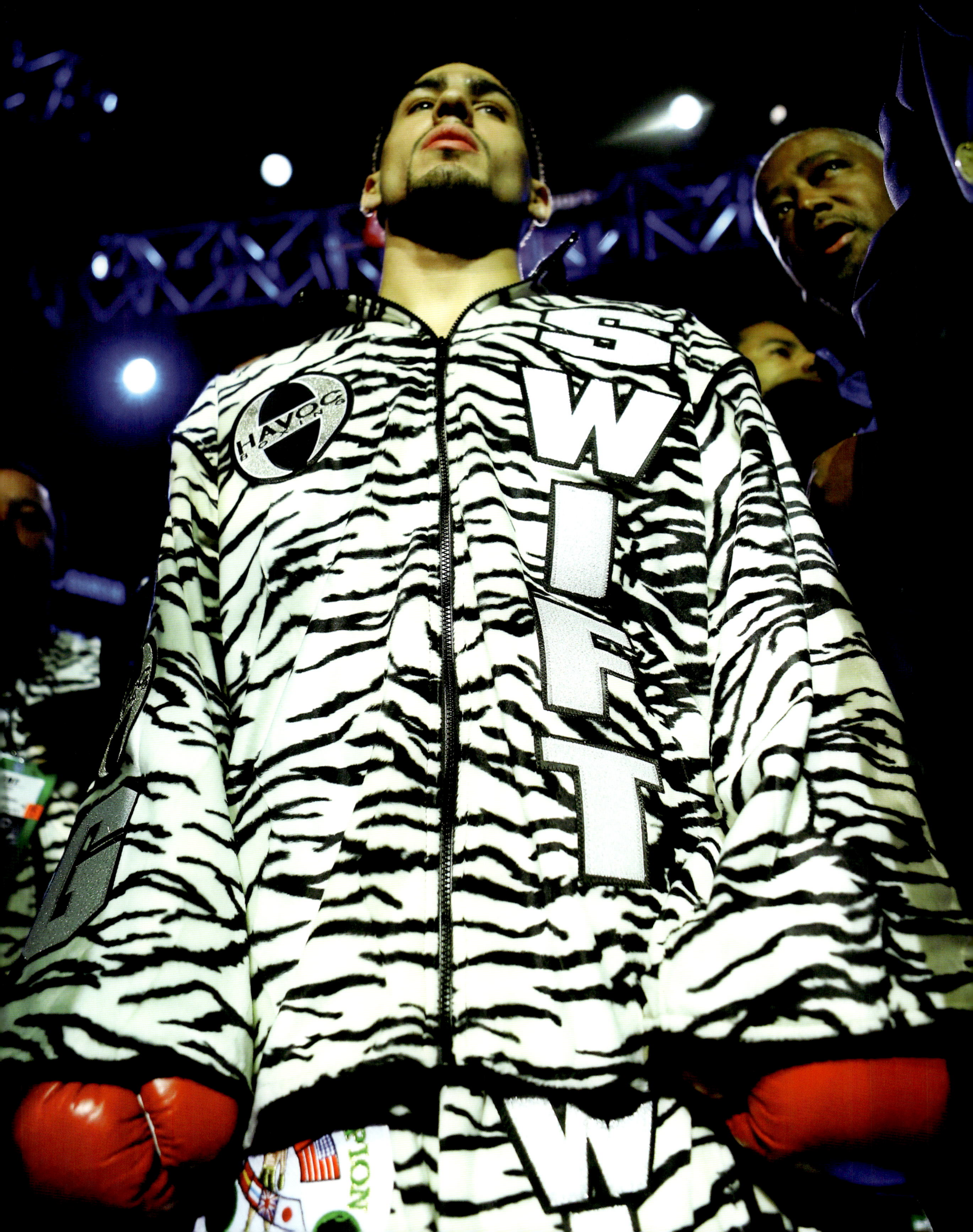

HAVOC
BOXING
S
W
I
F
T
S
W

DZINE: BORN, CARLOS ROLON, 1970
[PAUL KASMIN GALLERY NYC 2014]

PALM OF VICTORY [PATTERNED RGBES], 2014 - ACRYLIC, CRYSTALLINE, FLOCKING AND QUARTZ CRYSTALS ON WOOD PANEL / 40 X 40 X 2 1/2 INCHES
COURTESY OF PAUL KASMIN GALLERY

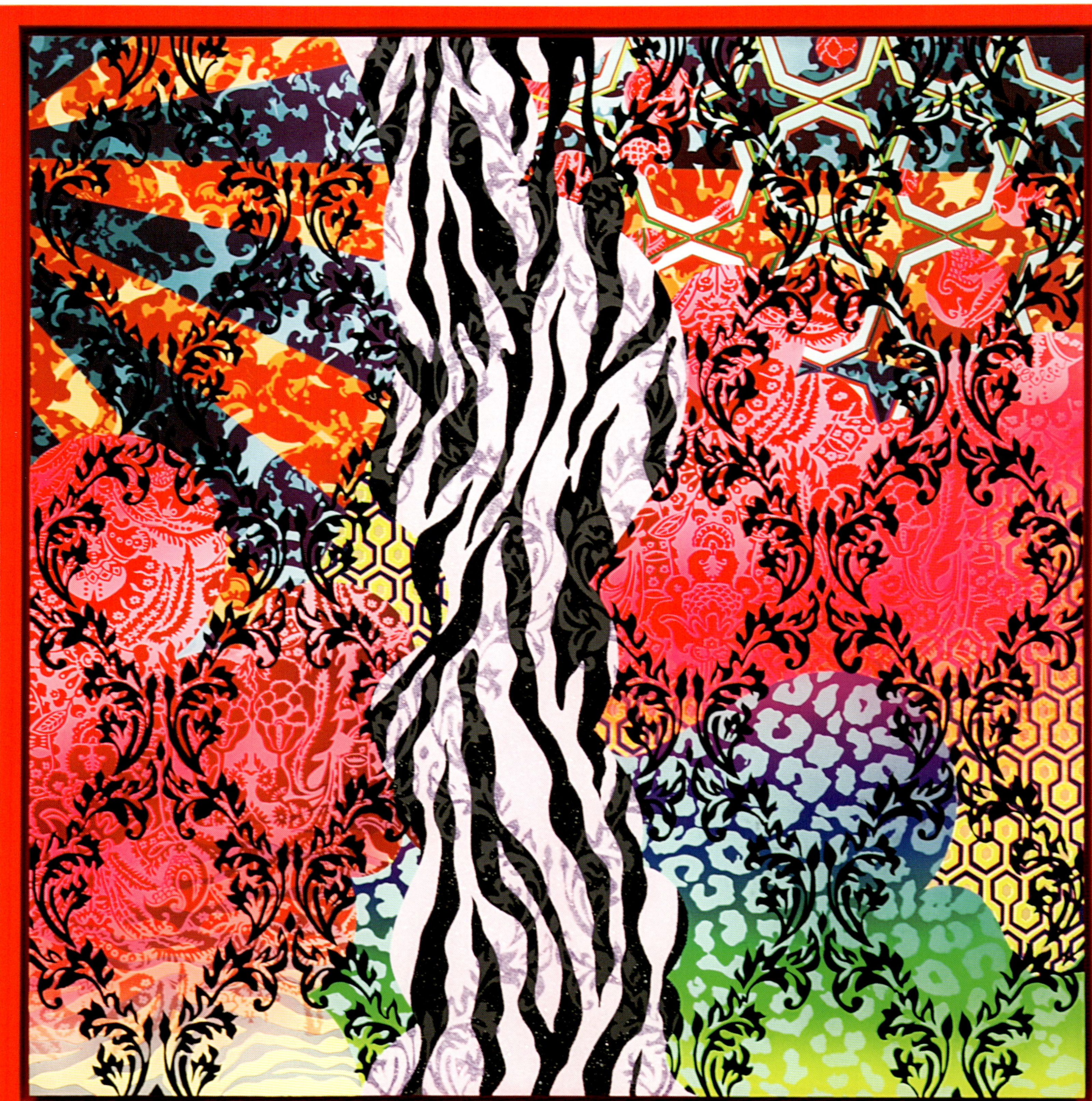

CAMACHO, 2014 - SEQUINS, FRINGE, GOLD GLASS BEADS, CLEAR GLASS BEADS, FELT AND VINTAGE FABRIC MOUNTED ON WOOD PANEL / 36 X 36 X 2 1/2 INCHES
COURTESY OF PAUL KASMIN GALLERY

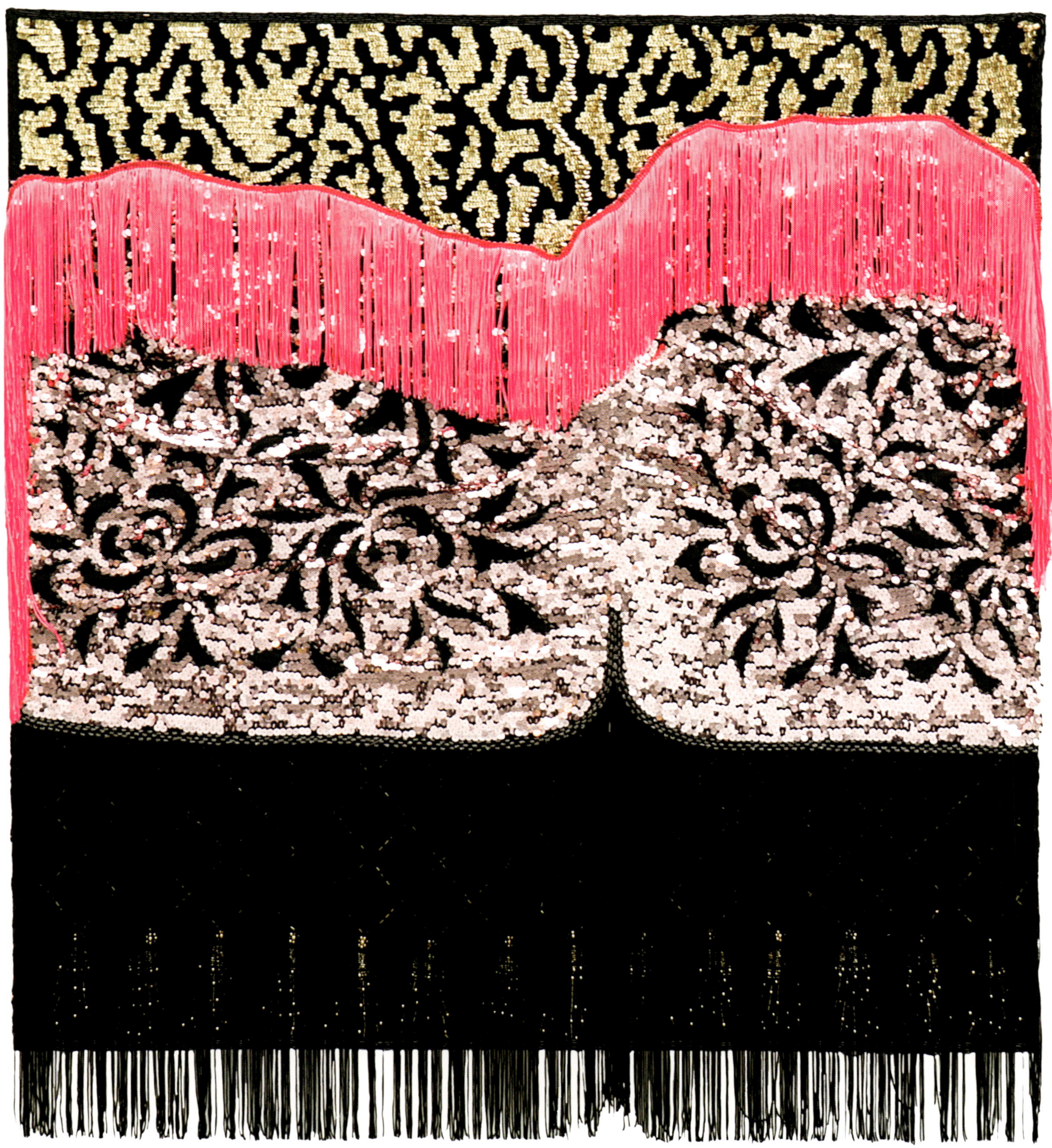

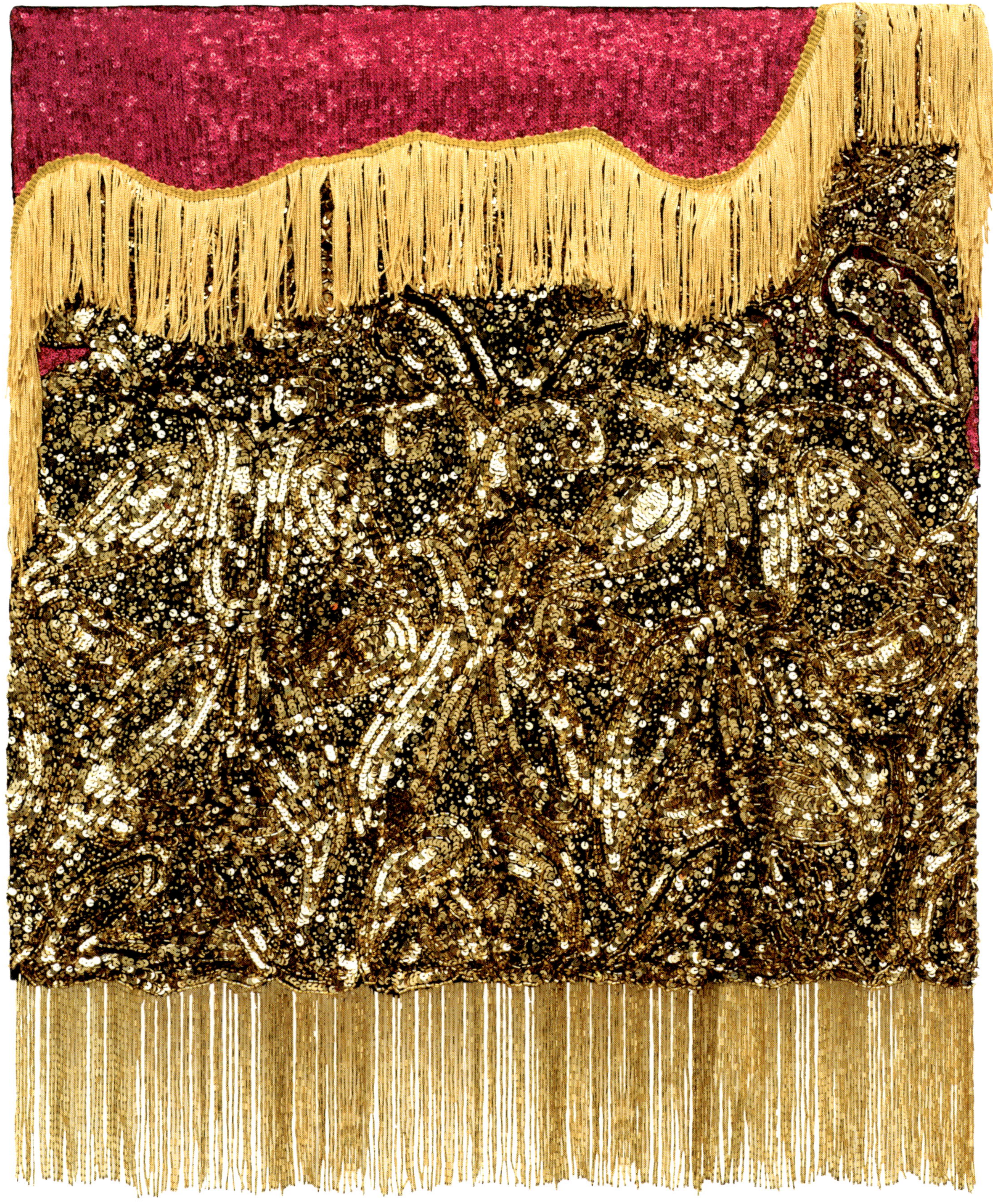

GOLDEN BOY, 2014 - SEQUINS, FRINGE, GOLD GLASS BEADS, FELT AND VINTAGE FABRIC MOUNTED ON WOOD PANEL / 24 X 24 X 2 1/2 INCHES
COURTESY OF PAUL KASMIN GALLERY

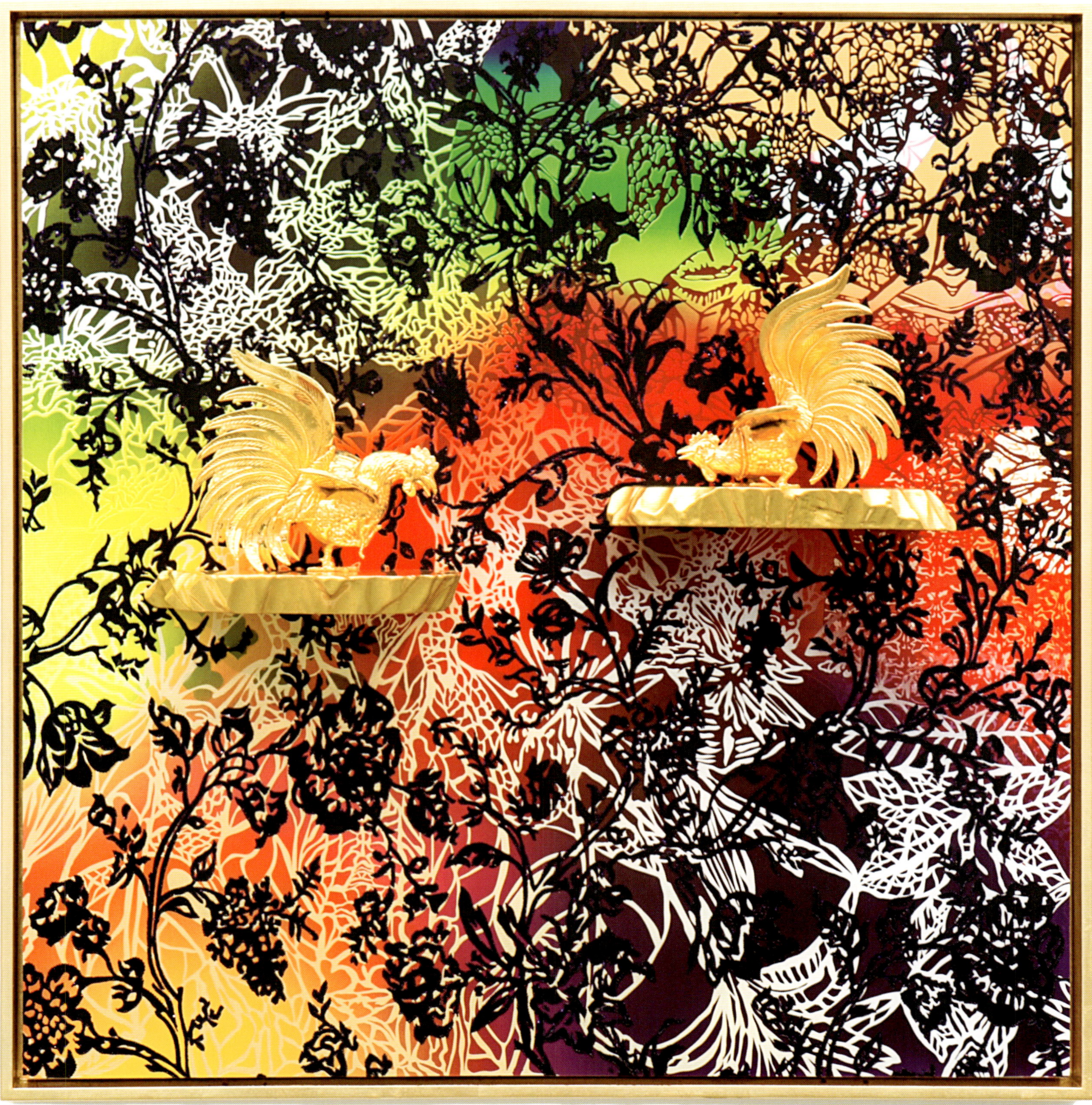

COCKFIGHT [CLUB GALLISTICO], 2014 - ACRYLIC, QUARTZ CRYSTALS, SPANISH CEDAR, 24 KT. GOLD LEAF, METAL AND GOLD PLATING ON WOOD PANEL / 40 X 40 X 2 1/2 INCHES
COURTESY OF PAUL KASMIN GALLERY

UNTITLED [BELT CREST], 2014 - ACRYLIC, CRYSTALLINE, AND QUARTZ CRYSTAL ON WOOD PANEL / 40 X 40 X 2 1/2 INCHES
COURTESY OF PAUL KASMIN GALLERY

[OPPOSITE] *HEAVYWEIGHT*, 2014 - ACRYLIC, CRYSTALLINE, QUARTZ CRYSTALS ON WOOD PANEL / 92 X 116 X 4 INCHES
COURTESY OF PAUL KASMIN GALLERY

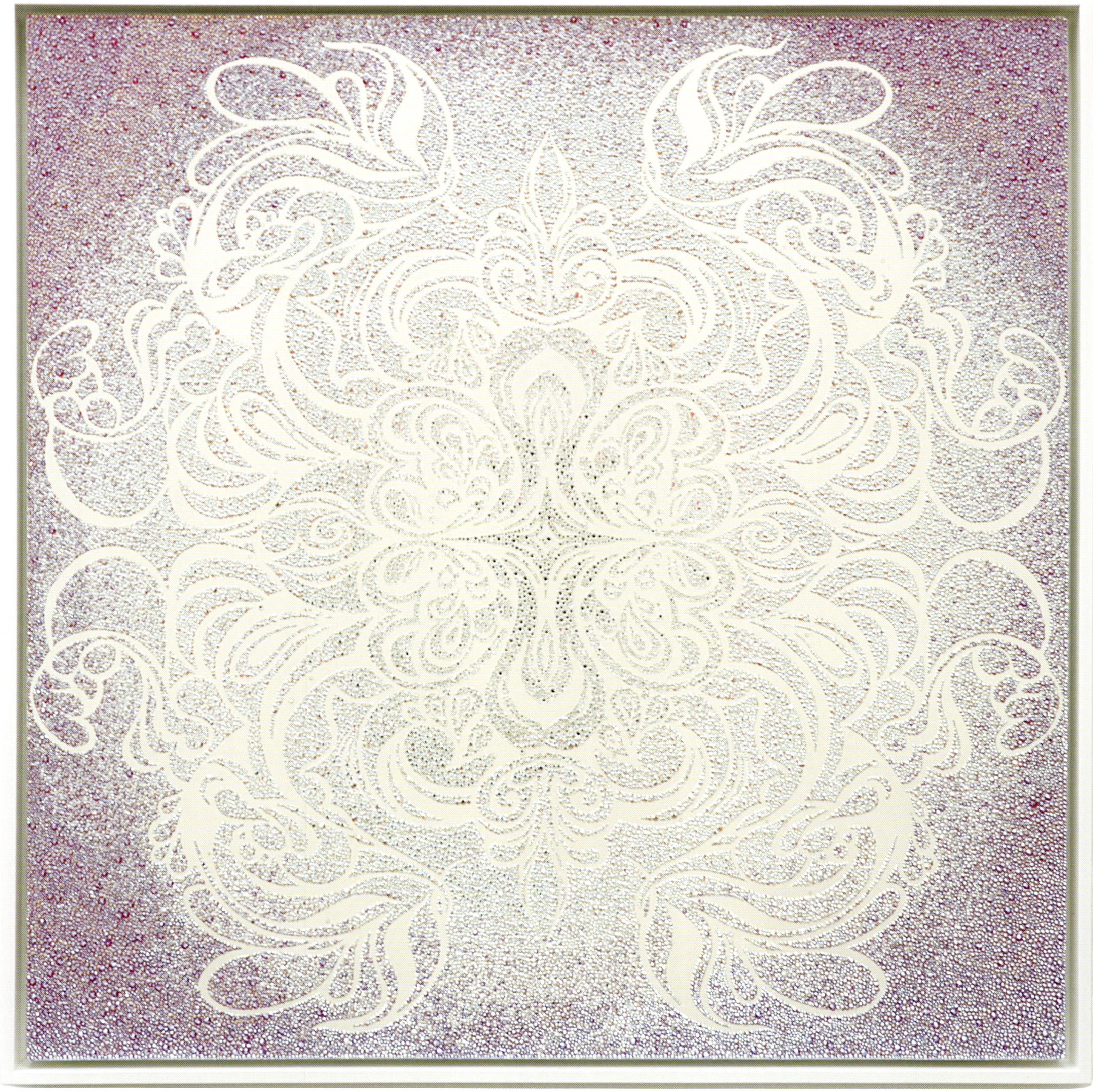

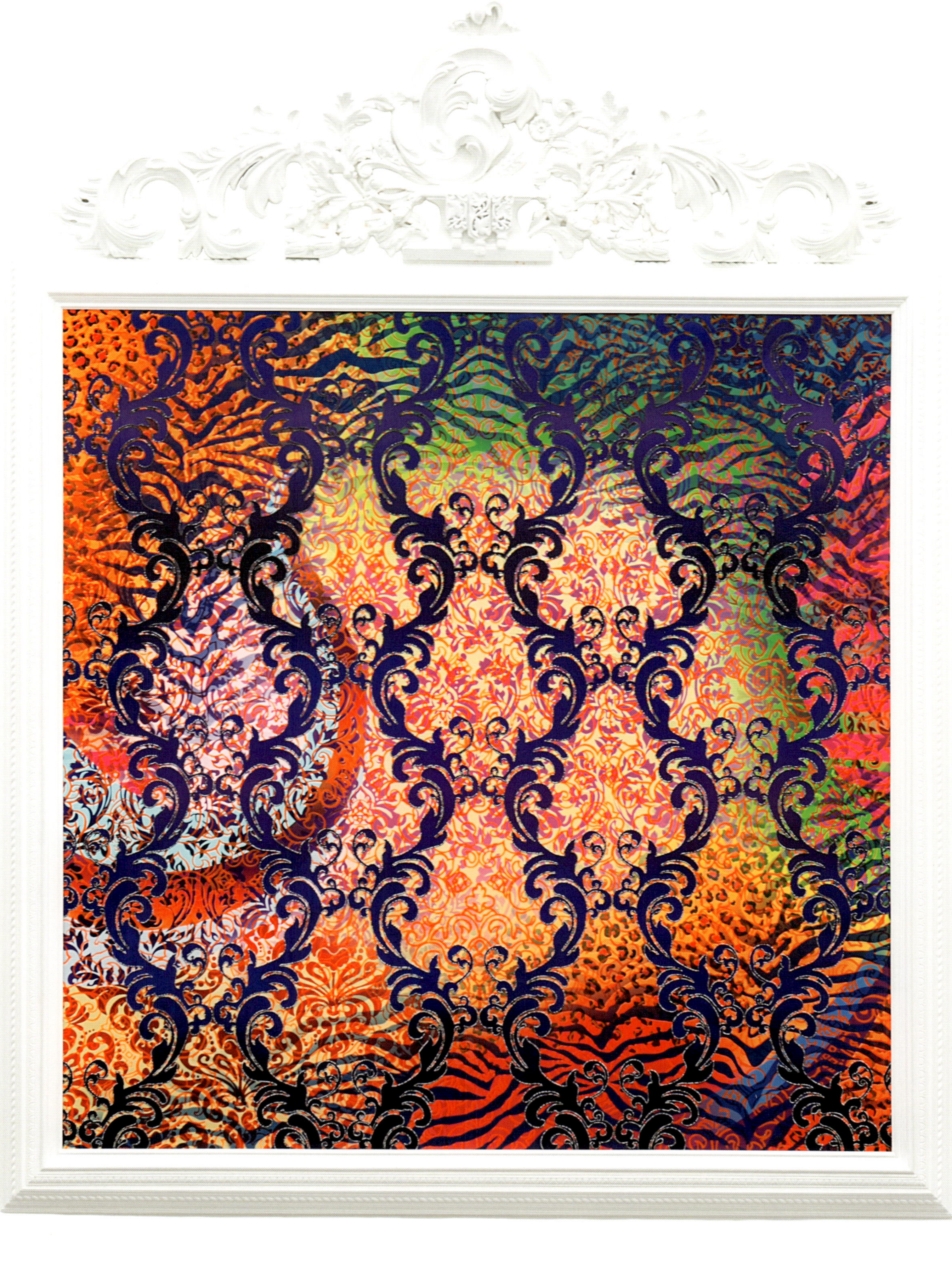

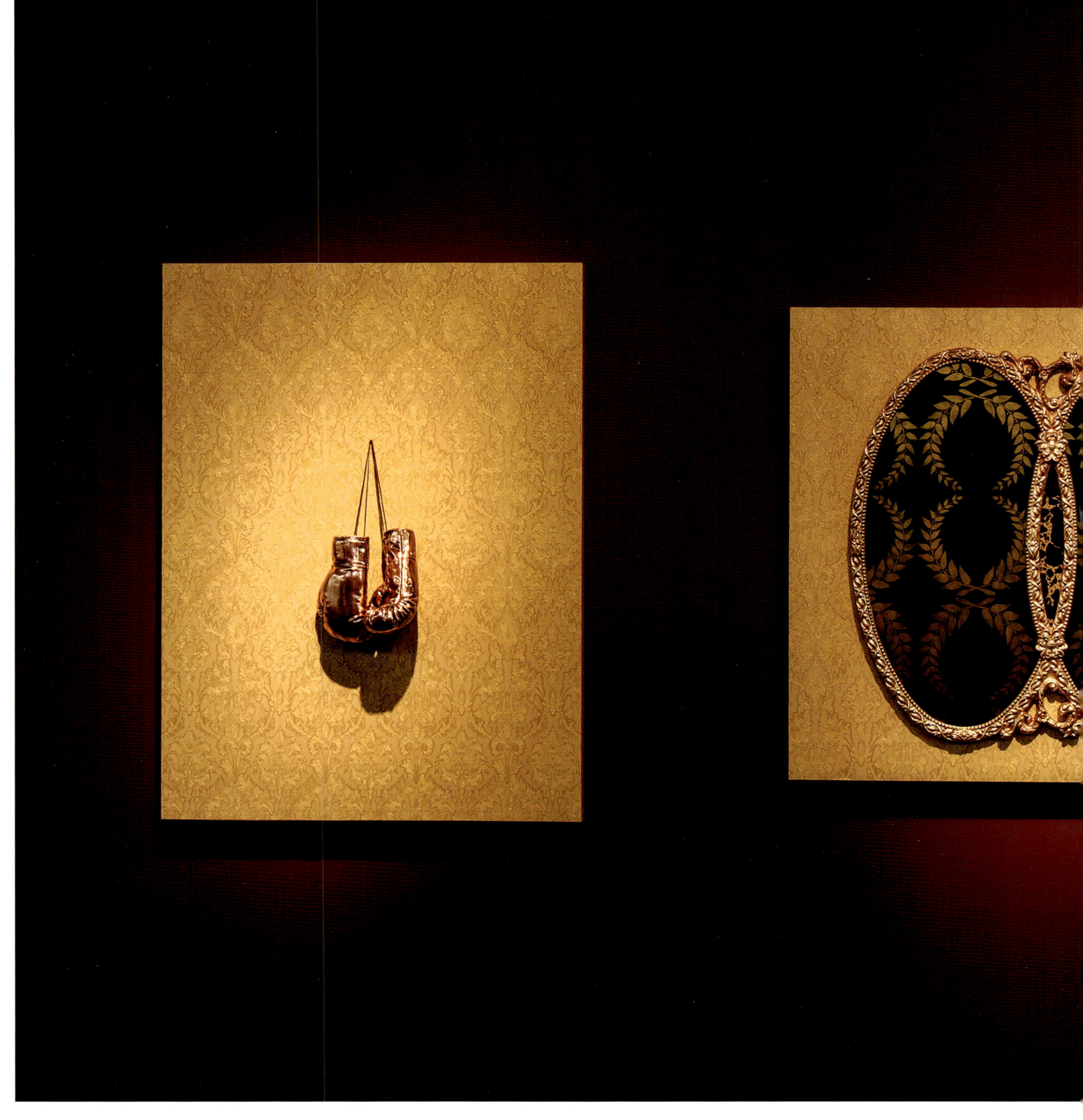

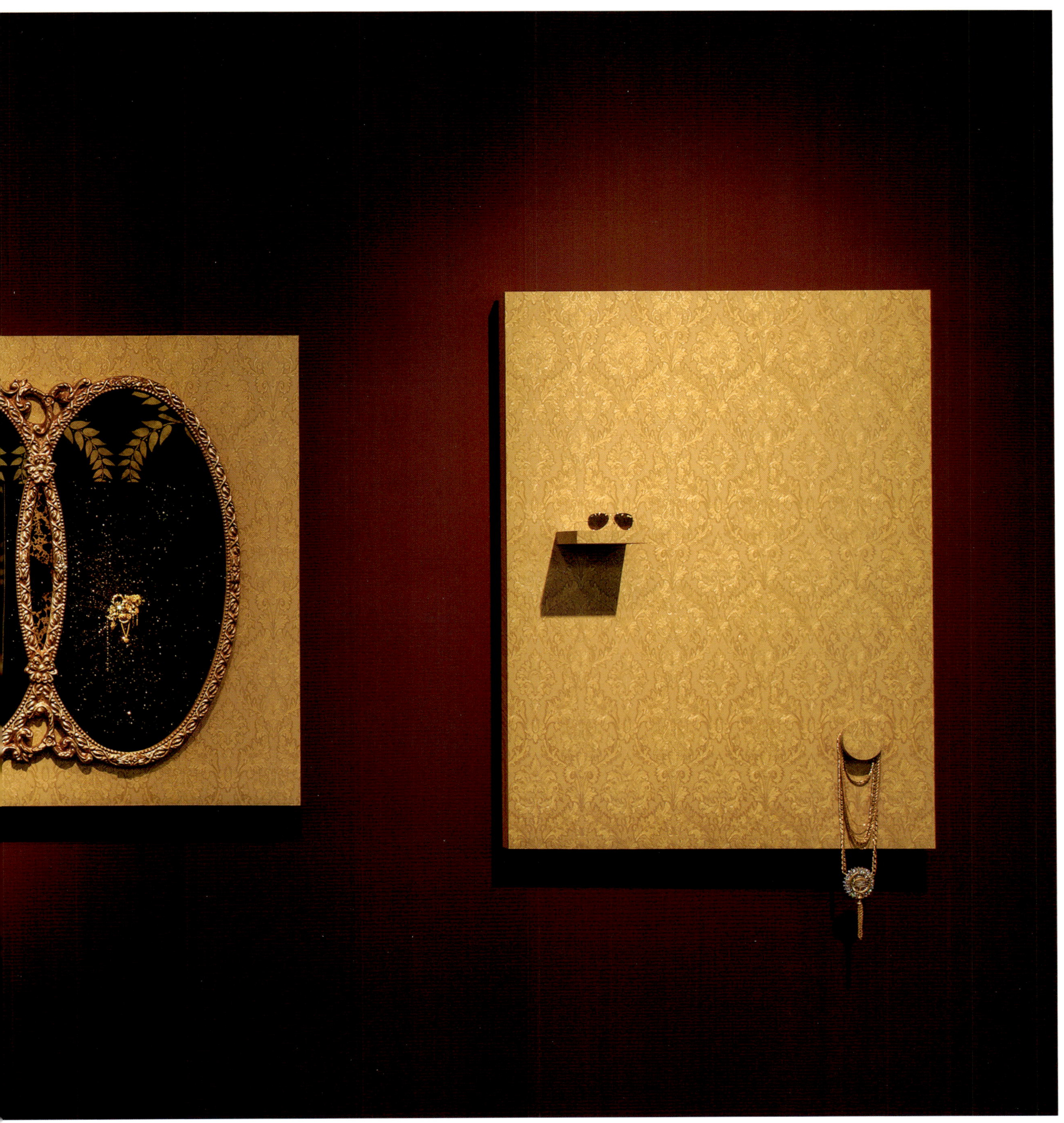

MY FATHER'S WISHES [NO.1, NO.2, NO3], 2014 - WALLPAPER, WOOD, MIRROR, 24 KT. GOLD LEAF, QUARTZ CRYSTALS, METAL SUNGLASSES AND BRONZED BOXING GLOVES
NO.1: 50 X 64 INCHES / NO.2: 80 X 54 INCHES / NO.3: 50 X 64 INCHES
COURTESY OF PAUL KASMIN GALLERY

194

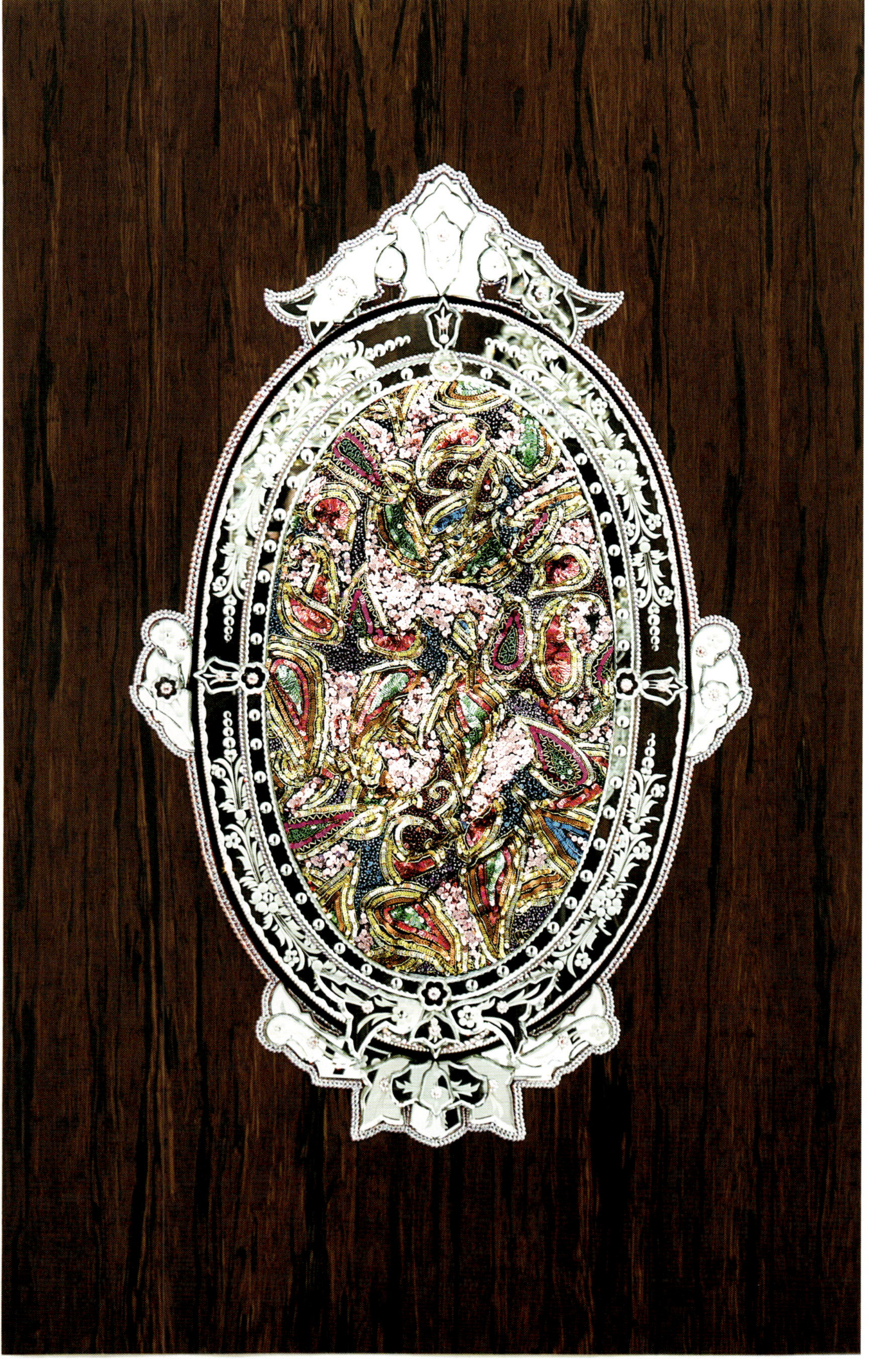

UNTITLED [TROPHY JACKET NO. 3], 2014 - SEQUINS, BLACK GLASS BEADS, COTTON, VINTAGE FABRIC, MIRROR AND QUARTZ CRYSTALS MOUNTED ON WOOD PANEL / 44 X 66 X 6 INCHES
COURTESY OF PAUL KASMIN GALLERY

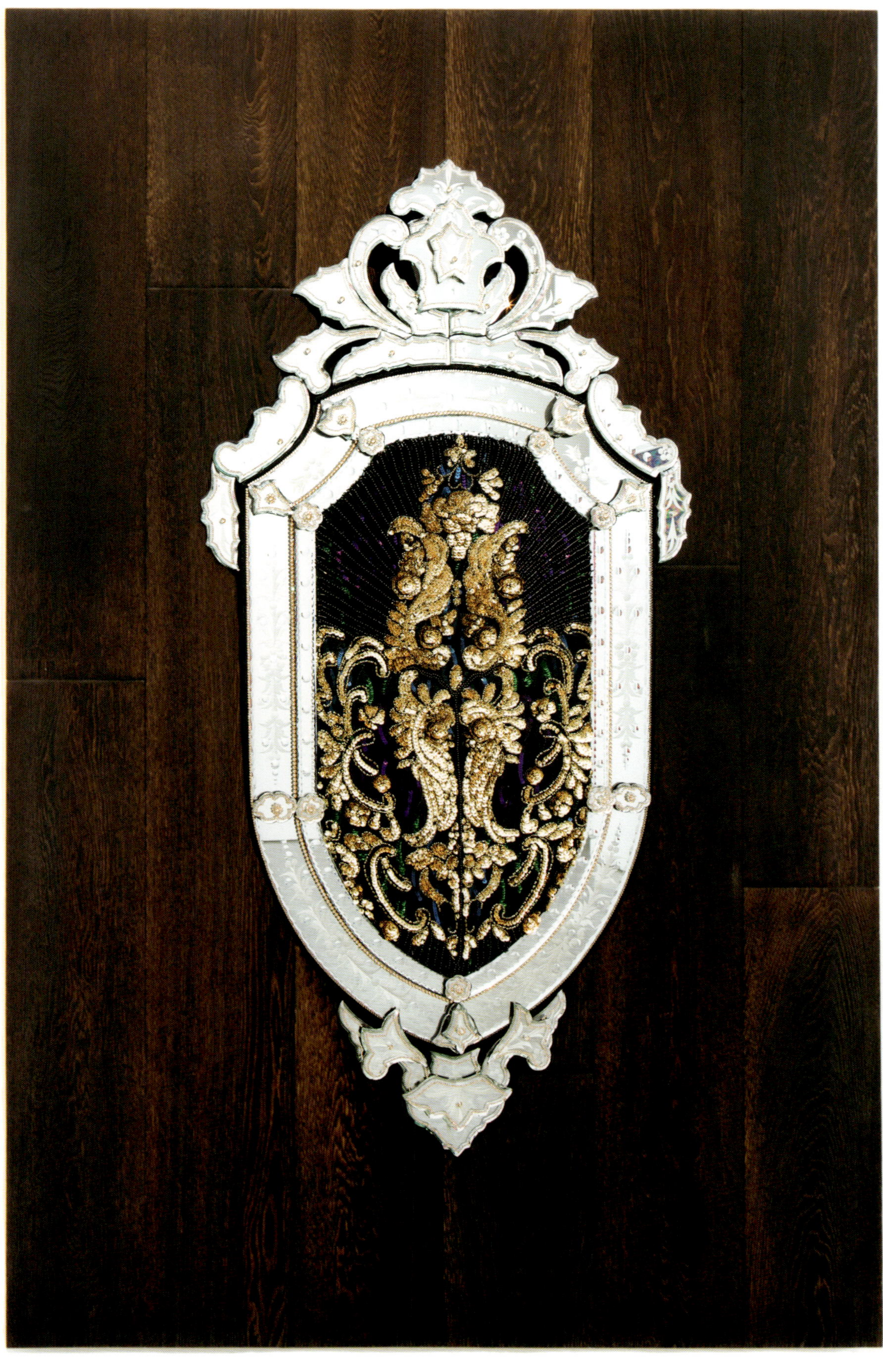

UNTITLED [TROPHY JACKET NO. 4], 2014 - SEQUINS, GOLD PLATED CHAINS, GOLD GLASS BEADS, CLEAR GLASS BEADS, COTTON, VINTAGE FABRIC, MIRROR AND QUARTZ CRYSTALS MOUNTED ON WOOD PANEL
60 X 66 X 6 INCHES
COURTESY OF PAUL KASMIN GALLERY

196

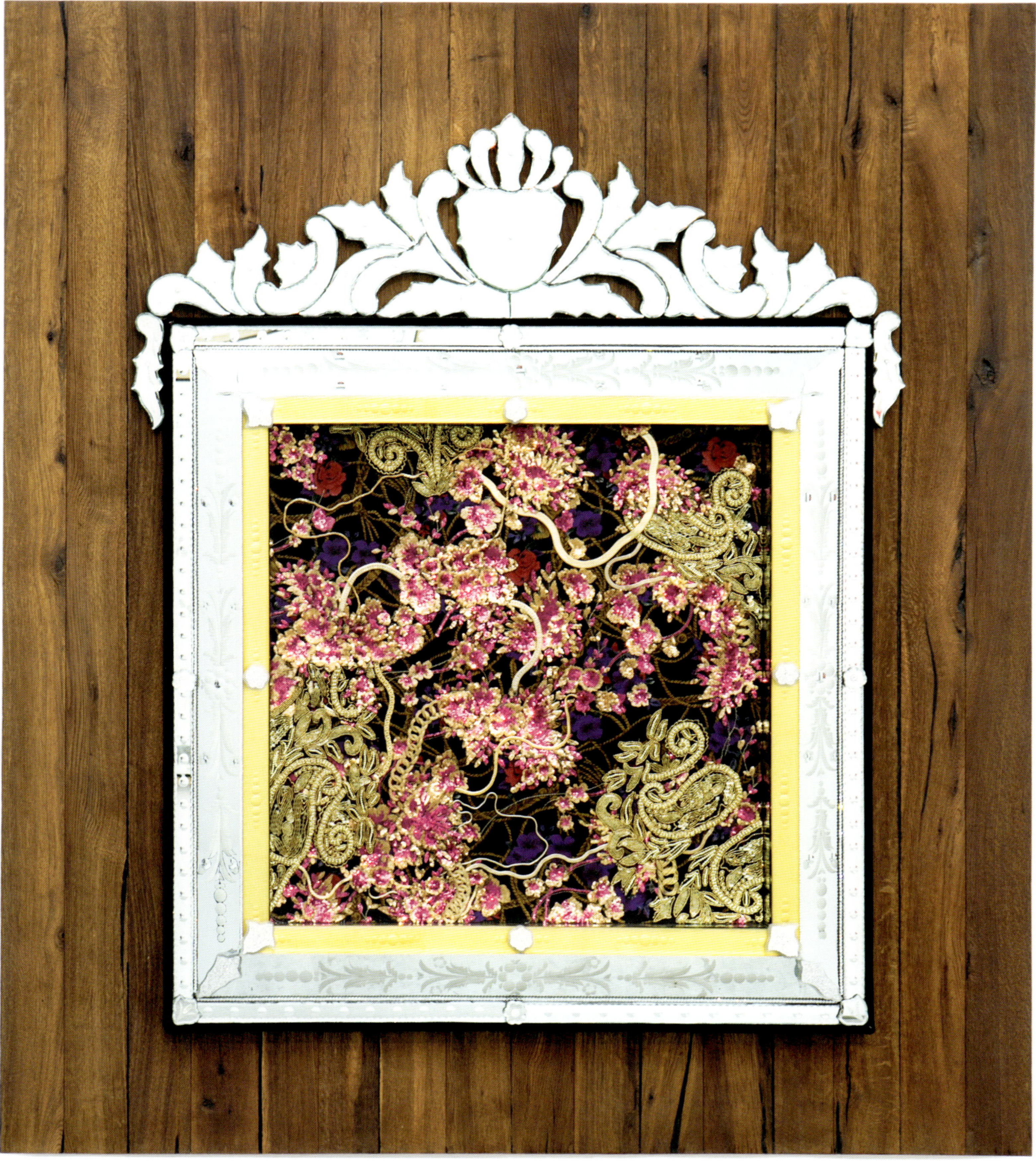

MOMENTS LIKE THISNEVER FAIL., 2014 - MIRROR, QUARTZ CRYSTAL AND 24 KT. GOLD LEAF MOUNTED ON WOOD PANEL / 64 X 64 X 2 1/2 INCHES
COURTESY OF PAUL KASMIN GALLERY

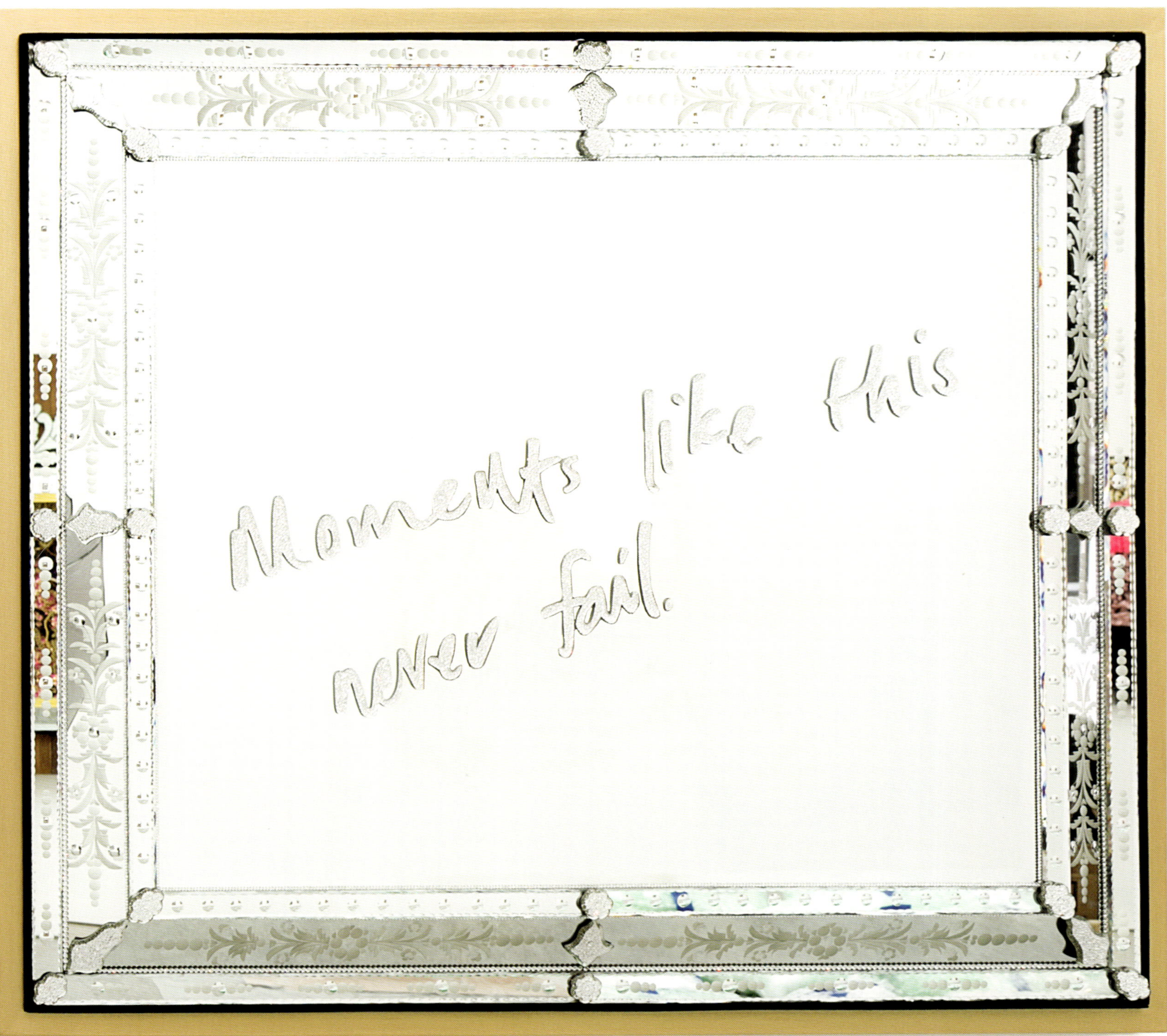

ORO [BASEMENT WALL], 2014 - BRONZE MIRROR, RESIN AND CRYSTALLINE ON WOOD PANEL / 40 X 40 X 3.5 INCHES
COURTESY OF PAUL KASMIN GALLERY

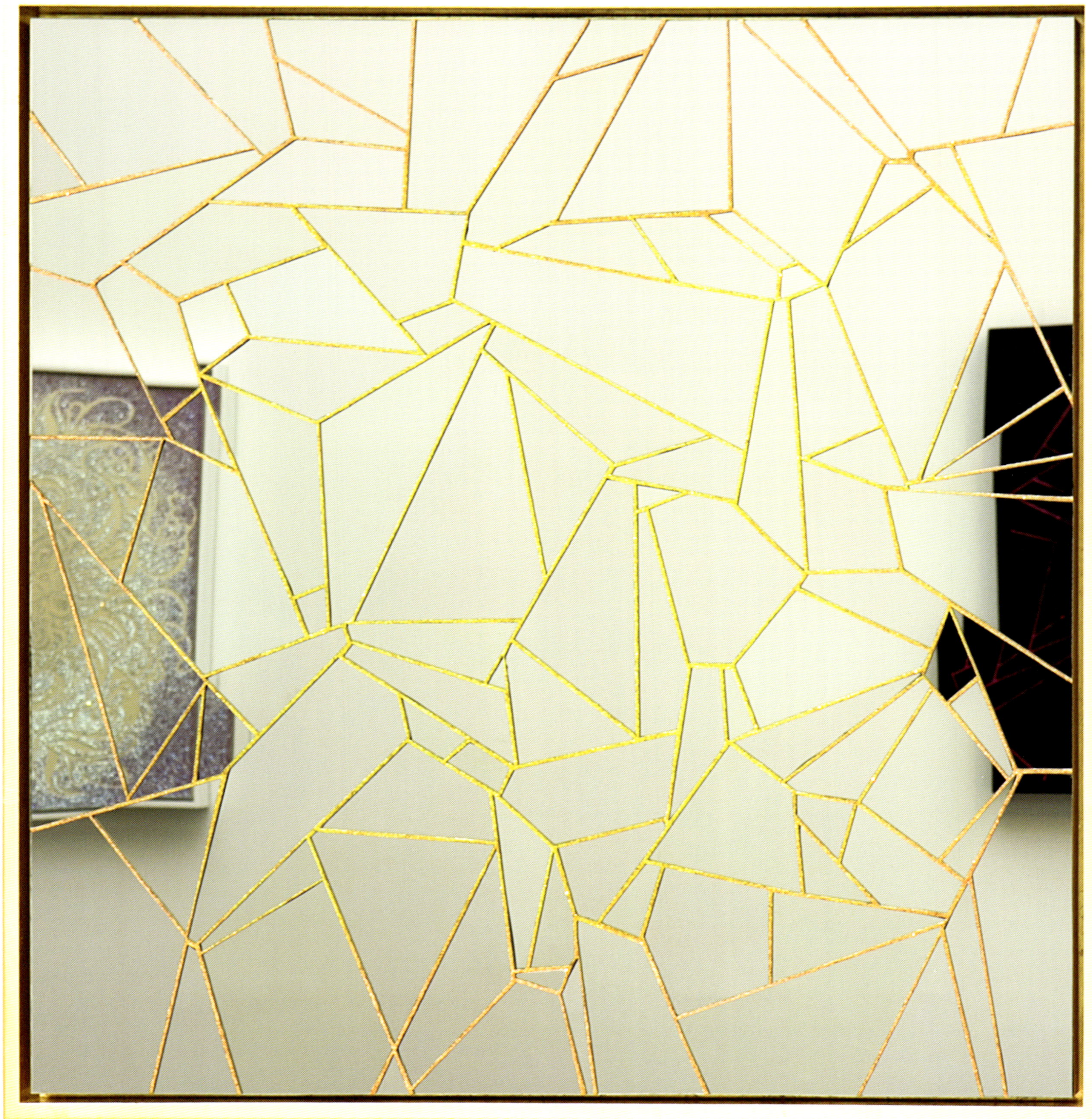

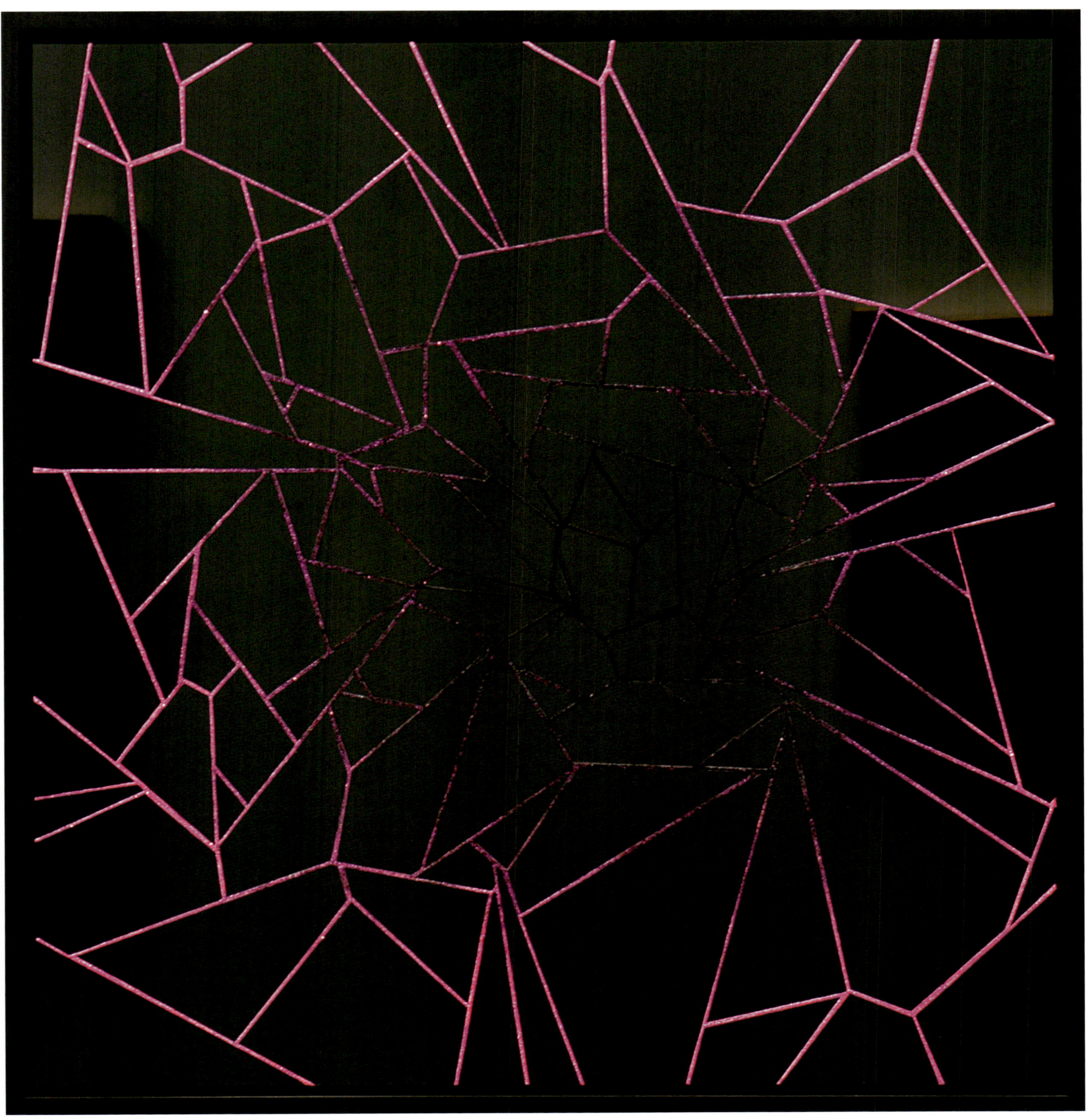

UNTITLED [BLACK VELVET PURPLE HOLE IN THE WALL], 2014 - BLACK MIRROR, RESIN AND CRYSTALLINE ON WOOD PANEL / 40 X 40 X 3 1/2 INCHES
COURTESY OF PAUL KASMIN GALLERY

UNTITLED [CUSTOM BOXING BELT], 2013 - ACRYLIC, QUARTZ CRYSTALS, VINTAGE JEWELRY, VELCRO, METAL, CANVAS MOUNTED ON BONDED LEATHER
[IN COLLABORATION WITH SARTONK] / DIMENSIONS VARIABLE
COURTESY OF PAUL KASMIN GALLERY
PHOTO BY LYLE OWERKO

[OPPOSITE] *ARTHUR ABRAHAM*, 2013 - C-PRINT IN CUSTOM FRAME [UNIQUE] / 122 X 203 CM
COURTESY OF PAUL KASMIN GALLERY

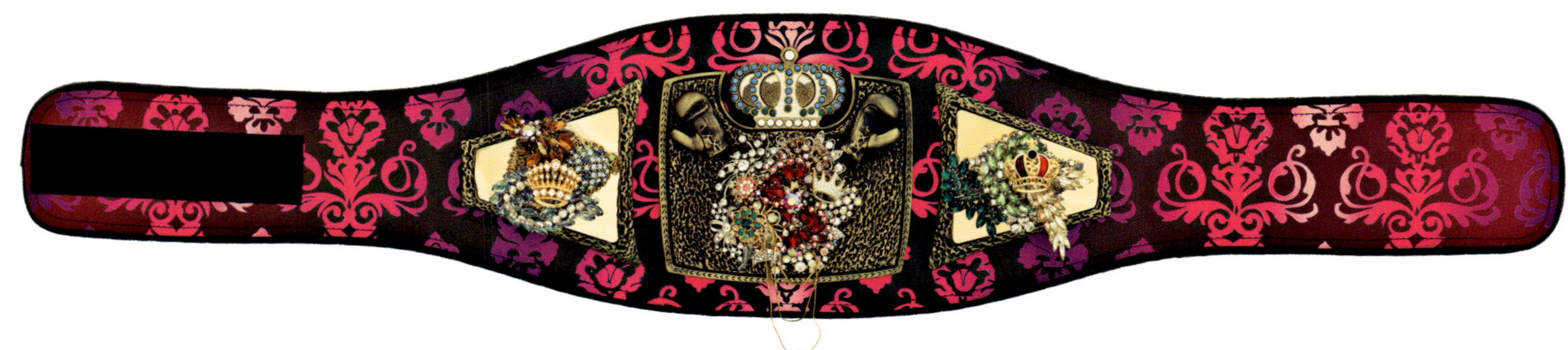

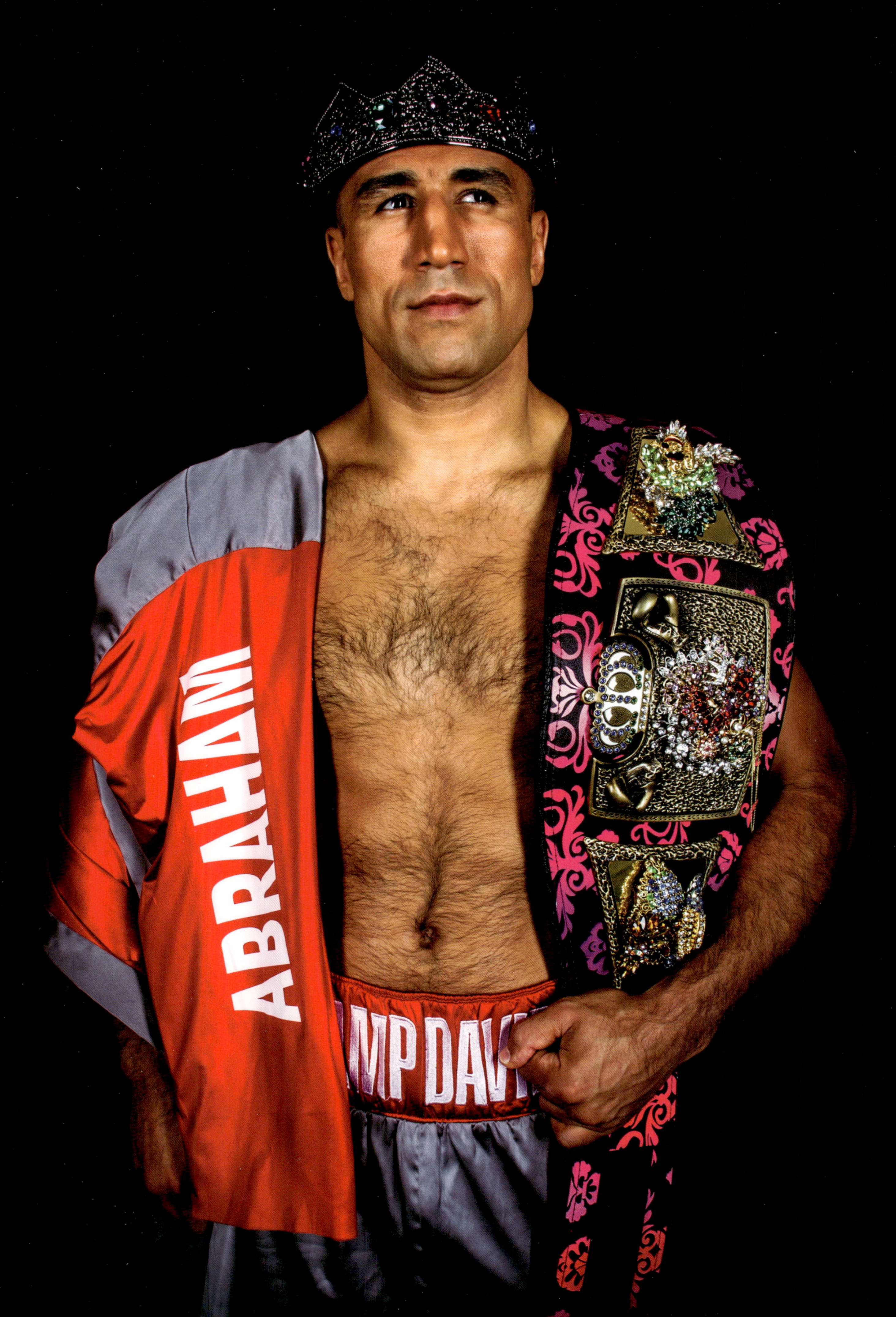
ABRAHAM
MP DAV

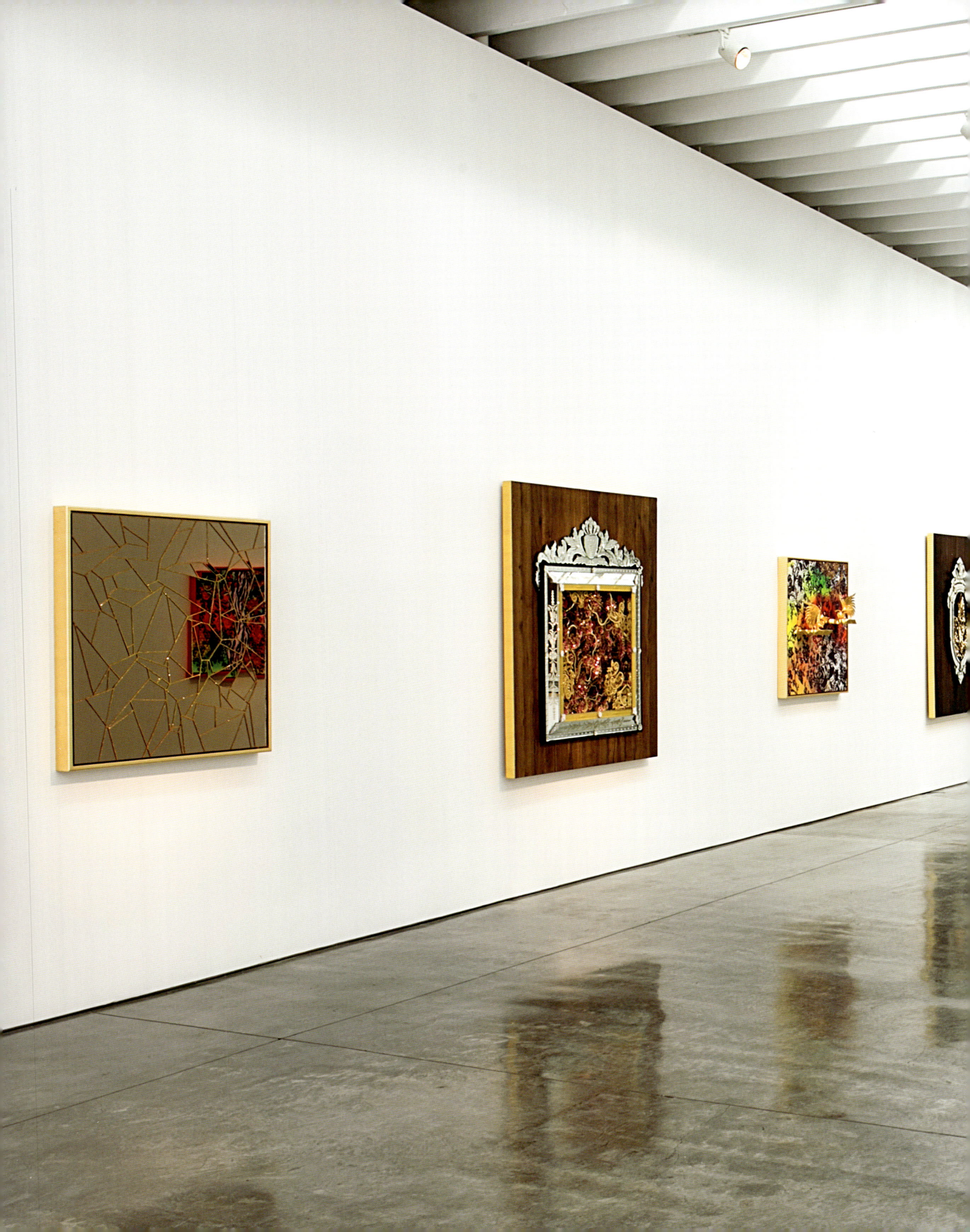

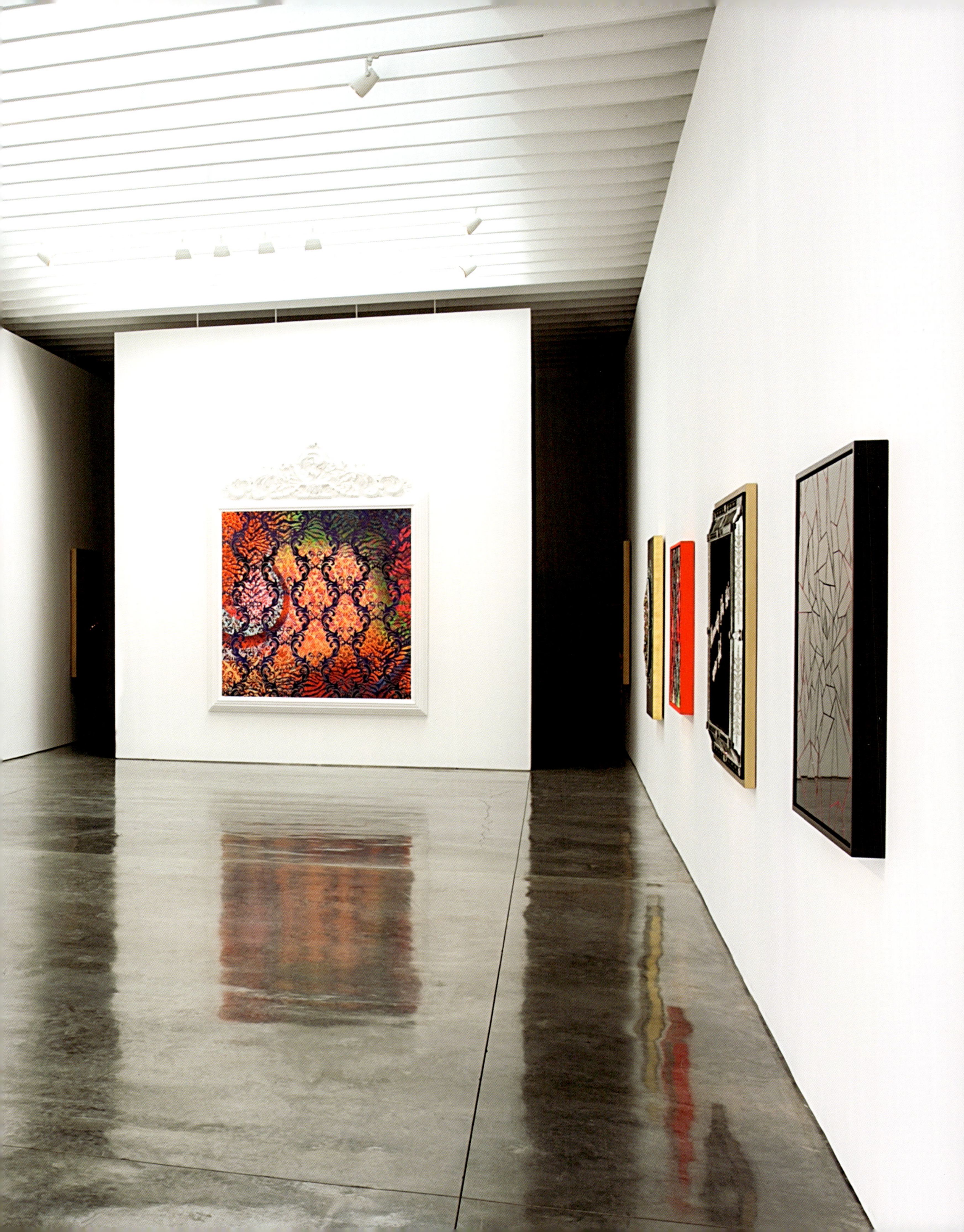

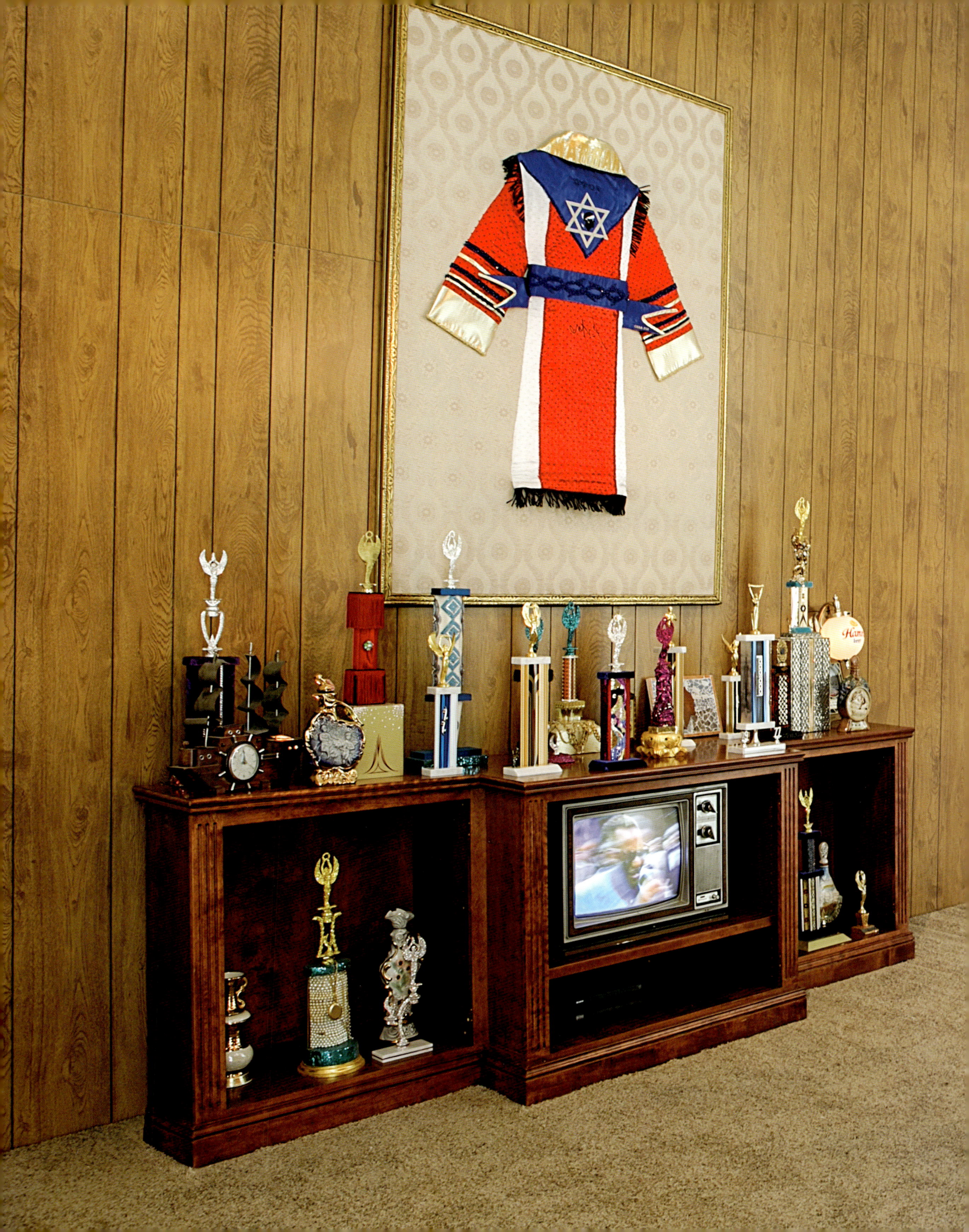

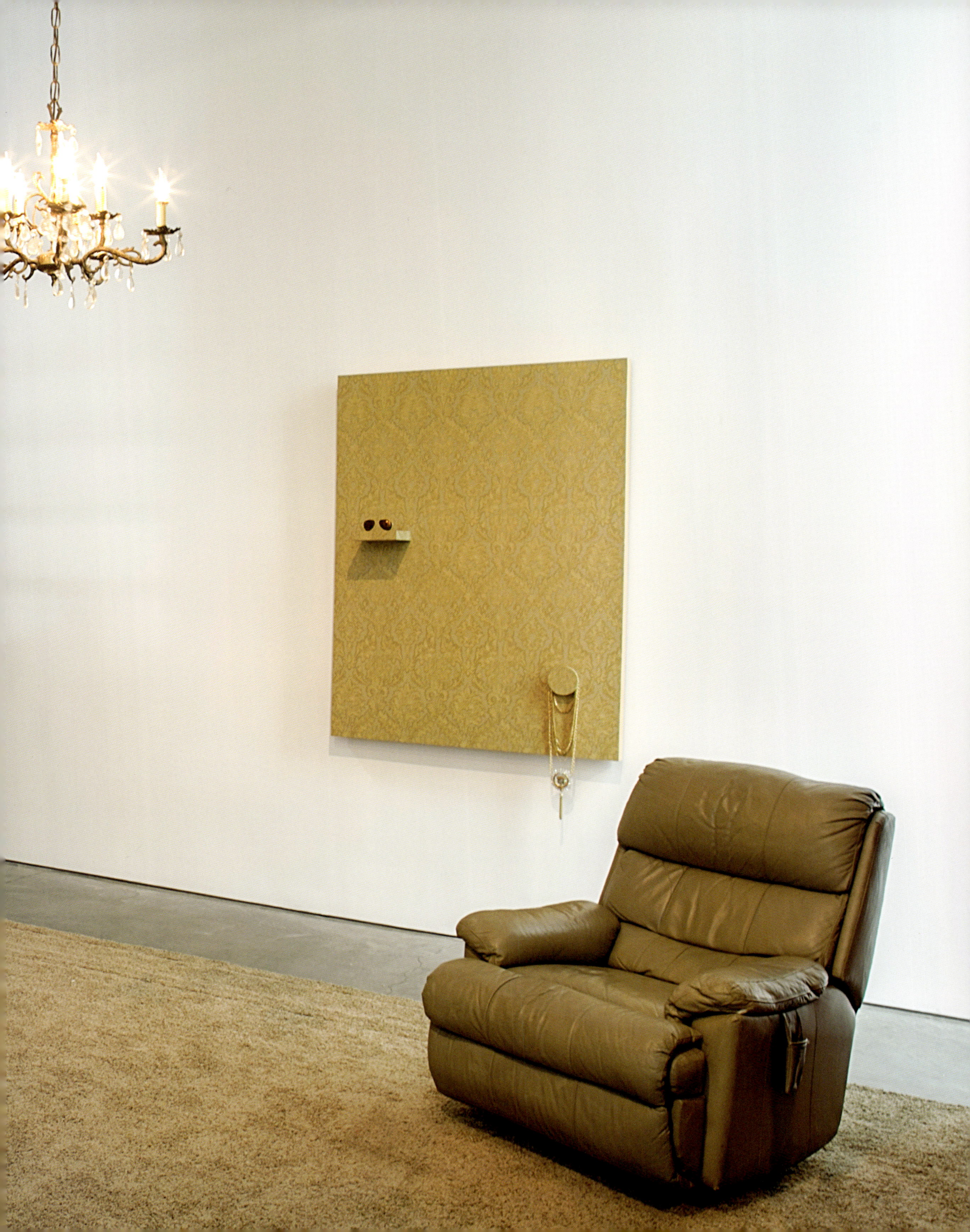

FRANKLIN SIRMANS

Franklin Sirmans is the Terri and Michael Smooke Department Head and Curator of Contemporary Art at the Los Angeles County Museum of Art and the current artistic director of Prospect.3 New Orleans, which will open in October 2014. At LACMA, Sirmans has organized *Color and Form, Robert Therrien, Ends and Exits: Contemporary Art from the Collections of LACMA and the Broad Art Foundation* and coorganized the exhibition *Human Nature: Contemporary Art from the Collection.* He has also organized the museum's presentations of *Blinky Palermo: Retrospective, 1964-1977, Ai Weiwei's Circle of Animals, Glenn Ligon: America* and his own shows on *Vija Celmins* and *Steve Wolfe.*

Sirmans is currently at work on *Futbol: The Beautiful Game* (opens February 2014), N*oah Purifoy: Junk Dada* (spring 2015), *Toba Khedoori* and *Rage Against the Machine: From the Other Story to Sensation—How the 90s Changed the Face of Contemporary Art.*

From 2006 to 2010, Sirmans was the Curator of Modern and Contemporary Art at The Menil Collection in Houston, TX, where he organized exhibitions including *NeoHooDoo: Art for a Forgotten Faith, Maurizio Cattelan: Is There Life Before Death, Steve Wolfe: On Paper* and *Vija Celmins: Television and Disaster, 1964-66.* Sirmans was the 2007 recipient of the David C. Driskell Prize awarded by the High Museum of Art, Atlanta. Prior to 2006, Sirmans held editorial positions at Dia Center for the Arts, *Flash Art Magazine* and *Art AsiaPacific.* He has written extensively for catalogues in addition to articles and reviews in publications such as *The New York Times, Time Out New York, Essence, Parkett* and *Grand Street.* He has also lectured at colleges and universities and art institutions.

CHRISTOPHER BEDFORD

Prior to joining the Rose Art Museum as the Henry and Lois Foster Director in September of 2012, Christopher Bedford was Chief Curator at the Wexner Center for the Arts at The Ohio State University in Columbus. In his almost four years at the Wexner Center, Bedford organized numerous exhibitions including *Hard Targets* (a multimedia show exploring sports and masculinity); Mark Bradford, a major mid-career survey of the L.A.-based artist; a small Susan Philipsz show and an Alyson Shotz project. Major monographic exhibitions organized for the Wexner Center include Katy Moran, Erwin Redl, Tobias Putrih, Pipilotti Rist, Nathalie Djurberg, Ernst Caramelle, Elliott Hundley, Paula Hayes, Sarah Morris, David Smith, Omer Fast and Paul Sietsema. For the two years prior to joining the Wexner Center, Bedford was with the Los Angeles County Museum of Art (LACMA) as assistant curator in the Department of Contemporary Art, where he curated *Contemporary Projects 11: Hard Targets—Masculinity and Sport* (which inspired a similar traveling show organized and circulated by Independent Curators International, and which was a smaller version of the Wexner Center show). Before going to LACMA, Bedford served as a curatorial assistant and then consulting curator in the department of sculpture and decorative arts at the Getty Museum in L.A. Along with co-curators Jennifer Wulffson and Kristina Newhouse,Bedford was the recipient of the 2008 Fellows of Contemporary Art Curators' Award for the exhibition *Superficiality and Superexcrescence,* currently on view at OTIS College of Art and Design in Los Angeles. Bedford has published essays, book reviews, editorials and exhibition reviews in *The Burlington Magazine, Artforum, Artforum.com,* A*rt in America, Tema Celeste, Sculpture Journal, Frieze, The Art Book, Afterall,* O*ctober, Word & Image,* and *caa.reviews,* as well as numerous essays in anthologies and exhibition catalogues. He is currently working on edited volumes for Duke University Press, MIT Press, and Sculpture Journal, and is a contributing editor to the Los Angeles-based contemporary art journal *X-TRA.* A citizen of the UK, Bedford holds a B.A. in art history from Oberlin College and an M.A. in art history from Case Western Reserve University, and is currently on leave from work on his PhD in art history at the Courtauld Institute of Art, University of London.

BIBLIOGRAPHY [HISTORY]

Boddy, Kasia. *Boxing: A Cultural History.* London: Reaktion, 2009.

"Collections." *The Met.* The Metropolitan Museum of Art, 2013. Web.<http://www.metmuseum.org/collections>.

"Collection online." *The British Museum.* The British Museum, 2013. Web. <http://www.britishmuseum.org/research/collection_online/search.aspx>.

Egan, Pierce. *Boxiana; or, Sketches of Ancient and Modern Pugilism, from the Championship of Cribb to the Present Time: Vol II.* London: Sherwood, Jones, and Co. 1824.

Frost, K.T. "Greek Boxing." *The Journal of Hellenic Studies.* 26 (1906): 213-225. JSTOR. Web. <http://www.jstor.org/stable/624373>.

Heinz, W. C. *The Professional.* New York: Da Capo, 2001. Print.

Holland, Gary. "A London Revival." *BBC News.* BBC, 13 Nov. 2007. Web. <http://www.bbc.co.uk/london/content/articles/2007/11/13/boxing_london_revival_feature.shtml>.

Jensen, Erik N. *Body by Weimar: Athletes, Gender, and German Modernity.* Oxford: Oxford University Press, 2010.

Kimball, George, John Schulian, and Colum McCann. *At the Fights: American Writers on Boxing.* New York: Library of America, 2011.

Kleiner, Fred S., Richard G. Tansery, Christian J. Mamiya. *Gardner's Art Through the Ages.* 11th ed. London: Thomson/Wadsworth, 2001.

Liebling, A. J. *The Sweet Science.* New York: Viking, 1956.

Mailer, Norman. *The Fight.* Boston: Little, Brown, 1975.

"Max Schmeling (1905-2005)." *PBS.* PBS, 9 Feb. 2005. Web. 15 Sept. 2013. <http://www.pbs.org/wgbh/amex/fight/peopleevents/p_schmeling.html>.

Murray, Stephen Ross. "Boxing Gloves of the Ancient World." *Journal of Combative Sport.* July 2010. (2010). Web. 2013. <http://ejmas.com/jcs/2010jcs/jcsart_murray_1007.html>.

Oates, Joyce Carol. *On Boxing.* Garden City, NY: Dolphin/Doubleday, 1987.

Olver, Ron, Nigel Collins, Thomas Hauser, Arthur Krystal, Michael Poliakoff, Jeffrey Thomas Sammons, and E.C. Wallenfeldt. "Boxing (sport)." *Encyclopedia Britannica Online.* Encyclopedia Britannica, 2013. Web.<http://www.britannica.com/EBchecked/topic/76377/boxing>.

Scott, David H. T. *The Art and Aesthetics of Boxing.* Lincoln: University of Nebraska, 2008.

"Search All Collections." *Yale Center for British Art.* Yale, 2013. Web.<http://britishart.yale.edu/collections/search>.

"The Collection." *MoMA.* The Museum of Modern Art, 2013. Web.<http://www.moma.org/explore/collection/index>.

THANK YOU
Casey, Paolo and Mila. My entire family in Chicago and Puerto Rico. Tony Arcabascio, Andrea Albertini, The entire staff at Carlos Rolon Studio/Dzine Studio, Inc., Paul Kasmin Gallery; New York, Salon 94; New York, Galerie Henrik Springmann; Berlin, Leeahn Gallery; Korea. All of the artists included or who gave freely based on the love and idea behind this project. All of the foundations, museums and galleries who helped facilitate images and contributed – Your contribution is what shaped this book.

Last but not least…. Howard Cosell
DOWN GOES FRAZIER! DOWN GOES FRAZIER! DOWN GOES FRAZIER!

BOXED. A Visual History and the Art of Boxing
Carlos Rolon/Dzine

Art Direction / Design
TONY ARCABASCIO

Texts
FRANKLIN SIRMANS, CHRISTOPHER BEDFORD, CARLOS ROLON/DZINE, BRITTANY REILLY, ZOE LARKINS

Photography
CHRIS MOSIER, HOLGER KEIFEL, CHERYL DUNN, LYLE OWERKO, JEFF ELSTONE, NATHAN KEAY

Project Management for the artist and Dzine Studio Inc
BRITTANY REILLY, ZOE LARKINS, SALON 94 AND PAUL KASMIN GALLERY

[DAMIANI]

**Damiani
Bologna, Italy
info@damianieditore.com
damianieditore.com**

PAUL KASMIN GALLERY

**Paul Kasmin Gallery
293 Tenth Avenue
New York City 10001
paulkasmingallery.com**

All exhibition artworks courtesy of Paul Kasmin Gallery, New York

---

ISBN 978-88-6208-354-6

Printed in March 2014 by Grafiche Damiani, Italy.